WERNER KELLER

THE BIBLE AS HISTORY

ARCHAEOLOGISTS SHOW THE TRUTH OF THE OLD TESTAMENT

Translated by
WILLIAM NEIL

New material translated by
Veronica Zundel

A LION/SPCK BOOK

Copyright of the German edition © 1989 ECON Verlag GmbH, Düsseldorf, Vienna, New York

Copyright of the English translation © 1991 Lion Publishing

Published by
Lion Publishing plc
Sandy Lane West, Oxford, England
ISBN 0 7459
The Society for Promoting Christian Knowledge
Holy Trinity Church, Marylebone Road, London, England
ISBN 0 281 04544 5

Text first published as *Und die Bibel hat doch Recht,* Germany, 1955
First published in English 1956, Hodder & Stoughton
Fully revised 1980, Hodder & Stoughton
This updated and illustrated edition 1991, Lion Publishing

Translated by William Neil and Veronica Zundel

Copyright of Bible translations
(Old Testament) *The Holy Bible New International Version,*
copyright 1973, 1978, 1984, International Bible Society,
Anglicisation copyright 1979, 1986, Hodder & Stoughton Ltd
(Apocrypha) *Good News Bible,*
copyright 1966, 1971, 1976 American Bible Society,
published by Bible Society/Collins

British Library Cataloguing in Publication Data
Applied for

Printed and bound in Germany

Photographs

American Schools of Oriental Research, New Haven, Connecticut (149); Archaeological Museum, Istanbul (272); Ingrid Asmus, Linz (72, 110, 111, 128); Arthaud-Mikael Audrain (31 left, 36, 120); Aviation Française du Levant (44 left); Gunther Baumann, München (178); Antonia Benedek (31, 39); F.S. Bodenheimer (124 b); Erwin Böhm, Mainz (147 left); Werner Braun, Jerusalem (70, 71); Trustees of the British Museum (25 right, 34 above, 37, 106 below, 177 right, 228 right, 262, 265 above, 280); P.J. Cools O.P. (148 b); Volker Eid, Bamberg (129, 137); Ernst Fahmüller, Dachau (16, 17 below, 18 above, 24, 32, 41 right, 65, 72/73, 90, 95, 100 above, 101, 104, 107 below right, 109 below, 112, 113, 116 right, 146, 186, 196, 274, 275, 284, 289 b); Herbert Fasching, St. Pölten (68, 69, 75, 76/77, 80 above, 81, 82/83, 87, 91, 98/99, 105, 122/123, 130, 156/157, 158, 159, 162, 163, 165, 176, 185, 188/189, 194, 197, 201 right, 202/203, 207, 208, 220, 251, 299, 301, jacket); Joachim Feist, Pliezhausen (33 above, 61); John Freeman (301); Generaldirektion der Altertümer in Nordsyrien, Aleppo (237); Nelson Glueck (241 right); Ewing Golloway, New York (34 below); Erhard Gorys, Krefeld (168, 182 below, 183, 211, 244, 255); Irak-Museum, Baghdad (15 right, 23); Israel-Museum, Jerusalem (147 right); Laenderpress, Erich Lessing (173; Seton Lloyd (56); Archives Photographiques, Musée du Louvre, Paris (14, 15 left, 38, 89 right, 160, 161 below, 229 above, 230, 231 right, 236, 258, 259, 268, 290 right); Foto Marburg (264, 273); Metropolitan Museum of Art, New York (161 above); Middle East Archives, Tel Aviv (121); Werner Neumeister, München (2, 66/67, 77 below, 200, 201 left, 206, 210, 297, 298, back jacket 4); Jean-Louis Nou, Paris (85, 153 above, 214 below, 216/217, 221, 266, 267, 294/295, 296); Oriental Institute of the University of Chicago (30, 167, 277 below); Palestine Archaeological Museum (166); Palestine Exploration Fund (228 left, 229 below); André Parrot (44 right, 45); Hans Pazelt, München (17 above, 20/21, 25 left, 33 below, 53 below, 58/59, 114/115, 134, 150 above, 152, 153 below, 157 above, 214 above, 215, 271, 282, 283, 285, 287, 288, 289 above, 300); Philadelphia University Museum (22); A.H. Philpot (241 left); Paul Popper, London (79); J.B. Pritchard (192, 193, 240); Radio Times Hulton Picture Library (181); Rijksmuseum van Oudheden; Leiden (88); Beno Rothenberg (148 above); Anton Schnell, Germering-Unterpfaffenhofen (9, 18 below, 19, 40, 41 above left, 41 below left, 46, 47, 48, 49, 50, 51, 52, 53 above, 54, 55, 60, 62, 63 left, 64, 80, 102, 103, 131, 150 below, 177 left, 182 above, 198, 199, 209, 231 left, 245, 250, 256, 257, 277 above, 278, 292); Achim Sperber, Hamburg (191, back jacket 2); Staatliche Museen zu Berlin (124 above, 265 below); Frank Teichmann, Stuttgart (42/43, 63 right, 74, 76, 84, 94, 119, 125, 126, 127, 132/133, 135, 136, 138, 139, 140/141, 151, 155, 169, 179); Eberhad Thiem, Lotos Film, Kaufbeuren (11, 13, 26/27, 28/29m 35m 89 left, 92/93, 96, 97, 100 below, 106/107, 107 below left, 108, 109 above, 116 left, 117, 142, 143, 144, 145, 170/171, 172, 174, 175, 187, 204, 205, 212, 213, 224, 225, 226, 227, 232/233, 234, 235, 238, 239, 242, 243 right, 246/247, 248, 249, 252, 253, 260/261, 279, back jacket 2); Trustees of Sir Henry S. Wellcome (254, 265 below); G.E. Wright (180 left, 241 middle, 273 right).

Drawings, maps and charts

W.F. Albright and G.E. Wright, The Biblical Archaeologist (219); W. Andrae, Das wiedererstandene Assur (260); A.H. Layard, Ninveh and its Remains (242); C.R. Lepsius, Denkmäler aus Ägypten und Äthiopien (7273); A. Rowe, the Topography and History of Beth-Shan (180); E. Unger, Babylon, die heilige Stadt (276); Annegrete Vogrin with Manfred Derler, Graz (70, 164, 190, 193, 244, 251, 255); Joachim Zwick, Giessen (10, 56, 78, 120, 166, 218, 240, 263, 281, 291, 293, 298).

Photograph opposite title page:

View from the Mount of Olives over the southern area of the Temple Mount, and the excavations of the southern part of Herod's wall. On the spot where the al-Aqsa Mosque is now, Solomon's Palace may well have stood.

PREFACE

When a non-theologian writes a book about the Bible it is a rare enough occurrence to entitle the reader to ask for some explanation of how the writer managed to make himself master of his subject.

As a journalist I have been for many years exclusively concerned with the results of modern science and research. In 1950 in the course of my ordinary routine work I came across the reports of the French archaeologists Professors Parrot and Schaeffer on their excavations at Mari and Ugarit. Cuneiform tablets discovered at Mari on the Euphrates were found to contain Biblical names. As a result, narratives of the patriarchs which had been for a long time regarded as merely pious tales were unexpectedly transferred into the realm of history. At Ugarit on the Mediterranean, evidence of the Canaanite worship of Baal had for the first time come to light. By a coincidence, a scroll of Isaiah discovered in a cave by the Dead Sea was in the same year dated as pre-Christian. These sensational reports—and indeed in view of the significance of these finds it is not too much to use the word 'sensational'— awakened in me the desire to come to closer grips with Biblical archaeology, the most recent and, generally speaking, least known province in the field of investigation into the ancient world. I therefore ransacked German and foreign literature for a comprehensive and intelligible summary of the results of previous research. I found none for there was none to find. So I went to the sources myself in the libraries of many lands—aided in this bit of real detective work by my wife's enthusiasm—and collected all the hitherto scientifically established results of investigations which were to be found in the learned works of Biblical archaeologists. The deeper I went into the matter the more exciting it became.

The door into the historical world of the Old Testament had been already thrown open by a Frenchman, Paul-Emile Botta, in 1843. In the course of excavations at Khorsabad in Mesopotamia he suddenly found himself confronted by reliefs of King Sargon II of Assyria, who ravaged Israel and led its people off into captivity. Accounts of this conqueror's campaigns deal with the conquest of Samaria, which is also described in the Bible.

For a century now, American, English, French and German scholars have been digging in the middle East, in Mesopotamia, Palestine and Egypt. All the great nations have founded institutes and schools specifically for this type of research. The Palestine Exploration Fund began in 1869, the German Palestine Association in 1877, the Dominican Ecole Biblique de St. Etienne in 1892. The German Oriental Society followed in 1898: then in 1900 the American schools of Oriental Research and in 1901 the German Protestant Institute of Archaeology.

In Palestine, places and towns which are frequently mentioned in the Bible are being brought back once more into the light of day. They look exactly as the Bible describes them and lie exactly where the Bible locates them. On ancient inscriptions and monuments scholars encounter more and more characters from Old and New Testaments. Contemporary reliefs depict people whom we have hitherto only known by name. Their features, their clothes, their armour take shape before our eyes. Colossal figures and sculptures show us the Hittites with their big noses; the slim tall Philistines; the elegant Canaanite chiefs with their 'chariots of iron' which struck terror into the hearts of the Israelites; the kings of Mari, contemporary with Abraham, with their gentle smiles. During the thousands of years that divide us from them the Assyrian kings have lost nothing of their fierce and forbidding appearance: Tiglath Pileser III, well known as the Old Testament 'Pul'; Sennacherib who destroyed Lachish and laid siege to Jerusalem; Esarhaddon who put King Manasseh in chains, and Ashurbanipal the 'great and noble Asnapper' of the book of Ezra.

As they have done to Nineveh and Nimrod—old-time Calah—or to Ashur and Thebes, which the prophets called No-Amon, the scholars have also awakened from its ancient slumber the notorious Babel of Biblical story with its legendary tower. In the Nile delta archaeologists have found the cities of Pithom and Raamses, where the resentful Hebrews toiled as slaves. They have laid bare strata which tell of the flames and destruction which accompanied the children of Israel on their conquering march into Canaan. In Gibeah they found Saul's mountain stronghold, whose walls once echoed to the strains of David's harp. At Megiddo they came upon the vast stables of King Solomon, who had '12,000 horsemen'.

These breathtaking discoveries, whose significance it is impossible to grasp all at once, make it necessary for us to revise our views about the Bible. Many events which previously passed for 'pious tales' must now be judged to be historical. Often the results of investigation correspond in detail with the Biblical narratives. They do not only confirm them, but also illumine the historical situations out of which the Old Testament grew. At the same time the chances and changes of the people of Israel are woven into a lively colourful tapestry of daily life in the age in which they lived, as well as being caught up into the political, cultural and economic disputes of the nations and empires which struggled for power in Mesopotamia and on the Nile, from which the inhabitants of the tiny buffer state of Palestine were never able completely to detach themselves for over 2,000 years.

The opinion has been, and still is widely held that the Bible is nothing but the story of man's salvation, a guarantee of the validity of their faith for Christians everywhere. It is however at the same time a book about things that actually happened. Admittedly in this sense it has limitations, in that the Jewish people wrote their history in the light of their relationship to Yahweh, which meant writing it from the point of view of their own guilt and expiation. Nevertheless the events themselves are historical facts and have been recorded with an accuracy that is nothing less than startling.

Thanks to the findings of the archaeologists many of the Biblical narratives can be better understood now than ever before. There are, of course, theological insights which can only be dealt with in terms of the Word of God. But as Professor André Parrot, the world-famous French archaeologist, has said: 'How can we understand the Word, unless we see it in its proper chronological, historical and geographical setting?'

Until now, knowledge of these extraordinary discoveries was confined to a small circle of experts. Only fifty years ago Professor Friedrich Delitzsch of Berlin was asking 'Why all this effort in these distant, barren and dangerous lands? Why all this costly rummaging among the rubble of past ages when we know there is neither gold nor silver to be found there? Why this mad competition among different countries to get control of these dreary looking mounds for the sole purpose of digging them up?' The German scholar Gustav Dalman gave him the right answer from Jerusalem itself when he expressed the hope that one day all that the archaeologists had 'experienced and seen in their scientific labours would be turned to good account and would help to solve the practical problems of school and church'. This latter hope has so far however remained unfulfilled.

No book in the whole history of mankind has had such a revolutionary influence, has so decisively affected the development of the western world, or had such a worldwide effect as the 'Book of Books', the Bible. Today it is translated into 1,120 languages and dialects, and after 2,000 years gives no sign of having exhausted its triumphal progress.

In gathering together and working over the material for this book, which I in no way claim to be complete, it seemed to me that the time had come to share with those who read their Bibles and those who do not, with churchmen and agnostics alike, the exciting discoveries which have resulted from a careful examination of the combined results of scientific investigation along many different lines. In view of the overwhelming mass of authentic and well-attested evidence now available, as I thought of the sceptical criticism which from the eighteenth century onwards would fain have demolished the Bible altogether, there kept hammering on my brain this one sentence: 'The Bible is right after all!'

Werner Keller
Hamburg, September 1955

CONTENTS

The Coming of the Patriarchs

> *Remember the days of old; consider the generations long past. Ask your father and he will tell you, your elders, and they will explain to you. When the Most High gave the nations their inheritance, when he divided all mankind, he set up boundaries for the peoples according to the number of the sons of Israel. For the Lord's portion is his people, Jacob his allotted inheritance. In a desert land he found him, in a barren and howling waste.*
>
> Deuteronomy 32:7–10

IN THE 'FERTILE CRESCENT'

If we draw a line from Egypt through the Mediterranean lands of Palestine and Syria, then following the Tigris and Euphrates, through Mesopotamia to the Persian Gulf, the result is an unmistakable crescent.

Four thousand years ago this mighty semi-circle around the Arabian Desert, which is called the 'Fertile Crescent', embraced a multiplicity of civilizations lying side by side like a lustrous string of pearls. Rays of light streamed out from them into the surrounding darkness of mankind. Here lay the centre of civilization from the Stone Age right up to the Golden Age of Graeco-Roman culture.

About 2000BC, the further we look beyond the 'Fertile Crescent', the deeper grows the darkness and signs of civilization and culture decrease. Over the Eastern Mediterranean already a light is shining—it is the heyday of the Minoan kings of Crete, founders of the first sea-power known to history. For 1,000 years the fortress of Mycenae had protected its citizens, and a second Troy had long been standing upon the ruins of the first. In the nearby Balkans, however, the Early Bronze Age had just begun. In Sardinia and Western France the dead were being buried in vast stone tombs. These megalithic graves are the last great manifestation of the Stone Age.

In Britain they were building the most famous sanctuary of the Megalithic Age—the Temple of the Sun at Stonehenge—that giant circle of stones near Salisbury which is still one of the sights of England about which many tales are told. In

'Long ago your forefathers lived beyond the River ...' (Joshua 24:2).

The Euphrates, together with the other great river of Mesopotamia, the Tigris, is named in the Bible as one of the four rivers of Paradise (Genesis 2:14).

A view of the Euphrates near Dura Europos in Syria.

Right **The 'Fertile Crescent' is essentially made up of river oases. It is no accident that early civilizations are 'river cultures'. The preconditions for advanced cultural achievements include not only fertile land, but also the challenge of directing the vagaries of nature. Great rivers present just such a challenge. Wresting the maximum productivity from such rivers through irrigation systems, dams, canals, is beyond the capabilities of a clan or tribe. It demands a larger, organized community life, in other words a state. And only this can produce an advanced culture.**

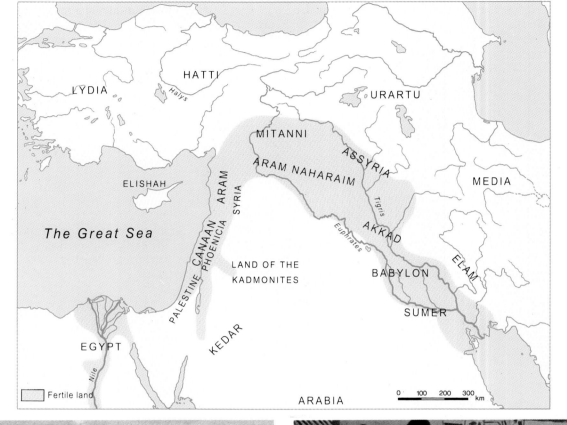

Germany they were tilling the soil with wooden ploughs.

At the foot of the Himalayas the flickering lamp of an isolated outpost of civilization in the Indus valley was fast going out. Over China over the vast steppes of Russia, over Africa, darkness reigned supreme. And beyond the waters of the Atlantic lay the Americas in twilight gloom.

But in the 'Fertile Crescent' and in Egypt, on the other hand, cultured and highly developed civilizations jostled each other in colourful and bewildering array. For 1,000 years the Pharaohs had sat upon the throne. About 2000BC it was occupied by the founder of the Twelfth Dynasty, Amenemhet I. His sphere of influence ranged from Nubia, south of the second cataract of the Nile, beyond the Sinai peninsula to Canaan and Syria. Along the Mediterranean coast lay the wealthy seaports of the Phoenicians. In Asia Minor the powerful kingdom of the ancient Hittites stood on the threshold of its history. In Mesopotamia, between Tigris and Euphrates, the kingdom of Akkad, founded by Sargon I, which existed from about 2340 to 2198, held in tribute all the smaller kingdoms from the Persian Gulf to the sources of the Euphrates. Its legacy was taken up by the kingdom of the Third Dynasty of Ur, whose rulers used the title 'King of Sumer and Akkad'.

Egypt's mighty pyramids and Mesopotamia's massive temples had for centuries watched the busy life around them. For 2,000 years fields in the artificially irrigated valleys of the Nile, the Euphrates and the Tigris had been exporting corn, vegetables and choice fruits. Everywhere throughout the 'Fertile Crescent' and in the empire of the Pharaohs the art of cuneiform and hieroglyphic writing was commonly known. Poets, court officials and civil servants practised it. For commerce it had long been a necessity.

The endless traffic in commodities of all sorts which the great import and export firms of Mesopotamia and Egypt despatched by caravan routes or by sea from the Persian Gulf to Syria and Asia Minor, from the Nile to Cyprus and Crete and as far as the Black Sea, is reflected in their business correspondence, which they conducted on clay tablets or papyrus. Out of all the rich variety of costly wares the most keenly sought after were copper from the Egyptian mines in the mountains of Sinai, silver from the Taurus mines in Asia Minor, gold and ivory from Somaliland in East Africa and from Nubia on the Nile, purple dyes from the Phoenician cities on the coast of Canaan, incense and rare spices from South Arabia, the magnificent linens which came from the Egyptian looms and the

Below left **The Egyptians were very well aware that Egypt was 'a gift of the Nile', as Herodotus puts it. As a result, in Egyptian temples, the stones at the base—as if to represent the foundation of the whole religious cult—are always dedicated to the gods of the Nile, who offer their gifts.**

Below right **Particularly impressive is the vision of the afterlife created by Sennodiem, a necropolis builder who lived in barracks in the desert town of Deir el-Medina and erected his grave there. He expects to farm by a river with irrigation canals, to plough together with his wife dressed in festive clothes, to sow and to harvest. Luxuriant trees bear their fruit on the shore, shrubs and flowers are in bloom, and in the bay a small boat is moored.**

wonderful vases from the island of Crete.

Literature and learning were flourishing. In Egypt the first novels and secular poetry were making their appearance. Mesopotamia was experiencing a Renaissance. Philologists in Akkad, the great kingdom on the lower Euphrates, were compiling the first grammar and the first bilingual dictionary. The story of Gilgamesh, and the old Sumerian legends of Creation and Flood were being woven into epics of dramatic power in the Akkadian tongue which was the language of the world. Egyptian doctors were producing their medicines in accordance with text-book methods from herbal compounds which had proved their worth. Their surgeons were no strangers to anatomical science. The mathematicians of the Nile by empirical means reached the conclusion about the sides of a triangle which 1,500 years later Pythagoras in Greece embodied in the theorem which bears his name. Mesopotamian engineers were solving the problem of square measurement by trial and error. Astronomers, admittedly with an eye solely on astrological prediction, were making their calculations based on accurate observations of the course of the planets.

Peace and prosperity must have reigned in this world of Nile, Euphrates and Tigris, for we have never yet discovered an inscription dating from this period which records any large-scale warlike activities.

Then suddenly from the heart of this great 'Fertile Crescent,' from the sandy sterile wastes of the Arabian desert, there burst in violent assaults on the North, on the north-west, on Mesopotamia, Syria and Palestine a horde of nomadic tribes of Semitic stock. In endless waves these Amorites, 'Westerners' as their name implies, surged against the kingdoms of the 'Fertile Crescent'.

The Third Dynasty of Ur collapsed in about 1950BC under their irresistible attack. The Amorites founded a number of states and dynasties. One of them was eventually to become supreme: the First Dynasty of Babylon, which was the great centre of power from 1830 to 1530BC. Its sixth king was the famous Hammurabi.

Meantime one of these tribes of Semitic nomads was destined to be of fateful significance for millions upon millions throughout the world up to the present day. It was a little group, perhaps only a family, as unknown and unimportant as a tiny grain of sand in a desert storm: the family of Abraham, forefather of the patriarchs.

UR OF THE CHALDEES

Terah took his son Abram, his grandson Lot son of Haran, and his daughter-in-law Sarai, the wife of his son Abram, and together they set out from Ur of the Chaldeans to go to Canaan. But when they came to Haran, they settled there.

GENESIS 11:31

... and they went forth with them from Ur of the Chaldees—Christians have been hearing these words for almost 2,000 years. Ur, a name as mysterious and legendary as the bewildering variety of names of kings and conquerors, powerful empires, temples and golden palaces, with which the Bible regales us. Nobody knew where Ur lay. Chaldea certainly pointed to Mesopotamia. No one could have guessed that the quest for the Ur which is mentioned in the Bible would lead to the discovery of a civilization which would take us farther into the twilight of prehistoric times than even the oldest traces of man which had been found in Egypt.

Today Ur is a railway station about 120 miles north of Basra, near the Persian Gulf, and one of the many stops on the famous Baghdad railway. Punctually the train makes a halt there in the grey light of early morning. When the noise of the wheels on their northward journey has died away, the traveller who has alighted here is surrounded by the silence of the desert.

His glance roams over the monotonous yellowish-brown of the endless stretch of sand. He seems to be standing in the middle of an enormous flat dish which is only intersected by the railway line. Only at one point is the shimmering expanse of desolation broken. As the rays of the rising sun grow stronger they pick out a massive dull red stump. It looks as if some Titan had hewn great notches in it.

To the Bedouins this solitary mound is an old friend. High up in its crevices the owls make their nests. From time immemorial the Arabs have known it and have given it the name Tell al Muqayyar, 'The Mount of Steps'. Their forefathers pitched their tents at its base. Still as from time immemorial it offers welcome protection from the danger of sandstorms. Still today they feed their flocks at its base when the rains suddenly charm blades of grass out of the ground.

Once upon a time—4,000 years ago—broad fields of corn and barley swayed here. Market gardens, groves of date-palms and fig trees stretched as far as the eye could see. The lush green fields and beds were interlaced by a system of dead

This pink granite head, excavated in 1970 at the Temple of Amun in Karnak, portrays Sesostris III, one of the Pharaohs of the Middle Kingdom. The internal political turmoil of the 'first intermediate period', after the collapse of the Old Kingdom, left Egypt no energy for foreign affairs. Even when the Theban prince Mentuhotep Nebhepetre succeeded in uniting the two kingdoms in about 2040BC, and so founding the Middle Kingdom, the first priority was to stabilize the country internally. It was not until the twelfth dynasty that Egypt reached out across its southern border into Nubia, with the main aim of gaining control of that region's gold and precious stone-mining industries. There were no immediate excursions into the Near East, even though contemporary propaganda talks repeatedly of 'thrashing the Asiatics'. Egypt instead confined itself to establishing a strict and well-defended border with the Isthmus of Suez, to forestall uncontrolled incursions of Bedouins from Sinai, Syria and Palestine. Only Sesostris III (1878–41BC) undertook a few expeditions into the Near East, which clearly had no lasting success.

In any case the contemporary Egyptian portrayal of the Asiatics as enemies may well be deceptive, since there was extensive trade with the Near East: timber and resin, semi-precious stones, silver and tin, objets d'art and slaves were sought-after commodities in Egypt; payment was chiefly in Nubian gold.

straight canals and ditches, a masterpiece of irrigation. Away back in the Stone Age experts among the natives had utilized the water of the great rivers. Skilfully and methodically they diverted the precious moisture at the river banks and thereby converted desert wastes into rich and fruitful farmland.

Almost hidden by forests of shady palms the Euphrates flowed in those days past this spot. This great life-giving river carried a heavy traffic between Ur and sea. At that time the Persian Gulf cut much deeper into the estuary of the Euphrates and the Tigris. Even before the first pyramid was built on the Nile, a high temple was towering into the blue skies on the site of Tell al Muqayyar. Four mighty cubes, built one upon the other in diminishing size, rose up into a 25 metre tower of gaily coloured brick. Above the black of the foundation block, its sides 62.5 metres by 43 metres long, shone the red and blue of the upper stages, each studded with trees. The uppermost stage provided a small plateau, on which was enthroned the high temple, shaded by a golden roof.

Silence reigned over this sanctuary, where priests performed their offices at the shrine of Nannar, the moon-god. The stir and noise of wealthy metropolitan Ur, one of the oldest cities of the world, hardly penetrated into it.

In the year 1854 a caravan of camels and donkeys, laden with an unusual cargo of spades, picks and surveyor's instruments, approached the lonely red mound, under the leadership of the British consul in Basra. Mr. J. E. Taylor was inspired neither by a lust for adventure nor indeed by any motive of his own. He had undertaken the journey at the instigation of the Foreign Office, which in its turn was complying with a request from the British Museum that a search should be made for ancient monuments in Southern Mesopotamia, where the Euphrates and the Tigris came closest together just before entering the Persian Gulf. Taylor had often heard in Basra about the strange great heap of bricks that his expedition was now approaching. It seemed to him a suitable site to investigate.

About the middle of the nineteenth century all over Egypt, Mesopotamia and Palestine investigations and excavations had started in response to a suddenly awakened desire to get a scientifically reliable picture of man's history in this part of the world.

Up till then the Bible had been the only historical source for our knowledge of the Near East

The victory stela (carved slab or obelisk) of King Naramsin of Akkad (about 2389–53BC) in the Louvre shows the ruler exaggeratedly large and adorned with the horned helmet of the gods, as a conqueror and the representative of a powerful kingdom.

before the sixth century BC. Only the Bible had anything to say about a period of history which stretched back into the dim twilight of the past. Peoples and names cropped up in the Bible about which even the Greeks and the Romans no longer knew anything.

Scholars swarmed impetuously into these lands of the Ancient East about the middle of last century. With astonishment the scientific age heard of their finds and discoveries. What these men with infinite pains extracted from the desert sand by the great rivers of Mesopotamia and Egypt deserved indeed the attention of mankind. Here for the first time science had forced open the door into the mysterious world of the Bible.

The French vice-consul in Mosul, Paul-Emile Botta, was an enthusiastic archaeologist. In 1843 he began to dig at Khorsabad on the Tigris and from the ruins of a 4,000 year old capital proudly brought to light the first witness to the Bible: Sargon, the fabulous ruler of Assyria. *In the year that Tartan came unto Ashdod, when Sargon the king of Assyria sent him . . .* says Isaiah 20:1.

Two years later a young English diplomat and excavator, A. H. Layard, uncovered Nimrud (Kalchu), the city which the Bible calls Calah (Genesis 10:11) and which now bears the name of the Nimrod of the Bible, *a mighty hunter before the Lord. The first centres of his kingdom were Babylon, Erech, Akkad and Calneh, in Shinar. From that land he went to Assyria, where he built Nineveh, Rehoboth Ir, Calah and Resen . . .* (Genesis 10:10–11).

Shortly after that, excavations under the direction of an English major, Henry Creswicke Rawlinson, one of the foremost Assyriologists, unearthed Nineveh, the Assyrian capital with the famous library of King Ashurbanipal. This is the Nineveh whose wickedness the biblical prophets constantly denounced (Jonah 1:2).

In Palestine the American scholar Edward Robinson devoted himself in 1838 and 1852 to the reconstruction of the topography of the ancient world.

From Germany, Richard Lepsius, later director of the Egyptian Museum in Berlin, recorded the monuments of the Nile area during an expedition which lasted from 1842–46.

After the Frenchman Champollion deciphered Egyptian hieroglyphics in 1822, Rawlinson, the discoverer of Nineveh, was successful in solving the riddle of cuneiform writing after 1850. The ancient documents were beginning to talk!

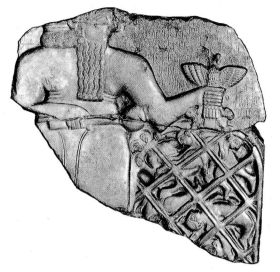

L et us return to the caravan which is approaching Tell al Muqayyar. Taylor pitches his tents at the foot of the red mound. He has neither scientific ambitions nor previous knowledge. Where is he to begin? Where is the best spot to deploy his native diggers? The great brick mound, architectural masterpiece of a shadowy past though it might be, conveys nothing to him. Perhaps in the heart of it lies something which might eventually be exhibited in the museum and might interest the London experts. He thinks vaguely of old statues, armour, ornaments or even perhaps buried treasure. He takes a closer look at the curious staged tower. Step by step he taps its surface. No indication of a hollow cavity within. The great edifice appears to be completely solid. Thirty feet above him the wall of the lowest block rises straight and sheer out of the sand. On its northern face three ramps of steps—two against the wall and one running at right angles to them—lead to the first terrace, above which tower a second and third.

Taylor clambers up and down, crawls along the ledges on hands and knees in the broiling sun, finding only broken tiles. One day, bathed in sweat, he reaches the topmost platform and a few owls fly startled from the dilapidated walls. Nothing more. However he is not discouraged. In his efforts to get to the heart of the secrets of the ruin he makes a decision which today we can only deeply regret. He takes his labour gangs away from the base and sets them to work at the top.

What had survived for centuries, what had withstood sandstorm and blazing sun alike, became now the victim of tireless pickaxes. Taylor gives orders to pull down the top story. The work of destruction begins at the four corners simulta-

Left **The 'vulture stela', originating from about 2500BC, was discovered in several fragments at Tell Loh. On the piece shown here, the god Ningirsu holds a net full of captured enemies. One of them has pushed his head through the mesh and seems about to receive a blow from the god's club. The stela is a record of the victory of Eannatum of Lagash, the 'steward of the god' who was avenging military inroads made by the kingdom of Umma.**

Right **One of the oldest pictorial stelae of Sumeria is this fragment of the 'lion hunt stela'. It was found in the shrine of Eanna at Uruk and has been dated to 3000BC, when the first princely cities were established in Mesopotamia. So it is a local ruler who is shown here engaged in a hunt; and perhaps the scene should also be taken metaphorically to signify the conquest of enemies, as on contemporary cylindrical seals.**

Plan of the city of Ur

1 Wall around the temple enclosure of the shrine of Nannar
2 Ziggurat
3 Entrance courtyard
4 Temple of Ningal, the consort of the moon god
5 Storehouse
6 Palace
7 Royal graves of the First Dynasty
8 Royal graves of the Third Dynasty
9 Excavated living quarters
10 Temple of Enki
11 Harbour temple
12 Palace of the High Priestess Bel-Shalti-Nannar
13 Fortress
14 North harbour
15 West harbour

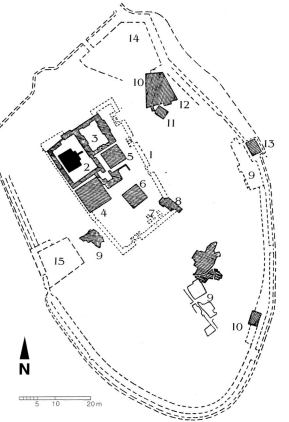

The central staircase of the ziggurat at Ur leads in a straight line up to the high temple of the moon god Nannar on the uppermost platform.

further results from Tell al Muqayyar and the expedition was abandoned.

It was seventy-five years later before the world learned what priceless treasures were still lying on this spot.

As far as the experts were concerned Tell al Muqayyar was once more forgotten. But it was by no means neglected. No sooner had Taylor left than hordes of other visitors arrived. The broken walls and above all the top tier of the mound, which Taylor's gangs had shattered, provided inexpensive building material for the Arabs who over the years came from far and near and departed with as many bricks as their pack-mules could carry. These bricks, fashioned by men's hands thousands of years before, still bore plainly the names of Ur-Nannu, the first great builder, and of Nabonidus, the Babylonian conqueror who restored the staged tower which they called the Ziggurat. Sandstorms, rain, wind and the heat of the sun have all added their quota to the process of destruction.

During the First World War when British troops on the march to Baghdad in 1915 camped near this ancient structure they found that its former appearance had been completely altered. It had become so flat due to dilapidation and theft in the intervening years since 1854 that one of the soldiers was able to indulge in a piece of daredevilry. The once steeply raked step-formation of the tower had disappeared so completely that he was able to ride his mule right to the summit of the mound.

By a lucky chance there was an expert among the officers of the party, R. Campbell Thompson, of the Intelligence Staff of the army in Mesopotamia. In peace time he had been an assistant in the British Museum. Thompson rummaged with an expert eye through the huge heap of bricks and was shocked at the deterioration of the material. Examination of the terrain led him to suppose that there were further areas worth investigating in the neighbourhood of the Tell, ruins of settlements which lay buried under the sand. Thompson recorded all this with great care and sent an urgent message to London. This prompted them to blow the dust off the insignificant looking little clay cylinders which had almost been forgotten and to look at them again with greater attention. The inscriptions on them were then found to contain some extremely important information as well as a curious story.

Almost 2,500 years before Taylor someone

neously. Day after day masses of bricks crash dully down the sides to the ground. After many weeks the chattering voices on the top of the mound are suddenly hushed, the clanging and banging of the pickaxes stop abruptly. Falling over each other in their haste a few men rush down the side of the mound and up to Taylor's tent. In their hands they hold little bars, cylinders made of baked clay. Taylor is disappointed. He had expected more. As he carefully cleans his finds he recognizes that the clay rolls are covered over and over with inscriptions—cuneiform writing! He understands none of it but he is highly delighted. The cylinders, carefully packed, are despatched to London. The scholars on Thames-side are however not impressed—and small wonder. These were the years when the experts were looking to North Mesopotamia, where, under their fascinated gaze, the emergence from the hills of Nineveh and Khorsabad on the upper Tigris of the palaces and colossal reliefs of the Assyrians, as well as thousands of clay tablets and statues, was enough to put everything else in the shade. What significance compared with them had the little clay cylinders from Tell al Muqayyar? For two years more Taylor hopefully continued his search. But there were no

else had been searching and rummaging on the same spot and with the same concern—Nabonidus, king of Babylon in the sixth century BC, venerator of the past, man of renown, ruler of a mighty kingdom and archaeologist rolled into one. In his day he established that *the Ziggurat was now old*. But his tactics were different from Taylor's. *I restored this Ziggurat to its former state with mortar and baked bricks.* When the weakened structure of the staged tower had been restored he had caused the name of the first builder, which he had discovered, to be cut out on these little clay cylinders. His name, as the Babylonian had been able to decipher from a damaged inscription, had been King Ur-Nammu. Ur-Nammu? Was the builder of the great staged tower king of the Ur that the Bible mentions? Was he the ruler of Ur of the Chaldees?

It seemed highly probable. The same biblical name had cropped up several times since then. Ancient records which had been recovered from other sites in Mesopotamia also mentioned Ur. It appeared from these cuneiform writings that it was the capital city of the great Sumerian people.

At once the battered remnants of Tell al Muqayyar aroused eager interest. Scholars from the Museum of Pennsylvania University joined the archaeologists from the British Museum in fresh investigations. The staged tower on the lower Euphrates might hold the secret of this unknown Sumerian people—and of the Ur of the Bible. But it was not until 1923 that a joint American and British team of archaeologists could set out. They were spared the tiresome journey on the backs of swaying camels. They went by the Baghdad railway. Their

Above **Ur-Nammu, the founder of the Third Dynasty of Ur, built temple towers in several towns of his kingdom, and these are probably the first to display the characteristic step-formation of the ziggurat. The ziggurat of Ur survives up to the height of its second platform. Staged towers of this kind form the background to the biblical story of the Tower of Babel.**

Below **In the sixth century BC the late Babylonian king Nabonidus had the shrine of the moon god restored. The inscriptions added in the restoration allowed Tell al Muqayyar to be identified as the biblical 'Ur of the Chaldeans' from which Abraham's journeyings began.**

The ziggurat of Choga Zambil in Susiana (southern Iran) was built about the middle of the thirteenth century BC by the Elamite king Untashgal. Partially restored, it still towers up to a height of 25 metres (opposite page). Originally there were five levels, of which the highest formed the temple of the chief god of what was once Dur Untashi, Inshushinak. Unlike the Mesopotamian pattern, the stairs leading to the temple platform are not open, but are built into the stages of the tower (right). Apart from bricks bearing the founder's records in cuneiform writing, the walls also bore glazed decorative studs. Small glass plates formed the temple roof, representing a starry sky. Around the ziggurat the excavators found further temples (above).

equipment likewise went by train: trucks, rails, picks, spades, baskets.

The archaeologists had enough funds at their disposal to turn up the whole countryside. They begin their carefully planned excavation on a large scale. Since considerable funds might be expected, they reckon on taking several years. In charge of the expedition is Sir Charles Leonard Woolley. The forty-three year old Englishman had already won his spurs on expeditions and digs in Egypt, Nubia and Carchemish on the upper Euphrates.

Now this talented and successful man makes Tell al Muqayyar his life's work. Unlike the zealous but unsuspecting Taylor several decades before, his chief aim is not directed to the staged tower at all. He is possessed with a desire above all to investigate these flat mounds which rise all around him out of the vast sandy plain.

Woolley's trained eye had not failed to note their striking configuration. They look like little Table Mountains. Flat on top, they slope downwards in an almost uniform pattern. Similar mounds exist in great numbers, large and small, in the Middle East, on the banks of the great rivers, in the midst of fertile plains, by the wayside on the routes followed by caravans from time immemorial. No one has yet been able to count them. We find them from the delta of the Euphrates and Tigris on the Persian Gulf to the highlands of Asia Minor where the river Halys tumbles into the Black Sea, on the eastern shores of the Mediterranean, in the valleys of the Lebanon, on the Orontes in Syria and in Palestine by the Jordan.

These little eminences are the great quarries for archaeological finds, eagerly sought and often

inexhaustible. They are not formed by the hand of Nature, but are artificially created, piled high with the legacy of countless generations before us; vast masses of rubble and rubbish from a bygone age which have accumulated from the remains of huts and houses, town walls, temples or palaces. Each one of these hills took shape gradually in the same way through a period of centuries or even millennia. At some point after men had first settled there the place was destroyed by war or was burned down or was deserted by its inhabitants. Then came the conquerors or new settlers and built upon the selfsame spot. Generation after generation built their settlements and cities, one on top of the other, on the identical site. In the course of time the ruins and rubble of countless dwellings grew, layer by layer, foot by foot, into a sizeable hill. The Arabs of today call such an artificial mound a *Tell*. The same word was used even in ancient Babylon. Tell means 'mound'. We come across the word in the Bible in Josh. II:13. During the conquest of Canaan, where cities *that stood on their mounds* are spoken of, it is these *Tulul*, which is the plural of *Tell*, which are meant. The Arabs

Overleaf **Of the once gigantic ziggurat in the town of Dur Kurigalzu, east of Baghdad, there remains little more than a 57-metre-high, bizarrely weathered stump. Even so, in the formless ruin, the building techniques of a staged tower of the fourteenth century BC can be clearly deciphered. The core is built of unfired mud bricks. To achieve better bonding and withstand the enormous weight, builders added a layer of reeds roughly after each eighth or ninth course of bricks. As a reinforcement to prevent the steeply sloping walls from drifting apart, ten centimetres of thick reed rope were stretched horizontally through the whole body of the wall. The dilapidation of the ziggurat probably set in when thieves removed the fired cladding bricks.**

The Third Dynasty of Ur was founded towards 2100BC by Ur-Nammu. Some huge building projects in Ur are associated with his name, including the ziggurat of the moon god Nannar. It is to this god that Ur-Nammu is sacrificing in the reliefs on a stela, which should probably be taken as a record of the building work. In the fragmentary lower section of the stela the ruler follows the moon god and carries on his shoulder building tools for the erection of the ziggurat. Evidently it was during his time that the staged tower received the form which became standard in later eras.

error in establishing a date in this way is at the outside about fifty years.

Priceless information was lost in the course of the first great excavations of last century because no one paid any attention to these apparently worthless bits of broken pottery. They were thrown aside. The only important things seemed to be great monuments, reliefs, statues or jewels. Much that was of value was thus lost for ever. The activities of Heinrich Schliemann, the antiquary, are an example of this sort of thing. Fired with ambition he had only one end in view: to find Homer's Troy. He set his gangs of labourers on to digging straight down. Strata, which might have been of great value in establishing dates, were thrown aside as useless rubbish. At length Schliemann unearthed a valuable treasure amid general acclamation. But it was not, as he thought, the treasure of Priam. His find belonged to a period several centuries earlier. Schliemann had missed the reward of his labours, that would have meant so much to him, by digging past it and going far too deep. Being a business man Schliemann was an amateur, a layman. But the professionals were, to begin with, no better. It is only in this century that the archaeologists have been working by the stratigraphic method of excavation, with the goal of establishing a chronology of cultures represented by different layers (strata). Beginning at the top and working down through the Tell they examine every square inch of the ground. Every tiny object, every piece of pottery is scrutinized. First vertical cuts are made through the mound of deposits. They serve to establish the 'stratigraphic profile'. The different coloured strata lie open like a cut cake and the trained eye of the expert is able at a rough glance to place in their historical perspective whatever ancient human habitations lie embedded there. It was in accordance with this tried method that the Anglo-American expedition started work at Tell al Muqayyar in 1923.

make a clear distinction between a Tell and a natural eminence, which they call a *Jebel*.

Every Tell is at the same time a silent history book. Its strata of occupation are for the archaeologist like the leaves of a calendar. Page by page he can make the past come to life again. Every layer, if we read it aright, tells of its own times, its life and customs, the craftsmanship and manners of its people. This skill on the part of excavators in deciphering the message of the strata has reached astonishing heights of achievement.

Stones, hewn or rough, bricks or traces of clay betray the nature of the building. Even decayed and weathered stones or the remains of brick dust can indicate exactly the ground plan of a building. Dark shadows show where once a fireplace radiated its warming glow. Broken pottery, armour, household utensils and tools which are to be found everywhere among the ruins, afford further help in this detective work on the past.

Today the different shapes, colours and patterns of pots and vases can be so clearly distinguished that pottery has become archaeology's Number One measurement of time. Single potsherds, sometimes only fragments, make it possible to give a precise dating. As far back as the second millennium BC the greatest margin of

In early December there arose a cloud of dust over the rubble heap which lay east of the Ziggurat and only a few steps from the broad ramp up which ancient priests in solemn procession had approached the shrine of Nannar the moon-god. Fanned by a light wind it spread across the site until it seemed as if the whole area around the old staged tower was shrouded in fine mist. Powdery sand whirling up from hundreds of spades indicated that the great dig had started.

From the moment when the first spade struck the ground an atmosphere of excitement hovered over every shovelful. Each spadeful was like a journey into an unknown land where no-one knew beforehand what surprises lay ahead. Excitement gripped even Woolley and his companions. Would some important find richly reward them for their toil and sweat upon the hill? Would Ur give up its secrets to them? None of these men could guess that for six long winter seasons, till the spring of 1929, they would be kept in suspense. This large-scale excavation deep in Southern Mesopotamia was to reveal bit by bit those far off days when a new land arose out of the delta of the two great rivers and the first human settlers made their home there. Out of their painstaking research, carrying them back to a time 7,000 years before, events and names recorded in the Bible were more than once to take solid shape.

The first thing, they brought to light was a sacred precinct with the remains of five temples, which had once surrounded King Ur-Nammu's Ziggurat in a semi-circle. They were like fortresses, so thick were their walls. The biggest one, which was 100 x 60 yards square, was dedicated to the moon-god. Another temple was in honour of Nin-Gal, goddess of the moon and wife of Nannar. Every temple had an inner court surrounded by a series of rooms. The old fountains were still standing, with long water troughs coated with bitumen. Deep grooves made with knives on the great brick tables showed where the sacrificial animals had been dissected. They were cooked as a common sacrificial meal on the hearths of the temple kitchens. Even the ovens for baking bread were there. 'After 3,800 years,' noted Woolley in his diary, 'we were able to light the fire again and put into commission once more the oldest kitchen in the world.'

Nowadays churches, law courts, tax offices and factories are quite separate establishments. It was otherwise in Ur. The sacred area, the Temple precinct, was not reserved exclusively for the worship of the gods. The priests had many other things to do besides their holy office. As well as receiving the sacrifices they collected the tithes and the taxes. That did not take place however without written confirmation. Every payment was noted on a little clay tablet—probably the first tax receipts ever issued. The amounts received were entered by scribes in weekly, monthly and yearly totals.

Minted currency was as yet unknown. Taxes were paid in kind: every inhabitant of Ur paid in his own coin. Oil, cereals, fruit, wool and cattle made their way into vast warehouses, perishable articles went to the temple shops. Many goods were manufactured in factories owned by the temple, for example in the spinning-mills which

In the early Sumerian shrine of Eanna was found a large alabaster vase, more than a metre in overall height. The reliefs on it show a kind of harvest festival: crops and herds are being brought to the treasury and storerooms of the temple. Unfortunately the portrait of the goddess is not completely preserved; it may be Innin to whom the procession is dedicated.

the priests managed. One workshop produced twelve different kinds of fashionable clothing. Tablets found in this place gave the names of the mill-girls and their quota of rations. Even the weight of the wool given to each worker and the number of garments made from it were meticulously recorded. In one of the legal buildings they found copies of the sentences carefully stacked exactly as they are in the administrative offices of modern law courts.

For three winter seasons the Anglo-American expedition worked on at the site of ancient Ur, and still this extraordinary museum of man's early history had not yielded up all its secrets. Outside the temple area the excavators had a further surprise.

South of the staged tower, as they were clearing away a series of mounds, there suddenly emerged from the rubble solid structures: row upon row of walls and facades one after the other. As the sand was cleared away it revealed a complete checkerboard of dwellinghouses whose ruins were in places still 10 feet high. Between them ran little alleyways. Here and there open squares broke the line of the streets.

Several weeks of hard work were necessary and endless loads of rubble had to be removed before the diggers were faced with an unforgettable sight: under the red slopes of Tell al Muqayyar lay a whole city, bathed in the bright sunshine, awakened from its long sleep after many thousand years by the patient burrowing of the archaeologists. Woolley and his companions were beside themselves with joy. For before them lay Ur, the *Ur of the Chaldees* to which the Bible refers.

And how well its citizens lived, and in what spacious homes! No other Mesopotamian city has revealed such handsome and comfortable houses.

Compared with them the dwelling-houses which have been preserved in Babylon are modest, in fact miserable. Robert Koldewey, during German excavations there at the beginning of this century, found nothing but simple mud brick erections, one story high with three or four rooms surrounding an open courtyard. That was how people lived about 600BC in the much admired and extolled metropolis of Nebuchadnezzar the Great of Babylon. But 1,500 years before that the citizens of Ur were living in large two-storied villas with thirteen or fourteen rooms. The lower floor was solidly built of burnt brick, the upper floor of mud brick. The walls were neatly coated with plaster and whitewashed.

A visitor would pass through the door into a small entrance hall where there was a basin to

Only a small portion of the residential areas of the ancient city of Ur has been excavated. The streets and alleys lead between houses which are frequently grouped around small courtyards, and often set into one another in complicated arrangements. Between them lie workshops, shops, tiny shrines and places of worship; even a school has been found. This, so it is believed, is where Abraham once lived.

wash the dust off hands and feet. He then continued into the inner court, which was laid out in attractive paving. Round it were grouped the reception room, the kitchen, living rooms and private rooms and the domestic chapel. Up a stone staircase, which concealed a lavatory, he would reach a gallery from which branched off the rooms belonging to members of the family and the guest rooms.

From beneath the debris of brick and plaster there emerged into the light of day all the things that these patrician houses had contained in the way of domestic appliances for ordinary use. Countless shreds of pots, jugs, vases and small clay tablets covered with writing combined to form a mosaic from which piece by piece a picture of everyday life in Ur could be reconstructed. *Ur of the Chaldees* was a powerful, prosperous, colourful and busy capital city at the beginning of the second millennium BC.

One idea was very much in Woolley's mind. Abraham is said to have come from *Ur of the Chaldees*—he must therefore have been born in one of these two-storied

patrician houses and must have grown up there. Woolley wandered through these alleyways, past the walls of the great temple, and as he looked up he glimpsed this huge staged tower with its black, red and blue blocks and its fringe of trees. 'We must radically alter', he writes enthusiastically, 'our view of the Hebrew patriarch when we see that his earlier years were passed in such sophisticated surroundings. He was the citizen of a great city and inherited the traditions of an old and highly organized civilization. The houses themselves reveal comfort and even luxury. We found copies of the hymns which were used in the services of the temples and together with them mathematical tables. On these tables were anything from plain addition sums to formulae for the extraction of square and cube roots. In other texts the writers had copied out the old building inscriptions to be found in the city and had compiled in this way a short history of the temples.'

Abraham—no simple nomad, this Abraham, but son of a great city of the second millennium BC.

That was a sensational discovery and one difficult to grasp. Newspapers and magazines carried photographs of the crumbling old staged

Alongside its incredibly rich and sumptuous treasures, the royal cemetery of the First Dynasty of Ur also revealed a gruesome fact: servants, courtiers and soldiers apparently followed their dead lord into the grave. From the skull of one of the jewel-laden women (above) it has been possible to create an impressive reconstruction of how she looked when alive (left). Most of the finds are exhibited in the Iraq Museum in Baghdad.

tower and the ruins of the metropolis. They caused a tremendous sensation. People looked with astonishment at a drawing which bore the title: 'A House of the time of Abraham'. Woolley had had this done by an artist. It is a genuine reconstruction in accordance with the finds. It shows the inner court of a villa-type house; two tall jars stand on a tiled pavement; a wooden balustrade running round the upper story shuts off the rooms from the courtyard. Was the old familiar picture of the patriarch Abraham, as it had been held for generations, which saw him surrounded by his family and his cattle, suddenly to be called in question?

Woolley's idea did not remain unchallenged. Very soon theologians and even archaeologists registered their dissent.

One of the most famous bonuses of the richly furnished pit graves in the royal cemetery of Ur is the so-called 'standard', now in the British Museum. 20.3 centimetres high and 48.3 centimetres wide, the wooden chest is decorated with mosaics of mussel shells, red limestone and lapis lazuli, depicting a historical event. In the

lower frieze of one face of the chest, four chariots with a driver and an armed guard charge over their fallen enemies. In the middle row of pictures, warriors march into battle, overcome their opponents and lead them away.
Above, the prisoners are brought before the victorious ruler.

In favour of Woolley's idea were the words of Genesis I:31: *And Terah took Abraham his son and Lot . . . and they went forth . . . from Ur of the Chaldees.* But there are other references in the Bible which point to somewhere else. When Abraham sends his old servant from Canaan to the city of Nahor, to fetch a wife for his son Isaac, he calls this place Nahor his *country* (Genesis 24:4), his

father's household and *native land* (Genesis 24:7). Nahor lay in the north of Mesopotamia. After the conquest of the Promised Land Joshua addressed the people in these words: *Long ago your fore-fathers, including Terah the father of Abraham and Nahor, lived beyond the River . . .* (Joshua 24:2). In this case the *river* means as in other places in the Bible, the Euphrates. The city of Ur was excavated

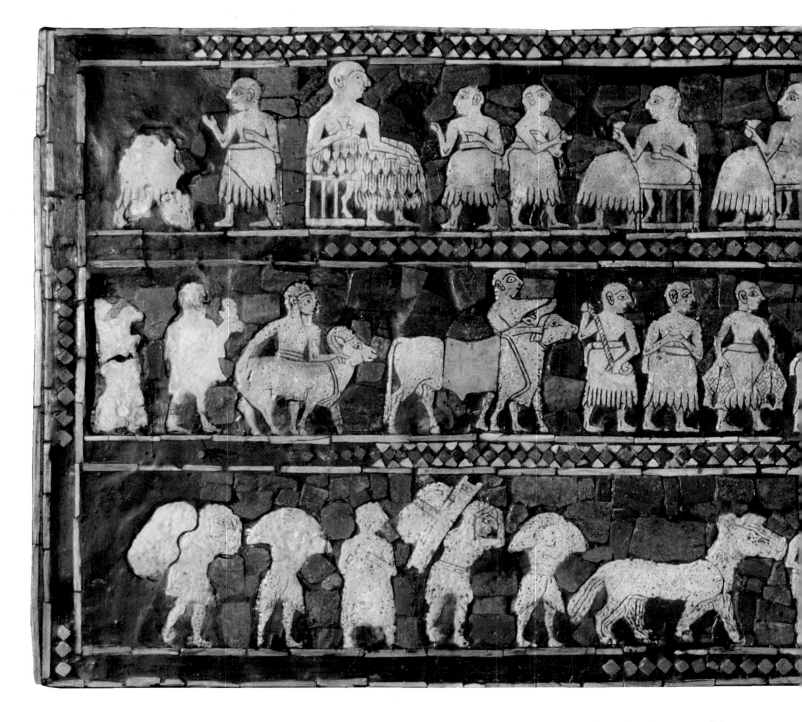

on the right bank of the Euphrates: looked at from Canaan it lay on this side, not on the other side of the *river*. Had Woolley been too hasty in his conclusions? What reliable evidence had the expedition produced? What proof was there that Terah and his son Abraham lived actually in the city of Ur?

'The earlier journey from Ur of the Chaldees to Haran has, apart from the discovery of the city itself, no archaeological foundation,' declares Professor W.F. Albright of Johns Hopkins University. This scholar, who himself conducted successful excavations and was in his time regarded as one of the foremost authorities on the archaeology of Palestine and the Middle East, went further. 'The remarkable fact that the Greek translations (of the

Bible) nowhere mention Ur but read instead the more natural "Land (of the Chaldees)" might mean that the removal of Abraham's native place to Ur is possibly secondary and was not generally known in the third century BC.'

Ur emerged from the shadowy past as one of the major cities of the Sumerians, who were among the oldest and most significant cultures in Mesopotamia. As we know, the Sumerians were not Semites like the Hebrews. When the great invasion of Semitic nomads streamed out of the Arabian desert about 2000BC its first encounter in the south was with the extensive plantations of Ur, its houses and its canals. It is possible that some recollection of that great journey through the lands of the 'Fertile Crescent,' in which Ur was

On the 'peace side' of the so-called standard of Ur, the upper frieze shows a festive meal, at which a lyre player and a musician are performing. In the middle band, fat stock and fish are delivered. The bottom row shows bringers of tribute, who are leading wild asses and carrying bundles.

The glassy, staring eyes of this group of petitioners speak of fear and dread at the inconceivable world of the gods. They come from the Temple of Abu at Tell Asmar, once Eshunna, north-east of Baghdad. The twelve votive statues made of marble from Mosul were discovered hidden under the floor of the temple, in the course of excavations carried out from 1930 to 1936 by the University of Chicago.

involved, has resulted in its being mentioned in the Bible. Painstaking research, particularly excavations in the following two decades, make it almost certain that Abraham cannot ever have been a citizen of the Sumerian metropolis. It would conflict with all the descriptions which the Old Testament gives of the kind of life lived by the patriarch: Abraham is a tent dweller, he moves with his flocks from pasture to pasture and from well to well. He does not live like a citizen of a great city—he lives the life of a typical nomad.

As we shall see, it was much farther to the north of the 'Fertile Crescent' that the stories of the biblical patriarchs emerged out of their mystical obscurity on to the plane of history.

DIGGING UP THE FLOOD

The Lord then said to Noah, 'Go into the ark, you and your whole family, because I have found you righteous in this generation. Seven days from now I will send rain on the earth for forty days and forty nights, and I will wipe from the face of the earth every living creature I have made' . . . And after the seven days the floodwaters came on the earth.

GENESIS 7:1, 4, 10

When we hear the word Flood, almost immediately we think of the Bible and the story of Noah's Ark. This wonderful Old Testament story has travelled round the world with Christianity. But although this is the best known tradition of the Flood it is by no means the only one. Among people of all races there is a variety of traditions of a gigantic and catastrophic Flood. The Greeks told the Flood story and connected it with Deucalion: long before Columbus many stories told among the natives of the continent of America kept the memory of a great Flood alive: in Australia, India, Polynesia, Tibet, Kashmir and Lithuania tales of a Flood have been handed down from generation to generation up to the present day. Are they all fairy tales and legends, are they all inventions?

It is highly probable that they all reflect the same world wide catastrophe. This frightful occurrence must, however, have taken place at a time when there were human beings on earth who could experience it, survive it, and then pass on an account of it. Geologists thought that they could

Left The large trench in the royal cemetery of Ur, in which Sir Leonard Woolley stumbled on the 'Flood-layer'. Above and below the layer of clay, nearly three metres thick, traces of human settlement were found, which led Woolley to conclude that there was a catastrophic flood about 4000BC.

Right Sir Leonard Woolley excavating in Ur.

solve this ancient mystery by pointing to the warm periods in the earth's history, between the Ice Ages. They suggested that when the huge ice-caps covering the continents, some of them many thousand feet high, gradually began to melt, the level of the sea rose to four times its normal height all over the world. This great additional volume of water altered land contours, flooded low lying coastal areas and plains, and annihilated their population, their animals, and their vegetation. But all these attempts at explanation ended in speculation and theory. Possible hypotheses satisfy the historian least of all. He constantly demands unambiguous factual evidence. But there was none: no scientist, whatever his line, could produce any. Actually it was by a coincidence—during research into something quite different—that unmistakable evidence of the Flood appeared, as it were, of its own accord. And that happened at a place we have already got to know: at the excavations at Ur.

For six years American and British archaeologists had been examining the ground at Tell al Muqayyar, which by that time looked like one vast building site. When the Baghdad train stopped there for a moment, travellers looked with amazement at the soaring sandhills which had resulted from the diggings. Waggon loads of soil were removed, carefully searched, and put through the riddle. Rubbish thousands of years old was treated like precious cargo. Perseverance, conscientiousness, and painstaking effort had in six years yielded a handsome dividend. The Sumerian temples with their warehouses, workshops and law courts and the villa-type dwelling houses were followed, between 1926 and 1928, by discoveries of such magnificence and splendour that everything else so far paled into insignificance.

In a mound of rubble 15 metres high, to the south-east of the shrine of Nanna, the excavators laid bare the royal burial palace of Ur. The pit graves of the First Dynasty were veritable treasure chests, for they were filled with all the costly things that Ur in its heyday possessed. Golden drinking cups and goblets, wonderfully shaped jugs and vases, bronze tableware, mother of pearl mosaics, lapis lazuli and silver surrounded these bodies which had mouldered into dust. Harps and lyres rested against the walls. A young man, 'Hero of the land of God' as an inscription described him, wore a golden helmet. A golden comb decorated with blossom in lapis lazuli adorned the hair of the beautiful Sumerian 'Lady Shubad'. Even the famous tombs of Nofretete and Tutankhamun contained no more beautiful objects. 'The graves of the kings of Ur' are moreover 1,000 years older at least.

As well as these precious contents the vaults had another aspect which sends a shiver down the spine of the twentieth-century observer. In the vaults were found teams of oxen with the skeletons still in harness and each of the great waggons was laden with artistic household furniture. The whole retinue had clearly accompanied the prince in death, as could be gathered from the richly clad and ornamented skeletons with which they were surrounded. The tomb of the Lady Shubad had twenty such skeletons, other vaults had as many as seventy.

What can have happened here so long ago? There was not the slightest indication that they were victims of a violent death. In solemn procession, it would seem, the attendants with the oxdrawn treasure-waggons accompanied the body to the tomb. And while the grave was being sealed outside they composed their dead master for his last rest within. Then they took some drug, gathered round him for the last time and died of their own free will—in order to be able to serve him in his future existence.

For two centuries the citizens of Ur had buried their princes in these tombs. When they came to open the lowest and last tomb the archaeologists of the twentieth century AD found themselves transported into the world of 2800BC.

The Arabs who inhabit the Iraqi lowlands on the lower Euphrates still live in houses woven from reed stalks according to the traditional pattern used from time immemorial.

As the summer of 1929 approached the sixth season of digging at Tell al Muqayyar was drawing to a close. Woolley had put his native diggers once more on the royal cemetery. He wanted to be certain whether the ground under the deepest royal grave had fresh discoveries in store for the next season's excavation.

After the foundations of the tomb had been removed, a few hundred thrusts of the spade made it quite plain that further layers of rubble lay below. How far into the past could these silent chronometers take them?

When had the very first human settlement arisen on virgin soil under this mound? Woolley had to know. To make certain he very slowly and carefully sank shafts and stood over them to examine the soil which came up from the underlying strata. 'Almost at once,' he wrote later in his diary, 'discoveries were made which confirmed our suspicions. Directly under the floor of one of the tombs of the kings we found in a layer of charred wood ash numerous clay tablets, which were covered with characters of a much older type than the inscriptions on the graves. Judging by the nature of the writing the tablets could be assigned to about 3000BC. They were therefore two or three centuries earlier than the tombs.'

The shafts went deeper and deeper. New strata with fragments of jars, pots and bowls kept coming up. The experts noticed that the pottery remained surprisingly enough unchanged. It looked exactly like what had been found in the graves of the kings. Therefore it seemed as if for centuries Sumerian civilization had undergone no radical change. They must, according to this conclusion, have reached a high level of development astonishingly early.

When after several days some of Woolley's workmen called out to him 'We are on ground level' he let himself down on to the floor of the shaft to satisfy himself. Traces of any kind of settlement did in fact abruptly break off in the shaft. The last fragments of household utensils lay on the smooth flat surface of the base of the pit. Here and there were charred remains. Woolley's first thought was: 'This is it at last'. He carefully prodded the ground on the floor of the shaft and stopped short: it was clay, pūre clay of a kind that could only have been deposited by water! Clay in a place like that? Woolley tried to find an explanation: it must be the accumulated silt of the Euphrates in bygone days. This stratum must have come into existence when the great river thrust its delta far out into the Persian Gulf, just as it still does, creating new land out of the sea at the river

mouth at the rate of 75 feet a year. When Ur was in its heyday, the Euphrates flowed so close to it that the great staged tower was reflected in its waters and the Gulf was visible from the temple on its summit. The first buildings must therefore have sprung up on the mud flats of the delta.

Measurements of the adjacent area and more careful calculations brought Woolley eventually however to quite a different conclusion.

'I saw that we were much too high up. It was most unlikely that the island on which the first settlement was built stood up so far out of the marsh.'

The foot of the shaft, where the layer of clay began, was several yards above the river level. It could not therefore be river deposit. What was the meaning then of this remarkable stratum? Where did it come from? None of his associates could give him a satisfactory answer. They decided to dig on and make the shaft deeper.

Woolley gazed intently as once more basket after basket came out of the trench and their contents were examined. Deeper and deeper went the spades into the ground, 3 feet, 6 feet—still pure clay. Suddenly at nearly 10 feet the layer of

clay stopped as abruptly as it had started. What would come now?

The next baskets that came to the surface gave an answer that none of the expedition would have dreamt of. They could hardly believe their eyes. They had expected pure virgin soil. But what now emerged into the glaring sunshine was rubble and more rubble, ancient rubbish and countless potsherds. Under this clay deposit almost 10 feet thick they had struck fresh evidence of human habitation. The appearance and quality of the pottery had noticeably altered. Above the clay-stratum were jars and bowls which had obviously been turned on the potter's wheel, here on the

Above **At Kurna the Euphrates and the Tigris unite in the Shatt al-Arab waterway. The palm groves on its banks form the largest enclosed date-growing area in the world.**

Below **After high water, the Euphrates leaves behind substantial deposits of mud, which the scorching summer heat dries to rock hard lumps.**

From earliest times a type of boat known as a guffa was used on the Euphrates. These round vessels were woven out of willow branches and made watertight either by covering the bottom with as-phalt—the 'bitumen' or 'pitch' which Noah used for the ark—or by stretching animal skins over them. A relief from the palace of the Assyrian king Sennacherib (704–681BC) in Nineveh shows a boat of this 'guffa' type, covered with skins, rowed by four men (above).

Right **The Euphrates marshes are the scene of battles depicted on a relief from Sennacherib's palace in Nineveh.**

contrary they were hand-made. No matter how carefully they sifted the contents of the baskets, amid increasing excitement, metal remains were nowhere to be found, the primitive implement that did emerge was made of hewn flint. It must belong to the Stone Age!

That day a telegram from Mesopotamia fla-shed what was perhaps the most extraordinary message that had ever stirred men's imaginations 'We have found the Flood'. The incredible discov-ery at Ur made headline news in the United States and in Britain.

The Flood—that was the only possible expla-nation of this great clay deposit beneath the hill at Ur, which quite clearly separated two epochs of settlement. The sea had left its unmistakable traces in the shape of remains of little marine organisms embedded in the clay. Woolley had to confirm his conclusions without delay: a chance coinci-dence—although the odds were against it—might conceivably have been making fools of them. Three hundred yards from the first shaft he sank a second one.

The spades produced the same result: pots thrown on the wheel—a layer of clay—fragments of hand-made pottery.

Finally to remove all doubt, Woolley made them dig a shaft through the rubble where the old settlement lay on a natural hill, that is to say, on a considerably higher level than the stratum of clay.

Just at about the same level as in the two other shafts the sherds of wheel-turned vessels stopped suddenly. Immediately beneath them came hand-made clay pots. It was exactly as Woolley had supposed and expected. Naturally the intermedi-ate layer of clay was missing. 'About sixteen feet

below a brick pavement,' noted Woolley, 'which we could with reasonable certainty date about 2700BC we were among the ruins of that Ur which had existed before the Flood.'

How far did the layer of clay extend? What area was affected by the disaster? A proper hunt now started for traces of the Flood in other parts of Mesopotamia. Other archaeologists discovered a further important check-point near Kish, south-east of Babylon, where the Euphrates and the Tigris flow in a great bend towards each other. There they found a similar band of clay, but only 18 inches thick. Gradually by a variety of tests the limits of the Flood waters could be established. According to Woolley the disaster engulfed an area north-west of the Persian Gulf amounting to 400 miles long and 100 miles wide, looking at the map we should call it today 'a local occurrence'—for the inhabitants of the river plains it was how-ever in those days their whole world.

After endless enquiry and attempts at some explanation, without achieving any concrete re-sults, any hope of solving the great riddle of the Flood had long since been given up. It seemed to lie in a dark and distant region of time which we could never hope to penetrate. Now Woolley and his associates had through their tireless and patient efforts made a discovery which shattered even the experts: A vast catastrophic inundation, resembling the biblical Flood which had regularly been described by sceptics as either a fairy tale or a legend, had not only taken place but was more-over an event within the compass of history.

At the foot of the old staged tower of the Sumerians, at Ur on the lower Euphrates, anyone could climb down a ladder into a narrow shaft and see and touch the remains of a gigantic and catastrophic Flood which had deposited a layer of clay almost to feet thick. Reckoning by the age of the strata containing traces of human habitation, and in this respect they are as reliable as a calen-dar, it could also be ascertained when the great Flood took place.

It happened about 4000BC.

It was in the library of Ashurbanipal at Nineveh that the cuneiform tablets of the Epic of Gilgamesh were discovered. Only a massive mound of ruins now betrays the place where once there stood the capital city of the Assyrians, destroyed by the Medes and Babylonians in 612BC.

A FLOOD-STORY FROM OLD BABYLONIA

So God said to Noah, 'I am going to put an end to all people, for the earth is filled with violence because of them. I am surely going to destroy both them and the earth. So make yourself an ark of cypress wood; make rooms in it and coat it with pitch inside and out.'

GENESIS 6:13–14

About the turn of the century, long before Woolley discovered Ur, another find had aroused great interest and given rise to lively discussions about the nature of Holy Scripture.

From the dim recesses of the Ancient East an old mysterious story came to light: a heroic epic, of 300 quatrains, inscribed on twelve large clay tablets, which told of the wonderful experiences of the legendary king Gilgamesh.

The text was astonishing: Gilgamesh told a tale exactly like the Bible—of a man who was said to have lived before and after a mighty and disastrous Flood.

Where did this splendid and remarkable epic come from?

During excavations in the fifties of last century British archaeologists had found these twelve clay tablets, together with about 20,000 others, all in a good state of preservation, among the ruins of the library at Nineveh, which was reckoned to be the most famous in the ancient world. King Ashurbanipal had it built in the seventh century BC high above the banks of the Tigris in old Nineveh. Today on the other side of the river the oil-derricks of Mosul tower into the sky.

A priceless treasure in packing cases started out on its long journey from Nineveh to the British Museum.

But it was not for several decades that the true value of these texts was revealed when they could finally be deciphered. At the time there was no one in the world who could read them. Despite every effort the tablets held their peace. Shortly before 1900 in the modest laboratories of the British Museum the old texts began, after an interval of twenty-five centuries, to unfold anew one of the finest narratives of the Ancient East. Assyriologists heard for the first time the Epic of Gilgamesh. It is written in Akkadian, the language of diplomacy in the second millenium BC. The form in which it existed in the library at Nineveh was given to it by a poet who probably lived in the twelfth century BC. Numerous further finds of clay tablets, not only in Sumerian and Akkadian, but also in the Hittite and Hurrite languages, testify to the wide distribution of the poetic Epic of Gilgamesh.

Its hero was in all likelihood a historical character, the king of a Sumerian kingdom whose capital was Uruk in southern Babylonia, who may have lived in the so-called 'Early Dynastic Period' in the first half of the third millenium BC.

Shattered by the death of his friend Enkidu, Gilgamesh wants to avoid the fate of death himself. He sets out on a long adventurous journey to find his ancestor Utnapishtim, from whom he hopes to learn the secret of everlasting life which the gods have bestowed on him. When he reaches the island on which Utnapishtim lives, Gilgamesh complains to him about his terror of death and asks him about death and life. According to the cuneiform writing on the eleventh tablet from the library at Nineveh, Utnapishtim tells Gilgamesh that he once lived in Shuruppak on the banks of the Euphrates and was a true worshipper of the god Ea. When the gods decided to destroy mankind by a Flood Ea warned his devotee Utnapishtim and issued this command:

> O man of Shuruppak, son of Ubar-Tutu, tear down thy house, build a ship; abandon wealth, seek after life; scorn possessions, save thy life. Bring up the seed of all kinds of living things into the ship: the ship which thou shalt build. Let its dimensions be well measured.

We all know the wonderful story which follows. For what the Sumerian Utnapishtim is said to have experienced, the Bible tells us about Noah.

> So God said to Noah . . . So make yourself an ark of cypress wood . . . You are to bring into the ark two of all living creatures, male and female, to keep them alive with you. (Genesis 6:13ff)

To make the comparison easier let us set side by side what Utnapishtim says of his great experience and what the Bible tells us of Noah and the Flood.

In accordance with the command of the god Ea, Utnapishtim builds the ship and says:

> On the fifth day I decided upon its plan.
> *This is how you are to build it: The ark is to be 450 feet long, 75 feet wide and 45 feet high. (Genesis 6:15)*
>
> The floor came to a 'field' in size (about 3600 square metres).
> The walls were each ten times twelve ells in height.
> I gave it six storeys and divided the breadth seven times.
> *Make a roof for it and finish the ark to within 18 inches of the top. Put a door in the side of the ark and make lower, middle and upper decks. (Genesis 6:16)*
> Its interior I divided into nine.

The eleventh tablet of the Epic of Gilgamesh from the library of Ashurbanipal in Nineveh contains Utnapishtim's account of the Flood.

. . . make rooms in it (Genesis 6:14)

6 sar of bitumen I poured into the kiln.
. . . coat it with pitch inside and out. (Genesis 6:14)

When Utnapishtim had finished building his ship he arranged a sumptuous banquet. He slaughtered deer and oxen for his helpers and dispensed *cider, beer, oil and wine to the people as if it were running water.* Then he continues:

All that I had I loaded, of the seed of all living things.
I brought into the ship my whole family and kinsfolk.
The cattle of the field, the beasts of the field, all craftsmen—I made them go up into it.
And Noah and his sons, and his wife and his sons' wives entered the ark to escape the waters of the flood.
Pairs of clean and unclean animals, of birds and of all creatures that move along the ground, male and female, came to Noah and entered the ark, as God had commanded Noah. (Genesis 7:7–9)

I went into the ship and closed my door.
Then the Lord shut him in. (Genesis 7:16)

As soon as a gleam of dawn shone in the sky, came a black cloud from the foundation of heaven. Inside it Adad thundered.
And after seven days the floodwaters came on the earth.
. . . on that day all the springs of the great deep burst forth, and the floodgates of the heavens were opened. (Genesis 7:10–11)
Adad's rage reached to the heavens: turning all light to darkness.

The gods are terrified by the Flood and flee to the upper reaches of heaven where the god Anu has his abode. They *cower like dogs . . . moan . . . complain . . . sit down and cry*—a description worthy of Homer!

But the Flood rages on unceasing, as Gilgamesh learns:

Six days and nights
Raged the wind, the flood, the cyclone devastated the land.
For forty days the flood kept coming on the earth, and as the waters increased they lifted the ark high above the earth. The waters rose and increased greatly on the earth, and the ark floated on the surface of the water. They rose greatly on the earth,

and all the high mountains under the entire heavens were covered. (Genesis 7:17–19)

When the seventh day came, the cyclone, the flood, the battle was over,
Which had battled like an army. The sea became calm, the cyclone died away, the flood ceased.
But God remembered Noah and all the wild animals and the livestock that were with him in the ark, and he sent a wind over the earth, and the waters receded. (Genesis 8:1)
Now the springs of the deep and the floodgates of the heavens had been closed, and the rain had stopped falling from the sky. The water receded steadily from the earth. At the end of the hundred and fifty days the water had gone down. (Genesis 8:2, 3)

And all mankind had turned to clay. The ground was flat like a roof.
Every living thing that moved on the earth perished—birds, livestock, wild animals, all the creatures that swarm over the earth, and all mankind. (Genesis 7:21)

And all mankind had turned to clay. Utnapishtim, the Sumerian Noah, is recording what he himself claimed to have lived through. Babylonians, Assyrians, Hittites and Hurrites who translated or read aloud or narrated these words had no more notion that they were describing something that actually happened, than did the modern Assyriologists who painfully deciphered them from the cuneiform tablets.

Today we know that the Flood story on the eleventh tablet of the Epic of Gilgamesh has a predecessor in the Old Babylonian Atramchasis Epic, which itself must have its origins in an eye-witness account. Only someone who had himself seen the desolation caused by a catastrophe of this kind could have described it with such striking force.

The great layer of mud, which covered every living thing like a shroud and levelled the ground until it was as *flat as a roof*, must have been seen with his own eyes by someone who had had a marvellous escape. The exact description of the great storm argues for this assumption. Utnapishtim expressly mentions a southern gale, which corresponds closely with the geographical situation. The Persian Gulf, whose waters were flung over the flat country by the gale, lies south of the estuary of the Tigris and Euphrates. To the last detail the weather conditions which he describes are characteristic of an unusual atmospheric disturbance. The appearance of black clouds and a roaring noise—sudden darkness in broad daylight—the howling of the southern gale as it drives the water in front of it. Any meteorologist recognize at once that this is a description of a cyclone. Modern weather experts recognize that, in tropical regions, coastal areas, islands, but above all alluvial river flats are subject to a spiral type of tidal wave which leaves devastation and destruction in its wake, and which is often caused by cyclones, accompanied by earthquakes and torrential rain.

All along the coast of Florida, in the Gulf of Mexico, and on the Pacific there is today an up-to-date alarm system with all the latest equipment. But for southern Mesopotamia in 4000BC even a modern alarm system would not have been of much use. Sometimes cyclones produce an effect which takes the shape of the Flood. There is an example in recent times.

In 1876 a cyclone of this nature, accompanied by tremendous thunderstorms, swept across the Bay of Bengal and headed for the coast at the mouth of the Ganges. Up to 200 miles from its centre ships at sea had their masts splintered. It was ebb-tide along the coast. The receding water was seized by the broad high sweep of the cyclone and a gigantic tidal wave reared itself up. It burst into the Ganges area and sea water 50 feet high swept inland—141 square miles were buried and 215,100 people died.

Utnapishtim tells a horrified Gilgamesh what happened when the disaster was over:

> I opened the window and the light fell on my face.
> *After forty days Noah opened the window he had made in the ark . . . (Genesis 8:6)*

> The ship lay upon Mount Nisir. Mount Nisir held the ship and allowed it not to move.
> *And on the seventeenth day of the seventh month the ark came to rest on the mountains of Ararat. (Genesis 8:4)*

Old Babylonian cuneiform texts describe with care where Mt. Nisir is to be found. It lies between the Tigris and the lower reaches of the river Zab, where the wild and rugged mountain ranges of Kurdistan rise sharply from the flat country bordering the Tigris. The alleged resting place corresponds perfectly with the last lap of the great catastrophe which burst inland from the south. We are told that Utnapishtim's home was in Shuruppak. It lay near the present day Fara in the

Left **The 4.7-metre-high colossus known as the 'hero with the lion', from the palace of the Assyrian king Sargon II (721–705) at Khorsabad (Dur Sarrukin) is thought to represent Gilgamesh (Louvre, Paris).**

Below **Fragment of a cuneiform tablet bearing part of the Epic of Gilgamesh, found in 1955 in Megiddo, Israel.**

Uruk, the biblical Erech, founded by Nimrod, was the royal city of Gilgamesh, who is said to have built the town wall, nearly ten kilometres in length. In the centre of the area occupied by the town is the Eanna area dedicated to the mother god Innin, with its ziggurat erected by Ur-Nammu. In contrast to Ur this is not a staged tower, but consists of a single terrace 55 metres long and 14 metres high.

middle of the flat fenland where Tigris and Euphrates part company. A tidal wave from the Persian Gulf must have carried a ship from here right to the Kurdistan mountains.

Despite the precise descriptions in the Epic of Gilgamesh, Mt. Nisir has never tempted the curious to search for the remains of this giant ship. Instead, Mt.Ararat, which belongs to the biblical tradition, has been the goal chosen by a series of expeditions.

Mt. Ararat lies in Eastern Turkey, near the borders of Russia and Iran. Its snow capped summit is over 16,000 feet high.

Last century, many years before any archaeologist turned a spadeful of Mesopotamian soil, the first expeditions were making their way to Mt. Ararat. A shepherd's story had started them off.

At the foot of Ararat lies the little Armenian village of Bayzit, whose inhabitants have for generations recounted the remarkable experience of a mountain shepherd who was said to have seen one day on Ararat a great wooden ship. A report from a Turkish expedition in 1833 seemed to confirm the shepherd's story since it mentioned a wooden prow of a ship which in the summer season stuck out of the south glacier.

The next person to claim to have seen it was Dr. Nouri, Archdeacon of Jerusalem and Babylon.

This agile ecclesiastical dignitary undertook a journey in 1892 to discover the sources of the Euphrates. On his return he told of the wreckage of a ship in the eternal ice: 'The interior was full of snow: the outer wall was of a dark red colour.' In the First World War a Russian flying officer, by name Roskowitzki, announced that he had spotted from his plane 'the remains of wreckage of a fair-sized ship' on the south flank of Ararat. Although it was the middle of the war, Czar Nicholas II despatched a search party without delay. It is supposed not only to have seen the ship but even to have photographed it. All proof of this however perished, presumably in the Revolution.

During the Second World War likewise, several aerial observations were reported by a Russian pilot and four American fliers.

These latter reports brought into the field the American historian and missionary Dr. Aaron Smith of Greensborough, an expert on the Flood. As a result of years of labour he has collected a complete history of the literature on Noah's Ark. There are 80,000 works in seventy-two languages about the Flood, of which 70,000 mention the legendary wreckage of the Ark.

In 1951 Dr. Smith spent twelve days with forty companions to no purpose on the ice-cap of Ararat. 'Although we found no trace of Noah's

Ark,' he declared later, 'my confidence in the biblical description of the Flood is no whit the less. We shall go back.'

Encouraged by Dr.Smith the young French Greenland explorer Jean de Riquer climbed the volcanic peak in 1952. He too came back without accomplishing anything. Despite this, further expeditions prepared themselves for an attempt on Mt.Ararat.

Fernand Navarra from France, searching for the most famous ship in history, succeeded to his great surprise in salvaging three fragments of a wooden beam embedded in solid ice on top of the mountain. The timber was at least 5,000 years old, although whether this was actually a relic of Noah's Ark it is of course impossible to say.

No tradition of the early days of Mesopotamia is in such close agreement with the Bible as the Flood-story in the Epic of Gilgamesh. In some places we find almost verbal correspondence. Yet there is a significant and essential difference. The familiar story in Genesis knows of one God only. The oddly amusing and primitive conception has disappeared of a heaven overcrowded with gods, many of whom bear all too human characteristics, who weep and wail, and are afraid of each other and cower like dogs.

The Epic of Gilgamesh had its origin in the same great area, the 'Fertile Crescent', in which the Bible likewise had its birth. As a result of the discovery of the clay-stratum at Ur it is certain that the old Mesopotamian epic deals with a traditional event: the Flood disaster about 4000BC in Southern Mesopotamia is vouched for by archaeology. But is that Babylonian Flood identical with the Flood of biblical tradition?

Above left **Some of the temples of the Eanna area in Uruk originate from as far back as the early Sumerian period.**

Below left **The high terrace consecrated to the chief heavenly god Anu, with its 'White Temple', is the second most important shrine of Uruk after the Eanna area.**

Right **A frieze of moulded bricks depicting mountain gods pouring out water once adorned the facade of the temple of Innin at Uruk, built in the fourteenth century BC. Parts of the facade have been reconstructed in the museums of Berlin and Baghdad.**

Overleaf **The snow-clad mountain of Ararat in eastern Turkey.**

ABRAHAM LIVED IN THE KINGDOM OF MARI

The Lord had said to Abram, Leave your country, and your people, and your father's household and go to the land I will show you.

GENESIS 12:1

The country of which the Bible is speaking in this case is Haran. Terah, his son Abram, his daughter-in-law Sarai, and his grandson Lot lived there (Genesis 11:31).

What was actually meant by Haran was until the twentieth century quite unknown. We knew nothing of its early history.

A chance find led to excavations in 1933, which here also gave rise to a great and exciting discovery and added considerably to our knowledge. They brought the Haran of the Bible and the kind of life lived by the patriarchs quite unexpectedly into a historical context.

On the line between Damascus and Mosul, where it cuts the Euphrates, lies the small unknown town of Abu Kemal. Since, as a result of the First World War, Syria was placed under a French mandate, there was a French garrison in the place.

The aerial photograph (left) shows the extensive palace of King Zimri-Lim of Mari. The centre of the structure consists of two great courtyards, approached from the north, which were attached to a throne room and a shrine. Other rooms too (altogether 260 have been counted) were grouped around courtyards. The north-western corner of the buildings, particularly strongly fortified, is taken to be the king's private apartments, of which the workshop of the palace scribes probably also formed part. In the southern part of the palace the storehouses with their large storage jars have been preserved (right). A room between the two great courtyards held the archives of cuneiform writings.

Over the broad Euphrates plain in midsummer 1933 lay a brooding, paralysing heat. Lieut. Cabane, the station-commander, expected, when he was called into the orderly room, that it was merely another of these quarrels among the Arabs that he was supposed to settle. He had had more than enough of that already. But this time the excitement in the office seemed to be about something different. Eventually he managed to extract through the interpreter the following story: These people had been burying one of their relatives. They were digging the grave on a remote hillside, by name Tell Hariri, when out popped a stone corpse!

Perhaps, thought Lieut. Cabane, this might be something that would interest the museum at Aleppo. At any rate it was a pleasant change from the endless monotony of this God-forsaken post.

In the cool of the evening he drove out to Tell Hariri, which lay about 7 miles to the north of Abu

Kemal near the Euphrates. The Arabs led him up the slope to the broken statue in a flat earthen trough which had so upset them the day before. Cabane was no expert, but he knew at once that the stone figure must be very old. Next day it was taken by French soldiers to Abu Kemal. The lights were on till long after midnight in the little command-post. Cabane was writing a detailed report on the find to his superior officer, to Henry Seyrig, Director of Antiquities in Beirut, and to the Museum at Aleppo.

Months went past and nothing happened. The whole thing seemed to be either unimportant or forgotten. Then at the end of November came a telegram from Paris, from the Louvre. Cabane could hardly believe his eyes and read the message again and again. In a few days important visitors from Paris would be arriving: Professor Parrot, the well known archeologist, accompanied by scientists, architects, assistants and draughtsmen.

At the foot of the staircase leading to the shrine in Zimri-Lim's palace the excavators found the statue of a man with a toga-style garment. The inscription on the shoulder of this almost lifesize figure in black stone identifies it as a portrait of the governor Ishtupilum, who probably held office about 2200BC.

Right **This statuette of King Lamgi-Mari, who probably ruled before the middle of the seconnd millennium BC, was found in the temple of Ishtar at Mari. His name and rank are carved into his right shoulder; his fringed ceremonial robe is drawn over his left shoulder. His hands are folded in a gesture of prayer.**

On the fourteenth of December Tell Hariri was buzzing like a bee-hive. The archaeologists had begun their detective-work. First of all the whole mound was carefully measured and photographed in detail. Soundings were taken for echoes, specimens of soil were removed and submitted to expert opinion. December went by and the first weeks of the New Year. The twenty-third of January 1934 was the decisive day.

As they were digging carefully through the outer crust of the Tell there appeared out of the rubble a neat little figure which had some writing pricked out on the right shoulder. Everyone bent over it, fascinated. *I am Lamgi-Mari... king... of Mari... the great... Issakk... who worships his statue... of Ishtar.*

Slowly, word by word, this sentence rings in the ears of the silent circle as Professor Parrot translates it from the cuneiform. This is an unforgettable moment for him and his companions. An

45

Right **The throne room or audience room in the palace of Zimri-Lim at Mari could only be reached from a large ceremonial courtyard by a semi-circular outside staircase jutting out of the building. The traces of wall painting which remain show the king involved in religious rites; a ruler of this period always had an additional function as a high priest, or even as a semi-divine figure.**

Below left and right **While palaces and temple buildings have been excavated in Mari, the residential**

areas have remained virtually un-explored. Our information on the living conditions of the citizens must therefore come from models of houses. This tower-like house in the Aleppo Museum (left), an apparently two-storeyd apartment which yet has no dividing floor, is an example of a frequently recurring type. The lower room is divided from the 'tower' by a windowed wall. The round house in the Damascus Museum (right) appears considerably more archaic. The tradition represented by this model of early dynastic origin undoubtedly has its roots in prehistoric times. In the middle of the round building lies a square room (or court?) with a hearth and benches, surrounded by four small rooms with antechambers, of which one is roofed but provided with a chimmey hole.

almost uncanny scene and probably unique in the history of archaeology with its surprises and adventures!

The monarch had solemnly welcomed the strangers from distant Paris and introduced himself to them. It was as if he wanted politely to show them the road into his kingdom of long ago which lay in a deep sleep beneath him, and of whose pomp and power the Parisian scholars had as yet no conception.

Carved in stone, a marvellous piece of sculpture, King Lamgi Mari stood before Parrot: a commanding broad-shouldered figure upon its base. But the face lacks that incredible arrogance which is so typical of the portraits of other conquerors from the ancient East, the Assyrians, who

without exception look fierce and bad tempered. The king of Mari is smiling. He carries no weapons, his hands are folded in an attitude of worship. His robe, which leaves one shoulder bare, like a toga, is richly decorated with fringes.

Hardly ever has an excavation been so crowned with success from the word 'go', and the first groping efforts. Mari, the royal city, must be lying slumbering under this mound.

Scholars had for a long time been familiar with the royal city of Mari which features in many old inscriptions from Babylonia and Assyria. One text maintained that Mari was the tenth city to be founded after the Flood. The great spade-offensive against Tell Hariri began.

With considerable intervals the digging went on from 1933 to 1939. For the greater part of the year the tropical heat made any activity impossible. Only in the cooler months of the rainy season, from the middle of December to the end of March, could anything be done.

The excavations at Tell Hariri brought a wealth of new discoveries to a chapter of the history of the Ancient East which is still unwritten.

No one knew as yet how close a connection the finds at Mari would prove to have with quite familiar passages in the Bible.

Year by year reports of the expedition provided fresh surprises.

In the winter of 1933–34 a temple of Ishtar the goddess of fertility was exposed. Three of Ishtar's

royal devotees have immortalized themselves as statues in the shrine which is inlaid with a mosaic of gleaming shells: Lamgi-Mari, Ebin-il, and Idi-Narum.

In the second season of digging the spades came upon the houses of a city. Mari had been found! However great was the satisfaction with their success, far more interest, indeed astonishment was aroused by the walls of a palace which must have been unusually large. Parrot reported: 'We have unearthed 69 rooms and courts, and there are still more to come.' One thousand six hundred cuneiform tablets, carefully stacked in one of the rooms, contained details of household management.

The record of the third campaign in 1935–36 noted that so far 138 rooms and courtyards had been found but that they had not yet reached the outer walls of the palace. Thirteen thousand clay tablets awaited deciphering. In the fourth winter a temple of the god Dagan was dug up and also a Ziggurat, the typical Mesopotamian staged tower. Two hundred and twenty rooms and courtyards

were now visible in the palace and another 8,000 clay tablets had been added to the existing collection.

At last in the fifth season, when a further forty rooms had been cleared of rubble, the palace of the kings of Mari lay in all its vast extent before Parrot and his assistants. This mammoth building of the third millennium BC covered almost ten acres.

Columns of lorries had to be commissioned to remove the cuneiform tablets from the palace archives alone. There were almost 24,000 documents. The great find of the tablets at Nineveh was put in the shade, since the famous library of the Assyrian king, Ashurbanipal, amounted to a 'mere' 22,000 clay texts.

To get a proper picture of Mari palace aerial photographs were taken. These pictures taken from a low altitude over Tell Hariri gave rise to almost incredulous amazement when they were published in France. This palace at Mari was, around 2000BC, one of the greatest sights of the world, the architectural gem of the Ancient East. Travellers came from far and near to see it. *I have*

This view of the imposing walls of Zimri-Lim's palace at Mari shows surviving parts of the original wall structure up to a height of five metres. The inner walls are as massive as the outer, a fact explained by the continuing preponderance of the use of unfired bricks. Among the great treasures salvaged from the ruins is the archive of clay tablets containing approximately 25,000 texts. They give an account not only of the goods that were traded in Mari and throughout the widespread trading network from Anatolia to the lands of the Gulf, but also of the caravans and nomadic shepherd tribes of the patriarchal age. Information on the positions of springs and oases and even lists of provisions for particular stretches of road give a graphic portrayal of daily life on the trade routes.

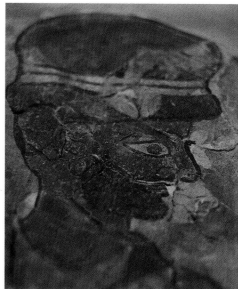

seen Mari, wrote an enthusiastic merchant from the Phoenician seaport of Ugarit.

The last king to live there was Zimri-Lim. The armies of the famous Hammurabi of Babylon subjugated the kingdom of Mari on the central reaches of the Euphrates and destroyed its mighty capital about 1700 BC.

Under the wreckage of roofs and walls were found the fire-pans of the Babylonian warriors, the incendiary squad who set fire to the palace.

But they were not able to destroy it completely. The walls were left standing to a height of 15 feet. 'The installations in the palace kitchens and bathrooms,' wrote Professor Parrot, 'could still be put into commission without the need of any repair, four thousand years after its destruction.' In the bathrooms they found the tubs, cake-moulds in the kitchens, even charcoal in the ovens.

The sight of these majestic ruins is an overwhelming experience. A single gate on the north side ensured easier control and better defence. Passing through a medley of courts and passages one reaches the great inner courtyard and broad daylight. This was the centre both of official life and the administration of the kingdom. The monarch received his officials as well as couriers and ambassadors in the neighbouring audience-chamber, large enough to hold hundreds of people. Broad corridors led to the king's private apartments.

One wing of the palace was used exclusively for religious ceremonies. It contained also a throne-room, approached by a marvellous staircase. A long processional way passed through several rooms to the palace chapel in which stood the image of the mothergoddess of fertility. From a vessel in her hands flowed perpetually 'the water of everlasting life'.

The entire court lived under the king's roof. Ministers, administrators, secretaries and scribes had their own roomy quarters.

There was a Foreign Office and a Board of Trade in the great administrative palace of the kingdom of Mari. More than 100 officials were involved in dealing with the incoming and outgoing mail, which amounted to thousands of tablets alone.

Wonderful frescoes added a decorative effect to the palace. Even to this day the colours have hardly lost any of their brilliance. They seem to have been laid on only yesterday but in fact they are the oldest paintings in Mesopotamia—1,000 years older than the renowned coloured frescoes in the splendid edifices of the Assyrian rulers at Khorsabad, Nineveh and Nimrod.

The size and grandeur of this unique palace corresponded to the land that was governed from it. Through these many thousands of years the palace archives have preserved the record.

Notices, public papers, decrees, accounts, scratched out on clay by the busy styli of well-paid scribes 4,000 years ago, had to be brought to life again with tireless industry. In Paris, Professor Georges Dossin, of the University of Liège, and a host of Assyriologists wrestled with the problem of deciphering and translating them.

Opposite page and above left **In the temple of Ishtar at Mari excavators found forty-five gypsum fragments which were painstakingly re-assembled into a figure almost a metre tall. The sacred statue portrays one of the early kings of Mari from before 2500BC; the inscription on his shoulder (above left) names him as Ikunshamagan. His eyebrows and pupils are inlaid in dark steatite, while his eyeballs are made of mussel shells.**

Above right **The rectangular courtyard in the palace of Zimri-Lim extended in front of a shrine, probably dedicated to Ishtar; at all events the traces of the wall painting with which the walls were decorated are related to her. This male head in the Aleppo Museum is part of a sacrificial procession with oxen. The paintings, originating from about 1800BC, are executed in a type of watercolour on a plaster coating; the palette is restricted to black, white and various shades of ochre.**

In the sacred precincts of the palace of Zimri-Lim at Mari excavators found a 45-centimetre-tall statue of a goddess pouring water, which now forms part of the treasures of the Aleppo Museum. Carved from white stone, she once had inlaid eyes, and her hair still shows traces of reddish painting. Her wavy robe, engraved with fishes, points symbolically to the life-giving element. In addition, the pitcher in the goddess' hands is connected to a water pipe inside the figure; so water, fed by an overhead tank, must once have gushed out of the vessel. The cultic scenes in the wall paintings of the court show similar motifs.

Each document contains a little piece of the mosaic which makes up the true facts about the kingdom of Mari.

Numerous orders for the construction of canals, locks, dams, and embankments make it plain that the prosperity of the country largely depended on the widespread system of irrigation, which was constantly under the supervision of government engineers, who saw to its care and maintenance.

Two tablets contain a list of 2,000 craftsmen, giving their full names and the names of their guilds.

The news service in Mari functioned so quicky and successfully that it would bear comparison with modern telegraphy. Important messages were sent by means of fire signals from the frontier of Babylon right up to present day Turkey in a matter of a few hours, a distance of more than 300 miles.

Mari lay at the intersection of the great caravan routes from West to East and North to South. It is not surprising therefore that the traffic in goods, which extended from Cyprus and Crete to Asia Minor and Mesopotamia, necessitated a lively correspondence on clay concerning imports and exports. But the tablets do not merely record everyday matters. They also give an impressive account of religious life, of New Year Festivals in honour of Ishtar, auguries with the entrails of animals, and interpretation of dreams. Twenty-five gods made up the Mari pantheon. A list of sacrificial sheep, which Zimri-Lim presented, refers to these occupants of heaven by name.

From countless individual bits of evidence on these tablets we can form a picture of this masterpiece of organization and administration which the kingdom of Mari constituted in the eighteenth century BC. What is astonishing is that neither in their sculptures nor in their paintings is there any indication of warlike activity.

The inhabitants of Mari were Amorites who had been settled there for a long time, and who preferred peace. Their interests lay in religion and ceremonial, in trade and commerce. Conquest, heroism, and the clash of battle meant little to them. As we can still see from statues and pictures, their faces radiate a cheerful serenity.

That did not mean, however, that they were absolved from the necessity of defending and safeguarding their territory by force of arms. On their frontiers lived tribes of Semitic nomads, who found the lush pastures, market gardens and cornfields of Mari a constant temptation. They were always crossing the border, grazing their cattle over wide stretches of the countryside, and disturbing the population. They had to be watched. Frontier posts were therefore established as a check on this danger, and any incident was immediately reported to Mari.

In Paris the Assyriologists were deciphering a clay tablet from the archives of Mari. They read with astonishment a report from Biennium, an officer of the desert police:

Say to my lord: This from Biennium, thy servant. Yesterday I left Mari and spent the night at Zuruban. All the Benjamites were sending fire-signals. From Samanum to Ilum-Muluk, from Ilum-Muluk to Mishlan, all the Benjamite villages in the Terqa district replied with fire-signals. I am not yet certain what these signals meant. I am trying to find out. I shall write to my lord whether or not I succeed. The city guards should be strengthened and my lord should not leave the gate.

In this police report from the central reaches of the Euphrates in the nineteenth century BC

Below **From the temple of Ishtar in Mari comes a whole row of small bas-relief figures, about eleven centimetres tall, made of mussel shell. Undoubtedly they formed the inlays of a frieze which must have been similar to the so-called 'standard' of Ur. The triumphal procession contains not only these long-robed warriors with battle-axes, but also prisoners and a chariot. The work has been dated to the first half of the third millennium BC.**

Left **This little seated figure, now in the Damascus Museum, also comes from the temple of Ishtar at Mari. The body is made of light gypsum, the eyes are mussel shell and lapis lazuli, and the hair is painted on in black. The figure, twenty-six centimetres tall, sits cross-legged on a cushion and may have once held a stringed instrument, as the fracture site on the chest suggests. The dedication to the goddess Ishtar provides the figure's name: Ur-Nanshe, singer to King Ib-Luli of Mari. The level at which the statue was found and its style lead to the conclusion that this priestly court musician served around 2700–2600 BC.**

The excavations at Tell Mardikh, south of Aleppo, will take another few decades. This view across part of the area occupied by ancient Ebla (above) ranges over peaceful pasture land from the 'Acropolis' to one of the city gates (opposite page, bottom). In the upper town, which held at least three palaces as well as shrines (opposite page, top), only a fraction has been investigated. Soundings have revealed a six-fold stratification, ranging from 3500 to 60 BC. The commercial town appears to have experienced a particular boom between 2400 and 2250 BC. This is evidenced by the remains of the splendid furnishings of Palace G, as well as by a comprehensive clay-tablet archive which gives detailed information on widespread trading networks. Of course the translators are still wrestling with the special position of the language of Ebla, and the peculiar variants of the old Sumerian script, which had to be adapted to the local dialect.

there appears the name of one of the tribes known to us from the Bible: *Benjamites*.

There is frequent mention of these Benjamites. They seem to have give the ruler of Mari so many headaches and caused so much trouble that periods of a king's reign were even called after them.

I n the Mari dynasties the years of each reign were not numbered but were identified with some notable event, for example the building and consecration of new temples, the erection of great dams to improve irrigation, the strengthening of the banks of the Euphrates or a national census. Three times the chronological tables mention the Benjamites:

The year in which Iahdulim went to Hen and laid hands upon the territory of the Benjamites, is referred to in the reign of King Iahdulim of Mari and *The year that Zimri-Lim killed the dâvidum of the Benjamites*, and *The year after Zimri-Lim killed the dâvidum of the Benjamites . . .* in the reign of the last monarch of Mari, Zimri-Lim.

A n elaborate correspondence between governors, district commissionaries, and administrators takes place over the single question: Dare we take a census of the Benjamites?

In the kingdom of Mari a census of the people was not uncommon. It provided a basis for taxation and for enlistment for military service. The population was summoned by districts and a nominal roll was made of every man liable for call-up.

The proceedings lasted several days, during which free beer and bread were distributed by

government officials. The administration in the palace of Mari would fain have included the Benjamites in this but the district officers had their doubts. They advised against it since they understood only too well the temper of these roaming and rebellious tribes.

Reference the proposal to take a census of the Benjamites, about which you have written me, begins a letter from Samsi-Addu to Iasmah-Addu in Mari. *The Benjamites are not welldisposed to the idea of a census. If you carry it out their kinsmen the Ra-ab-ay-yi, who live on the other bank of the river, will hear of it. They will be annoyed with them and will not return to their country. On no account should this census be taken!*

Thus the Benjamites lost their free beer and bread and also escaped paying taxes and military service.

The Old Testament too gives us accounts of censuses of this sort. Already before setting out for the Promised Land, Moses on Sinai is supposed, on the command of the Lord, to have carried out a census of all men over twenty capable of bearing arms, according to their tribes (Numbers 1–2). When David orders a similar count of men of military age, this seems unthinkable to his kinsman and commander-in-chief Joab; and it arouses God's anger and is seen as an expression of royal arrogance (2 Samuel 24). The Israelites loved their freedom above all else. Registration and the prospect of being called up were equally hateful to them. Even in the year AD6 the census carried out by Governor Cyrenius almost led to open revolt.

I n Paris the mention of Benjamites gave rise to conjecture and anticipation along a particular line.

Not without reason, for on other clay tablets the Assyriologists dealing with these reports of governors and district commissioners of the Mari empire came across one after another a whole series of familiar sounding names from biblical history—names like Peleg, and Serug, Nahor and Terah and—Haran.

These are the generations of Shem, says Genesis 11. *Peleg lived 30 years and begat Reu: And Reu lived two and thirty years and begat Serug: And Serug lived thirty years and begat Nahor: And Nahor lived nine and twenty years and begat Terah: And Terah lived seventy years and begat Abram, Nahor, and Haran.*

Names of Abraham's forefathers emerge from these dark ages as names of cities in north-west Mesopotamia. They lie in Padan-Aram, the plain of Aram. In the centre of it lies Haran, which must

have been a flourishing city in the early part of the second millenium BC. Haran, the home of Abraham, father of the patriarchs, the birthplace of the Hebrew people, is here for the first time historically attested, for contemporary texts refer to it. Further up the same Balikh valley lay the city with an equally well-known biblical name, Nahor, the home of Rebecca, wife of Isaac.

Abraham was now old and well advanced in years, and the Lord had blessed him in every way. He said to the chief servant in his household, the one in charge of all that he had, 'Put your hand under my thigh. I want you to swear by the Lord, the God of heaven and the God of earth, that you will not get a wife for my son from the daughters of the Canaanites, among whom I am living, but will go to my country and my own relatives and get a wife for my son Isaac . . .' Then the servant . . . taking with him all kinds of good things from his master . . . set out for Aram Naharaim and made his way to the town of Nahor. (Genesis 24:1–4, 10)

The biblical city of Nahor is unexpectedly drawn into a recognizable historical setting. Abraham's servant set out for the land of the kings of Mari. The instructions of his master, according to the biblical tradition, clearly indicate a precise knowledge of northern Mesopotamia, including Nahor.

If we follow the dates given in the Bible we find that Abraham left his native place, Haran, 645 years before the Exodus of the people of Israel from Egypt. They wandered through the desert towards the Promised Land under the leadership of Moses in the thirteenth century BC. This date is, as we shall see, assured by archaeology. Abraham must therefore have lived about 1900BC. At that time, according to the evidence ot the palace

These two reliefs from Ebla show a motif of battle with animals, which enjoyed great popularity in the whole of Mesopotamia from the third millennium BC, and which also appears in the Epic of Gilgamesh: a bearded hero of superhuman strength is overcoming lions, bulls or mythical creatures, and occasionally he himself wears the mask

archives, Haran and Nahor were both flourishing cities.

The documents from the kingdom of Mari produce startling proof that the stories of the patriarchs in the Bible are not 'pious legends'—as is often too readily assumed—but things that are described as happening in a historical period which can be precisely dated.

THE LONG JOURNEY TO CANAAN

He took his wife Sarai, his nephew Lot, all the possessions they had accumulated and the people they had acquired in Haran, and they set out for the land of Canaan, and they arrived there.

GENESIS 12:5

of the animals involved (left).
Also from Ebla is this relief frieze of praying figures in ceremonial clothes (above). The little mythical being (above right), a bison with a human face, consists of a core of wood overlaid with gold, with hair made of steatite. The finds from Ebla are on display in the Aleppo Museum.

The road from Haran, the home of the patriarchs, to the land of Canaan runs south for more than 600 miles. It follows the river Balikh as far as the Euphrates, thence by a caravan route thousands of years old via the oasis of Palmyra, the Tadmor of the Bible, to Damascus, and from there in a south-westerly direction to the Lake of Galilee. It is one of the great trade routes that have always led from Euphrates to Jordan, from the kingdom of Mesopotamia to the Phoenician seaports on the Mediterranean and the distant Nile lands in Egypt.

Anyone nowadays wanting to follow Abraham's route must cross the border between Turkey and Syria and that between Syria and Israel. To go by car from Damascus to Palestine is, particularly in springtime, an unforgettable experience.

The first city of any size that Abraham must have struck on his journey is still standing today: Damascus.

The ancient city with its narrow streets and dark bazaar-alleys, with its mosques and its Roman remains, lies in the centre of a wide and fertile plain. When the Arabs speak of Paradise they think of Damascus. What other Mediterranean city can compare with this place, which every spring is decked with an incredible mantle of gay blossom? In all the gardens and in the hedgerows beyond the city walls apricots and almonds are a riot of pink. Flowering trees line the road which climbs gently as it heads for the south-west. Tilled fields alternate with olive groves and large mulberry plantings. High above, to the right of the road, rises the El Barada river, to which the land owes its fertility. Here mighty Hermon thrusts its steep slopes 10,000 feet into the heavens above the flat and verdant plain. From the side of this famous mountain ridge, to the south, gushes the source of the Jordan. Towering over both Syria and Palestine and visible from afar it seems to have been placed there by Nature as a gigantic boundary stone between them. Even in the blazing heat of summer its peak remains covered in snow. The

Galilee. A few minutes later comes the frontier. Syria lies behind. The road crosses a small bridge. Under the arch a fast moving narrow current hurries on its way. It is the Jordan: we are in Palestine, in the young state of Israel.

After a few miles between dark basalt rocks the bright blue of the Lake of Galilee sparkles up at us from far beneath. It was on this lake, where time seems to have stood still, that Jesus preached from a boat off Capernaum. Here he told Peter to cast his nets and raise the great draught of fishes. Two thousands years before that the flocks of Abraham perhaps grazed on its shores. For the road from Mesopotamia to Canaan went past the Lake of Galilee.

Canaan is the narrow mountainous strip of land between the shores of the Mediterranean and the borders of the desert, from Gaza in the south right up to Hamath on the banks of the Orontes in the north.

Canaan was the 'Land of Purple'. It owed its name to a product of the country which was highly prized in the olden days. From earliest times the inhabitants had extracted from a shellfish (*Murex*), which was native to these parts, the most famous dye in the ancient world, purple. It was so uncommon, so difficult to obtain and therefore so expensive, that only the wealthy could afford it. Purple robes were throughout the Ancient East a mark of high rank. The Greeks called the manufacturers of purple and the purple-dyers of the Mediterranean Phoenicians. The country they called Phoenicia, which meant 'purple' in their language.

The Land of Canaan is also the birthplace of two things which have radically affected the whole world: the word 'Bible' and our alphabet. A Phoenician city was godparent to the Greek word for 'book': from Byblos, the Canaanite seaport, comes *biblion* and hence, later, 'Bible'. In the ninth century BC the Greeks took over from Canaan the letters of our alphabet.

The part of the country which was to become the home of the Israelite people was named by the Romans after Israel's worst enemies: Palestine comes from *Pelishtim*, as the Philistines are called in the Old Testament. They lived in the southernmost part of the coast of Canaan. *All Israel from Dan to Beersheba* (1 Samuel 3:20) is how the Bible describes the extent of the Promised Land, that is, from the sources of Jordan at the foot of Hermon to the hills west of the Dead Sea, and the Negeb in the south.

Above **A peasant village now nestles in the ruins of ancient Haran.**

Below **Abraham's journeys from Ur to Haran and through Palestine to Egypt.**

Opposite **Statuette of a bearded figure carrying a sacrificial animal, from Mari, early second millennium.**

effect becomes even more impressive as on the left of the road the green fields disappear. Monotonous grey-brown hills, streaked with dried up river beds, pile up towards the distant shimmering horizon where the scorching Syrian Desert begins—the home of the Bedouins. The road climbs gradually for an hour and a half. Fields and groves become rarer. The green is more and more swallowed up by the sandy grey of the desert.

Behind a ridge suddenly appear the hills of

Below **In the villages of the upper Euphrates the peasants live in beehive-shaped houses, which have existed here from ancient times.**

Previous pages **The name and the ruins of the town of Palmyra, with its almost endless colonnades, originate from the Graeco-Roman period. However, under the name of Tadmor, the settlement is mentioned as early as the nineteenth century BC. A century later it is included in the list of trading partners of Mari. The Bible too refers to it by the same name. The Assyrian king Tiglath-Pileser I counts it among the Aramaean cities, and it is under this rule that Tadmor seems to have enjoyed its greatest flowering, which however has not yet been sufficiently confirmed archaeologically.**

If we look at a globe of the world, Palestine is only a tiny spot on the earth's surface, a narrow streak. It is possible to drive comfortably in a single day round the borders of the old kingdom of Israel: 150 miles from north to south, 25 miles across at its narrowest point, 9,500 square miles in all, its size was about that of the island of Sicily. Only for a few decades in its turbulent history was it any bigger. Under its renowned kings David and Solomon its territory reached to the arm of the Red Sea at Ezion-Geber in the south, and far beyond Damascus into Syria on the north. The present state of Israel (within its pre–1967 boundaries) with its 8,000 square miles is smaller by a fifth than the old kingdom.

There never flourished here crafts and industries whose products were sought after by the world at large. Traversed by hills and mountain chains, whose summits rose to over 3,000 feet, surrounded in the south and east by scrub and desert, in the north by the mountains of the Lebanon and Hermon, in the west by a flat coast with no natural harbours, it lay like a poverty stricken island between the great kingdoms on the Nile and the Euphrates, on the frontier between two continents. East of the Nile delta Africa stops. After a desolate stretch of 100 miles of desert Asia begins, and at its threshold lies Palestine.

When in the course of its eventful history it was constantly being dragged into the affairs of the wider world, it had its position to thank for it. Canaan is the link between Egypt and Asia. The most important trade route of the ancient world passes through this country. Merchants and caravans, migratory tribes and peoples, followed this road which the armies of the great conquerors were later to make use of. Egyptians, Assyrians, Babylonians, Persians, Greeks and Romans one after another made the land and its people the plaything of their economic, strategic and political concerns.

It was in the interests of trade that the giant on the Nile in the third millennium BC was the first great power to stretch out its tentacles towards Canaan.

We brought 40 ships, laden with cedar trunks. We built ships of cedarwood: One 'Pride of Two Lands' ship of 150 feet: And of meru-wood, two ships 150 feet long: We made the doors of the king's palace of cedarwood. That is the substance of the world's oldest advice note from a timber importer about 2700BC. The details of this cargo of timber in the reign of Pharaoh Snefru are scratched on a tablet of hard black diorite, which is carefully preserved in the museum at Palermo. Dense woods covered the

slopes of Lebanon then. The excellent wood from its cedars and meru, a kind of conifer, were just what the Pharaohs needed for their building schemes.

Centuries before Abraham's day there was a flourishing import and export trade on the Canaanite coast. Egypt exchanged gold and spices from Nubia, copper and turquoise from the mines at Sinai, linen and ivory, for silver from the Taurus, leather goods from Byblos, painted vases from Crete. In the great Phoenician dye-works well-to-do Egyptians had their robes dyed purple. For their society women they bought a wonderful lapislazuli blue—eyelids dyed blue were all the rage—and stibium, a cosmetic which was highly thought of by the ladies for touching up their eyelashes.

In the sea-ports of Ugarit (now Ras Shamra) and Tyre there were Egyptian consuls; the coastal fortress of Byblos became an Egyptian colony; monuments were erected to the Pharaohs and Phoenician princes adopted Egyptian names.

If the coastal cities presented a picture of cosmopolitan life which was busy, prosperous and even luxurious, a few miles inland lay a world which provided a glaring contrast. The Jordan mountains have always been a trouble-spot. Bedouin attacks on the native population, insurrection and feuds between towns were unending. Since they also endangered the caravan route along the Mediterranean coast, Egyptian punitive expeditions had to bring the unruly elements to heel. The inscription on the tomb of the Egyptian Uni gives us a clear picture of how one of these expeditions was organized about 2350BC Uni, an army commander, received orders from Pharaoh Phiops I to assemble a striking force against Bedouins from Asia who were attacking Canaan. His report on the campaign reads as follows:

His Majesty made war on the desert peoples and His Majesty gathered an army: in the south beyond Elephantine . . . all over the north . . . and among the Jertet, Mazoi, and Jenam Nubians. I was entrusted with the whole campaign. The morale of this multicoloured fighting force comes in for high praise, and in the course of it we learn what sort of attractions Canaan offered in those days in the way of loot: *None of them stole the sandals off anyone who came their way . . . None of them stole food from any of the cities . . . None of them stole any goats.* Uni's war-diary proudly announces a great victory and in passing gives us valuable information about the country: *The king's army returned in good order, after laying waste the country of the desert peoples, . . . after destroying their fortresses . . . after cutting*

down their fig-trees and vines . . . and carrying off a large number into captivity. His Majesty sent me five times to ravage the land of the desert peoples with these troops every time they revolted.

Semites thus made their first entry into the land of the Pharaohs as P.O.W.'s where they were contemptuously described as 'Sand-dwellers'. Chu-Sebek, adjutant to King Sesostris III of Egypt, wrote in his war-diary 500 years later the following account which has been preserved at Abydos on the Upper Nile, where it was chiselled out on a monument: *His Majesty proceeded northwards to crush the Asiatic Bedouins . . . His Majesty went as far as a place called Sekmem . . . Sekmem collapsed together with the whole miserable country of Retenu.*

The Egyptians called Palestine and Syria together *Retenu. Sekmem* is the biblical town of Shechem, the first town which Abraham struck on entering Canaan (Genesis 12:6).

During the Middle Kingdom the whole of Canaan came under the suzerainty of the Pharaohs. Thanks to the archaeologists we possess a unique document from this epoch, a gem of ancient literature. The author: a certain Sinuhe of Egypt. Scene: Canaan. Time: between 1971 and 1928 BC under Pharaoh Sesostris I.

Sinuhe, a nobleman in attendance at court, becomes involved in a political intrigue. He fears for his life and emigrates to Canaan:

As I headed north I came to the Princes' Wall, which was built to keep out the Bedouins and crush the Sandramblers. I hid in a thicket in case the guard on the wall, who was on patrol at the time, would see me. I did not move out of it till the evening. When daylight came . . . and I had reached the Bitter Lake, I collapsed. I was parched with thirst, my throat was red hot. I said to myself: This is the taste of death! But as I made another effort and pulled myself on to my feet, I heard the bleating of sheep and some Bedouins came in sight. Their leader, who had been in

The Euphrates is formed by two sources, the Karasu and the Murat-Suyu in the highlands of East Anatolia. It then cuts in deep gorges through the eastern Taurus range towards the south, where it crosses the Syrian/Iraqi tableland.

61

The northern Syrian town of Aleppo dates from earliest antiquity. In the first half of the second millennium BC it was the capital of the influential state of Jamchad. The citadel preserves traces of every era of its long history.

Egypt, recognized me. He gave me some water and boiled some milk, and I went with him to his tribe. They were very kind to me.

Sinuhe's escape had been successful. He had been able to slip unseen past the great barrier wall on the frontier of the kingdom of the Pharaohs which ran exactly along the line which is followed by the Suez Canal today. This 'Princes' Wall' was even then several hundred years old. A priest mentions it as far back as 2650BC: *The Princes' Walls are being built to prevent the Asiatics forcing their way into Egypt. They want water . . . to give to their cattle.* Later on the children of Israel were to pass this wall many times: there was no other way into Egypt. According to Genesis 12:10ff Abraham must have been the first of them to see it when he immigrated to the land of the Nile during a famine.

Sinuhe continues: *Each territory passed me on to the next. I went to Byblos, and farther on reached Kedme where I spent eighteen months. Ammi-Enschi, the chief of Upper Retenu made me welcome. He said to me: 'You will be well treated and you can speak your own language here.' He said this of course because he knew who I was. Egyptians who lived there had told him about me.'*

We are told in great detail of the day to day experiences of this Egyptian fugitive in North Palestine. *Ammi-Enschi said to me: 'Certainly, Egypt is a fine country, but you ought to stay here with me and what I shall do for you will be fine too.'*

He gave me precedence over all his own family and gave me his eldest daughter in marriage. He let me select from among his choicest estates and I selected one which lay along the border of a neighbouring territory. It was a fine place with the name of Jaa. There were figs and vines and more wine than water. There was plenty of honey and oil; every kind of fruit hung on its trees. It had corn and barley and all kinds of sheep and cattle. My popularity with the ruler was extremely profitable. He made me a chief of his tribe in the choicest part of his domains. I had bread and wine as my daily fare, boiled meat and roast goose. There were also desert animals which they caught in traps and brought to me,

Left **Damascus, the capital of Syria and from time immemorial one of the most important centres of the Orient, lies on the eastern slopes of Anti-Lebanon in the middle of an oasis watered by the river Barada.**

Above **Steep ravines cut furrows through the Golan Heights east of the Sea of Galilee.**

apart from what my hunting dogs collected ...
There was milk in every shape and form. Thus many years went by. My children grew into strong men, each of them able to dominate his tribe.

Any courier coming from Egypt or heading south to the royal court lived with me. I gave

Byblos was regarded in ancient times as the oldest city in the world, and indeed it must already have played an important role as a port and trading city towards the end of the fourth millennium BC. For thousands of years Byblos pursued the closest possible connections with Egypt, for it was from here that the precious cedar wood from Lebanon was shipped. Solomon procured timber from Byblos for the Temple in Jerusalem. The pluralistic culture of the Phoenicians displays particularly strong Egyptian influences here, most notably in the so-called 'obelisk temple' of the god Reshef (below), whose courtyard contains at least twenty small obelisks.

hospitality to everyone. I gave water to the thirsty, put the wanderer on the right way, and protected the bereaved.

When the Bedouins sallied forth to attack neighbouring chiefs I drew up the plan of campaign. For the prince of Retenu for many years put me in command of his warriors and whichever country I marched into I made ... and ... of its pastures and its wells. I plundered its sheep and cattle, led its people captive and took over their stores. I killed its people with my sword and my bow thanks to my leadership and my clever plans.

Out of his many experiences among the 'Asiatics' a life and death duel, which he describes in detail, seems to have made the deepest impression on Sinuhe. A 'Strong man of Retenu' had jeered at him one day in his tent and called him out. He was sure he could kill Sinuhe and appropriate his flocks and herds and properties. But Sinuhe, like all Egyptians, was a practised bowman from his earliest days, and killed the 'strong man', who was armed with shield, spear and dagger, by putting an arrow through his throat. The spoils that came to him as a result of this combat made him even richer and more powerful.

At length in his old age he began to yearn for his homeland. A letter from his Pharaoh Sesostris I summoned him to return: . . . *Make ready to return to Egypt, that you may see once more the Court where you grew up, and kiss the ground at the two great gates . . . Remember the day when you will have to be buried and men will do you honour. You will be anointed with oil before daybreak and wrapped in linen blessed by the goddess Tail. You will be given an escort on the day of the funeral. The coffin will be of gold adorned with lapis-lazuli, and you will be placed upon a bier. Oxen will pull it and a choir will precede you. They will dance the Dance of the Dwarfs at the mouth of your tomb. The sacrificial prayers will be recited for you and animals will be offered on your altar. The pillars of your tomb will be built of lime-stone among those of the royal family. You must not lie in a foreign land, with Asiatics to bury you, and wrap you in sheepskin.*

Sinuhe's heart leapt for joy. He decided to return at once, made over his property to his children and installed his eldest son as 'Chief of his tribe'. This was customary with these Semitic nomads, as it was with Abraham and his progeny. It was the tribal law of the patriarchs, which later became the law of Israel. *My tribe and all my goods belonged to him only, my people and all my flocks, my fruit and all my sweet trees. Then I headed for the south.*

He was accompanied right to the frontier posts of Egypt by Bedouins, thence by representatives of Pharaoh to the capital south of Memphis. The second stage was by boat.

What a contrast! From a tent to a royal palace, from a simple if dangerous life back to the security and luxury of a highly civilized metropolis. *I found his Majesty on the great throne in the Hall of Silver and Gold. The King's family were brought in. His Majesty said to the Queen: 'See, here is Sinuhe, who returns as an Asiatic and has become a Bedouin.' She gave a loud shriek and all the royal children screamed in chorus. They said to his Majesty: 'Surely this is not really he, my lord King.' His Majesty replied: 'It is really he.'*

I was taken to a princely mansion, writes Sinuhe enthusiastically, *in which there were wonderful things and also a bathroom . . . there were things from the royal treasure house, clothes of royal linen, myrrh and finest oil; favourite servants of the King were in every room, and every cook did his duty. The years that were past slipped from my body. I was*

shaved and my hair was combed. I shed my load of foreign soil and the coarse clothing of the Sand-ramblers. I was swathed in fine linen and anointed with the finest oil the country could provide. I slept once more in a bed. Thus I lived, honoured by the King, until the time came for me to depart this life.

The Sinuhe story does not exist in one copy only. An astonishing number of them has been found. It must have been a highly popular work and must have gone through several 'editions'. Not only in the Middle Kingdom but in the New Kingdom of Egypt it was read with pleasure, as the copies found indicate. One might call it a 'best-seller', the first in the world, and about Canaan, of all places.

The scholars who came across it again at the turn of the century were as delighted with it as Sinuhe's contemporaries had been 4,000 years before. They regarded it however as a well-told story, exaggerated like all Egyptian writings and completely without foundation. The Tale of Si-nuhe became a mine of information for learned Egyptologists, but not for historians. They were so busy disputing about the clarification of the text, the letters, the construction and connection of the sentences that the contents were forgotten.

Meantime Sinuhe came into his own. For we now know that the Egyptian had written a factual account of the Canaan of the patriarchal period. It is to hieroglyphic texts dealing with Egyptian campaigns that we owe the first evidence we possess about Canaan. They agree with Sinuhe's description. Similarly, the Egyptian nobleman's

Above **No usable timber grows in Egypt; the sycamore-fig is too crooked, the palm too fibrous. For shipbuilding, houses and palaces, even for straight coffin wood, the Egyptians were from earliest times dependent on imports. The cedars of Lebanon provided the most sought-after beams and planks. Egypt would pay almost any price for this wood, and the Phoenician coastal towns, above all Byblos, became rich on it. If the lively trade was interrupted by political factors, Egypt experienced the re-sulting wood shortage as a major disaster. 'No one travels to Byblos any more, what shall we do to get cedars for our mummies?' was the complaint during the devastating economic crisis of the 'first inter-regnum'. The trade with the Phoe-nicians also fell victim to the Hittite invasion. It is significant that at Karnak, King Sethos I portrays the felling of cedar trees as the most important result of his campaign in Canaan.**

Overleaf **A view over the Sea of Galilee towards Magdala and Tiberias.**

story shows in some places almost literal correspondence with verses of the Bible which are often quoted. *For the Lord thy God bringeth thee into a good land* says Deuteronomy 8:7—*It was a fine country* says Sinuhe. *A land* continues the Bible *of wheat and barley and vines and fig trees . . . Barley and wheat, figs and vines were there* Sinuhe tells us. And where the Bible says: *A land of oil, olive and honey, a land wherein thou shalt eat bread without scarceness*, the Egyptian text reads: *There was plenty of honey and oil. I had bread as my daily fare.*

The description which Sinuhe gives of his way of life among the Amorites, living in a tent, surrounded by his flocks and herds, and involved in conflict with presumptuous Bedouins whom he has to drive away from his pastures and his wells, corresponds with the biblical picture of life in patriarchal times. It is reported of Abraham and his son Isaac, too, that they were locked in conflict with others over their wells.

A bout 1900BC Canaan was but thinly populated. Properly speaking it was no-man's land. Here and there in the midst of ploughed fields a fortified keep could be seen. Neighbouring slopes would be planted with vines or with fig trees and date palms. The inhabitants lived in a state of constant readiness. For these widely scattered little townships, like veritable islands, were the object of daring attacks by the desert nomads. Suddenly, and when least expected, these nomads were upon them, with indiscriminate butchery, carrying off their cattle and their crops. Just as suddenly they would disappear again into the vast recesses of the desert plains to the south and east. There was endless war between the settled farmers and cattle breeders and these plundering hordes who had no fixed abode, whose home was a goatshair tent somewhere out under the open skies of the desert.

In the twenties, remarkable sherds were found on the Nile, the chief funds being at Thebes and Saqqara. Archaeologists in Berlin obtained some of them, others went to Brussels, and the rest went to the great museum at Cairo. Under the careful hands of experts the fragments were reassembled into vases and statuettes, but the most astonishing thing about them was the inscriptions.

The writing is full of menacing curses and maledictions like:
'Death strike you at every wicked word and thought, every plot, angry quarrel and plan.' These and other unpleasant wishes were generally addressed to Egyptian court officials and other eminent people,

In his excavations of the mound of ruins at Azor near Jaffa, begun in 1958, Jean Perrot found numerous ossuaries from the Chalcolithic era. The majority of these containers for bones, made from fired clay, are shaped like houses and thus allow us to draw inferences about building methods of the fourth millennium BC in Canaan. Beams formed the framework of the facade, while others bore the roof and supported the side walls.

but also to rulers in Canaan and Syria.

In accordance with an old superstition it was believed that at the moment the vase or statuette was smashed the power of the person cursed would be broken. It was common to include within the spell the family, relatives, even the home town of the victim of the curse. The magical texts include names of cities like Jerusalem (Genesis 14:19), Askelon (Judges 1:18), Tyre (Joshua 19:29), Hazor (Joshua 11:1), Bethshemesh (Joshua 15:10), Aphek (Joshua 12:18), Achsaph (Joshua 11:1) and Shechem (Sichem). Here is a convincing proof that these places mentioned in the Bible existed already in the nineteenth and eighteenth centuries BC, since the vases and statuettes date from that time. Two of these towns are said to have been visited by Abraham. He calls on

Melchizedek *King of Salem* (Genesis 14:18) at Jerusalem. Jerusalem is well enough known, but where was Sichem?

It was at the terebinth grove at Mamre that Abraham pitched his tent and erected an altar. King Herod the Great enclosed this historic site with a perimeter wall built of mighty blocks of ashlar.

I n the heart of Samaria lies a broad flat valley, dominated by the high peaks of Gerizim and Ebal. Well cultivated fields surround Ashkar, a small village in Jordan. Nearby at the foot of Gerizim in Tell el Balata the ruins of Sichem were discovered.

It was due to the German theologian and archaeologist Professor Ernst Sellin that during excavations in 1913–14 strata from very early times came to light.

Sellin came across remains of walls dating back to the nineteenth century BC. Bit by bit the

picture emerged of a mighty surrounding wall with strong foundations, entirely built of rough boulders, some of them 6 feet in diameter. Archaeologists call this type a 'cyclops-wall'. The wall was further strengthened by an escarpment. The builders of Sichem fortified the 6 feet thick wall with small turrets and provided an earth wall in addition.

The remains of a palace also emerged out of the ruins. The square cramped courtyard, surrounded by a few rooms with solid walls, hardly deserved the name of palace. Adjoining it was a temple, its entrance flanked by two towers. All the Canaanite towns whose names are so familiar, and which the Israelites feared so greatly in the early days, looked like Sichem in the first half of the second millenium BC. Since then a whole series of these towns have been excavated. For thousands of years they have been buried deep in the ground, now they stand clearly before us. Among them are many towns whose walls the patriarchs might have seen: Bethel and Mizpah, Gerar and Lachish, Gezer and Gath, Askelon and Jericho.

The Canaanite towns were fortresses, places of refuge in time of danger, whether it was from sudden attack by nomadic tribes or civil war among the Canaanites themselves. Towering perimeter walls built of these great boulders invariably enclose a small area, not much bigger than St. Peter's Square in Rome. Many of these town-forts may even at this time have had a water supply, but they were not towns in which a large population could have made a permanent home. Compared with the palaces and great cities in Mesopotamia or on the Nile they look tiny. Most of the towns in Canaan could have gone into the palace of the kings of Mari comfortably.

In Tell el-Hesi, (possibly the biblical Eglon) the ancient fortifications enclosed an area of just over an acre (half a hectare). In Tell es-Zakariyah (Aseka) less than ten acres (four hectares) and in Tell el-Safi (Gath) twelve acres (five hectares); Tell el-Mutesellim (Megiddo) was, including the lower town, about twice as big. The built-up area of Geser, on the road from Jerusalem to Jaffa, occupied twenty acres (nine hectares). Even in Jericho the inner fortified wall, the Acropolis proper, enclosed a space of little more than five acres. Yet Jericho was one of the strongest fortresses in the country. Only on the coast of Canaan were there larger cities: Acre reached twenty hectares, Ashkelon as much as fifty-five.

Bitter feuds between the tribal chiefs were the order of the day. There was no supreme authority. Every chieftain was master in his own territory.

No one gave him orders and he did what he pleased. The Bible calls the tribal chieftains 'kings'. As far as power and independence were concerned that is what they were.

Between the tribal chiefs and their subjects the relationship was patriarchal. Inside the wall lived only the chief, the aristocracy, Pharaoh's representatives, and wealthy merchants. Moreover they alone lived in strong, solid, mostly one-story houses with four to six rooms built round an open courtyard. Upper class homes with a second story were comparatively rare. The rest of the inhabitants—craftspeople, vassals, servants, and serfs—lived in simple mud or wattle huts outside the walls. They must have had a miserable life.

Since the days of the patriarchs two roads meet in the plain of Shechem. One goes down into the rich valley of the Jordan. The other climbs over the lonely hills southwards to Bethel, on past Jerusalem and down to the Negeb, or the Land of the South as the Bible calls it. Anyone following this road would encounter only a few inhabited areas in the central highlands of Samaria and Judah: Shechem, Bethel, Jerusalem and Hebron. Anyone choosing the more comfortable road would find the larger towns and more important fortresses of the Canaanites in the lush valleys of the Plain of Jezreel, on the fertile coast of Judah and amid the luxuriant vegetation of the Jordan valley.

Abraham, as the Bible tells us, chose for his first exploration of Palestine the lonely and difficult road that points over the hills towards the south. For here the wooded hillsides offered refuge and concealment to a stranger in a foreign land, while the clearings provided pasture in plenty for his flocks and herds. Later on it was up here that the migrating clans settled, who were to become the strongest tribes of the people of Israel. However tempting were the fertile valleys of the plain, the clans were still a long way from being a match for the Canaanite local rulers with their chariots.

ABRAHAM AND LOT IN THE LAND OF PURPLE

Now there was a famine in the land, and Abram went down to Egypt to live there for a while because the famine was severe.

GENESIS 12:10

We have to thank the dryness of the sands of the Egyptian desert for preserving a considerable variety of hieroglyphic texts, among which is to be found a wealth of written evidence of the immigration of Semitic families into the Nile valley. The best and clearest proof is however a picture.

Halfway between the old cities of the Pharaohs, Memphis and Thebes, 200 miles south of Cairo, there lies on the banks of the Nile amid green fields and palm groves the little settlement of Beni-Hasan. Here in 1890 a British expert, Percy A. Newberry, was given an assignment by the Cairo authorities to investigate some old tombs. The expedition was financed by the Egyptian Exploration Fund.

The tombs were located at the outer end of a desert wadi, where the remains of old quarries and a temple carved from the rock also lay. One of them was the last resting place of the Egyptian provincial ruler Khnum-hotpe. Hieroglyphs indicated the name of the occupant. He was the ruler of this district of the Nile, which at one time was called Gazelle Province. Khnum-hotpe lived under Pharaoh Sesostris II (1878–1840BC).

Newberry freed the entrance of sand and debris and found his way into a huge rock chamber. Pillars in the shape of rolls of papyrus supported the ceiling. The walls were bright with gorgeous coloured paintings on a thin limewashed plaster. These depicted scenes from the life of the nobleman telling of harvest, hunting, dancing and sport. In one of the pictures on the north wall, immediately next to an over life-size portrait of the nobleman, Newberry discovered a frieze with foreign-looking figures. They were wearing a different type of clothing from the ordinary Egyptians, they were fairer-skinned and had sharper features. Two Egyptian officials in the foreground were obviously introducing this group of foreigners to the prince. What sort of people were they?

Hieroglyphs on a written document in the hand of one of the Egyptians gave the explanation: they were 'Sand-dwellers', Semites. Their leader was called Abishai. With thirty-six men, women

and children of his tribe Abishai had come to Egypt. He had brought gifts for the prince, among which special mention was made of some costly stibium for the nobleman's wife.

Abishai is a genuine Semitic name. After the conquest of Canaan by Joshua the name occurs in the Bible during the reign of the second king of Israel: *David then asked . . . Abishai son of Zeruiah, Joab's brother* (1 Samuel 26:6). So the Abishai of the Bible was the brother of Joab, the commander-in-chief and cousin of David, under whom Israel was a large kingdom.

The artist whom Prince Khnum-hotpe entrusted with the decoration of his tomb has depicted the 'Sand-dwellers' with such care that the smallest detail is faithfully noted. This lifelike and unusually striking picture gives the impression that this family of Semites had just stopped for a second, and that suddenly men, women and children would start off again and continue their journey. Abishai at the head of the column makes a slight obeisance and salutes the prince with his right hand, while his left hand leads a tame horned goat with his shepherd's crook.

The shepherd's crook was so characteristic of the nomads that the Egyptians in their picture-writing used it for the name of these foreigners.

The style and colour of their clothing are faithfully reproduced. Square woollen blankets, reaching in the case of the men to the knee and in the case of the women to the calf, are caught up on one shoulder. They consist of highly coloured striped material and serve as cloaks. Does that not remind us of the famous *coat of many colours* which Jacob, much to the annoyance of his other sons, bestowed upon his favourite son Joseph? (Genesis 37:3). The men's hair is trimmed into a pointed beard. The women's hair falls loosely over breast and shoulders. It is fastened by a narrow white ribbon round the forehead. The little curls in front of the ears seem to have been a concession to fashion. The men are wearing sandals, the women have dark brown half-length boots. They carry their water ration in artistically embroidered containers made of animal skins. Bows and arrows, heavy throw-sticks and spears serve as their weapons. Even their favourite instrument has been brought with them on their long journey. One of the men is playing the eight-stringed lyre. According to the instructions given in the Bible some of the Psalms of David were to be accompanied on this instrument: *To be sung to eight strings* is the heading of Psalms 6 and 12.

We may imagine that Abraham and his family on their way to Egypt looked something like this

The excavations at Tel Beersheba (opposite page, bottom), begun in 1969, brought to light among other remains an Israelite royal fortress with a military storage depot next to a monumental town gate (bottom right corner of map). The small Canaanite ivory figure (above), which probably had a religious function, dates from about 2000BC.

caravan of Semitic nomads on the grave paintings in Beni-Hasan. When he reached the Egyptian frontier a similar scene must have taken place. For the procedure for admitting foreign visitors was exactly the same at all the other frontier posts as in the case of the lord Khnum-hotpe.

It was thus no different long ago from what it is now to travel in a foreign country. Certainly there were no passports but formalities and officialdom made life difficult for foreign visitors even then. Anyone entering Egypt had to state the number in his party, the reason for his journey and the probable length of his stay. All the particulars were carefully noted down on papyrus by a scribe using red ink and then sent by messenger to the frontier officer who decided whether an entrance permit should be granted. This was however not left to his own judgment. Administrative officers at the court of Pharaoh issued from time to time precise directives, even to the point of specifying which grazings were to be put at the disposal of immigrant nomads.

In times of famine Egypt was for Canaanite nomads their place of refuge and often their only salvation. When the ground dried up in their own

country, the land of the Pharaohs always afforded sufficient juicy pastures. The Nile with its regular annual flooding took care of that.

On the other hand the proverbial wealth of Egypt was often a temptation to thieving bands of daring nomads who were not interested in finding pasture but were much more concerned with the bursting granaries and sumptuous palaces. Often they could only be got rid of by force of arms. As a protection against these unwelcome invaders and to keep a closer check on the frontier, the erection of the great 'Princes' Wall' was begun in the third

High above the Nile at Beni Hasan the princes of the 'Gazelle Province' at the time of the Eleventh and Twelfth Dynasties erected their rock tombs (right). The large painted halls (left) served the cult of the dead; the grave pits lie deep under the floor.

millennium BC. It consisted of a chain of forts, watchtowers and strongpoints. It was only under cover of darkness that the Egyptian Sinuhe with his local knowledge was able to slip through unobserved. Six centuries later, at the time of the Exodus from Egypt, the frontier was also strongly guarded. Moses knew only too well that escape from the country in defiance of Pharaoh's orders was impossible. The sentries would at once have sounded the alarm and summoned the guards. Any attempt to break through would have been nipped in the bud by sharpshooters and comman-

dos in armoured chariots and would have ended in bloodshed. That was the reason why the prophet knowing the country chose another quite unusual route. Moses led the children of Israel southwards, as far as the Red Sea, where there was no longer any wall.

After their return from Egypt Abraham and Lot separated: *The land could not support them while they stayed together, for their possessions were so great that they were not able to stay together. And quarrelling arose between Abram's herdsmen and the herdsmen of Lot . . . So Abram said to Lot, 'Let's not*

Above The Egyptians regarded only their own race as 'real human beings'. Foreigners were notoriously depicted as 'weaklings'. Particular mistrust was reserved for the 'sandramblers', Near Eastern nomads who in times of need often came to the eastern Nile delta to beg for pasture and water rights. From the Middle Kingdom on, border traffic across the Isthmus of Suez was very strictly controlled; the particulars of commercial travellers, shepherds or those seeking work were thoroughly checked. Qualified craftspeople, for instance Asiatic women weavers, or salesmen offering exotic goods, could get a visa by making a written application; even so their journey through the country would continue to be monitored.

This supervision devolved upon the provincial princes of the time. Prince Khnumhotep, in his rock tomb at Beni Hasan, commissioned a painting of the entry of a Semitic caravan into the Gazelle Province. The master of the hunt is handing his employer the entry application of the 'foreign prince Abishai' and his thirty-seven-strong clan, who want to import eye make-up, a highly desirable commodity in Egypt. The Semites are faithfully depicted, with their colourful woven garments, their sharp features and their carefully arranged hair and beards.

have any quarrelling between you and me, or between your herdsmen and mine, for we are brothers. Is not the whole land before you? Let's part company. If you go to the left, I'll go to the right; if you go to the right, I'll go to the left.' (Genesis 13:6–9).

In making Abraham the ancestor of the Israelites, Ishmaelites and Edomites, while it makes his nephew Lot father of the Moabites and Ammonites, the biblical account attempts to explain the various relationships between Israel and its neighbours.

Abraham left the choice to Lot. Lot, taking everything for granted, like so many young people, chose the best part, in the neighbourhood of the Jordan. It was *well-watered . . . towards Zoar.* (Genesis 13:10) and blessed with luxuriant tropical vegetation *like the garden of the Lord, like the land of Egypt* (Genesis 13:10).

From the wooded mountain chain in the heart of Palestine Lot made his way downhill to the east, wandered with his family and his flocks southwards along the Jordan valley and finally pitched his tent in Sodom. South of the Dead Sea lay an extremely fertile plain, the *Valley of Siddim (the Salt Sea)* (Genesis 14:3). The Bible lists five towns in this valley, *Sodom, Gomorrah, Admah, Zeboiim, and Zoar* (Genesis 14:2). It also knows of a warlike incident in the history of these five towns: Four kings *went to war against Bera king of Sodom, Birsha king of Gomorrah, Shinab king of Admah, Shemeber king of Zeboiim, and the king of Bela, (that is, Zoar)* (Genesis 14:2). For twelve years the kings of the Vale of Siddim had paid tribute to King Kedorlaomer. In the thirteenth year they rebelled. Kedorlaomer sought help from three royal allies. A punitive expedition would bring the rebels to their senses. In the battle of the nine kings, the kings of the five towns in the Vale of Siddim were defeated, their lands were ravaged and plundered.

Among the captives of the foreign kings was Lot. He was set free again by his uncle Abraham. *When Abram heard that his relative had been taken*

Right **In the Wadi el-Arabah, south of Sodom.**

Opposite **View of the Negev Desert across the Wadi el-Arabah towards the highlands of Trans-jordan, along the plateau of which the old 'king's highway' runs.**

captive, he called out the 318 trained men born in his household and went in pursuit as far as Dan. During the night Abram divided his men to attack them and he routed them, pursuing them as far as Hobah, north of Damascus. He recovered all the goods and brought back his relative Lot and his possessions, together with the women and the other people (Genesis 14:14–16).

Among the inhabitants of that stretch of country the memory of that punitive expedition has remained alive to this day. It is reflected in the name of a road which runs eastward of the Dead Sea and parallel with it, traversing what was in ancient times the land of Moab and leading to the north. The nomads of Jordan know it very well. Among the natives it is called, remarkably enough, the 'King's Way'. We come across it in the Bible, where it is called 'the king's high way' or 'the high way'. It was the road that the children of Israel wished to follow on their journey through Edom to the 'Promised Land' (Numbers 20:17, 19). In the Christian era the Romans used the 'King's Way' and improved it. Parts of it now belong to the network of roads in the state of Jordan. Clearly visible from the air the ancient track shows up as a dark streak across the country.

A fter the tale of Abraham's hospitality (Genesis 18) there follows the portrayal of the destruction of Sodom and Gomorrah:

Then the Lord said, 'The outcry against Sodom and Gomorrah is so great, and their sin so grievous . . .' Then the Lord rained down burning sulphur on Sodom and Gomorrah—from the Lord out of the heavens. Thus he overthrew those cities and the entire plain, including all those living in the cities— and also the vegetation in the land. But Lot's wife looked back and she became a pillar of salt . . . He looked down towards Sodom and Gomorrah, to-wards all the land of the plain, and he saw dense smoke rising from the land, like smoke from a furnace. (Genesis 18:20; 19:24–26, 28)

The calamity which is the subject of this powerful biblical story of divine punishment for incorrigible sin has probably in all ages made a deep impression on men's minds. Sodom and Gomorrah have become synonymous with vice and godlessness. When men have talked in terms of utter annihilation, again the fate of these cities has always sprung to their minds. Their imaginations have constantly been kindled by this inexplicable and frightful disaster, as can well be seen

from the many allusions to it in ancient times. Remarkable and quite incredible things are said to have happened there by the Dead Sea, the 'Sea of Salt', where according to the Bible the catastrophe must have happened.

During the siege of Jerusalem in AD70 it is said that the Roman army commander Titus sentenced certain slaves to death. He gave them short shrift, had them bound together by chains and thrown into the sea at the foot of the mountains of Moab. But the condemned men did not drown. No matter how often they were thrown into the sea they always drifted back to the shore like corks. This inexplicable occurrence made such a deep impression upon Titus that he pardoned the unfortunate offenders. Flavius Josephus, the Jewish historian who lived latterly in Rome, repeatedly mentions a 'Lake of Asphalt'. Greeks lay stress on

the presence of poisonous gases, which are reported as rising from all parts of this sea. The Arabs say that in olden times no bird was able to reach the opposite side. The creatures, as they flew across the water, would suddenly drop dead into it.

These and similar traditional stories were well enough known, but until the middle of the nineteenth century we had no first hand knowledge of this old mysterious sea in Palestine. No scientist had investigated it or even seen it. In 1848 the

Left **One of the three sources of the Jordan rises near the biblical city of Dan. Here the young river flows through a nature reserve.**

Above **The Jordan in Upper Galilee.**

United States took the initiative and equipped an expedition to solve the riddle of the Dead Sea. One autumn day in that year the beach of the little coastal town of Akka, less than 10 miles from present-day Haifa, was black with spectators who were engrossed in an unusual manoeuvre.

W. F. Lynch, a geologist and leader of the expedition, had brought ashore from the ship which was lying at anchor two metal boats which he was now fastening on to large-wheeled carts. Pulled by a long team of horses, the trek began.

Left **At one of the three sources of the Jordan in the Hermon mountains, the water springs from a grotto which was dedicated by the Greeks to the god Pan. Herod the Great erected a temple to Caesar Augustus here, and his son Philip elevated the town, which he gave the name Caesarea Philippi, to the status of capital of his kingdom.**

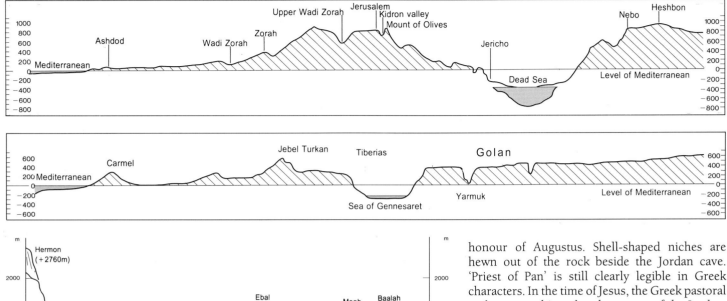

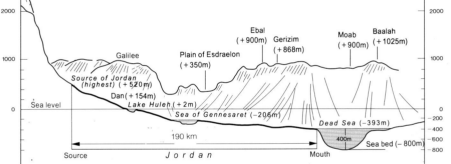

Above Two cross sections of the geological structure of Palestine.

Below From its source in the Hermon mountain range, to its mouth in the Dead Sea, the Jordan falls 913 metres over a distance of 190 kilometres.

Opposite page **Between the bare mountains of Palestine and the East Bank, the Jordan winds its snake-like way from the Sea of Galilee in endless meanderings through the 'zor', the 'thickets by the Jordan' (Jeremiah 12:5), to the Dead Sea.**

Three weeks later after indescribable difficulties they had succeeded in getting the waggons over the hills of Southern Galilee. The two boats took the water against Tiberias. When Lynch set up his theodolite at the Lake of Galilee, the result produced the first big surprise of the expedition. To begin with he thought he had made an error of calculation, but a cross check confirmed the result. The surface of the Lake, which played so notable a part in the life of Jesus, is 676 feet below the level of the Mediterranean. What then could be the height of the source of the Jordan, which flows through the Lake?

Some days later W. F. Lynch stood on the slopes of snow-capped Hermon. Among remains of broken columns and gateways lies the little village of Baniya. Local Arabs led him through a thick clump of oleanders to a cave, half choked with rubble, on the steep limestone flank of Hermon. Out of its darkness gushed a stream of pure water. This is one of the sources of the Jordan. The Arabs call the Jordan Nahr esh-Sheri'a el Kebire, the 'Great River'. This was the site of Panium where Herod built a temple of Pan in

honour of Augustus. Shell-shaped niches are hewn out of the rock beside the Jordan cave. 'Priest of Pan' is still clearly legible in Greek characters. In the time of Jesus, the Greek pastoral god was worshipped at the source of the Jordan. There the goat-footed Pan raised his flute to his lips as if he wanted to send the Jordan on its way with a tune. Only 3 miles west of this source lay Dan, which is frequently mentioned in the Bible as the most northerly point in the country. There too is another source of the Jordan where its clear waters spring out of the southern slopes of Hermon. A third stream rushes out of a wadi higher up. The bottom of the wadi just above Dan is 1,500 feet above sea level.

When the Jordan on its way south reaches little Lake Huleh 12 miles away, the river bed is only 6 feet above sea level. Then the river rushes down the next 6 miles to the Lake of Galilee. In the course of its descent from the slopes of Hermon to this point, a distance of only 25 miles, it has dropped 2,275 feet.

From Tiberias the members of the American expedition in their two metal boats followed the endless windings of the Jordan downstream. Gradually the vegetation became sparser and the thick undergrowth extended no farther than the banks. Under the tropical sun an oasis came into view on their right—Jericho. Soon afterwards they reached their goal. There before them, embedded between almost vertical precipices, lay the vast surface of the Dead Sea.

The first thing to do was to have a swim. But when they jumped in they felt as if they were being thrown out again. It was like wearing life-jackets. The old stories were therefore true. In this sea it is impossible to drown. The scorching sun dried the men's skins almost at once. The thin crust of salt which the water had deposited on their bodies made them look quite white. No shellfish, no fish, no seaweed, no coral—no fishing boat had ever rocked on this sea. Here was neither a harvest from the sea nor from the land. For the banks were equally bare and desolate. Huge deposits of coagulated salt made the beach and the rockface above it sparkle in the sun like diamonds. The air was filled with sharp acrid odours, a mixture of petroleum and sulphur. Oily patches of asphalt—the Bible calls them 'tar pits' (Genesis 14:10)—float on the waves. Even the bright blue sky and the all powerful sun could not breathe any life into this forbidding looking landscape.

For twenty-two days the American boats went back and forth across the Dead Sea. They tested the water and analysed it, they took innumerable soundings. The mouth of the Jordan, at the Dead Sea, lies 1,280 feet below sea level. If there were any connection with the Mediterranean, the Jordan and the Lake of Galilee, 65 miles away, would disappear. A vast inland sea would stretch almost up to the shores of Lake Huleh.

'When a storm sweeps up through this rocky basin,' observed Lynch, 'the waves strike the sides of the boats like blows from a hammer. But the weight of the water is such that a short time after the wind has died down the sea is calm again.'

The world learned for the first time from the report of the expedition two astonishing facts. The Dead Sea is over 1,200 feet in depth. The bottom of the sea is therefore about 2,500 feet below the level of the Mediterranean. The water of the Dead Sea contains 30% of solid ingredients, mostly sodium chloride, i.e. cooking salt. The normal ocean has only 3.3 to 4% salt. The Jordan and many smaller rivers empty themselves into this basin of approximately 50 x 10 miles which has not a solitary outlet. Evaporation under the broiling sun takes place on the surface of the sea at a rate of over 230 million cubic feet per day. What its tributaries bring to it in the way of chemical substances remains deposited in this great basin of 500 square miles.

It was only after the turn of the century that, keeping pace with excavations in other parts of Palestine, interest was also awakened in Sodom and Gomorrah. Archaeologists began their quest for the vanished cities that were said to have existed in the Vale of Siddim in biblical times. At the furthermost south-east point of the Dead Sea remains of a large settlement were found. The place is still called Zoar by the Arabs. The scientists were delighted, for Zoar was one of the five wealthy cities in the Vale of Siddim, which had refused to pay tribute to the four foreign kings. But

exploratory digging which was immediately undertaken proved a disappointment.

The date of the ruins that came to light showed it to be a town which had flourished there in the Middle Ages. There was no trace of the ancient Zoar of the king of Bela (Genesis 14:2) or of its neighbours. Nevertheless there were plentiful indications in the environs of mediaeval Zoar that there had been a numerous population in the country in very early times.

The excavation of Tell Mardikh in northern Syria, begun in 1975, caused a great sensation. Here the Italian scholar Giovanni Pettinato found Ebla, a city of the third millennium BC with an advanced civilization and, for the conditions of those times, an exceptionally differentiated social structure. Among the texts he found in the rich archive of clay tablets at Ebla, Pettinato deciphered, as well as other names vouchsafed to us by the Bible, the names of the cities of Sodom, Gomorrah, Admah and Zeboiim on the Dead Sea.

O n the eastern shore of the Dead Sea the peninsula of el-Lisan protrudes like a tongue far into the water. El-Lisan means 'the tongue' in Arabic. The Bible expressly mentions it when the country is being divided up after the Conquest. The frontiers of the tribe of Judah are being carefully outlined. In the course of this Joshua gives an unusually illuminating description of their southern limits; in describing the area allotted to the tribe of Judah he says: *Their southern boundary started from the bay at the southern end of the Salt Sea, crossed south of Scorpion Pass, continued on to Zin . . .* (Joshua 15:2)

The ground falls away under the surface of the water at a prodigious angle, dividing the sea into two parts. To the right of the peninsula the ground slopes sharply down to a depth of 1,200 feet. Left of the peninsula the water remains remarkably shallow. Soundings taken in the last few years established depths of only 50—60 feet.

Geologists added to these discoveries and observations a conclusive piece of evidence, which explains the occasion and the result of the biblical story of the annihilation of Sodom and Gomorrah.

The American expedition under Lynch in 1848 produced the first information about the prodigious drop of the Jordan on its short course through Palestine. This plunging of the river bed until it is far below sea level is, as later investigation established, a unique geological phenomenon. 'There may be something on the surface of

Above **View from the Judean desert towards the Dead Sea, whose surface lies a whole 400 metres below that of the Mediterranean.**

Below and opposite **In the Bible the Dead Sea is called the 'Salt Sea'. On account of its high evaporation it has a salt content of over 26 per cent, making it impossible for any form of life to survive in the water and creating impressive deposits of salt on the banks of the sea.**

Overleaf **View across the Dead Sea towards the highlands of Trans-jordan.**

another planet which is similar to the Jordan Valley, but on our planet there certainly is nothing,' wrote George Adam Smith, the Scottish Old Testament scholar, in his 'Historical Geography of the Holy Land'. 'No other part of the globe, which is not under water, lies deeper than 300 feet below sea level.'

The Jordan Valley is only part of a huge fracture in the earth's crust. The path of this crack has meantime been accurately traced. It begins far north, several hundred miles beyond the borders of Palestine, at the foot of the Taurus mountains in Asia Minor. In the south it runs from the south shore of the Dead Sea through the Wadi el-Arabah to the Gulf of Aqabah and only comes to an end beyond the Red Sea in Africa. At many points in this vast depression signs of intense volcanic activity are obvious. In the Galilean mountains, in

the highlands of Transjordan, on the banks of the Jabbok, and on the Gulf of Aqabah great fields of lava and huge strata of basalt have been deposited on top of the limestone.

The subsidence released volcanic forces that had been lying dormant deep down along the whole length of the fracture. In the upper valley of the Jordan near Bashan there are still the towering craters of extinct volcanoes; great stretches of lava and deep layers of basalt have been deposited on the limestone surface. From time immemorial the area around this depression has been subject to earthquakes. There is repeated evidence of them

and the Bible itself records them. Did Sodom and Gomorrah sink when perhaps a part of the base of this huge fissure collapsed still further to the accompaniment of earthquakes and volcanic eruptions? And did the Dead Sea then take on a further extension towards the south, and did the Valley of Siddim become part of the lake?

And Lot's wife—*looked back, and she became a pillar of salt* (Genesis 19:26).

T he nearer one gets to the south end of the Dead Sea the more wild and desolate it becomes. Landscape and mountain grow

Right **Flocks of sheep in the mountains of the Judean wilderness above the Dead Sea.**

Left **To the south of the Judean wilderness stretches the Negev desert, 'a dry and thirsty land', as its name implies. In older translations of the Bible this desert is called 'the South'.**

eerier and more forbidding. The hills stand there silent and everlasting. Their scarred slopes fall sheer and steep down to the sea, their lower reaches are crystal white. The unparalleled disaster which once took place here has left an imperishable and oppressive mark. Only occasionally is a band of nomads to be seen heading inland along one of the steep and rugged wadis.

Where the heavy oily water comes to an end in the south the harsh rockface on either side breaks off abruptly and gives place to a salt-sodden swamp. The reddish soil is pierced by innumerable channels and can easily become dangerous for the unwary traveller. Sweeping southwards the

bogland merges into the desert Wadi el-Arabah, which continues down to the Red Sea.

To the west of the southern shore and in the direction of the biblical 'Land of the South', the Negeb, stretches a ridge of hills about 150 feet high and 10 miles from north to south. Their slopes sparkle and glitter in the sunshine like diamonds. It is an odd phenomenon of nature. For the most part this little range of hills consists of pure rock salt. The Arabs call it Jebel Usdum, an ancient name, which preserves in it the word Sodom. Many blocks of salt have been worn away by the rain and have crashed downhill. They have odd shapes and some of them stand on end,

looking like statues. It is easy to imagine them suddenly seeming to come to life.

These strange statues in salt remind us vividly of the biblical description of Lot's wife who was turned into a pillar of salt. And everything in the neighbourhood of the Salt Sea is even to this day quickly covered with a crust of salt.

In the Realm of the Pharaohs

> *Now Joseph had been taken down to Egypt. Potiphar, an Egyptian who was one of Pharaoh's officials, the captain of the guard, bought him from the Ishmaelites who had taken him there. The Lord was with Joseph and he prospered... So Pharaoh said to Joseph, 'I hereby put you in charge of the whole land of Egypt.'*
>
> Genesis 39:1–2a; 41:41

JOSEPH IN EGYPT

The tale of Joseph, who was sold by his brothers to Egypt and later as grand vizier became reconciled to them, is undoubtedly one of the finest stories in the world's literature.

After a while his master's (Potiphar's) wife took notice of Joseph and said, 'Come to bed with me!' But he refused... (Genesis 39:7–8). When her husband came home, she said, *'This Hebrew has been brought to use to make sport of us!'* (Genesis 39:17).

Nothing new under the sun—smirked the Egyptologists whenever they started work on the translation of the 'Orbiney Papyrus'. What they were deciphering from hieroglyphics was a popular story about the time of the Nineteenth Dynasty which bore the discreet title: *The Tale of the Two Brothers.*

Once upon a time there were two brothers... The name of the elder one was Anubis, the younger was called Bata. Anubis owned a house

and a wife and his younger brother lived with him as if he were his own son. He drove the cattle out to the fields and brought them home at night and slept with them in the cowshed. When ploughing time came round the two brothers were ploughing the land together. They had been a few days in the fields when they ran out of corn. The elder brother therefore sent the younger one off: 'Hurry and bring us corn from the city.' The younger brother found his elder brother's wife having a hair-do. 'Up,' he said, 'and give me some corn, for I have to hurry back to the field. My brother said: "Quick, don't waste any time."' He loaded up with corn and wheat and went out with his burden... Then said she to him: 'You have so much energy! Every day I see how strong you are... Come! Let us lie down for an hour!—It might give you

The mighty pyramids of Gizeh, with the graves of kings Cheops, Chephren and Mykerinos, became a landmark of the realm of the Pharaohs.

pleasure, and I shall also make you fine clothes.'
Then the young man was as angry as a southern
panther at this wicked suggestion that had been
made to him. He said to her: 'What a disgraceful
proposal you have just made . . . Never do it
again and I shall say nothing to anyone.' So
saying he slung his load on his back and went
out to the fields. The wife began to be frightened
about what she had said. She got hold of some
grease paint and made herself up to look like
someone who had been violently assaulted. Her
husband . . . found his wife lying prostrate as a
result of the outrage. Her husband said to her:
'Who has been with you?' She replied: 'No
one . . . apart from your young brother. When he
came to fetch the corn he found me sitting alone
and said to me: "Come, let us lie down for an
hour! Do up your hair." But I paid no attention to
him. "Am I not your mother! and is your elder
brother not like a father to you!" I said to him.
But he was afraid and struck me to stop me
telling you about it. If you leave him alive now I
shall die.' Then his brother grew as wild as a
southern panther. He sharpened his knife . . . to
kill his younger brother . . .

The story of an adulteress, in the heart of an
Egyptian tale, as the prototype of the biblical story
of Joseph? Scholars argued the pros and cons
based on the text of the 'Orbiney Papyrus' long
after the turn of the century. On the debit side,
there was not the slightest trace of Israel's sojourn
in Egypt apart from the Bible itself. Historians and
professors of theology alike spoke of the 'Legend
of Joseph'. Egypt was just the kind of country from
which one might hope for and even expect contemporary documentation about the events recorded in the Bible. At any rate this ought to be true as
far as Joseph was concerned, for he is said to have
been Pharaoh's grand vizier and therefore a most
powerful man in Egyptian eyes.

No country in the Ancient East has handed
down its history so faithfully as Egypt. Right back
to about 3000BC we can trace the names of the
Pharaohs practically without a break. We know
the succession of dynasties in the Old, Middle and
New Kingdoms. No other people have recorded so
meticulously their important events, the activities
of their rulers, their campaigns, their erection of
temples and palaces, as well as their literature and
poetry.

But this time Egypt gave the scholars no
answer. As if it were not enough that they found
nothing about Joseph, they discovered far fewer
documents and monuments from his time than

This relief from the tomb of Haremhab in Sakkara near Memphis
shows Syrians and Libyans pre-
senting petitions to a high-ranking
Egyptian official. They kneel or
prostrate themselves; one is lying
on his stomach, another even lies
on his back! (Rijksmuseum van
Oudheden, Leiden.)

from previous centuries. The records stopped
suddenly about 1650BC. Only in 1575BC did
substantial contemporary evidence appear once
again. How could this absence of almost any
information whatever over so long a period be
explained, especially from such a highly developed people and civilization?

Something incredible and frightful befell the
Nile country about 1730BC. Suddenly, like
a bolt from the blue, warriors in chariots
drove into the country like arrows shot from a
bow, endless columns of them in clouds of dust.
Day and night horses' hooves thundered past the
frontier posts, rang through city streets, temple
squares and the majestic courts of Pharaoh's
palaces. Even before the Egyptians realized it, it
had happened: their country was taken by surprise, overrun and vanquished. The giant of the
Nile who never before in his history had seen
foreign conquerors lay bound and prostrate.

The rule of the victors began with a bloodbath.
The Hyksos, Semitic tribes from Canaan and Syria,
knew no pity. With the fateful year 1730BC the
thirteen hundred year rule of the dynasties came
to an abrupt end. The Middle Kingdom of the
Pharaohs was shattered under the onslaught of
these Asian peoples, the 'rulers of foreign lands'.
That is the meaning of the name Hyksos.

The memory of this political disaster

Tell el-Daba in the eastern Nile delta, where a fortress of the Hyksos period and a Canaanite temple have been excavated.

remained alive among the Nile people, as a striking description by the Egyptian historian Manetho, who lived at the time of the Ptolemies, testified: *We had a king called Tutimaeus. In his reign, it happened. I do not know why God was displeased with us. Unexpectedly from the regions of the East, came men of unknown race. Confident of victory they marched against our land. By force they took it, easily, without a single battle. Having overpowered our rulers they burned our cities without compassion, and destroyed the temples of the gods. All the natives were treated with great cruelty for they slew some and carried off the wives and children of others into slavery. Finally they appointed one of themselves as king. His name was Salitis and he lived in Memphis and made Upper and Lower Egypt pay tribute to him, and set up garrisons in places which would be most useful to him . . . and when he found a city in the province of Sais which suited his purpose (it lay east of the Bubastite branch of the Nile and was called Avaris) he rebuilt it and made it very strong by erecting walls and installing a force of 240,000 men to hold it. Salitis went there every summer partly to collect his corn and pay his men their wages, and partly to train his armed troops and terrify foreigners.*

It is thought that Avaris can be identified with

Left **The chariot, originating in the Near East and then adopted in Egypt, at first had little practical use there; it was simply used for state processions. Ceremonial chariots used in these events have survived in the tomb of Tutankhamun. It was a mark of Joseph's exceptional status in Egypt that the king allowed him to ride in 'his second chariot'.**

Right **On the occasion of major temple festivals, the Pharaoh would bestow 'gold of honour' on deserving officials—from the window where he made his royal appearances. Golden collars, staffs of office, signet rings and bracelets were emblems of dignity and power in the administrative hierarchy. This relief from a stela of Marmin, guardian of the royal harem, shows one of these 'award ceremonies' conducted by King Sethos I. (Louvre, Paris.)**

The biblical story of Joseph and the sojourn of the sons of Jacob, who received the name Israel from Yahweh, in Egypt probably come into this period of turbulent conditions on the Nile under the rule of the foreign Hyksos. It is therefore not surprising that no contemporary Egyptian information has come down to us. Nevertheless there is indirect proof of the authenticity of the Joseph story. The biblical description of the historical background is authentic. Equally genuine is the colourful Egyptian detail. Egyptology confirms this.

Spices and aromatic products are brought to Egypt by the Ishmaelites, the Arabian merchants who sell Joseph there (Genesis 37:25). There was a heavy demand for these things in the Nile country. They were used in religious services, where the wonderfully fragrant herbs were burned as incense in the temples. The doctors found them indispensable for healing the sick, and priests required them for embalming the bodies of the nobility.

Potiphar was the name of the Egyptian to whom Joseph was sold (Genesis 37:36). It is a thoroughly characteristic native name. In Egyptian it is *Pa-di-pa-rê*, 'the gift of the god Rê'.

Joseph's elevation to be viceroy of Egypt is reproduced in the Bible exactly according to protocol. He is invested with the insignia of his high office, he receives the ring, Pharaoh's seal, a costly linen vestment, and a golden chain (Genesis 41:42). This is exactly how Egyptian artists depict this solemn ceremony on murals and reliefs.

Above **Arab nomadic shepherds encamped by the Nile with their characteristic dark goatskin tents.**

Opposite **The huge oasis of Fayum is among the most fertile areas of Egypt. It lies in a depression below sea level and is watered by the so-called 'River of Joseph' (below right). This is often described as a 'canal', but it is in fact a natural branch of the Nile. Before the kings of the Middle Kingdom regulated its waters in about 1800BC, this river annually turned Fayum, which had no drainage, into a substantial lake bristling with crocodiles.**

As viceroy Joseph rides in Pharoah's 'second chariot' (Genesis 41:43, AV). In the time of the Hyksos the fast war chariot reached Egypt. The luxury model of it is the ostentatious chariot as we know it from the grave of Tutankhamun and many other pictorial records from the time of the New Kingdom. The ceremonial chariot harnessed to thoroughbred horses was in those days the Rolls Royce of the governors. The first chariot belonged to the ruler, the 'second chariot' was occupied by his chief minister.

Joseph married in accordance with his rank (Genesis 41:45)—his wife's name Asenath means 'belonging to the goddess Neith'—and thereby became the son-in-law of an influential man Potipherah, the priest of Heliopolis. Heliopolis is the On of the Bible and it lay on the right bank of the Nile a little to the north of present-day Cairo.

Joseph was thirty years of age when he *went throughout the land of Egypt* (Genesis 41:45). The Bible says no more about this but there is a spot by the Nile which still bears his name.

The town of Medinet-el-Faiyum, lying 80 miles south of Cairo in the middle of the fertile Faiyum, is extolled as the 'Venice of Egypt'. In the lush gardens of this huge flourishing oasis grow oranges, mandarins, peaches, olives, pomegranates and grapes. Faiyum owes these delicious fruits to the artificial canal, over 200 miles long, which conveys the water of the Nile and turns this district, which would otherwise be desert, into a paradise. This arm of the Nile is not only to this day called 'Bahr Yusuf', 'Joseph's Canal', by the fellahin, but is known by this name throughout Egypt. People say that it was the Joseph of the Bible, Pharaoh's 'Grand Vizier' as Arab legends would describe him, who planned it.

The Bible depicts Joseph as an able administrator who as grand vizier guides the Egyptian people through difficult times by his counsel and actions, making provision in years of plenty for years of want. Thus he gathers in corn and lays it up in granaries against times of need.

The seven years of abundance in Egypt came to an end, and the seven years of famine began, just as

90

Above **The tomb of Menena, at Shech Abd el-Kurna to the west of ancient Thebes, enjoys great popularity with tourists on account of its charming scenes of everyday life. The tomb's owner was an official of the land registry and superintendent of the royal domains. Since the annual flooding of the Nile area obliterated all boundaries between adjoining lands, the fields had to be newly measured every year. According to the size of the fields and their productivity after flooding, officials then calculated how much produce had to be delivered as 'taxes in kind' to the royal silos. On the extreme left Menena, wearing his robes of state, carrying writing materials and accompanied by his assistants, arrives at the cornfield of a peasant, who first of all offers him presents and refreshment. A rope with knots at regular intervals serves as a tape measure. The harvest too must be supervised, so that none of the farmers or labourers can make off with a sheaf for his own use. But the most important task is to record the exact amount of grain. The corn is transferred from one pile to another with 'bushels', or measuring shovels. It is a measure of the inflated bureaucracy of Egypt that four men are shovelling and eight taking note of the results.**

Joseph had said. There was famine in all the other lands, but in the whole of Egypt there was food. (Genesis 41:53, 54)

Years of drought, bad harvests and famine are well attested in the lands of the Nile. In very early times, for example at the beginning of the third millennium, there is said to have been a seven year famine according to a rock inscription of the Ptolemies. King Zoser sent the following message to the governor of the great cataracts of the Nile at Elephantine: *I am concerned about the people in the palace. My heart is heavy over the calamitous failure of the Nile floods for the past seven years. There is little fruit; vegetables are in short supply; there is shortage of food generally. Everybody robs his neighbour... Children weep, young folk slouch around. The aged are depressed, they have no power in their legs, they sit on the ground. The court is at its wits' end. The storehouses have been opened but everything that was in them has been consumed.* Traces have been found of the granaries which existed even in the Old Kingdom. In many tombs there were little clay models of them. Apparently they were making provision for possible years of famine among the dead.

When Jacob learned that there was corn in Egypt, he said to his sons, 'Why do you just keep looking at each other?' He continued, 'I have heard that there is corn in Egypt. Go down there and buy some for us, so that we may live and not die. Then ten of Joseph's brothers went down to buy corn from Egypt.' (Genesis 42:1–3)

This is the reason for the great journey which led to the reunion with the brother who had been sold as a slave and to the migration of the Israelites into Egypt. The viceroy brought his father, broth-

ers and other relatives into the country: ... *the members of Jacob's family, which went into Egypt, were seventy in all... they arrived in the region of Goshen* (Genesis 46:27–8). The viceroy had obtained permission from the highest authority for his family to cross the frontier, and what the Bible records corresponds perfectly with the guidelines under which the government admitted to Egyptian territory nomads who had been forced to migrate by famine.

Pharaoh said to Joseph, 'Your father and your brothers have come to you, and the land of Egypt is before you; settle your father and your brothers in the best part of the land. Let them live in Goshen. And if you know of any among them with special ability, put them in charge of my own livestock.' (Genesis 47:5–6)

A frontier official writes to his superiors on papyrus: *I have another matter to bring to the attention of my lord and it is this: We have permitted the transit of the Bedouin tribes from Edom via the Menephta fort in Zeku, to the fen-lands of the city of Per-Atum ... so that they may preserve their own lives and the lives of their flocks on the estate of the king, the good Sun of every land ...*

Per-Atum, that crops up here in a hieroglyphic text, is the biblical Pithom in the land of Goshen, later one of the bond-cities of Israel in Egypt (Exodus 1:11).

In cases of this sort the Egyptian frontier police, like the higher officials, were carefully graded in a chain of command right up to the court. The procedure to be followed was of a standard pattern: Petitioners for pasture land, refugees from famine stricken countries, were accepted and almost always directed into the same area. It lay on the delta, on the right bank of the

From the earliest days of the Egyptian state there is archaeological evidence of large silos for holding stockpiles of grain. This not only guaranteed food throughout the year and seed corn for the next, but also provided for times of shortage when the Nile floods failed. Wall paintings in tombs from the Old Kingdom and wooden models from the Eleventh Dynasty confirm the importance of such measures.

It was in the New Kingdom at the latest that storage was transferred, at least in part, to the great temples. Extensive storehouses were built in the sacred areas around the temples; those around the temple of the dead built by Rameses II in western Thebes provide a well-preserved example. If after a number of 'fat years' there was a surplus of grain which threatened to overflow the silos, grain could be sold to needy Bedouins or exported elsewhere. Egypt made good money from this trade and the temple economy flourished. The biblical story of Joseph shows an awareness of these circumstances and the important position of the central organizer.

Nile in the biblical 'Land of Goshen'. The seat of government of the Hyksos rulers was also in the delta.

The children of Israel must have appreciated life in the Land of Goshen. It was—exactly as the Bible describes it (Genesis 45:18; 46:32; 47:3)—extremely fertile and quite ideal for cattle breeding. When Jacob died at a ripe old age something happened to him which was quite as unknown and uncommon in Canaan and Mesopotamia as among his own family, who considered it a very remarkable proceeding. His body was embalmed.

Then Joseph directed the physicians in his service to embalm his father Israel. So the physicians embalmed him, taking a full forty days for that was the time required for embalming. And the Egyptians mourned for him seventy days. (Genesis 50:2–3)

We can read in Herodotus, the 'father of history', who travelled through Egypt in the fifth

For a space of 400 years, during which, politically, the face of the 'Fertile Crescent' was completely altered, the Bible is silent. In these four centuries there took place a vast rearrangement of the disposition of national groups. They interrupted the history of the Semitic kingdoms that for 1,000 years had maintained their sway on the Euphrates and the Tigris. The great island of civilization in the Middle East was rudely dragged from its self-sufficient existence. Foreign peoples with foreign ways surged in from distant and hitherto unknown lands. For the first time it felt the clash with the outside world.

Egypt shook off the foreign yoke of the Hyksos rulers, and the Pharaohs of the Eighteenth Dynasty entered on the glorious New Kingdom. The prelude to the reawakening of the giant of the Nile opens with a remarkable motif: the roaring of hippopotami.

A papyrus fragment tells how the ambassador of the Hyksos king Apophis went from Avaris to the prince of the City of the South. The City of the South was Thebes and its prince was the Egyptian Sekenenrê, who paid tribute to the foreign overlords on the upper delta. The prince in astonishment asked the emissary of the Asiatic occupying power: *'Why have you been sent to the City of the South? Why have you made this journey?'* The messenger replied: *'King Apophis—may he have long life, health and prosperity!—bids me say to you: Get rid of the hippopotamus pool in the east end of your city. I cannot sleep for them. Night and day the noise of them rings in my ears.'* The prince of the City of the South was thunderstruck because he did not know what answer to give to the ambassador of King Apophis—may he have long life, health and prosperity!* At last he said: *'Very well, your master—may he have long life, health and prosperity!—will hear about this pool in the east end of the City of the South.'* The ambassador however was not to be so easily put off. He spoke more plainly: *'This matter about which I have been sent must be dealt with.'* The prince of the City of the South then tried in his own way to get round the determined ambassador. He was well aware of the ancient equivalent of the present day slap-up lunch as a means of creating a friendly atmosphere and goodwill. Accordingly he saw to it that the Hyksos commissioner was *supplied with good things, with meat and cakes.* But his luck was out. For when the ambassador departed he had a promise from the prince in his saddle-bag, written on papyrus: *'All that you have told me to do I shall do. Tell him that.'* Then the prince of the City of the South summoned his highest officials and his leading officers and repeated to them the message

Even in fertile Egypt there was no guarantee of full stomachs. It is true that official chronicles give us no reports of disasters, but there are plenty of indications of lean times. The flooding of the Nile, on which alone the fertility of the almost rainless land depended, was not always sufficient; when it was not, the harvest was scanty. If the floods failed altogether, hunger followed, and if this happened several times in succession, there was famine.

An early record of such penury is provided by a relief from the approach to the pyramid of King Una at Sakkara, originating from about 2300BC. It shows emaciated figures squatting on the ground, weak and infirm, their bones sticking out. They are evidently receiving help; the king's stockpiling system is proving itself. Many provincial rulers, too, could boast: 'In my time there was no hunger. When lean years came, I kept the people alive...' The organized stockpiling system in Egypt also benefited its Asiatic neighbours, when need arose in their regions. But they could expect no charitable handouts; they had to pay.

century BC, how closely this description corresponds with Egyptian practice. Later on Joseph was buried in the same way.

Under the Egyptian Pharaohs a 'Sand-dweller' could never have become viceroy. Nomads bred asses, sheep and goats and the Egyptians despised none so much as breeders of small cattle. *For all shepherds are detestable to the Egyptians* (Genesis 46:34). Only under the foreign overlords, the Hyksos, would an 'Asiatic' have the chance to rise to the highest office in the state. Under the Hyksos we repeatedly find officials with Semitic names. On scarabs dating from the Hyksos period the name 'Jacob-Her' has been clearly deciphered. 'And it is not impossible,' concluded the great American Egyptologist James Henry Breasted at the beginning of the twentieth century, 'that a leader of the Israelite tribe of Jacob gained control for a time in the Nile valley in this obscure period. Such an occurrence would fit in surprisingly well with the migration to Egypt of Israelite tribes which in any case must have taken place about this time.'

FOUR HUNDRED YEARS' SILENCE

Now the Israelites settled in Egypt in the region of Goshen. They acquired property there and were fruitful and increased greatly in number.

GENESIS 47:27

that King Apophis—*may he have long life, health and prosperity!*—*had sent him. Then one and all remained silent for quite a while . . .* At this point the papyrus text breaks off. The end of the story is unfortunately missing, but we can reconstruct the sequel from other contemporary evidence.

In the Cairo Museum lies the mummy of Sekenenrê. When it was discovered at Deir-el-Bahri near Thebes, it attracted special attention from medical men, for there were five deep sword cuts in the head. Sekenenrê had lost his life in battle.

It sounds like a fairy tale, yet it is an attractive possibility that the roaring of hippopotami at Thebes should have unseated the Hyksos rulers up in the delta. The roaring of a hippopotamus is probably the most extraordinary casus belli in world history.

Kamose, the son of Sekenenrê, led the rebellion against the hated oppressors with as much determination as circumspection. Stelae from Karnak tell us the story. Egyptian battalions marched once more down the Nile. They were accompa-

nied by a well-equipped fleet of galleys which headed north down the sacred river. In 1580 BC, after years of furious attacks, Avaris, the chief fortress of the Hyksos in the delta, fell amid bloody and savage fighting. Ahmose I, the younger brother of Kamose, was the glorious liberator of Egypt. A namesake of his, Ahmose, an officer in the new Royal Egyptian Navy, has left us a record of this decisive battle on the walls of his tomb at El-Kab. After a detailed description of his career he adds laconically: *Avaris was taken: I captured one man and three women, four people in all. His Majesty gave them to me as slaves.*

This naval officer had also something to say about the military side of things: *Sharuhen was besieged for three years before his Majesty captured it.* This was also a profitable occasion for Ahmose: *I collected two women and one labourer as my booty. I was given gold for my bravery, as well as the prisoners for my slaves.*

Sharuhen was, on account of its commanding position in the Negeb, an important strategic point south of the brown mountain chains of Judah. It

A highly exceptional documentary record of a time of need is provided by the so-called 'famine stela', an inscribed block of stone on the granite island of Sehel, in the midst of the rapids of the first cataract at Aswan. The inscription comes much later, from the time of the Ptolemies. But it gives an account of a seven-year drought under the rule of King Djoser, who reigned about 2700BC. The provincial prince of Aswan, the report says, finally instigated the building of a temple to the creator god Khnum, who was responsible for the luxuriant gushing forth of the sources of the Nile.

From about 1650BC Egypt experienced foreign government by rulers from the Near East who were known as Hega Hasut (Hyksos in Greek), 'rulers of foreign lands'. By about 1560BC a family of Upper Egyptian princes from Thebes had gained enough power to turn against the Nubians in the South and subsequently against the Hyksos in the North. The military success of one of these princes, Kamose, was crowned in about 1550BC by his younger brother Ahmose, with the conquest of Avaris and the founding of the New Kingdom.

A record of this event is provided by this costly royal battle-axe made of gold, amber and niello (silver on which incisions have been filled with a black composite); it is inlaid with semi-precious stones and enamel. One side of the axe-head (right) shows the given name and royal name of the king, the killing of an Asiatic, and a griffin—symbol of the Theban war god, Month. The other side (left) portrays the king as a Sphinx with the head of a decapitated Asiatic in its lion's claws; it also symbolizes the new union of Upper and Lower Egypt by the heraldic plants of the time and the goddesses who were thought to crown the monarchs. At the top it shows the god Heh, who offers 'millions of years of rule'. The ceremonial axe was the victory sceptre of the hero of freedom and re-founder of the realm. It was found in the tomb of the king's mother, Ahhotep, at Dra Abul Nega in western Thebes. Also in her tomb was a bead bracelet with the name of Ahmose (opposite page).

Overleaf **A troop of forty Nubian bowmen, who served as mercenaries in Egypt. This group of models comes from the grave of Mesekti, who lived about 2000BC, in Assiut.**

has been identified with Tell el-Agul, which Flinders Petrie, the famous British archaeologist, excavated from 1930–1934.

The multi-coloured army of mercenaries which the Egyptians controlled, consisting of Negroes, Asiatics, and Nubians, marched on northwards through Canaan. The Pharaohs of the New Kingdom had learned a lesson from the bitter experience of the past. Never again would their country be taken by a surprise attack. Egypt lost no time in creating a buffer-state far in advance of its frontier posts. Palestine became an Egyptian province. What had once been consular stations, trading posts, and messengers' quarters in Canaan and on the Phoenician coast became permanent garrisons, fortified strong points and Egyptian fortresses in a subjugated land.

After a history of more than 2,000 years the giant of the Nile stepped out of the shadows of his Pyramids and Sphinxes and claimed the right to take an active part in affairs beyond his own border and to have some say in the outside world. Egypt matured more and more into a world-power. Previously, everyone who lived outside of the Nile valley was contemptuously described as 'Asiatics', 'Sandramblers', cattle-breeders—people not worthy of the attention of a Pharaoh. Now however the Egyptians became more affable. They began communications with other countries. Hitherto that had been unthinkable. Among the diplomatic correspondence in the archives of the palace of Mari there is not one single item from the Nile. Tempora mutantur—times change.

Their advance brought them eventually to Syria, indeed to the banks of the Euphrates. There, to their astonishment, they came up against people of whose existence they had no idea. The priests searched in vain through the ancient papyrus rolls in the temple archives, and studied without result the records of the campaigns of earlier Pharaohs. Nowhere could they find even a hint about the unknown kingdom of Mitanni. Its foundation is attributed to an extremely active and creative people, the Hurrians, named as *Horites* in the Bible about the time of Abraham (Genesis 14:6, etc).

In the neighbourhood of the oil-wells of Kirkuk in Iraq, where now derricks draw immeasurable wealth from the earth, archaeologists from U.S.A. and Iraq came across a large settlement, the old Hurrian city of Nuzu. Stacks of tablets which

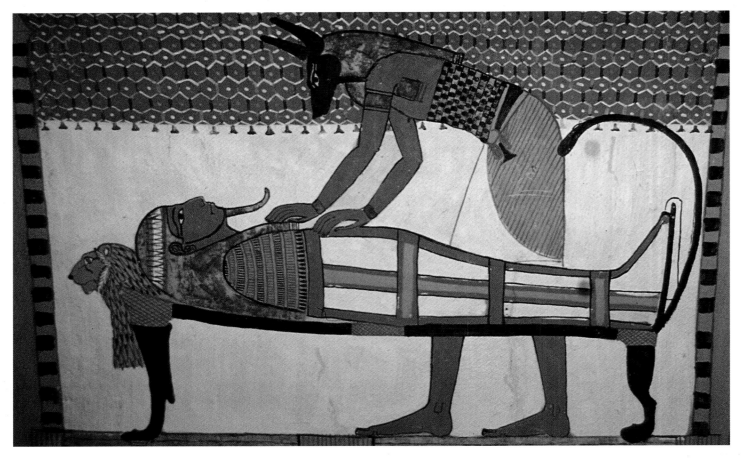

Above **One of the paintings in the tomb of Sennoiem at Deir el-Medina shows the jackal-headed desert god Anubis, who is attending to and guarding the body as it lies in state. The painstaking and expensive process of embalming high-ranking corpses was the province of specially trained doctors. These enjoyed priestly status, and for their work they wore masks of Anubis. In the Genesis story, the 'anointing' which Joseph bestowed on his father Jacob when he died in Egypt signified more than simply the use of preservative oils. The viscera were removed to be buried separately in jars, and the body was dehydrated by the use of sodium salts and wrapped in mummy cloths.**

have been salvaged, and among these principally marriage contracts and wills, contained extremely interesting information: the biblical Horites were not a Semitic people. Their home was among the mountains round the Black Sea. The names on many Hurrian documents indicate that at least the princely caste must be reckoned as Indo-Aryan. It is even certain that as far as their outward appearance was concerned they belonged to the brachycephalous type like present day Armenians.

In the north of Mesopotamia the Hurrites had built up the powerful kingdom of Mitanni between the upper reaches of the Euphrates and the Tigris. Their kings had collected round them an aristocracy of warlike charioteers and they bore Indo-Aryan names. The aristocracy of the country was called Marya, which is the equivalent of 'Young Warriors'. Marya is an old Indian word and their temples were dedicated to old Indian gods. Magic incantations from the Rigveda were intoned in front of the images of Mithras, the victorious champion of Light against Darkness, of Indra, who ruled the storms, and of Varuna, who governed the eternal order of the universe. The old gods of the Semites had crashed from their pedestals.

The Hurrites were completely devoted to their horses, they were 'horse-daft'. They held the first Derbys in the world along the banks of their great rivers. Advice on the breeding and care of stud animals, directions for the training of cavalry

horses, instructions on breaking-in young horses, regulations for feeding and training in racing stables fill veritable libraries of clay tablets. These are works on equitation which can bear comparison with any modern textbook on horse-breeding. As far as the Marya, these aristocratic charioteers, were concerned, horses were of more account than human beings.

It was with this state of Mitanni that Egypt had now a common frontier, nevertheless one on which there was to be no peace. Local feuds were unending. Raids on one side or the other constantly involved Egyptian archers in angry passages with the charioteers. In the course of these expeditions sometimes it was Egyptian striking forces, sometimes columns of Mitanni, who struck deep into the enemy's territory. The valleys of the Lebanon, the banks of the Orontes and the Euphrates were the scenes of endless battles and bloody mêlées. For almost a century the two great kingdoms were at each other's throats.

Shortly before 1400BC the warlike Mitanni proposed a peaceful settlement with the Egyptians. The enemy became a friend. What was the reason for the unexpected desire for peace on the part of the warlike Mitanni?

The impulse came from outside. Their kingdom was suddenly threatened with war on two fronts. A second powerful opponent began to storm the frontiers with his armies from Asia Minor in the north-west. This was a nation about which scholars until this century knew hardly anything, but which plays a considerable part in the Old Testament—the Hittites.

It was among the Hittites that Abraham pitched his tent near Hebron, south of the hills of Judah, and it was from them that he bought the land where he laid his wife Sarah to rest (Genesis 23:3ff). Esau, much to the distress of his parents Isaac and Rebecca, married two Hittite women (Genesis 26:34), and King David himself is said to have taken *the wife of Uriah, the Hittite* (2 Samuel 11). We are told by the prophet Ezekiel that Hittites were partly responsible for founding Jerusalem: *Your ancestry and birth were in the land of the Canaanites; your father was an Amorite and your mother a Hittite.* (Ezekiel 16:3, 45).

Right **The continuance of family life was one of the fundamental hopes the Egyptians cherished for the afterlife. So the necropolis builder Inherchaui commissions a self-portrait with his wife and children in his tomb at Deir el-Medina. It is the children, too, who must take responsibility for the religious care of the tomb, for ensuring the attendance of the priests of the dead, and for supplying food and drink to maintain the lives of their deceased parents.**

Opposite page, below '**And the Egyptians mourned for him seventy days' (Genesis 50:3). The prescribed mourning of the dead performed by professional women mourners, as depicted on the wall painting in the tomb of Ramose in western Thebes, is easily imagined.**

The rediscovery of the Hittite people who had sunk into complete oblivion took place in the heart of Turkey shortly after the turn of the century.

In the highlands east of Ankara, the capital, the river Halys makes a huge bend on its way to the Black Sea. Almost exactly in the middle lies Boghaz-Keui: *Boghas* in Turkish means a gorge and *Keui* is a village. Near this 'Village in the gorge' the German Egyptologist Professor Hugo Winckler discovered in 1905 a number of cuneiform texts, among which was also a peculiar type of hieroglyphics. They aroused tremendous interest and not only among scholars. The general public learned with amazement just what kind of people these biblical 'sons of Heth' were. The translations of the cuneiform writings brought to the notice of the world at large the hitherto unknown Indo-Germanic Hittites and their vanished empire.

Two years later a fresh expedition set out from Berlin for Boghaz-Keui. This time it was under the direction of the President of the Archaeological Institute of Berlin, Otto Puchstein. The great pile of ruins above the village was carefully examined. This was the site of royal Chattusas, the proud capital of the Hittite empire. What remained of it was a vast ruin of walls, temples, fortified gateways—the remnants of a great city. Its walls enclosed an area of 425 acres. Chattusas was almost as big as mediaeval Nuremberg. At the city gates were life-size reliefs. It is to these effigies, carved out of black basalt as hard as iron, that we are indebted for our knowledge of the appearance of Hittite kings and warriors: their long hair hung over their shoulders like a full-bottomed wig. On top sat a high dented cap. Their short aprons were fastened with a wide belt and their shoes had pointed toes.

When Subbiluliuma, king of the Hittites, marched south-east with a powerful army about 1370BC the days of the kingdom of Mitanni were already numbered despite all their clever dynastic politics. Subbiluliuma crushed the kingdom of the warlike charioteers, compelled it to pay tribute, and then passed on farther to the mountains of the Lebanon in the north of Canaan. Overnight, as it were, Egypt had a new equally powerful neighbour in Syria, thirsting for victory.

A delightful document has come down to us from this period. Prince Mursilis, son of Subbiluliuma, tells in his autobiography of an episode at the Hittite Court, which must have made such a

Among the most famous memorials of the realm of the Hittites are these rock reliefs of Yazilikaya, created about 1260BC. They portray Hurrite gods, whose names are listed in hieroglyphics. In one large scene the god Sharumma embraces the king.

lasting impression on him that he had it recorded.

Anches-en-Amun, the wife of Pharaoh Tutankhamun, had become a widow. She had very famous parents, Akhnaten and Nofretete. We know her from wonderful Egyptian representations as a slight young thing. But she must have been a woman who knew what she wanted and used all her natural charm to further the aims of her people in the realm of high politics. Using the inviting bed and throne of the Pharaohs as a bait—and what an attractive one—she tried to take the wind out of the sails of her powerful new neighbours by discouraging their warlike intentions. Hittite warriors had just made an attack on Amqa, the fertile country between Lebanon and Anti-Lebanon.

Mursilis dictated: *When the Egyptians heard of the attack on Amqa they were alarmed. To make matters worse their lord (Tutankhamun) had just died. But the widowed queen of Egypt sent an ambassador to my father and wrote him the following letter: 'My husband is dead and I have no son. I am told that you have many sons. If you send me one of your sons he could become my husband. I do not wish to take one of my servants and make a husband of him.' When my father heard this he summoned his nobles to a council and said: 'I have never in all my life come across anything like this.' He despatched his chamberlain Hattu-Zitis: 'Go and find out if this is true. Perhaps they are trying to deceive me. There*

may in fact be a prince. Bring me back reliable information.' The Egyptian ambassador, the honourable Hanis, came to my father. Since my father had instructed Hattu-Zitis before he left for Egypt: 'Perhaps they have a prince of their own: They may be trying to deceive us. They may not need one of my sons at all to occupy the throne.' The queen of Egypt now replied to my father in a letter: 'Why do you say, they may be trying to deceive me? If I had a son would I write to a foreign country in a manner that is humiliating both for me and my people? You do not trust me, otherwise you would not say such a thing. He who was my husband is dead and I have no sons. Am I to take one of my servants and make him into my husband? I have written to no other country, I have only written to you. They tell me you have so many sons. Give me one of your sons and he shall be my husband and king over the land of Egypt.' Since my father was so fine a king, he complied with the lady's request and sent her the son she asked for.

Fate prevented the successful conclusion of this unusual offer of marriage. The royal throne and the bed of Anches-en-Amun both remained empty, since the candidate for both was murdered on his way to Egypt.

S eventy-five years later another offer of marriage on this same Halys-Nile axis had a happy ending, although the prelude to it, which was the din of battle and the clash of weapons, pointed to a different conclusion. Rameses II, who was called the 'Great', set out with his army for Palestine and Syria. He intended to deal with the hated Hittites once and for all.

In the valley of the Orontes, where today fields of cotton stretch far and wide and the old Crusader castle 'Krak des Chevaliers' keeps an eye on the fertile plain of Bukea, there lay in those days the city of Kadesh, a little to the south of the dark green of Lake Homs. Before its walls four Egyptian armies threw themselves on the swift war-chariots

Hattusa (Boghaskoi) was probably the oldest royal residence of the Hittites. The mighty fortress had walls in places eight feet thick. The so-called Lion Gate has been dated to about 1800BC.

glad to hear these unusual tidings which were quite unheard of in Egypt. He therefore sent forth the army and the dignitaries to receive her.'

A large delegation was despatched to the north of Palestine to bring back the bride. Yesterday's enemies became brothers: *So the daughter of the great Prince of Hatti came to Egypt. Whilst the infantry, charioteers and dignitaries of His Majesty accompanied them, they mingled with the infantry and charioteers from Hatti. The whole populace from the country of the Hittites was mixed up with the Egyptians. They ate and drank together, they were like blood-brothers...*

The great bridal train proceeded from Palestine to the city of Pi-Raamses-Meri-Imen in the Nile delta: *Then they brought the daughter of the Great Prince of Hatti... before His Majesty. And His Majesty saw that she was fair of countenance like a goddess... And he loved her more than anything else...*

Israelites too may could have been eye-witnesses of the ceremonial arrival of the bridal procession in the city of Pi-Raamses-Meri-Imen which means 'The House of Ramses the Beloved of the god Amun.' As the biblical description indicates however their presence in this city was by no means of their own accord. It is at this point also that the Bible resumes its narrative. Four hundred years which the Children of Israel had spent as immigrants in the land of the Nile have been passed over in silence. Bad news comes at the beginning of a new and significant chapter of the history of the biblical people now begins.

and infantry of the Hittites. The battle did not, as it happened, bring Rameses II the victory he had hoped for—he came in fact within an ace of being captured himself—but it put an end to these endless military incidents. In 1280BC the Hittites and the Egyptians concluded the first non-aggression and mutual defence pact in world history. The good understanding was cemented at top level by the marriage of Rameses II to a Hittite princess. Many lengthy inscriptions give in full and vivid detail the colourful background of what was in the circumstances an international event of the first order. Whether they are found on the walls of the temples at Karnak, Elephantine or Abu Simbel, or on the numerous monuments, they all tell the same story.

As far as self-advertisement and self-praise were concerned, Rameses II put all his predecessors in the shade. On the many temples he built, he had the battle of Kadesh recorded in full detail in words and pictures, celebrating it as a great victory. He also had the text of the peace treaty, too, which we know in its Akkadian cuneiform version from the clay tablet archive of Boghasköi, chiselled into a wall of the temple at Karnak and in the Ramesseum in western Thebes. His marriage to a Hittite princess, too, was immortalized in various temples including Karnak and Abu Simbel: *Then came a messenger to inform His Majesty. He said: 'Behold, even the great Prince of Hatti! Prince of the Hittites. His eldest daughter is on her way and she brings untold tribute of all kinds... They have reached His Majesty's frontiers. Let the army and the dignitaries come to receive her! Then His Majesty was greatly delighted, and the palace was*

Above **Rameses II in battle near Kadesh.**

Below **The so-called 'wedding stela' at Abu Simbel tells the story of the marriage of Rameses II to a Hittite princess.**

Opposite page **Tutankhamun with his consort Ankhesenamun. When widowed she offered her hand, and the throne of the Pharaohs, to a Hittite king's son.**

FORCED LABOUR IN PITHOM AND RAAMSES

Then a new king, who did not know about Joseph, came to power in Egypt... So they put slave masters over them to oppress them with forced labour, and they built Pithom and Raamses as store cities for Pharaoh.

EXODUS 1:8, 11

The new king who 'did not know about Joseph' was more likely to have been Rameses II than any of his predecessors. His ignorance is understandable. For Joseph lived centuries before him in the days of the Hyksos. The names of these Hyksos rulers who were so cordially detested by Egyptians have hardly been

Egypt's demand for bricks for scaffolding, ramps and walls must have reached a high point under Rameses II, when everywhere throughout the land one set of major building works followed another. The builders would have had difficulty finding labour for the unpopular work of producing mud bricks, and it was an easy solution to find foreigners whose lives could be 'made . . . bitter with hard labour in brick and mortar' (Exodus 1:14). In the tomb of the vizier Rechmire in western Thebes the manufacture of bricks is portrayed in detail. Water is scooped from a pool, the earth is moistened and worked into a stiff paste with mattocks, mixed with chopped blades of straw, moulded in small wooden boxes, tipped out and allowed to dry in the sun. Mud from the Nile is used as mortar. Overseers with sticks supervise the work and punish slackers.

Below A brick with the stamp of Rameses II on it.

recorded, far less the names of their dignitaries and officials.

Even if this pharaoh of the new dynasty, whether it was Rameses II or a predecessor, had known of Joseph, that is as far as he would have wanted it to go. Joseph was bound to be an object of contempt to any nationally conscious Egyptian for two reasons. One, that he was an 'Asiatic' and a miserable 'Sandrambler', and, two, that he was the highest official of the hated occupying power. From the latter point of view any appeal to Joseph would hardly have been a recommendation for Israel in the eyes of a pharaoh.

What forced labour meant in ancient Egypt, and what the Children of Israel experienced at the great building projects on the Nile, can be gathered from an old painting that Percy A. Newberry, the discoverer of the painting from the patriarchal period at Beni-Hasan, found in a rock tomb west of the royal city of Thebes.

On its walls there is a series of paintings from the life of a great dignitary, the vizier Rekhmirê,

showing what he had done for the benefit of his country. Several scenes shows him in charge of public works, including the manufacture of bricks. In the accompanying inscription the workers express themselves content with their provisions: *He provides us with bread, beer and every good thing.* Yet one of the Egyptian overseers is saying, *Be not idle.*

The picture is an impressive illustration of the biblical words: *The Egyptians . . . worked them ruthlessly. They made their lives bitter with hard labour in brick and mortar* (Exodus 1:13, 14). The forefathers of Israel were of shepherd stock, unused to work of any other kind, which was therefore twice as hard for them. Building and brick making were forced labour.

The 'classical' bond-cities of the children of Israel were Pithom and Raamses. Both names appear in slightly different form in Egyptian inventories. 'Per-Itum', 'House of the god Atum', is a town which was built by Rameses II. Pi-Raamses-Meri-Imen, which has already been mentioned, is the biblical Raamses. An inscription of the time of Rameses II speaks of 'PR', 'who hauled the stones for the great fortress of the city of Pi-Raamses-Meri-Imen'. Could this 'PR' perhaps refer to the Hebrews?

The question of where these bond-cities were situated remained a problem. It was known that the rulers of the New Kingdom had moved their seat from ancient Thebes northward to Avaris, in

the Nile delta, which was the place from which the Hyksos had also ruled the country. The new type of international power-politics made it seem advisable to be nearer the centre of things than was the case with Thebes, which lay much farther south. From the delta they could much more easily keep an eye on their dominions in Canaan and Syria. Pharaoh Rameses II gave his name to the new capital.

After a fair amount of guesswork and supposition archaeologists' picks put an end to all differences of opinion about the site of the bond-cities.

About half way down the Suez Canal, where it goes through what was the Lake of Crocodiles, Lake Timsah, a dried up watercourse known as Wadi Tumilat stretches westward till it strikes the easternmost arm of the Nile. About 100 kilometres from Cairo there lie two mounds of rubble. One is Tell er-Retabe, which many scholars identify with the biblical Pithom. Others consider Tell el-Mas-khuta, fifteen kilometres away, to be Pithom, whereas others consider it to be the biblical Succoth (Exodus 12:37; 13:20). At both sites temples have been discovered to the god Atum. At

Left **Beatings were a daily occurrence in the realm of the Pharaohs. The paintings in the tomb of Menena show peasant farmers being beaten during the collection of taxes.**

Right **Workers in ancient Egypt can hardly have looked so well groomed as those in the vizier Rechmire's paintings; they are more likely to have looked like the man on the scaffolding in this fragment from a tomb painting.**

In his long reign (1290–24 BC) Rameses II substantially altered the appearance of Egypt. His huge temple of the dead on the west side of Thebes (above) was only one of dozens of gigantic building projects.

To be sure the 'wholly divine one and victor of many battles' did not always stay as young-looking as his bust in the Museum of Cairo shows him (above right), but the Egyptian sculptors were aiming not at a realistic but at a timeless picture of the god-king.

Examinations of the mummy of Rameses II (opposite page) have revealed that this tenacious man, with the help of his doctors, survived many severe illnesses.

Tell el-Maskhuta, apart from remains of granaries, inscriptions have also been found which refer to storehouses.

Granaries, circular buildings about 25 feet in diameter with ramps leading up to the feeder, were not uncommon on the Nile. As grand vizier Joseph built granaries (Genesis 41:48ff) and as slave labourers his descendants built granaries in the land of Goshen.

The search for the other bond-city, Raamses, went on for a long time without success. Then nearly thirty years after the discovery of Pithom it was thought that it had finally been found.

Rameses II, the 'Great', has given the archaeologists many a hard nut to crack. Apparently his vanity was even greater than his passion for building. He never hesitated to deck himself in borrowed plumes: posterity would marvel at the great builder Rameses II! And indeed it did. The experts could hardly grasp at first how it came

about that on so many temples, public buildings and in other places they came upon the cipher of this Pharaoh. But when they examined the buildings a little more closely the explanation was plain. Many of these buildings must have been built centuries before Rameses II. To pander to his own vanity however he had decided to have his monogram carved on them all.

In the delta the search for the city of Pi-Raamses-Meri-Imen led from one mound to another. One excavated site after another, throughout the Nile delta, was thought to be the one they were looking for: Pithom, Heliopolis, Pelusium and others. When, between 1929 and 1932, Egyptologist Professor Pierre Montet of Strasbourg unearthed an unusual number of statues, sphinxes, columns, and fragments of buildings, near the present-day fishing village of San, thirty miles south-west of Port Said, all of them were stamped with the crest of Rameses II. He was

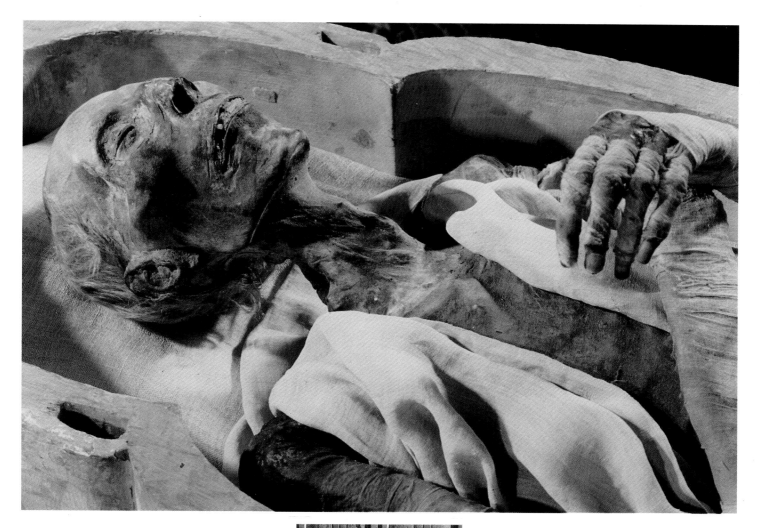

convinced that he had found the remains of Pi-Raamses, the biblical bond city of Raamses. But later it turned out that he was wrong; this was Tanis, capital city of the Twenty-first and Twenty-second Dynasties, to which numerous monuments had been transferred from the city of Raamses. Raamses itself had been discovered a few years before near the village of Kantir. German and Austrian archaeologists have now begun to uncover it.

The Israelites became the victims, in the truest sense of the word, of Pharaoh's lust for building. The position of their immigration area made it easier for them to be dragooned into forced labour. The Goshen of the Bible with its rich grazings began just a few miles south of the new capital and went as far as Pithom. Nothing could be simpler than to drag these

No royal name is found as frequently in the land of the Nile as that of the great Rameses. He 'signed' works of his predecessors as well as his own.

foreigners who lived, so to speak, on the doorstep of these great building projects, away from their flocks and tents and force them into servitude.

The ruins at Kantir no longer give any indication of the splendour of the former metropolis. What the columns of Israelite levies saw on their daily march to the building sites we can only gather from a contemporary papyrus letter. It is written by a schoolboy Pai-Bes to his teacher Amen-em-Opet: *I have come to Pi-Raamses of the Beloved of Amun and find it wonderful. A splendid city without a rival. Rê, the same god who founded Thebes, founded this according to the same plan. To live here is to have a glorious life. The countryside provides a wealth of good things. Every day they get fresh provisions and meat. Their pools are full of fish, their lagoons are thick with birds, their meadows are covered with green grass, the fruit from their well tilled fields has the taste of honey. Their storehouses are full of barley and corn and tower up to the sky.*

Rameses II built himself a completely new town in the eastern Nile delta to serve as his royal seat; the Israelites were among those who were forced to labour in its construction. But where was this town? It had been thought for a long time that Tanis was the city of Rameses, but the most recent excavations at Kantir, south of Tanis, provided irrefutable evidence that Pi-Ramses must have lain here.

The rulers of the Twenty-first Dynasty had used the city of Rameses as a quarry for their royal seat in Tanis, so the relics of Kantir do not look exactly impressive. For instance, of a colossal statue of Rameses II only the toes on their pedestal still remain. The position of the town, in intensively farmed arable land, and the high water table have hindered both the excavations and the preservation of significant finds, such as these smelting ovens for weapon production.

There are onions and chives to season the food, also pomegranates, apples, olives and figs from the orchards. Sweet wine from Kenkeme, which tastes nicer than honey. The Shi-Hor branch of the Nile produces salt and saltpetre. Their ships come and go. Everyday here there are fresh victuals and meat. People are glad to be able to live there and nobody cries: God help me! Simple folk live like great folk. Come! Let us celebrate there the festivals of heaven and the beginning of the seasons.

The biblical account describes how life in the barren wilderness blotted out the recollection of their forced labour from the minds of the children of Israel. All they remembered was the plentiful food of the delta: *If only we had died by the Lord's hand in Egypt! There we sat round pots of meat and ate all the food we wanted* (Exodus 16:3). *If only we had meat to eat! We remember the fish we ate in Egypt at no cost—also the cucumbers, melons, leeks, onions and garlic . . . If only we had meat to eat! We were better off in Egypt!* (Numbers 11:4–5, 18).

Discoveries during excavations, and contemporary texts, sometimes providing almost literal correspondence, seem very much to confirm the biblical picture. So much so that Professor William Foxwell Albright of America, a scholar with almost universal qualifications—as theologian, historian, philosopher, orientalist, archaeologist, and comparative philologist—can write in these terms: 'According to our present knowledge of the topography of the eastern delta the account of the start of the Exodus, which is given in Exodus 12:37 and Exodus 13:20, is topographically absolutely correct.' Further proofs of the essentially historical nature of the Exodus-story and of the journey in

At Tell ed-Daba, south-west of Kantir, excavations brought to light a powerful fortress from the Hyksos era (left). A shrine has been identified as a Canaanite temple of the dead, possibly built by Semitic settlers in the land of Goshen. The burial site of a horse (right) also points to a date around 1650BC. Whether Tell ed-Daba can be identified with the Hyksos royal seat of Avaris is still in dispute.

the area of Sinai, Midian and Kadesh can be supplied without great difficulty thanks to our growing knowledge of topography and archaeology.

We must content ourselves here with the assurance that the hypercritical attitude which previously obtained in respect of the earlier historical traditions of Israel has no longer any justification. Even the long-disputed date of the Exodus can now be fixed within reasonable limits . . . If we put it at about 1290BC we cannot go far wrong, since the first years of the reign of Rameses II (1301–1234BC) were to a large extent occupied with building activities in the city to which he has given his name—the Raamses of Israelite tradition. The striking correspondence between this date and the length of their stay given by Exodus 12:40 as 430 years—*Now the sojourning of the children of Israel, who dwelt in Egypt, was 430 years* (Exodus 12:40)—may be purely coincidental but it is very remarkable. According to this the migration must have taken place about 1720BC.

The reign of Rameses II is the time of the oppression and forced labour of Israel, but also the time at which Moses the great liberator of his people appears.

One day after Moses had grown up, he went out to where his own people were and watched them at their hard labour. He saw an Egyptian beating a Hebrew, one of his own people. Glancing this way and that and seeing no one, he killed the Egyptian and hid him in the sand. When Pharaoh heard of this, he tried to kill Moses, but Moses fled from Pharaoh and went to live in Midian, where he sat down by a well. (Exodus 2:11, 12, 15)

The huge mound of ruins at San el-Hagar in the eastern Nile delta has been the object of French research since as early as 1825. Despite this, up to now little more has been excavated than the town centre with its shrines and the rich tombs of the Twenty-first Dynasty. As the many stone blocks, obelisks and statues in this area bear names from the Old and Middle Kingdoms, the Hyksos period and above all Rameses II, there has long been confusion about the historical development of the town. The name of King Apophis suggested an identification with the Hyksos royal seat of Avaris, and until recently it was thought that the city of Rameses had been found here. Now that Kantir has been

Moses is a Hebrew who was born in Egypt, brought up by Egyptians, whose name can be connected with a Semitic root meaning 'bring or take out, remove, extract', but can also be interpreted as Egyptian. 'Moses' means simply 'boy, son'. A number of Pharaohs are called Thutmose, Ahmose and Amasis. And Thutmose was the name of the famous sculptor, among whose masterpieces the incomparably beautiful head of Nofretete is still the admiration of the world.

These are facts. Egyptologists know that. But the general public picks on the famous biblical story of Moses in the bulrushes, and it is not difficult for the eternal sceptic to produce it as an apparently valid argument against the credibility of Moses himself. 'It is simply the birth-legend of Sargon'—they say. But they add mentally: 'Plagiarism'.

Cuneiform texts have this to say of King Sargon, the founder of the Semitic dynasty of Akkad in 2360BC: *I am Sargon, the powerful king, the king of Akkad. My mother was an Enitu princess, I did not know any father . . . My mother conceived me and bore me in secret. She put me in a little box made of reeds, sealing its lid with pitch. She put me in the river . . . The river carried me away and brought me to Akki the drawer of water. Akki the drawer of water adopted me and brought me up as his son . . .*

The similarity with the biblical story of Moses is in fact astounding: *But when she could hide him no longer, she got a papyrus basket for him and coated it with tar and pitch. Then she placed the child in it and put it among the reeds along the bank of the Nile* (Exodus 2:3).

The basket-story is a very old Semitic folk-tale. It was handed down by word of mouth for many

centuries. The Sargon-Legend of the third millennium BC is found on Neo-babylonian cuneiform tablets of the first millennium BC. It is nothing more than the frills with which posterity has always loved to adorn the lives of great men. Who would dream of doubting the historicity of the Emperor Barbarossa, simply because he is said to be still sleeping under Kyffhüser?

Officials everywhere and all the time enjoy the protection of the state. So it was in the time of the Pharaohs. So it is today. It was for this reason that Moses had no choice but to flee from certain punishment after he had in righteous indignation killed the guard in charge of the labour gangs.

Moses does what Sinuhe had done before him. He flees eastward to get out of Egyptian territory. Since Canaan is occupied by Egypt Moses chooses for his exile the mountains of Midian east of the

Gulf of Aqabah, with which he had a remote connection. *Abraham took another wife, whose name was Keturah. She bore him ... Midian* (Genesis 25:1). The tribe of Midian is often called Kenites in the Old Testament (Numbers 24:21). The name means 'belonging to the coppersmiths'—Qain in Arabic, Qainâya in Aramaic means a smith. This designation connects up with the presence of metal in the neighbourhood of the tribal territory. The mountain ranges east of the Gulf of Aqabah are rich in copper, as the latest investigations of Nelson Glueck of America have indicated.

No country will willingly part with a cheap supply of forced foreign labour. Israel had to learn that too. Eventually we are

established as Rameses' former royal seat, which however had clearly been demolished, the older pieces can be explained as spoils which the kings of the Twenty-first Dynasty brought from there to speed up their building projects and beautify their capital city.

Overleaf **The Island of the Pharaohs in the Gulf of Aqabah. Across the Gulf lie the mountains of the biblical land of Midian, to which Moses fled from Egypt.**

The imperial expansion programme of Thutmosis II brought large areas of the Near East under Egyptian sovereignty. The extent to which the city-states of the area were really obliged to give forced tribute is uncertain. On one hand, in the tomb of the commanding officer Sobekhotep in western Thebes (above left) Semitic envoys are bringing precious articles of beaten gold, falling on their knees in a gesture of total submission; on the other hand, traders from Crete, which never belonged to Egypt, are shown in the same way. This suggests strongly that it is normal trading which is being shown here as a payment of tribute. After the invasion of the Hittites, Sethos I (opposite page) tried to subject at least the trading towns of the Mediterranean to Egyptian influence again. But he cannot have been as successful as the reports of victory on the temple of Karnak make him out to be. Rameses II was the first who could really claim to have subjected Semitic towns to his rule (above right).

told that it was the occurrence of plagues that compelled the Egyptians to give way. Whether they raged exactly at the time of Moses can so far neither be affirmed nor denied since no contemporary evidence on the subject has so far been found. But plagues are neither improbable nor unusual. Indeed they are part of Egypt's local colour. The water of the Nile 'was turned to blood'. 'And the frogs came up and covered the land of Egypt'. 'Flies' appear, 'lice', a 'cattle murrain' and 'boils'—finally 'hail', 'locusts' and 'darkness' (Exodus 7–10, AV). These things which the Bible describes are still experienced by the Egyptians, as, for example, the 'red Nile'.

Deposits from the Abyssinian lakes often colour the flood waters a dark reddish-brown, especially in the Upper Nile. That might well be said to look just like 'blood'. At the time of the floods 'frogs' and also 'flies' sometimes multiply so rapidly that they become regular plagues on the land.—Under the heading of 'lice' would come undoubtedly the dog-fly. These often attack whole areas in swarms, affect eyes, nose and ears, and can be very painful.

Cattle pest is known all over the world. The 'boils' which attack human beings as well as animals may be the so-called 'Nile-heat' or 'Nile-itch'. This is an irritating and stinging rash which often develops into spreading ulcers. This horrible skin disease is also used as a threatened punishment by Moses in the course of the journey

through the desert: *The Lord will afflict you with the boils of Egypt and with tumours, festering sores and the itch, from which you cannot be cured* (Deuteronomy 28:27).

'Hailstorms' are extremely rare on the Nile, but they are not unknown. The season for them is January or February. 'Swarms of locusts' on the other hand are a typical and disastrous phenomenon in the countries of the Orient. The same is true of sudden 'darkness'. The Khamsin, also called the Simoon, is a blistering hot wind which whirls up vast masses of sand and drives them before it. They obscure the sun, give it a dull yellowish appearance and turn daylight into darkness. Only the death of the 'first-born' is a plague for which there is no parallel (Exodus 12) and the statement in the Bible that the plague of *darkness in all the land of Egypt* affected only the Egyptians, but not the Israelites living in Egypt is, of course, incapable of any scientific explanation . . .

Forty Years in the Wilderness

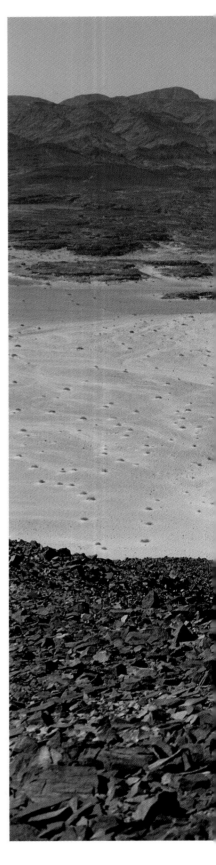

> *The Israelites journeyed from Rameses to Succoth.*
> Exodus 12:37
> *So God led the people around by the desert road towards the Red Sea.*
> Exodus 13:18
> *After leaving Succoth they camped at Etham on the edge of the desert.*
> Exodus 13:20
> *The Egyptians—all Pharaoh's horses and chariots, horsemen and troops—pursued the Israelites and overtook them as they camped by the sea near Pi Hahiroth, opposite Baal Zephon.*
> Exodus 14:9

ON THE ROAD TO SINAI

The first section of the route followed by the fugitives can easily be followed on the map. It is expressly noted that they did not travel in the direction of the *road through the Philistine country* (Exodus 13:17), which was the A1 route from Egypt to Asia via Palestine. This main highway for caravans and military expeditions ran almost parallel with the Mediterranean coast and was the shortest and best route, but the one which was most closely guarded. An army of soldiers and officials in the frontier posts kept a sharp watch on all traffic in both directions.

The main road was too risky. The Israelites therefore headed southwards. From Pi-Ramses on the eastern branch of the delta the first stage is Succoth in Wadi Tumilat. After Etham the next stage is Pi-Hahiroth. According to the Bible this place lay *between Migdol and the sea... directly opposite Baal Zephon* (Exodus 14:2). *Migdol* ap-pears also in Egyptian texts, it means a 'tower'. A fort which stood there guarded the caravan route to the Sinai area. All that remains of it has been excavated at Abu Hasan, 15 miles north of Suez.

Then Moses stretched out his hand over the sea, and all that night the Lord drove the sea back with a strong east wind and turned it into dry land. The waters were divided, and the Israelites went through the sea on the dry ground, with a wall of water on their right and on their left. (Exodus 14:21–22)

.... a detachment of Egyptian chariots, which was attempting to recapture the Israelites, was

In the Bible the desert is a land full of symbolic power. The conditions of life there set Israel a hard challenge. Later their sojourn in the desert became a standard-setting time to which they looked back idealistically.

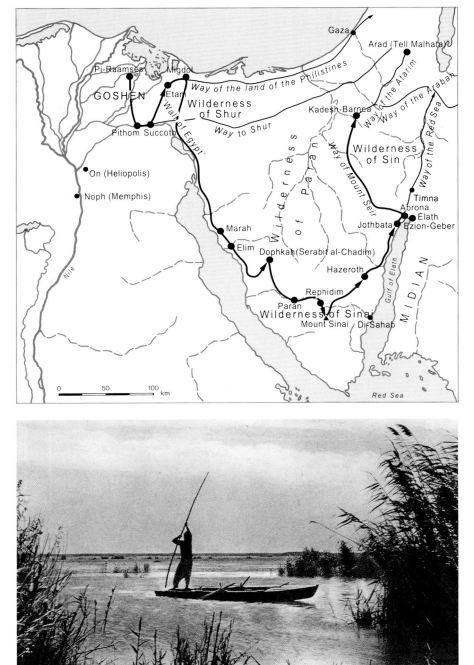

The first difficulty is one of translation. The Hebrew words *Yam Suph* are sometimes translated as the 'Red Sea', at other times as the 'Reed Sea'. The 'Reed Sea' is frequently mentioned: *For we have heard how the Eternal dried up the water of the Reed Sea before you when you left Egypt (Joshua 2:10: Moffatt's Translation)*. In the Old Testament up to Jeremiah it is called the 'Reed Sea'. The New Testament speaks only of the 'Red Sea' (Acts 7:36; Hebrews 11:29).

On the shores of the Red Sea there are no reeds. The Reed Sea proper lay further north. A reliable reconstruction of the situation that existed then is hardly possible, and that is the second difficulty. The building of the Suez Canal last century has altered the appearance of the landscape to an extraordinary degree. According to those calculations which seem to have most probability, the so called 'Miracle of the Sea' must have taken place in that area. What was once Lake Balah, for example, which lay south of the 'Way of the Land of the Philistines', disappeared when the canal was constructed and became marshland. In the time of Ramesses II the Gulf of Suez, in the south, was connected to the Bitter Lakes. Probably the connection extended up to Lake Timsah, the Lake of Crocodiles. In this area there was at one time a Sea of Reeds. The waterway to the Bitter Lakes could be forded at several points. Fords can actually be traced there. The flight from Egypt by way of the Sea of Reeds is therefore perfectly credible.

In early Christian times pilgrims surmised that the flight of Israel led them through the Red Sea. At that time they thought in terms of the northern end of the Gulf near the town of Es-Suwez, present-day Suez. The crossing could have taken place here too. Occasionally strong north-west winds drive the water at the northern extremity of the Gulf back so far that it is possible to wade across. In Egypt the prevailing wind is from the west. The east wind mentioned in the Bible is on the other hand typical of Palestine.

Then Moses led Israel from the Red Sea and they went into the Desert of Shur. For three days they travelled in the desert without finding water. When they came to Marah, they could not drink its water because it was bitter. (Exodus 15:22–23)
Then they came to Elim, where there were twelve springs and seventy palm trees, and they camped near the water. (Exodus 15:27)
And they took their journey from Elim and all the congregation of the children of Israel came unto the wilderness of Sin, which is between Elim and Sinai . . . (Exodus 16:1)

Where did the Israelites' wandering take them after their exodus from Egypt? The route is difficult to reconstruct and thus the subject of much dispute (above). The 'Sea of Reeds' could have been one of the inland waters between the Mediterranean and the Gulf of Suez, for instance the Bitter Lakes or Lake Timsah in the North (below).

swallowed up by the sea, the horses and their riders were drowned.

This 'Miracle of the Sea' has perpetually exercised men's minds. The difficulty which faced science and research for a long time was not to shed light on the escape itself, for which there were several real possibilities. The only dispute was about the scene of the event, and on this point it is barely possible even yet to get a clear picture.

Below **From the Sea of Reeds the Israelites moved on 'into the Desert of Shur. For three days they travelled in the desert without finding water. When they came to Marah, they could not drink its water because it was bitter' (Exodus 15:22–23). 75 kilometres south of Suez, near the west coast of the Sinai peninsula, lies Ain Hawara. Today only a group of palm trees indicates a small amount of underground water. Nevertheless it is believed that this can be identified as Marah.**

Above left **The second place where the Israelites encamped was Elim. Here 'there were twelve springs and seventy palm trees, and they camped there near the water' (Exodus 15:27). The oasis of Wadi Garandel on the west coast of the Sinai peninsula lies a day's journey from Ain Hawara and could be the biblical Elim.**

The laborious journey began—a nomadic existence in a barren scrub land that was to last for forty years.

With donkeys, goats and sheep only short stretches of about 12 miles a day could be covered. The goal each day was invariably the next water-hole.

Forty long years the children of Israel wandered round the edge of the desert from well to well, from water-hole to water-hole. From the stopping places which the Bible mentions the most important stages of the journey can be marked out.

The route is realistically and convincingly described in Numbers chapter 33. As we should expect with a mixed company of human beings and animals, they never moved far from the oases and pastures of the Sinai peninsula and the Negeb.

From the Nile to the mountains of the Sinai peninsula stretches an ancient beaten track. It was the road followed by the countless labour gangs and slave gangs who had been digging for copper and turquoise in the Sinai mountains since 3000BC. More than once in the course of these millennia the mines had been forsaken and lapsed for centuries into oblivion. Ramesses II remembered the treasure that was lying dormant and started up the mines once more.

It was along this road to the mines that Moses led his people. It begins at Memphis, crosses the top of the Gulf, at what is now Suez, and then bends south along a waterless stretch of 45 miles, without a single oasis or spring. The Bible expressly mentions that at the beginning of their journey they wandered for three days in the desert without water, then came to a well of undrinkable water, after which they soon reached a particularly rich oasis with *twelve wells and seventy palm trees*. This very exact biblical description helped the experts to find the historical route of the Exodus.

A 45-mile trek with herds of cattle and a large contingent of people would take three days. Nomads can cope with the problem of thirst for a period of this length. They have always their 'iron rations' for such an emergency, water in goatskin containers, like the patriarchal family in the mural

121

painting at Beni-Hasan. Forty-five miles from the northern tip of the Red Sea there is still a spring called 'Ain Hawarah' by the Bedouins. Nomads are very reluctant to stop here with their cattle. The water is not inviting for a long stay. It is salty and sulphurous, or 'bitter' as the Bible calls it. This is Marah of olden times.

Fifteen miles farther on to the South, exactly a day's march, lies Wadi Gharandel. A fine oasis with shady palms and plenty of water-holes. That is the biblical Elim, the second stopping place. After Elim begins the Wilderness of Sin, on the shore of the Red Sea, now known as the Plain of El Kaa. The children of Israel have come no great distance, but they are untrained and unused to privation after what was despite its rigours a well

'The Egyptians—all Pharaoh's chariots, horsemen and troops—pursued the Israelites...' (Exodus 14:9). From the Middle Kingdom on, horses in full festive caparisons and battle chariots were part of the display of the Pharaohs when they ventured out in public, whether hunting or going to war. 'Thrashing the Nubians' and

'thrashing the Asiatics' were also part of the government programme of every king. Even if, like Tutankhamun, he had no opportunity at all to do so, it still appears again and again in pictures. A typical feature is the chaotic disarray of the enemy, in contrast to the well-arranged fighting forces of the Egyptians.

fed and well ordered life in Egypt. It is no wonder that they gave tongue to their disappointment and complaints. However they were able to augment their scanty diet with two unexpected but most welcome items.

That evening quail came and covered the camp, and in the morning . . . when the dew was gone, thin flakes like frost on the ground appeared on the desert floor. When the Israelites saw it they said to each other, What is it? For they did not know what it was. Moses said to them, It is the bread the Lord has given you to eat. (Exodus 16:13–15)

The Exodus of the Israelites began in the spring, the time of the great bird migrations. From Africa, which in summer becomes unbearably hot and dry, the birds have from time immemorial migrated to Europe along two routes. One route goes via the west coast of Africa to Spain, the other via the Eastern Mediterranean to the Balkans. In the early months of the year, quails, together with other birds, fly across the Red Sea, which they must cross on the eastern route. Exhausted by their long flight, they alight on its flat shores to gather fresh strength for the next stage of their journey over the high mountains to the Mediterranean. Josephus (*Antiquities*, III, 1,5) describes an experience of this kind, and even today the Bedouins of this area catch the exhausted quails in spring and autumn by hand.

As far as the famous Manna is concerned, we have reliable information from the botanist. To anticipate: Anyone who is interested in manna will find it on the list of exports from the Sinai peninsula. Further, its supplier is registered in every botanical index of the Middle East, it is the Tamarix Mannifera, Ehr.

There is no lack of fully authenticated descriptions of its occurrence. The following eye-witness account is almost five hundred years old.

In every valley throughout the whole region of Mt. Sinai there can still be found Bread of Heaven, which the monks and the Arabs gather, preserve and sell to pilgrims and strangers who pass that way. These words were written in 1483 by Breitenbach, Dean of Mainz, in an account of his pilgrimage to Sinai. *This same Bread of Heaven,* he continues, *falls about daybreak like dew or hoarfrost and hangs in beads on grass, stones, and twigs. It is sweet like honey and sticks to the teeth. We bought a lot of it.*

In 1823 the German botanist G. Ehrenburg published a paper which even his colleagues received with incredulity. His explanation seemed indeed to ask people to believe too much, namely that this notorious manna in nothing more than a secretion exuded by tamarisk trees and bushes when they are pierced by a certain type of plant-louse which is found in Sinai.

A hundred years later an organized manna-expedition was under way. Friedrich Simon Bodenheimer and Oskar Theodor, botanical experts from the Hebrew University at Jerusalem, set out for the Sinai Peninsula, to clear up the disputed question of the existence of manna once and for all. For several months the two scientists investigated the dry water-courses and oases in the whole area of Mt. Sinai. Their report caused a sensation. They not only brought back the first photographs of manna and fully confirmed the

Above '**I have heard the grumbling of the Israelites. Tell them, "At twilight you will eat meat..." That evening, quail came and covered the camp' (Exodus 16:12–13). The biblical story is explained by the fact that flocks of migrating quails cross the Red Sea and rest on the coast of Sinai. In ancient Egypt, too, quails were a coveted catch, particularly when they descended in swarms on the grain fields. Hunters threw nets over them and could then grab the birds easily.**

Right **Manna was seen as a particularly miraculous food by the wandering Israelites. Yet it did not fall from heaven. The gelatinous, sweet-tasting drops of manna can still be found today in the early morning on the branches of the tamarisk. The first photograph of manna was taken by F.S. Bodenheimer on the 1927 Sinai expedition.**

Time and again more or less profound discussions have taken place over this question of the quails and the manna. What a vast amount of disbelief they have occasioned. The Bible is telling us about things that are miraculous and inexplicable! On the contrary quails and manna are perfectly matter of fact occurrences. We need only ask a naturalist or natives of these parts who can see the same thing happening today.

findings of Breitenbach and Ehrenburg, but also established the factual truth of the biblical description of the desert migration of the people of Israel.

Without the plant-louse mentioned first by Ehrenburg there would in fact be no manna at all. These little insects live primarily off tamarisks which are a type of tree indigenous to Sinai. They exude a peculiar resinous secretion, which according to Bodenheimer is about the same shape and size as a coriander seed. When it falls to the ground it is white in colour, but after lying for some time it becomes yellowish-brown. Naturally the two scientists did not fail to taste the manna. Bodenheimer's verdict was: 'The taste of these

crystallized grains of manna is peculiarly sweet. It is most of all like honey when it has been left for a long time to solidify.' *It was white like coriander seed and tasted like wafers made with honey,* says the Bible (Exodus 16:31).

The findings of the expedition likewise confirmed the other features of the biblical description of manna. *Each morning everyone gathered as much as he needed, and when the sun grew hot, it it melted away* (Exodus 16:21). Exactly in the same way today the Bedouins of the Sinai peninsula hasten to gather up their 'Mann es-Samâ', the 'Manna from Heaven', as early as possible in the morning, for the ants are keen competitors. 'They

Tamarisk trees near Bir Narib in central Sinai.

With the prevailing north winds on the Sinai Peninsula, only a small amount of rain falls on the coast and in the Sinai mountains. There are indeed a few oases in the mountains, for example in Wadi Feiran north of the Sinai range, but in most wadis the flocks of the Bedouins find only scanty vegetation, as in the area around the 'Smooth Mount'.

begin gathering when the ground temperature reaches 21 degrees centigrade,' says the report of the expedition, 'which is about 8.30 a.m. Until then the insects are inert.' As soon as the ants become lively, the manna disappears. That must have been what the biblical narrator meant when he said that it melted. The Bedouins prudently do not forget to seal the manna they have collected carefully in a pot, otherwise the ants pounce on it. It was just the same in Moses' day during the sojourn in the desert: *However, some of them . . . kept part of it until morning, but it was full of maggots and began to smell* (Exodus 16:20).

The incidence of the manna depends on favourable winter rains and is different from year to year. In good years the Bedouins of Sinai can collect 4 pounds per head in a morning—a considerable quantity which is quite sufficient to satisfy a grown man. Thus Moses was able to order

the children of Israel: *Each one is to gather as much as he needs.* Exodus 16:16).

The Bedouins knead the globules of manna into a purée which they consume as a welcome and nourishing addition to their often monotonous diet. Manna is indeed an exportable commodity, and if it is carefully preserved, forms an ideal 'iron ration' since it keeps indefinitely.—*So Moses said to Aaron, 'Take a jar and put an omer of manna in it. Then place it before the Lord to be kept for the generations to come.'* (Exodus 16:33).

The Israelites ate manna for forty years, until they came to a land that was settled; they ate manna until they reached the border of Canaan (Exodus 16:35). Tamarisks with manna still grow in Sinai and along the Wadi el Arabah right up to the Dead Sea.

So far we have listened to science. But the question that has to be asked is whether we have not at this point crossed the frontiers of science

and entered the territory of the unknown, the sphere of the miraculous? For it is clear beyond all possible doubt that the Bible does not intend us to think of this as something that happened in the normal course of events but as an act of God—especially in view of the incredibly large crowd who had to be provided for, the men alone numbering 603,550! The same thing is true of the quails.

They left the Desert of Sin and camped at Dophkah.
(Numbers 33:12)

Several hundred metres above the waters of the Red Sea lies the monotonous expanse of the Wilderness of Sin. On this torrid plateau the only things that break the bright yellow flatness of the sand are camel-thorns and sparse brushwood. Not a breath of wind or a breeze fans the traveller's brow. Anyone following the ancient beaten-track to the south-east encounters an unforgettable sight: directly ahead on the horizon a jagged mountain range rises abruptly from the plateau—the Sinai-massif. At closer quarters geological formations of unusual and rare ranges of colour meet the eye. Precipitous cliffs of pink and mauve granite thrust their way upwards to the blue sky. Between them sparkle slopes and gorges of pale amber and fiery red, streaked with lead-coloured veins of porphyry and dark-green bands of felspar. It is as if all the colour and beauty of a garden had been poured into this wild serrated symphony in stone. At the margin of the Wilderness of Sin the beaten-track ends abruptly and is lost in a wadi.

No one knew where to look for Dophkah until the turn of the century. The only clue was

The Sinai is primarily a desert of stone. Chalk and sandstone form the tableland in the north, slate and granite the jagged mountains in the south. There is only one large area of sand. It separates the the mountain ranges on the southern tip from the plateau stretching northwards from Jebel et-Tih.

127

From the beginning of the third millennium BC the Egyptians have mined turquoise, copper and malachite in Sinai. Rock inscriptions and stelae tell of the expeditions and their dangers from water and food shortage, as well as from attacks by Asiatic Bedouins. A temple to Hathor, the 'Mistress of Turquoise', is still standing at Serabit el-Chadim. Apart from the extremely popular cow goddess, the god of scribes and the moon, Thot, and the god of the eastern wilderness, Sopdu, were worshipped there, as well as the divine king Snofru, who did much to further mining expeditions around 2750BC.

contained in the name of the place itself. 'Dophkah,' so the subtleties of philology inform us, is related in Hebrew to the word for 'smelting operations'. Smelting operations take place where there are mineral deposits.

In the spring of 1904 Flinders Petrie, who had made a name for himself in England as a pioneer of biblical archaeology, set out from Suez with a long camel caravan. A veritable mass-formation of scholars, thirty surveyors, Egyptologists and assistants accompanied him. From the banks of the Suez Canal the expedition followed the line of the Egyptian beaten-track into the wilds of Sinai. Through the Wilderness of Sin as far as the mountains it followed the same route as Israel.

Slowly the caravan made its way along a wadi and round a sharp bend in the hills—suddenly time seemed to rush back three or four thousand years. The caravan was transported straight back into the world of the Pharaohs. Petrie ordered a halt. From a terrace in the rock face a temple projected into the valley. From the square columns at the gateway stared the face of a goddess with great cow's ears. A jumble of pillars with one

very tall one seemed to be growing out of the ground. The yellow sand round a number of little stone altars showed unmistakable evidence of the ashes of burnt offerings. Dark caverns yawned round the cliff-face and high above the wadi towered the solid massif of Sinai.

The cries of the drivers were silenced. The caravan stood motionless as if overpowered by the almost ghostly sight.

In the ruined temple Petrie found the name of the great Ramesses II carved on the walls. The expedition had reached Serabit el-Khadem, the ancient Egyptian mining and manufacturing centre for copper and turquoise. In all probability this is where we should look for the Dophkah of the Bible.

For two long years a camp in front of the old temple brought new life into the valley. Representations of cultic acts and pictures of sacrifices on the walls of the temple indicate that this had been a centre of worship of the goddess Hathor. An almost endless confusion of half choked galleries in the neighbouring wadis bore witness to the search for copper and turquoise. The marks of the work-

	Sinai 1500BC	Canaan 1000BC	Phoenicia Greece 750BC		Europe today
Oxhead	𐤀	K	𝋊	𐤀	A
Fence	⊟	⊟	⊟	⊟	H
Water	∿	⟨	⌇	∿	M
Human head	⌀	⊲	◁	▷	R
Horns	◡	W	W	⟨	S

men's tools were unmistakable. Tumbledown set-tlements which housed the workers lie in the immediate neighbourhood.

The pitiless sun beat down on this cauldron of a valley, filling it with unbearable heat and making the work of the expedition doubly difficult. A worker's life in these mines in the desert must have been, above all in summer, pure hell. An inscription from the reign of Amenemhet III about 1800BC told the party what it had been like.

Hor-Ur-Re, bearer of the royal seal and 'Min-

The rock inscriptions of Sinai (above the lower group of figures in the picture above) come from the second millennium BC and can undoubtedly be traced to western Semites. They are the beginnings of an alphabetic script, which was further developed in Canaan and Phoenicia and finally taken over by the Greeks: thus they are the origin of our own alphabet.

ister of Labour' under Pharaoh, is addressing the miners and slaves. He tries to cheer them on and encourage them: *Anyone should think himself lucky to work in this area.* But the reply is *Turquoise will always be in the mountain. But it is our skins we have to think about at this time of the year. We have already heard that ore has been quarried at this season. But really, our skin is not made for that sort of thing at this time of the year.* Hor-Ur-Re assures them: *Whenever I have brought men out to these mines my one consideration has always been the honour of His Majesty . . . I never lost heart at the sight of work . . . There was no talk of: 'O for a tough skin'. On the contrary, eyes sparkled . . .*

While the excavations in the old mines, the dwelling houses, and the temple precincts were in full swing, only a few paces from the sanctuary of the goddess fragments of stone tablets were dug out of the sand together with a statue of a crouch-ing figure. On both the tablets and the sculpture there were unusual markings. Neither Flinders Petrie nor the Egyptologists in the party could make anything of them. They were obviously written characters of a type never seen before.

The Wilderness of Sin. In this part of the Negev loess, a fine loamy soil deposit, forms a hard crust which prevents rain from soaking in. The water therefore runs down through natural drainage channels and and continually washes out the beds and banks of the nahals **(rain streams) formed by this process.**

Although the inscriptions give a pictographic impression—they are reminiscent of Egyptian hieroglyphics—they can hardly be said to be a picture language. There are too few different signs for that.

When all the circumstances of the find had been carefully gone into Flinders Petrie came to the following daring conclusion: 'Workmen from Retenu, who were employed by the Egyptians and are often mentioned, had this system of linear writing. The inference that follows from that is extremely significant, namely that about 1500BC these simple workmen from Canaan were able to write and that the type of writing is independent both of hieroglyphics and cuneiform. Further, it invalidates once and for all the hypothesis that the Israelites who came through this area from Egypt, were at that stage still illiterate.'

This explanation aroused considerable attention among antiquarians, palaeographers, and historians. All existing theories about the origin and first use of writing in Canaan were at once out

of date. It seemed incredible that the inhabitants of Canaan could have had their own type of script as far back as the middle of the second millennium BC. Only from the text of the Sinai tablets could it be proved whether Petrie was actually right. Immediately on his return to England Petrie had the tablets copied.

Paleographers from all countries pounced upon these awkward-looking scratched-out characters. No one was able to make any sense of them. It was not till ten years later that Sir Alan Gardiner, the brilliant and tireless translator of Egyptian texts, lifted the veil. He it was who first succeeded in deciphering parts of the inscriptions.

The repeated appearance of the notched 'shepherd's crook' helped him along. Eventually Gardiner conjectured that a combination of four or five signs which occurred several times represented ancient Hebrew words. The five characters 1-B-'-l-t he interpreted as '(dedicated) to (the goddess) Baalath'.

In the second millennium BC a female deity

with the name of Baalath was venerated in the seaport of Byblos. It was to this same goddess that the temple at Serabit-el-Khadem had been erected by the Egyptians. Only the Egyptians called her Hathor. Workmen from Canaan had dug for copper and turquoise beside her temple.

The chain of evidence was complete. The significance of the discovery at Sinai did not fully emerge until six years after Flinders Petrie's death, by which time it had had further exhaustive research and study.

Gardiner had only been able to decipher part of the strange characters. Thirty years later, in 1948, a team of archaeologists from the University of Los Angeles found the key which made it possible to give a literal translation of all the characters on the Sinai tablets. Without a doubt the inscriptions had their origin about 1500BC and are written in a Canaanite dialect.

What Flinders Petrie wrested from the burning sands of Sinai in 1905 nowadays meets the eye everywhere in a different form in newspapers, magazines, books—and the keys of a typewriter. For these stones in Serabit el-Khadem provided the ancestor of our alphabet. The two primary modes of expression in the 'Fertile Crescent,' namely hieroglyphics and cuneiform, were already quite ancient when a third fundamental way of expressing men's thoughts was born in the second millennium BC—namely the alphabet. Possibly stimulated by the picture language of their Egyptian comrades, these Semitic workmen in Sinai devised their own peculiar and quite different type of script.

The famous Sinai inscriptions are the first stage of the northsemitic alphabet, which is the direct ancestor of our present alphabet. It was used in Palestine, in Canaan, in the Phoenician Republics on the coast. About the end of the ninth century BC the Greeks adopted it. From Greece it spread to Rome and from there went round the globe. *Then the Lord said to Moses, 'Write this on a scroll as something to be remembered.'* (Exodus 17:14). The first time that the word 'write' is mentioned in the Old Testament is when Israel reaches the next stopping place after Dophkah. Previously the word is never used. The deciphering of the Sinai tablets shows up this biblical passage in a completely new light as a historical statement. Because we now know that three hundred years before Moses led his people out of Egypt to Sinai, men from Canaan had already been 'writing' in this area, in a language which was closely related to that of Israel.

AT THE MOUNTAIN OF MOSES

The whole Israelite community set out from the Desert of Sin, travelling from place to place as the Lord commanded. They camped at Rephidim... The Amalekites came and attacked the Israelites at Rephidim.

EXODUS 17:1, 8

Rephidim is now Feiran, extolled by the Arabs as the 'Pearl of Sinai'. Protected by the lonely but colourful rock barrier which surrounds it, this miniature paradise has presented the same appearance for thousands of years. A small grove of palm trees provides welcome shade. As they have always done since the days of their remote ancestors, the nomads bring their flocks here to drink and rest on the tiny grass carpet.

From the main camp Flinders Petrie organized parties to investigate the neighbouring territory. By dint of exhausting and difficult journeys he got to know the wadis and mountains right down to the shores of the Red Sea. He established that Feiran is the only oasis in the whole southern part of the massif. For the nomads who lived, and still live, here it is essential for existence and is their most precious possession. 'The Amalekites must have been trying to defend Wadi Feiran from the foreign invaders,' reflected Flinders Petrie. His next thought was: 'If the climate has not changed—and the proof of that lies in the fact that the sandstone pillars in Serabit-el-Khadem show no sign of erosion despite the thousands of years of their existence—the population must also be numerically the same. Today at a rough estimate 5,000 to 7,000 nomads live with their flocks on the Sinai peninsula. Israel must therefore have been about 6,000 strong since the battle with the Amalekites appears to have been indecisive.' *As long as Moses held up his hands, the Israelites were winning, but whenever he lowered his hands, the Amalekites were winning* (Exodus 17:11).

Bitter fighting continued all day *till sunset*, when at length Joshua won a decisive victory for Israel. Thereafter the way was open to the water supply in the oasis of Rephidim. Before that *there was no water for the people to drink* (Exodus 17:1). In this emergency Moses is said to have taken his rod and produced water by striking a rock (Exodus 17:6), an action which has been regarded, and not only by sceptics, as quite incomprehensible, although the Bible is merely once more recording

Ain Murra in the Wilderness of Sin. Wherever there are cavities in the ground, rainwater collects and forms natural cisterns where the Bedouins can water their flocks.

131

Right **At Jebel Katherin (St Catherine's Mount) the Sinai mountain range rises to 2637 metres; at Jebel Musa (Mount Moses) it reaches 2285 metres. Gneiss and granite, porphyry and syenite tower up here, forming an impressive backdrop to the highly revered St Catherine's Monastery. According to ancient tradition the religious community, founded in AD537 by Emperor Justinian I, guards the stump of the burning bush. It owns not only a unique collection of ikons but also a library of more than 3,000 manuscripts.**

Previous pages **View before sunrise from Mount Moses to the huge massif of the Sinai range.**

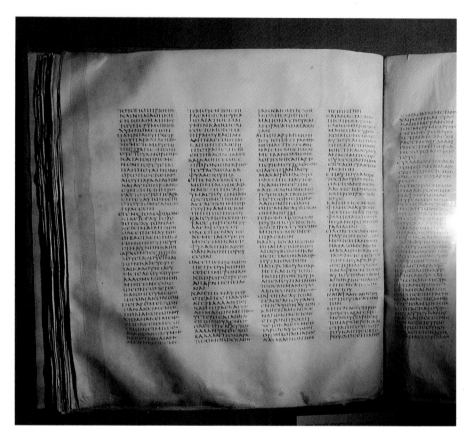

The Codex Sinaiticus, from the fourth century AD, is among the most important Greek manuscripts of the Bible. Discovered in the monastery of St Catherine in 1859 by Konrad von Tischendorf, it found its way to Leningrad as a gift from the monks to the Tsar. In 1933 it was sold to the British Museum.

a perfectly natural occurrence.

Major C. S. Jarvis, who was British Governor of Sinai in the 1930s, has seen it happen himself. He writes in his book *Yesterday and Today in Sinai*: 'Moses striking the rock at Rephidim and the water gushing out sounds like a genuine miracle, but the writer has actually seen this happen. Several men of the Sinai Camel Corps had halted in a dry wadi and were in process of digging about in the rough sand that had accumulated at the foot of a rock-face. They were trying to get at the water that was trickling slowly out of the limestone rock. The men were taking their time about it and Bush Shawish, the coloured sergeant, said: 'Here, give it to me!' He took the spade of one of the men and began digging furiously in the manner of N.C.O.'s the world over who want to show their men how to do things but have no intention of keeping it up for more than a couple of minutes. One of his violent blows hit the rock by mistake. The smooth hard crust which always forms on weathered limestone split open and fell away. The soft stone underneath was thereby exposed and out of its apertures shot a powerful stream of water. The Sudanese, who are well up in the activities of the prophets but do not treat them with a vast amount of respect

overwhelmed their sergeant with cries of: 'Look at him! The prophet Moses!' This is a very illuminating explanation of what happened when Moses struck the rock at Rephidim.'

C. S. Jarvis had witnessed a pure coincidence. For the men of the Camel Corps were Sudanese and not in any sense natives of Sinai, who might be expected to be familiar with the technique of producing water in this way. On the journey from Kadesh to Edom Moses employed this method of striking water once more. *Then Moses raised his arm and struck the rock twice with his staff,* as we are told in Numbers 20:11. *Water gushed out, and the community and their livestock drank.* He had obviously got to know this highly unusual method of finding water during his exile among the Midianites.

At the beginning of the Christian era many monks and hermits settled in Feiran, where Israel had had to cope with its first hostile attack under Moses. In the gullies and on the cliffs they built their tiny cells. A church was founded in Feiran and 25 miles south of the oasis a little chapel was erected at the foot of Jebel Musa.

The barbaric tribes of nomads however gave the hermits and monks of Sinai no peace. Many of them lost their lives in these repeated attacks. St. Helena, eighty year old mother of Constantine, the first Christian emperor, during a visit to Jerusalem in AD327, learned of the plight of the monks of Sinai and founded a tower of refuge which was erected at the foot of the mountain of Moses.

In AD530 the Byzantine emperor Justinian caused a strong defensive wall to be built round the little chapel at the mountain of Moses. Right up to the Middle Ages this fortified church at Jebel Musa was the goal of devout pilgrims who came to Sinai from every land. A legend tells how this notable spot came to be called 'St. Catherine's Monastery', which is the name it bears still.

Napoleon was instrumental in saving the masonry of this isolated early Christian fortress from collapse.

In 1859 the German theologian Constantine von Tischendorf discovered in the monastery at Sinai in a good state of preservation one of the most precious parchment manuscripts of the Bible, the famous 'Codex Sinaiticus'. It dates from the fourth Century AD and contains the New Testament and parts of the Old Testament.

The Czar accepted it as a gift, giving the monastery 9,000 roubles for it. Then this priceless possession found its way into the library at St.

Petersburg. Finally in 1933 the British Museum bought the 'Codex Sinaiticus' from the Soviet Government for £100,000.

The little chapel at the foot of Jebel Musa was built on the site where Moses according to the Bible encountered the Burning Bush: *Moses saw that though the bush was on fire it did not burn up* (Exodus 3:2).

Different attempts have been made to find a scientific explanation of this remarkable phenomenon. An expert on the botany of the Bible, Dr. Harold N. Moldenke, director and curator of the Botanical Garden in New York, has this to say: ' . . . Among the commentators who think that a natural explanation can be found, some think that the phenomenon of the bush that "burned with fire" and yet "was not consumed" can be explained as a variety of the gas-plant or Fraxinella, the Dietamnus Albus L. This is a plant with a strong growth about three feet in height with clusters of purple blossom. The whole bush is covered with tiny oilglands. This oil is so volatile that it is constantly escaping and if approached with a naked light bursts suddenly into flames . . . The most logical explanation seems to be that suggested by Smith. He puts forward the theory that the "flames" may have been the crimson blossoms of mistletoe twigs (*Loranthus Accaciae*) which grow on various prickly acacia bushes and acacia trees throughout the Holy Land and in Sinai. When this mistletoe is in full bloom the bush becomes a mass of brilliant flaming colour and looks as if it is on fire.'

> *After they set out from Rephidim, they entered the Desert of Sinai, and Israel camped there in the desert in front of the mountain. Then Moses went up to God. (Exodus 19:2–3)*
> *So Moses went down to the people and told them. And God spoke all these words: 'I am the Lord your God . . . You shall have no other gods before me.' (Exodus 19:25; 20:1–3)*

At Sinai something happened which is unique in the history of mankind. Here lie both the roots and the greatness of a faith without precedent or prototype which was strong enough to conquer the globe.

Moses, this child of a world which believed in a host of deities and in gods of all shapes and forms, proclaimed his faith in one God alone. Moses was the herald of monotheism—that is the true greatness of this incomprehensible miracle of Sinai. Moses—this unknown son and grandson of

desert nomads, brought up in a foreign land, 'went down unto the people and spake unto them'. Nomads in their goatshair tents, camping in the desert under the open sky, are the first to hear this astounding message, to accept it and transmit it. First of all for thirty-nine years, in the solitude of the desert, by gurgling springs, beside the still waters of shady oases, and facing the biting wind which sweeps across the sullen landscape, as they feed their sheep, their goats and their donkeys, they speak among themselves of the one great God, YHWH.

So begins the wonderful story of this world embracing faith. Simple shepherds, inured to hardship, carried the great new idea, the new faith, to their homeland, whence the message was one day to go out into the whole world and to all the peoples of the earth. The great nations and mighty empires of these far off days have long since disappeared into the dark recesses of the past. But the descendants of those shepherds who were the first to pledge their faith in one sole omnipotent God, are still alive today.

I am the Lord your God . . . You shall have no other gods before me. That was a word heard for the first time since man inhabited this planet. There was no pattern for this faith, no hint of it from other nations.

We can make this assertion with confidence thanks to archaeological discoveries in Egypt, the land in which Moses grew up and received his education, as well as in other lands of the Ancient East. Both the sun-worship of Akhnaten and the appearance in Mesopotamia of a blending of many deities into one sole god, Ninurta, god of war, are but vague preludes to monotheism. In all these conceptions what is lacking is the concentrated power and redemptive moral purpose rooted in the Ten Commandments, which Moses brought down from the lonely heights of Mt. Sinai into the hearts and minds of men.

It is only among the people of Israel out of the whole of the 'Fertile Crescent' that there is this awakening of the new idea of God in all its clarity and purity, untainted by magic, free from a variegated and grotesque imagery, and conceived as something other than a materialistic preparation for perpetuating the self beyond the grave. Without precedent and prototype is likewise the clear imperative of the Ten Commandments. The Israelites are bidden not to sin because they are under the obedience of Yahweh!

Above **The oasis of Ain el-Furtaga in the Sinai desert.**

Opposite page, above **The old pilgrims' way on Mount Moses.**

Opposite page, below **Bedouins with their camels in the Sinai mountains.**

In the oases of Ain Qedeis, which has kept its old name to this day, and of Ain el-Qudeirat, it is thought that the Kadesh-Barnea of the Bible has been rediscovered. In this area of springs towards the north of the Sinai Peninsula, a green island of vegetation is created in the heart of the wilderness. Set with olive trees and shrubs, these oases became the most important stopping-point in the progress of the Israelites towards the Promised Land.

UNDER DESERT SKIES

Then the Israelites set out from the Desert of Sinai.
NUMBERS 10:12

Israel had pledged itself to believe in one God and his laws. The portable palladium that they had constructed for him—the Ark of the Covenant—had been made out of acacia wood (Exodus 25:10), which is still indigenous to Sinai and widely used.

For almost a year they had lingered at Mt. Sinai. Now they set out again, heading north for Canaan. Kadesh, the next stage, which is a landmark in the long desert wanderings of the children of Israel, lies 150 miles from Sinai as the crow flies.

This stretch too can be accurately traced on the basis of the very precise topographical details given in the Bible. The route lies along the west side of the Gulf of Aqabah to the 'Wilderness of Paran' (Numbers 12:16)—now Bàdiet et-Tin, i.e. 'Wilderness of Loneliness'—and then continues along its eastern edge. Among the halts made on this journey (Numbers 33:16–36) Hazeroth and Ezion-Geber can be identified with certainty. Hazeroth is the presentday Ain Huderah, which lies near the Gulf. Ezion-Geber lies at the topmost point of the Gulf of Aqabah and is the place which was later to become a centre for shipping and industry in the days of King Solomon (1 Kings 9:26).

As they made their way along the shores of the Gulf the 'miracle' of the quails was repeated. Once more it was springtime, the time of bird migration, and again the description is true to nature: *Now a wind went out from the Lord and drove quail in from the sea. It brought them down all around the camp to about three feet above the ground* (Numbers 11:31).

They left Ezion Geber and camped at Kadesh, in the Desert of Zin. (Numbers 33:36)

Below Hebron the hill country of Judah falls away into a fairly flat plain, the southern part of which, towards the frequently mentioned 'Brook of Egypt', which is a ramification of wadis, is always very poorly supplied with water (Numbers 34:5; Joshua 15:4; 1 Kings 8:65). This is the Negev, the biblical 'Land of the South' (Numbers 13:17). Amid innumerable wadis—dried-up river beds which only run with water in the rainy season during the winter months—lies Kadesh. The old name Kadesh is preserved in the name of the little spring 'Ain Qedeis', from which passing Bedouins water their cattle. But this trickle of spring water can hardly have been sufficient to provide for 6,000 Israelites and their flocks for any length of time. Only about 5 miles to the north-west of Kadesh, however, lies the most ample supply of water in the whole area, 'Ain el-Qudeirât'. Wadi Qudeirât has this to thank for its fertility. It was from here that the children of Israel saw in the distance the land that had been

Above **Landscape to the north of Kadesh-Barnea.**

Overleaf **Ain Huderah, on the west bank of the Gulf of Aqabah, is identified with Hazerot, one of the resting-places on the Israelites' journey through the desert.**

The spies brought figs, pomegranates and grapes out of the Promised Land. Fig trees, too, were never lacking in the ornamental gardens which upper-class Egyptians laid out and had painted in their tombs (fragment of a tomb painting from the time of the Eighteenth Dynasty, in the British Museum). After the expeditions organized under Hatsheput and the military excursions of Thutmosis III into Asia, which brought many foreign plants and animals into Egypt, it was a mark of high living to cultivate exotic trees. One grave owner boasts of his 500 trees of twenty different kinds, including figs, pomegranates, avocados and rare vine varieties.

Water is carried to it by ship. If you go to Jaffa you will find that the fields are green. Go . . . and look for the pretty girl who is in charge of the vineyards. She will accept you as her mate and grant you her favours . . . You will be drowsy and indolent. They will steal . . . your bow, your knife, your quiver. Your reins will be slashed in the darkness . . . your chariot will be smashed to pieces. But you will say: bring me food and drink, I am happy here! They will pretend they are deaf and pay no attention. Come with me south to the region of Akka. Where is the hill of Schechem? Can this clever scribe tell me how to get to Hazor? What is special about its river? Now let me ask you about some other towns. Tell me what Kjn near Megiddo looks like, describe Rehob to me, give me a picture of Bethshan and Kiriath-El. Let me know how to get past Megiddo. How does one cross the Jordan? You see, concludes Hori, officer of the royal stables, *I have taken you through the whole of Palestine . . . have a good look at it, so that in future you will be able to describe it properly, and . . . you will . . . be made a councillor.* Government officials, soldiers, merchants had at least some clear notion of Palestine. Moses, who belonged to a poor shepherd folk, had first to find out about this country. He sent out scouts.

When Moses sent them to explore Canaan, he said, 'Go up through the Negev and on into the hill country. See what the land is like and whether the people who live there are strong or weak, few or many.' (Numbers 13:17–18)

promised to them, of which as yet they had been able to form no clear picture. It may be that their hasty departure from Egypt had prevented them from finding out about it before they left. Palestine was so well known to the inhabitants of the Nile country that anyone who was lacking in detailed knowledge of it was reckoned to be lacking in proper education. Aman-Appa, a 'commissioned scribe of the army' under Ramesses II, was even ridiculed for his ignorance about Palestine. Hori, an officer of the royal stables, replies to a letter from him in an extremely satirical vein and puts his geographical knowledge to the test: *Your letter is overloaded with big words. You have asked for it and you shall have it—and more than you bargained for. What we say is: If what you say is true, come and let us test you. We shall harness a horse for you which will bring you as fast as any jackal can run. Let us see what you can do. Have you not seen the country of Upe near Damascus? Don't you know its peculiarities, or those of its river? Have you not been to Kadesh? Have you never found your way to the Lebanon where the sky is dark in broad daylight? It is overgrown with cypresses, oaks and cedars which rise sky-high. I shall also mention a mysterious city, Byblos by name. What does it look like? Tell me too about Sidon and Sarepta. They talk about another city that lies in the sea, the port of Tyre is its name.*

Among the twelve scouts was Joshua, a man with great gifts as a strategist, as later became plain during the conquest of Canaan. They chose as the best spot to spy out the land the country round Hebron in the south of Judah. Forty days later the men reported back to Moses. As proof that they had done their job they brought fruit from the area they had scrutinized: figs and pomegranates. Incredulous astonishment greeted one gigantic bunch of grapes, cut at the 'Brook of Eshcol', for *two of them carried it on a pole between them* (Numbers 13:23). Posterity is equally sceptical because the narrative speaks of only one cluster. Surely it must have been a whole vine with all its fruit. The spies would cut it down with the grapes on it to keep them fresher. At all events the place of their origin according to the Bible is reliable. 'Brook of Eshcol' means '. . . of Grapes'; it lies south-west of Hebron and even today this district is rich in vines. Fine heavy bunches of from 10–12 pounds are no rarity. The scouts made their report and described Canaan, like Sinuhe 650 years ear-

Above **In the tomb of the royal cupbearer Wah, from the time of Thutmosis II, giftbearers bring a truss of pomegranates along with wine in every shape and form: bottled grapes, pressed wine or grape juice in a jug carried on a pole, fresh grapes in a basket and even a whole vine branch.**

Left **Vine-growing and the accompanying pressing is one of the most popular themes in Egyptian grave painting. In the tomb of Nacht the grape-pickers stand under a vine arbour with huge grapes. In a walled vat, grapes are trodden. The juice flows into a basin from which it is ladled to fill the jars.**

lier, as a land that *flows with milk and honey, only the people who live there are powerful, and the cities are fortified and very large* (Numbers 13:27, 28; Deuteronomy 1:28).

In their recital of the different inhabitants of the country they mention some we already know, Hittites, Amorites, Jebusites in and around Jerusalem, Canaanites and Amalekites with whom Israel had already come into conflict in Sinai. They also mention the 'children of Anak' or 'necklace people', members of the 'race of giants' (Numbers 13:22, 28, 33, AV). 'Anak' might mean 'long necked', and that is as much as the experts can tell us. It has been surmised that these 'giants' are possibly survivals of ancient presemitic elements in the population but there is no certainty in the matter.

Actually there were people from other countries living in Canaan at that time who must have been quite unknown to Israelites coming from Egypt. Whose 'children' they were, they intimated to posterity themselves on clay tablets which were accidentally discovered by a peasant woman at Tell el-Amarna in 1887. Further investigation produced eventually a collection of 377 documents in all. These are cuneiform letters from the royal archives of Amenophis III and his son Akhnaten who built himself a new capital at El-Amarna in central Egypt. The tablets contain correspondence from the princes of Palestine, Phoenicia and Southern Syria to the Foreign Office of both Pharaohs. They are written in Akkadian, the diplomatic language of the second millennium BC. Most of the writings are full of typically Canaanite words. This priceless find threw light for the first time on conditions in Palestine in the fifteenth and fourteenth centuries BC.

One of the letters runs: *To the King, my Lord,*

143

my Sun, my God, say: Thus (says) Suwardata, thy servant, the servant of the King and the dust under his feet, the ground on which thou dost tread: At the feet of the King, my Lord, the Sun of Heaven, seven times, seven times I prostrated myself, on my belly and on my back . . .

This is only the introduction. Nor is it in any way extravagant. On the contrary it is extremely formal, in accordance with contemporary protocol. Suwardata then comes to the matter in hand: *The King, my Lord, should know that the Hapiru have risen in the lands which the God of the King, my Lord, has given me, and that I have beaten them, and the King, my Lord, should know that all my brothers have left me; and that I and Abdi-Kheba alone are left to fight against the leader of the Hapiru. And Zurata, prince of Acco (Judges 1:31) and Indaruta, prince of Achsaph (Joshua 11:1) were the ones who hastened to my help in return for 50 chariots of which I have now been deprived. But behold, (now) they have been fighting against me and may it please the King, my Lord, to send the Janhamu, so that we can wage a proper war and restore the land of the King, my Lord, to its old frontiers . . .*

This letter from a prince of Canaan paints a picture which faithfully reflects the times. In these few sentences we can recognize unmistakably the intrigues and endless feuds both among the princes themselves and with the warlike nomadic tribes. The most interesting point about the letter, apart from the style and contents, is its author, Prince Suwardata. His name shows clearly that he was of Indo-Aryan descent. Prince Indaruta whom he mentions is also an Indo-Aryan. Though it may sound extraordinary, a third of these princely correspondents from Canaan have Indo-Aryan ancestry. Biryawaza of Damascus, Biridiya of Megiddo, Widia of Askelon, Birashshena of Shechem in Samaria have all Indo-Aryan names. Indaruta, the name of the prince of Achsaph, is in fact identical with names from the Vedas and other early Sanskrit writings. Abdi-Kheba of Jerusalem, who has been mentioned, belongs to a people often referred to in the Bible as Horites.

The reliability of this tradition has recently been illuminated by the discovery of Egyptian papyri of the fifteenth century BC, in which the land of Canaan is repeatedly called 'Khuru' after the Hurri, the Horites of the Bible. According to this the Hurrites must for a time at least have been widespread throughout the whole country as a 'knightly' upper class.

That night all the people of the community raised their voices and wept aloud. Why is the Lord bring-

ing us to this land only to let us fall by the sword?
Our wives and children will be taken as plunder.
(Numbers 14:1–3)

The reports that the spies brought back telling of the strongly fortified cities of Canaan, *large, with walls up to the sky* (Deuteronomy 1:28), and of their superbly armed inhabitants, were not exaggerated. Turreted fortresses built of 'Cyclops-walls' were to the children of Israel an unaccustomed and menacing sight. In the land of Goshen, which for many generations had been their home, there was only one fortified town, Raamses. In Canaan the fortresses were practically cheek by jowl. The country was plastered with them. Numerous strongpoints stared down from hilltops and mountain peaks, which made them look even more powerful and terrifying. Little wonder that the report of the scouts was shattering in its effect.

Israel was quite unskilled in the use and manufacture of implements of war. They had at their disposal nothing but the most primitive weapons—bows, javelins, swords, knives—to say nothing of horse-drawn chariots which the Canaanites possessed in vast numbers. Israel was still spoilt by the 'fleshpots of Egypt', for which especially the older people among them were continually sighing and bemoaning their lot. Despite their new faith and the experiences of the Exodus which they had shared together, they were not yet welded into a community which would be prepared to risk a clash with superior forces.

In view of these facts Moses wisely resolved not to carry out his original intention of marching upon Canaan from the south. Neither the time nor the people was ripe for the great moment. They must begin their roaming afresh, the time of testing and proving their mettle must be prolonged in order to allow these refugees and land-hungry wanderers to develop into a tough and compact national group schooled to bear any privation. A new generation must first emerge.

We know very little about the obscure period which now follows. Thirty-eight years—almost a generation, and time enough to mould a nation. This was the duration of their sojourn in the 'wilderness'. Frequently associated with the 'miracles' of the quails and the manna, this section of biblical chronology and topography sounds highly improbable. And with good reason, as would appear from systematic investigations, though on different grounds from those generally supposed. Actually there never was a 'sojourn in the wilderness' in the proper sense of the words.

Although the biblical data for this period are very scanty, we can obtain a sufficiently clear picture from the few places that can be scientifically established. According to this the children of Israel with their flocks spent a long time in the Negev, near the two sources of water at Kadesh. Once they went back again to the Gulf of Aqabah into the area of Midian and the Sinai peninsula. Compared with the deadly stretches of African sand-dunes in the Sahara, this tract of land has never been a proper desert. Examination of the terrain has established the fact that since neither the irrigation nor the rainfall has altered greatly, the 'wilderness' must have had at least the character of steppe country with possibilities for grazing and waterholes.

The archaeological activities of Nelson Glueck of the U.S.A. in the last few years have enhanced our knowledge of the general conditions of that period. According to him these regions were inhabited about the thirteenth century BC by semi-nomadic tribes who had brisk and flourishing trading and commercial relations with both Canaan and Egypt. Among them we should include the Midianites with whom Moses lived during his exile and one of whom, Zipporah, he married (Exodus 2:21).

Surprisingly enough quite recently we have had archaeological confirmation of two occurrences in the biblical account of the journey through the desert which nobody would have expected in this connection. In spite of all the planning and systematic work, chance nevertheless has its part to play in archaeology and chance does not always pay any attention to what the scholars expect! In this case it enabled the Israeli

Above **'They have made themselves an idol cast in the shape of a calf. They have bowed down to it...'** (Exodus 32:8). **In many cultures of the ancient world cattle were given particular honour. The strength of the bull and its fertility were regarded as divine, as was the protective motherliness of the cow. In Egypt the sacred bull was honoured as an incarnation of the creator god Ptah. The goddess Hathor also was worshipped in the form of a cow as the goddess of love, as mother and nourisher, and protectress against the dangers of the desert. A small sculpture in a bronze ceremonial bowl from the Eighteenth Dynasty shows her with the sun's disc between her horns.**

Opposite page **'Moses made a bronze snake...'** (Numbers 21:9). **Its strange earthbound life, the power and danger of its poison and its supposed immortality lent the snake the aura of a being both fear-inspiring and health-giving. In Egypt the cobra became a symbol of royalty, a goddess who protected the crown. It rears up threateningly on the Pharaoh's coronet and on the crowns of gods such as the golden falcon of Horus from Hierakonopolis.**

A procession carrying a religious image, on the granite sanctuary of the temple of Amun at Karnak. When a divinity, in the form of its image, went on a journey, perhaps to the annual marriage feast in the temple of the god's consort, it was placed in a precious shrine which was covered with cloths: by no means would the god expose himself to profane glances! Since Egyptian gods could only travel on the sacred Nile, the shrine had to be loaded onto the barge of the gods and this had to be taken to the river on carrying poles. The procession was led by the king, and shaven-headed priests shouldered the poles.

archaeologist Benno Rothenberg to discover a 'serpent of brass' and a tabernacle in the copper mine area of Timna (Wadi Arabah).

The 'serpent of brass' is a serpent idol to which magical powers were attributed (Numbers 21:9). It is reported that there was a similar idol in the temple at Jerusalem which was not removed until it was broken in pieces by King Hiskia (Hezekiah) of Judah, who reigned around 700BC (2 Kings 18:4). The serpent idol naturally reminds us of the Sumerian serpent staff on a vase dedicated to the god of life Ningizidda, and Aesculapius' staff of classical antiquity. Already at the beginning of this century a German scholar, H. Gressmann, had asserted that the 'brazen serpent' in the Bible must have been taken over from the Midianites with whom the Israelites were in contact during the journey through the desert.

According to the Bible, the Midianites were descended from Abraham's wife Keturah (Genesis 25:2–6) and Reuel (or Jethro), a priest of the Midianites, who was the father-in-law, adviser and co-celebrant 'before the Lord' (Exodus 2:16; 3:1;

18:1ff) of Moses. The Israelites are supposed to owe the strange cult of the brazen serpent to Reuel. It is not without a touch of dramatic effect that we note that it was at an archaeological site showing signs of Midianite occupation that Benno Rothenberg found an idol in the form of a brazen serpent five inches in length and partly decorated with gold. As though this sensational confirmation of an important part of the biblical accounts of the journey through the desert, which have been the object of so much discussion, were not enough, this small bronze serpent was found in the Holy of Holies of a tabernacle! That really was the crowning point of Rothenberg's discoveries, for the unearthing of a tabernacle was something of extraordinary importance, as ever since the nineteenth century biblical scholars of the most varied persuasions had expressed doubts concerning the existence of the tabernacle about which the Bible has so much to say (Exodus 25–31 and 35–39). It is true that some critics had fallen silent when a very small, transportable tabernacle was discovered on a relief on the Bel Temple at Palmyra

(Tadmor). At any rate the possibility of the existence of a tabernacle was no longer completely excluded, although the details of the biblical descriptions of tabernacles were still considered to be a back projection on to the period of the wandering in the desert of conditions in the Temple at Jerusalem. In any case, the nomads' shrine on the relief at Palmyra was extremely small and strictly speaking it is rather a representation of the Ark of the Covenant than of the Tabernacle which contained the Holy Ark.

The Midianite tabernacle unearthed by Rothenberg is quite different. Its measurements bring it much closer to the tabernacle described in the Bible. It was found on the site of an older, Egyptian place of worship dedicated to the goddess Hathor. The Midianites who, following the Egyptians, were mining copper on their own account at Timna, converted this place of worship into a shrine of their own religion and covered it with an awning of which Rothenberg found not only the holes into which the posts had been rammed at an angle but even some remnants of material.

Of course, details of the interior lay-out and arrangement of the biblical tabernacles still remain to be clarified. Thus, for example, the altar for burnt offerings is supposed to have been equipped with bronze fittings and *a grating...a bronze network* (Exodus 27:1–8), but at a very much later date not even King Solomon had at his disposal craftsmen who could carry out such work. He was obliged to request them from King Hiram of Tyre (2 Chronicles 2:6 and 12). The

horns of this altar in the tabernacle, as they are called (Exodus 27:2; 30:2) did not appear, according to the archaeological find in Israel, until the beginning of the time of the kings, that is to say not until the Temple had been built. It is only in connection with the time of the kings (cf 1 Kings 1:50; Psalm 118 (117); Jeremiah 17:1; Amos 3:14) that the Bible mentions them again. Whatever the truth of the matter, after Rothenberg's discovery, there is now *in principle* nothing to prevent us from supposing that at quite an early date Israel possessed a tabernacle and that it was more or less like that described in the Bible.

ON THE THRESHOLD OF THE PROMISED LAND

And he made them wander in the desert for forty years, until the whole generation of those who had done evil in his sight was gone.

NUMBERS 32:13

Not until the long years of their wanderings are approaching an end does the Bible take up the thread again of the story of the children of Israel. A new generation has sprung up and is ready to cross the threshold of the Promised Land. None of the men who led the Exodus out of Egypt will, according to the Bible, set foot in the land of promise—not even Moses himself.

The new plan of campaign is to conquer Canaan from the east, i.e. the territory east of the

Above left **The Baal image of Palmyra was also transported under a vellum cover, albeit on a camel according to the custom of the desert nomads! Likewise a 'curtain' (see Exodus 40:3) shielded from view the ark containing the tablets of the ten commandments in the tabernacle, or 'tent of meeting'. The box of acacia wood overlaid with gold, like the Egyptian idols, was carried carefully on gilded poles inserted into golden rings on the sides of the box (Exodus 25:10–22).**

Above right **In the tabernacle was an altar for burnt offerings (Exodus 27:1–8) and an altar for incense which was 'square... and two cubits high—its horns of one piece with it' (Exodus 30:1–2). Horned altars of this kind were widespread in the Near East. Several examples were found in Megiddo, dating from around the time of the Israelite entry into the land.**

147

Above **The Edomite royal town of Busera, the biblical Bozrah, during the excavations which began in 1971.**

Below **The river Arnon was 'the border of Moab, between Moab and the Amorites' (Numbers 21:13).**

Jordan. Nevertheless the road to Upper Transjordan from Kadesh is blocked by five kingdoms, which occupy the broad strip of land between the Jordan valley and the Arabian desert: in the north, beginning at the spurs of Hermon is the kingdom of Bashan, then the Amorite kingdom of Sihon, next, the kingdom of Ammon, then the kingdom of Moab, on the east side of the Dead Sea, and, right in the south, Edom.

Edom is therefore the first kingdom that has to be negotiated on the way to Upper Transjordan. The children of Israel ask permission to pass through:

> Moses sent messengers from Kadesh to the king of Edom . . . Please let us pass through your country. (Numbers 20:14, 17)

Main roads are the quickest roads to anywhere. In those days what corresponds to our trunk roads and motorways in the twentieth century was a road that ran right through the middle of Edom. This was the old 'King's Highway' which dated back to Abraham's time. *Please let us pass through your country . . . We will travel along the king's highway* (Numbers 20:17).

The settled population of the East always distrusts nomads, nowadays as much as long ago, even though Israel's emissaries declare expressly: *We will not go through any field or vineyard, or drink water from any well . . . We . . . will not turn to the right or to the left until we have passed through your territory . . . and if we or our livestock drink any of your water, we will pay for it* (Numbers 20:17, 19).

In the course of an expedition which lasted

several years Nelson Glueck confirmed the aptness of the biblical description of Edom. In the southern part of Trnsjordan, in the territories that had once belonged to Edom and Moab, he came across numerous traces of a settlement which dated from the beginning of the 13th century. Signs of cultivated ground, which were also discovered, suggested well stocked fields. It is therefore understandable that in spite of all assurances Edom refused the children of Israel permission to use the road and pass through their country.

Their hostility compelled Israel to go a long way round. They trek northwards along the western edge of Edom towards the Dead Sea. Punon, now called Kirbet-Feinan, an old copper-mine and Oboth, are visited for the sake of their water supplies. Then the Israelites follow the little river Sered, which marks the frontier between Edom and Moab, and reach Transjordan. They make a wide circle round Moab on the south-east side of the Dead Sea. By this time they have reached the river Arnon and the southern frontier of the kingdom of the Amorites (Numbers 21:13). Once more the Israelites ask for permission to use the 'King's Highway' (Numbers 21:22). Once more it is refused, this time by Sihon, king of the Amorites. A battle begins and the process of conquest by force of arms has started.

By defeating the Amorites the Israelites collect their first laurels. Conscious of their strength they push northwards over the river Jabbok and conquer the kingdom of Bashan in addition. Thus by their first determined attack they have become masters of Transjordan from the river Arnon to the banks of the Lake of Galilee.

Into the matter-of-fact description of this military offensive in Transjordan there has crept a reference to the 'iron bed' or 'stone sarcophagus' of a giant, King Og of Bashan (Deuteronomy 3:11), which may have puzzled many people. This mysterious and improbable-sounding passage in the Bible, has, however, a very natural and at the same time striking explanation. The Bible is preserving here in all faithfulness a memory which takes us back to Canaan's dim and distant past.

When the scholars were searching the Jordan country for evidence which would tie up with biblical history, they came upon remarkable structures such as archaeologists had already encountered in other countries. These consisted of tall stones, built in oval formation and every now and then roofed over with a heavy transverse block—the famous Great Stone Graves. They are also

biblical description of the 'iron bed' of the giant king. Further investigations have proved that dolmens are common in Palestine, principally in Transjordan above the river Jabbok, that is, in present day Ajlun. Well over a thousand of these ancient monuments are to be found among the coarse grass of the highlands. The country above the Jabbok, so the Bible tells us, is the kingdom over which King Og of Bashan is said to have reigned, Og who alone 'remained of the remnant of giants' (Deuteronomy 3:11, AV). Bashan, which was conquered by Israel, was also called 'the land of giants' (Deuteronomy 3:13, AV).

West of the Jordan the only dolmens to be found are in the neighbourhood of Hebron. The scouts, whom Moses sent out from Kadesh, *ascended by the south, and came unto Hebron . . . and there we saw the giants, the sons of Anak* (Numbers 13:22, 33, AV). They must have seen the stone graves which have now been discovered at Hebron in the vicinity of the Valley of Grapes.

Who the 'giants' really were is still quite unknown. Possibly they were a people who were much taller than the old established population around the Jordan. Clearly there was some racial memory of a taller type of man, which was enough to make a deep impression, and perhaps this is the reason why it appears in the Bible too.

These huge stone graves and the stories about giants once again bear witness to the colourful and varied history of the Land of Canaan, that narrow strip of land on the Mediterranean coast, into which from earliest times waves of alien peoples surged incessantly and left their mark behind them.

called megalithic graves or dolmens, and were once used for burying the dead. In Europe—they are found in North Germany, Denmark, England and North-west France—they are called locally 'Giants' Beds'. Since these massive monuments are also found in India, East Asia and even the South Sea Islands, they are ascribed to a great mass migration in early times.

In 1918 Gustav Dalman, the German scholar, discovered in the neighbourhood of Amman, the modern capital of Jordan, a dolmen which aroused unusual interest because it seemed to shed light on a factual biblical reference in quite an astonishing way. Amman stands precisely on the old site of Rabbath-Ammon. The Bible says about this giant King Og: *His bed was made of iron and was more than thirteen feet long and six feet wide* (Deuteronomy 3:11). The size of the dolmen discovered by Dalman corresponded approximately to these measurements. The 'bed' consists of basalt, an extremely hard grey-black stone. The appearance of such a burying-place may have given rise to the

From the air the route of the 'King's Highway' through the landscape of Jordan is still clearly recognizable, furrowed by deep valleys.

The news that Israel had conquered the whole of Jordan put King Balak of Moab into a panic. He was afraid that his own people too would be no match in physique or military skill for these tough sons of the desert. He convenes 'the elders of Midian' and incites them against the children of Israel (Numbers 22:4). They resolve to employ other than military measures. They will attempt to impose a check on Israel by means of magic. Incantations and curses, in the efficacy of which the peoples of the Ancient East firmly believed, will assuredly smash Israel's power. Balaam is summoned in haste from Pethor in Babylonia, where these black arts flourish. But Balaam, the great sorcerer and magician, fails. As soon as Balaam tries to utter a curse, a blessing upon Israel comes out instead (Numbers 23). Then the king of Moab throws the most dangerous

149

Above **Amman, the capital of the Kingdom of Jordan, lies on the site of the biblical Rabbat-Ammon or 'Rabbah of the Amonnites'. The seat of the Amonnite kings was situated on a height overlooking the deep gorge of Wadi Amman.**

Right **Once the boundary between Moab and Ammon, the highlands east of the Dead Sea, the Arnon cuts through a gully 500 metres deep.**

Opposite page **Dolmen (man-made rock mound, probably a prehistoric tomb) at Yehudiyya on the Golan Heights.**

trump card in existence into the balance, a wicked card that is to have a lasting effect on the lives of the children of Israel.

The Bible passage which contains a description of the abominable stratagem of King Balak is felt by many theologians to be embarrassing and therefore they prefer to gloss it over. The real question is, however, why such a scandalous affair appears in the Bible at all. The answer is simple: The event was one which was of the deepest and most fateful significance for the people of Israel. That is the reason why the narrator does not maintain a modest silence but gives a frank and candid account of what actually happened.

It was in the thirties that French archaeologists, working at the Mediterranean port of Ras Shamra—the 'White Haven' on the coast of Phoenicia—under the direction of Professor Claude Schaeffer of Strasbourg brought to light some evidence of Canaanite religious practices. Only then was it possible to estimate and understand the nature of the disaster that is recorded in Numbers 25.

While Israel was staying in Shittim, the men began to indulge in sexual immorality with Moabite women, who invited them to the sacrifices to their gods. (Numbers 25:1–2)

It is not the attractions of vice that the children of Israel are faced with. That is something that is and always has been universal. It was not professional prostitutes who led Israel astray. It was the daughters of the Moabites and the Midianites, their own wives and sweethearts. They enticed and seduced the men of Israel to take part in the rites of Baal, the fertility cult of Canaan. What Israel encountered, while still on the other side of

Jordan, was the voluptuous worship of the Phoenician gods.

The leaders of Israel struck swiftly and struck hard. They did not even spare their own men. Offenders were slaughtered and hanged. Phinehas, grand-nephew of Moses, who saw an Israelite taking a Midianite woman into his tent, took a javelin and *drove the spear through both of them— through the Israelite and into the woman's body* (Numbers 25:8). The people of Moab were spared since they were related to Israel—Lot, Abraham's nephew, was regarded as their ancestor (Genesis 19:37). But against the Midianites a war of extermination was let loose, the classical 'herem' or ban, as it is laid down in the Law (Deuteronomy 7:2ff; 20:13ff). *'Now kill all the boys. And kill every*

On Mount Nebo, from which Moses was allowed before his death to look into the Promised Land, a monastery was erected in the sixth century, with a basilica whose splendid mosaic floors have survived (opposite page, above). From the terrace of the ruined church there is a view across the lower Jordan valley with the oasis of Jericho (opposite page, below) and over the Dead Sea (left) as far as the Judean mountains.

woman who has slept with a man,' ordered Moses. Only the young girls were spared, everyone else was killed (Numbers 31:7, 17, 18).

> *Then Moses climbed Mount Nebo from the plains of Moab to the top of Pisgah, across from Jericho. There the Lord showed him the whole land.*
> *(Deuteronomy 34:1)*

Moses had now fulfilled his heavy task. From the bond-cities of Egypt, through the years of hardship and privation in the steppes right up to that moment he had had to travel a long and bitterly hard road. He had nominated as his successor Joshua, a tried and trusted man and an unusually gifted strategist, which was what Israel was most in need of. Moses had finished the course and could take his leave of the world. He was not allowed to set foot himself on the soil of the Promised Land. But he was allowed to glimpse it from afar, from Mt. Nebo.

To visit this biblical mountain means a journey of about 18 miles from Amman, capital of the kingdom of Jordan. The trip takes rather more than half an hour in a Land Rover, crossing the hill-country on the edge of the Arabian desert, through wadis and sometimes past ploughed fields, heading straight for the south-east in the direction of the Dead Sea.

On the broad barren plateau, 2,500 feet above sea level, a church was built in the Byzantine period. On the western edge the cliffs drop sharply down to the Jordan basin. A fresh breeze blows on the summit. Under the clear blue skies there stretches into the distance in front of the enchanted visitor a unique panorama.

To the south lie the broad waters of the Salt Sea with their silvery sheen. On the far bank rises a dreary desolate scene of stone humps and hillocks. Behind it towers the long chain of brownish white limestone mountains of the Land of Judah. Just where it begins, rising sharply out of the Negev, lies Hebron. In the west, towards the Mediterranean, when the weather is clear two tiny dots can be distinguished with the naked eye from the mountain range that stands out against the horizon—the towers of Bethlehem and Jerusalem. The eye wanders northward over the highlands of Samaria, past Galilee to the snow capped peaks of Hermon in the shimmering distance.

At the foot of Nebo narrow gorges slope downwards, brilliant with the green of their pomegranate trees and their orange coloured fruit. Then the ground sinks abruptly into the desolate steppe of the Jordan basin. A landscape of dazzling white chalk hills, almost as ghostly as the mountains of the moon and without a single blade of grass, flanks the mere 30 foot width of the river Jordan. The only comfort to the eye is a small green patch in front of the mountains that rise steeply on the west side of the Jordan—the oasis of Jericho.

This view from Nebo into Palestine, the Bible story tells us, was the last thing that Moses saw.

But beneath him on the broad steppe of Moab thin columns of smoke are rising heavenwards. Day and night campfires are burning among the mass of black goatshair tents. Joined to the hum of voices of all these men, women and children, the wind also carries over to the Jordan valley the bleating of grazing flocks. It is a peaceful scene. But it is only a moment of respite before the long yearned for day, the great calm before the storm which is decisively to affect the destiny of Israel and that of the land of Canaan.

The Battle
for the
Promised Land

After the death of Moses the servant of the Lord, the Lord said to Joshua son of Nun, Moses' assistant: 'Moses my servant is dead. Now then, you and all these people, get ready to cross the Jordan River into the land I am about to give to them—to the Israelites.'

Joshua 1:1–2

ISRAEL INVADES

About the same time as Israel was standing by the Jordan ready to march into the Promised Land, fate was advancing upon Mediterranean Troy and the days of the proud stronghold of King Priam were numbered. Soon the Homeric heroes of Greece, Achilles, Agamemnon and Odysseus would be arming for the fray— the hands of the timepiece of history were moving towards 1200BC. Israel could have chosen no better time for invasion. No danger threatened them from Egypt. Under Rameses II Egypt had indeed known a last period of glory during which it had consolidated its power in Palestine, but even the might of Egypt crumbled in the political upheavals which marked the transition between the Bronze and the Iron Ages. Its influence in Canaan declined rapidly.

Torn by internal feuds between the innumerable petty kingdoms and principalities of its city-states, and sucked dry by the corrupt politics of Egyptian occupation, Canaan itself had shot its bolt.

Ever since the expulsion of the Hyksos about 1550BC Palestine had been an Egyptian province. Under the Hyksos a feudal system had broken up the old patriarchal social structure as it had existed in the towns of Abraham's day. Under an aristocratic ruling class, which was self-centred and despotic, the people were reduced to the level of subjects without rights, and became mere plebeians. Egypt left this feudal system in Palestine unaltered. Native princes could do as they pleased: they had their own armies, which consisted of patrician charioteers and plebeian infantry. Bloody warfare between the city-states did not worry the Egyptians. All they were interested in was the payment of tribute, which was supervised by strict and inflexible Egyptian inspectors. Garrisons and defence posts tacitly lent their activities the necessary weight. Gaza and Joppa housed the most important Egyptian administrative centres. By means of labour levies—supplied by the feudal

View from the Crusader fort of Belvoir to the west, across the hill country of Lower Galilee with Mount Tabor.

lords—roads were built and maintained, the royal estates on the fertile plain of Jezreel south of Nazareth were managed and the glorious cedar forests of Lebanon were felled to the ground. The commissioners of the Pharaohs were corrupt. Often the troops' pay and rations were misappropriated. Whereupon they took the law into their own hands, and mercenaries from Egypt and Crete, Bedouins and Nubians plundered defenceless villages.

Under Egyptian rule the land of Canaan bled to death. The population shrank. Patrician houses of the thirteenth century BC are more primitive than they had been in earlier times, as is shown by excavations. Objets d'art and jewellery of any value are rarer, and gifts deposited with the dead in their tombs are of poorer quality. Fortress walls have lost their old solidity.

Only on the coast of Syria, protected on the landward side by the mountain ridges of the Lebanon and less affected by the quarrels of the princes, life in the maritime republics pursued its untroubled way. Whatever else happens seaports are always places where men can exchange what they have for what they want. About 1200BC an entirely new metal—as valuable to begin with as gold or silver—appeared on the price lists: iron. Since it came from the Hittite country, the Phoenicians were the first to deal in this metal, which was to give its name to one of the ages of man's history. The Egyptians had known about iron for nearly 2,000 years and valued it as an extremely unusual and rare commodity. The iron they knew however did not come from our planet at all but from

meteors. And the few expensive weapons that they managed to produce in this way were very properly called 'Daggers from Heaven'.

With the appearance of this new metal a new epoch, the Iron Age, was announced. The Bronze Age with its unique civilizing achievements died away and a great epoch of the ancient world came to an end.

At the end of the thirteenth century BC a great new wave of foreign peoples surged down from the northern Aegean. By land and water these 'Sea Peoples' flowed over Asia Minor. They were the fringes of a great movement of population to which the Dorian migration to Greece also belonged. The impetus of these foreigners—they were Indo-Germanic—was directed to Canaan and Egypt. For the time being Israel, waiting poised by the Jordan, had nothing to fear from them. And the Canaanites were divided and weak. Israel's hour had come. The biblical trumpets of Jericho gave the signal.

. . . and all the Israelites set out from Shittim and went to the Jordan . . . The priests who carried the ark of the covenant of the Lord stood on firm ground in the middle of the Jordan, while all Israel passed by until the whole nation had completed the crossing on dry ground . . . and camped at Gilgal, on the eastern border of Jericho. (Joshua 3:1,17; 4:19)

Below **From their last camp in Moab, the Israelites moved down into the Jordan valley near Jericho, to the north of the Dead Sea. Here they found a barren limestone plain in which the Jordan has carved out a flood plain a kilometre wide.**

Today there is a bridge over the river at this point: the Jordan is very narrow and has always been fordable in many places. The natives know exactly where these fords are. In the dry season the dirty yellow water at Jericho is only about 30 feet wide.

When Israel reached the Jordan they found it in full spate, *now Jordan is in flood all during harvest* (Joshua 3:15). As happened every year, the snow on Hermon had begun to melt. . . . *the water from upstream stopped flowing. It piled up in a heap (i.e. dammed) a great distance away, at a town called Adam . . . So the people crossed over opposite Jericho* (Joshua 3:16,17). A much frequented ford on the middle reaches of the Jordan, el-Damiyah, recalls the town 'Adam'. Should there be a sudden spate it can quite easily be dammed at such a place for a short time, and while it is blocked the lower part of the river is almost dried up.

Considerable damming of the Jordan has however often been attested as a result of earthquake. The last thing of this kind happened in 1927. As a result of a severe quake the river banks caved in, tons of soil crashed down into the river bed from the low hills that follow the Jordan's winding course. The flow of water was completely stopped for twenty-one hours. In 1924 the same thing happened. In 1906 the Jordan became so choked up with debris as the result of an earthquake that the river bed on the lower reaches near Jericho was completely dry for twenty-four hours. Arab records mention a similar occurrence in AD1267.

It is easy to see from the air why this part of the Jordan valley was so important thousands of years ago. To the east, between the river and the Arabian desert, stretches the hilly plateau of Jordan, which has always been the home of countless tribes of nomads and from which they have always been able to look across to the fertile pastures and ploughed fields of Canaan. It is a natural line of attack—the principal ford across the Jordan, easily negotiated by man and beast. But anyone trying to force his way in from the east had to face the first serious obstacle soon after crossing the river—Jericho, the strategic key to the conquest of Canaan.

When the trumpets sounded, the people shouted, and at the sound of the trumpet, when the people gave a loud shout, the wall collapsed; so every man

Above **Ain el-Duq is one of the springs which feeds the oasis of Jericho.**

charged straight in, and they took the city . . . Then they burned the whole city and everything in it. (Joshua 6:20,24)

Joshua's battle for this city has made it famous. Today a battle rages round it, but it is between experts armed with spades, picks and chronological tables. According to the Bible it took Joshua seven days to subdue Jericho. The battle of the archaeologists over what is left of it has lasted—with intervals—for more than eighty years now and is by no means settled.

The exciting and dramatic excavations at Jericho are rife with remarkable finds and unexpected discoveries, with surprises and disappointments, with assertions and counter-assertions, with disputes over interpretation and chronology.

The Jordan basin has a tropical climate. The village of Eriha, the modern successor of Jericho, gives the impression of being an oasis on the edge of a barren waste of chalk. Even palmtrees grow here although they are seldom found anywhere else in Palestine, except to the south of Gaza. The Bible too calls Jericho 'City of Palms' (Judges 3:13). Golden red clusters of dates shimmer among the green foliage. From ancient times the spring called 'Ain es-Sultan' has produced as if by magic this lush patch of vegetation. North of present day Jericho a mound of ruins is named after it, Tell es-Sultan. This is the battle ground of the archaeologists. Anyone wanting to examine it must buy a ticket. The site of the excavations lies behind a barbed wire fence.

The remains of Jericho have made Tell es-Sultan one of the most extraordinary scenes of discovery in the world, for it has long since been not merely a matter of investigating the fortress of biblical times. In this mound, under the strata of the Bronze Age, lie traces of the Stone Age, which take us back to the earliest times of all, to the days when man first built himself settled habitations. The oldest of Jericho's houses are 9,000 years old and, with their round walls, resemble Bedouins' tents. But the art of pottery was as yet unknown among their inhabitants. In 1953 a British expedition conducted excavations here, and the director of the enterprise, Dr. Kathleen M. Kenyon declared: 'Jericho can lay claim to being by far the oldest city in the world.'

Shortly after the turn of the century archaeologists directed their attention to this lonely mound of Tell es-Sultan. From 1907 to 1909 picks and spades carefully felt their way through layer after layer of this massive mound of ruins. When the two leaders of the German–Austrian expedition, Professor Ernst Sellin and Professor Karl Watzinger, made known what they had discovered, they caused genuine amazement. Two concentric rings of fortification were exposed, the inner ring surrounding the ridge of the hill. It is a masterpiece of military defence made of sun-dried bricks in the form of two parallel walls about 10 or 12 feet apart. The inner wall, which is particularly massive, is about 12 feet thick throughout. The outer ring of fortification runs along the foot of the hill and consists of a 6 foot thick wall, about 25–30 feet high, with strong foundations. The excavators were positive: these were the famous walls of Jericho. The two lines of fortification, their exact historical placing, the dates of their erection and destruction have given rise to a vehement dispute among the experts who advance the pros and cons in a welter of opinions, hypotheses and arguments. It began with the first announcement

The oasis of Jericho on the edge of the lifeless Jordan basin (left) offered a basis for human habitation right from the early Stone Age. Here, between the seventh and fourth millennia BC, a small walled town developed. Among its fortifications was a round stone tower (above), of which the original walls have been found up to a height of nine metres. A sloping shaft gives access to the inside, joining a stairway which leads to the top of the tower. Even given this spectacular discovery, the excavators were still disappointed not to find the walls of the 'City of Palms' (Deuteronomy 34:3) from the time of Joshua.

by Sellin and Watzinger and has continued ever since.

Both discoverers arrived themselves at what they called a 'considerable modification' of their first conclusion. They issued a joint statement in which they maintained that the outer wall 'fell about 1200BC, and therefore must be the city wall which Joshua destroyed'. To shed new light on the whole business a British expedition set out for Tell es-Sultan in 1930. After six years' digging further portions of the fortifications were exposed. Professor John Garstang as leader of the expedition noted every detail with the utmost precision. He described graphically the violence with which the inner circle of parallel fortifications had been destroyed: 'The space between the two walls is filled with fragments and rubble. There are clear traces of a tremendous fire, compact masses of blackened bricks, cracked stones, charred wood and ashes. Along the walls the houses have been burned to the ground and their roofs have crashed on top of them.'

After Garstang had consulted the most knowledgeable experts, the outcome of the second archaeological battle was that the inner ring was the more recent, therefore, the one which must have been destroyed by the Israelites. But that did not settle the matter. The wrangle about the Walls of Jericho continues. Garstang dates the destruction of the inner ring about 1400BC. Father Hughes Vincent, a leading archaeologist and one of the most successful investigators into Jerusalem's ancient past, also studied the evidence and dated the destruction of the walls between 1250 and 1200BC.

Today we know that both experts were mistaken. Since their day, archaeologists have developed methods which allow us to interpret and date excavated finds much better than was the case a few decades ago. Professor Garstang and Father Hughes Vincent both thought that walls from the *early* Bronze Age belonged to the *late* Bronze Age. Today we know that this is not so. The mistake occurred because wind and weather had largely carried away the more recent layers which covered the earliest remains. It is in one area only, at the highest place on Tell es-Sultan, on the northwest of the heap of ruins, that the remains of middle Bronze Age defence works, built on top of what is left of early Bronze Age walls, have been preserved at their full height. Scanty vestiges of late Bronze Age dwellings have been found only on the lower eastern slopes of the hill. We owe all this information to the great British archaeologist Kathleen M. Kenyon who by her extensive and successful excavations in Jericho during the fifties of the present century laid the foundations of our present-day knowledge. It was Kathleen M. Kenyon, too, who convincingly interpreted the very small amount of pottery found at Jericho. She was also able to interpret the information provided by the graves which constitute the only evidence concerning the late period of ancient Jericho.

According to her findings the walls of Jericho had to be rebuilt during the Bronze Age no less than seventeen times. The walls were repeatedly destroyed either by earthquakes or by erosion. Perhaps this weakness of the walls of Jericho found expression in the Bible account of how the children of Israel, in order to conquer Jericho, merely had to shout their war cry when the priest blew the trumpets. The middle Bronze Age city dated from the time of the Hyksos and came to an end at the same time as they, around 1550BC. Thereafter Jericho remained uninhabited for about a century and a half. It is only about the year 1400BC, as is shown by pottery, objects found in graves and the few late Bronze Age remains of dwellings on the eastern slope of the hill, that people began to settle there once more. This late Bronze Age town, of whose existence we have only such sparse evidence, was again deserted by its inhabitants, however, around 1325BC. Did they become the victims of conquerors of some kind who were subsequently absorbed in the melting-pot of 'Israel' and whose conquests were ultimately incorporated in the biblical account of the settlement of the land? For if it is the case that Israelites did not come to Jericho until the time of the occupation, i.e. about the middle or towards the end of the thirteenth century BC, they did not need to conquer the city for they found it uninhabited! Jericho was not rebuilt until the ninth century before Christ, in the days of King Ahab (1 Kings 16:34). As the Bible tells us (Joshua 6:26), it was as though a curse had lain on the place for centuries.

J ericho was the first strong point to be overcome on the way to the Promised Land. Archaeologists have been able on other sites to follow the further progress of the children of Israel towards their conquest of Canaan.

About 12 miles southwest of Hebron lay the Debir of the Bible. Defended by a strong enclosing wall it dominated the Negev. Excavations by W.F. Albright and M.G. Kyle of the U.S.A. in Tell Beit Mirsim since 1926 disclosed a layer of ashes and considerable destruction. The stratum of ashes contained sherds which undoubtedly date from the end of the thirteenth century BC. Immediately above the burst layer are traces of a new settlement by Israel. *Then Joshua and all Israel with him turned round and attacked Debir* (Joshua 10:38).

Thirty miles south-west of Jerusalem the Lachish of the Bible can be identified. It must have been an extraordinarily strong fortress for Canaan. In the thirties at Tell ed-Duweir a British expedition under James Lesley Starkey measured out an area of twenty-four acres which had at one time been built up and surrounded by a strong wall. This city also fell a victim to a conflagration which destroyed everything. A bowl which was salvaged

'Canaan is conquered with all its evil ... Israel is laid waste and has no offspring, Palestine has become a widow ...' Thus announces the 'Israel stela' in the Cairo Museum (opposite page), a victory declaration of King Merenptah (above) dated 1230BC. This is the first reference to the name of Israel in an Egyptian document. The word Israel is composed of six hieroglyphs in the middle of the penultimate line (detail, below).

from the ruins bears an inscription giving its date as the fourth year of Pharaoh Merenptah. That corresponds to the year 1230BC. *The Lord handed Lachish over to Israel* (Joshua 10:32).

I n the Cairo Museum there is a monument from a mortuary temple near Thebes, on which the victory of Pharaoh Merenptah over the Libyans is commemorated and celebrated. In order to augment his triumph, other notable victories which this ruler is said to have achieved are also mentioned. The end of the hymn of praise runs as follows: Canaan is despoiled and all its evil with it. Askelon is taken captive, Gezer is conquered, Yanoam is blotted out. The people of Israel is desolate, it has no offspring: Palestine has become a widow for Egypt.

This triumphal hymn, written in 1929BC, is in more than one respect valuable and illuminating. Here for the first time in human history the name 'Israel' is immortalized, and that by a foreigner and a contemporary. Israel is expressly described as a 'people' and moreover in connection with Palestinian placenames—surely a proof for the most hardened sceptic that Israel was already properly settled in Canaan in 1229BC and no longer completely unknown.

S hortly before 1200BC Israel had reached the goal which had for so long been the object of its aspirations. It is now in Canaan, but it is not yet in full control of the country. A trail of burnt out cities marks its path and indicates an extremely shrewd strategic plan. Joshua avoided the strongest fortresses like Gezer and Jerusalem. Obviously he followed the line of least resistance. The fertile plains and river valleys are likewise still in the hands of the Canaanites and will remain so for many generations to come. Israel has neither the armour to resist the dreaded chariots, nor the technique and experience required to war against strongly fortified cities. But it has secured a foothold in the more sparsely populated areas, the hill country on both sides of the Jordan is in its hands.

About ten miles north of the Lake of Galilee lay the mighty stronghold of Hazor, which was still quite powerful, although it had had to suffer, about 1300BC, at the hands of conquerors, probably the Egyptians under the Pharaoh Sethos I; *Joshua turned back and captured Hazor and put its king to the sword. (Hazor had been the head of all these kingdoms.)* (Joshua 11:10). The word 'beforetime' provides us with cause for reflection. The town, devastated probably by Sethos I, before its destruction by the Israelites, had indeed been richer and more flourishing than the Hazor they found. The more crucial event and the one which had the gravest consequences in the town's history was undoubtedly this destruction by Israel towards the

The old town of Hazor lies on a mighty tell 23 kilometres north of Tiberias. Its oldest levels of settlement go back to around 2000BC, and the enormous defensive walls too come from the Canaanite era. After Joshua's conquest of the town in the thirteenth century BC, work was limited to the development and walling of the upper town.

The plan above shows the citadel of Hazor, erected under Omri and his successors (1). Between the fortress and the adjoining buildings (2, 3) was a monumental gate (4) with 'proto-Aeolian' capitals. On the plan below can be seen the remains of a Bronze Age temple (1) and the massive walls of a palace or citadel (2). Solomon had the area levelled and built a twin-towered gate (3) with six rooms and a casemate wall (4). The three-aisled colonnaded hall comes from the ninth century BC (5, shown on the opposite page with the snow-capped Mount Hermon in the background). It probably served as a storehouse. King Ahab laid great emphasis on providing for his towns in case of siege. It was he, too, who commissioned the forty-metre-deep tunnel through the rock leading to the spring below the town. After a major fire in the eighth century BC, dwelling houses (6, 7) were built on the site, and all sorts of utensils have been found from these. The damage done by an earth tremor in 763BC was repaired, but from the devastation done by the Assyrian king Tiglath-Pileser III in 732BC, Hazor never recovered.

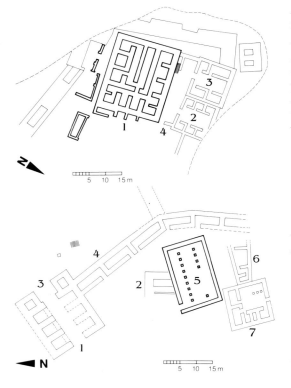

end of the thirteenth century BC.

The rediscovery of this royal city can be counted as one of the most surprising pieces of good fortune in recent biblical archaeology. John Garstang, the English archaeologist, had already identified as the site of old Hazor the extensive mound of rubble Tell el-Qedah, which stands out prominently to the west of the Jordan between Lake Huleh and the Lake of Galilee. But it was not until excavations, begun in 1953 under the auspices of the Hebrew University of Jerusalem and directed by Yigael Yadin of the James A. de Rothschild expedition, had continued over several seasons that the hitherto undisturbed Tell could be awakened from its dreams and induced to part with its closely guarded secrets. Bit by bit its layers began to tell the experts the long and exciting story of the chequered fortunes of Hazor.

No fewer than twenty-one stages of development can be distinguished: twenty-one cities growing up on top of one another, each built on the rubble of past generations and each in its turn levelled to the ground, destroyed by war or fire or the force of nature. Surmounted by its citadel and fortified area the city spread its lower reaches far out into the plain. An ingenious drainage system consisting of clay pipes looked after public sanitation. What has been discovered confirms in a striking way what the Bible has to say about the

powerful role that Hazor played in Canaan at the time of the Israelite conquest. Hazor was in fact not only one of the largest settlements of the country but also one of the strongest fortresses. In the thirteenth century BC it was destroyed, as the Book of Joshua records. A layer of burnt rubble indicates a great conflagration about that time. Many scholars do not hesitate to attribute this burnt rubble to Joshua and his hosts.

UNDER DEBORAH AND GIDEON

So the Lord gave Israel all the land he had sworn to give their forefathers, and they took possession of it and settled there.

JOSHUA 21:43

Immediately after the conquest an astonishing thing happened: the tribes of Israel dug their toes into the ground they had won. They can therefore no longer have been a typical nomadic people. Canaan had experienced invasions of nomads from time immemorial but they had always been merely episodes. The tribes would graze their flocks and then one day they would disappear as suddenly as they had come. Israel on the other hand became static, cultivating fields and clearing forests... 'If you are so numerous,' Joshua answered, '... go up into the forest and clear land for yourselves' (Joshua 17:15). They gave up their tents and built themselves huts: they settled down among the ruins of the houses in the towns they had conquered. In Debir, Bethshemesh and Bethel remains of their primitive and poverty-stricken furnishings were found on top of the strata which were deposited when the towns were burned down.

This break with the past is clearly recognizable from the excavations. Where previously patrician houses and palaces of the long established feudal barons had been standing, there now arose peasants' huts and fences. The massive defence walls show signs of having had necessary repairs done to them. But what the men of Israel replaced was of the thinnest masonry. The construction of a new system of strong defensive walls would have entailed forced labour and there was nothing the Israelites hated more. They regarded themselves as freemen, as independent farmers. Everyone did as he saw fit (Judges 17:6). Even the word generally used in Canaan meaning a bondsman was used by the Israelites in exactly the opposite sense to

Above **One of the few pictorial records of the courtly life of the kings of Canaanite cities was found in the excavations at Megiddo. This little ivory tablet probably served as a decorative mounting for a precious piece of furniture or utensil. The ruler sits on a throne flanked by winged sphinxes, with a footstool. He wears a floor-length robe trimmed with decorative borders and drinks from a bowl. From the right a triumphal procession approaches him, led by a crowned woman, perhaps a goddess of the city, who offers the king a lotus blossom. Behind her a female musician plays a nine-stringed lyre, then there follows an armed officer with two prisoners and finally a chariot and team of horses. Behind the throne stand servants with delicacies for a victory banquet.**

Right **The areas of the twelve tribes after Joshua's conquests.**

The Great Sea

Sor (Tyre)
ASHER
NAPHTALI
Laish (Dan)
Acco
ZEBULON
Ashteroth
ISSACHAR
Megiddo
MANASSEH
Shechem
EPHRAIM
Jaffa (Joppa)
DAN
GAD
BENJAMIN
Rabbath Ammon
Jerusalem
Gath
REUBEN
Ashkelon
JUDAH
Gaza
Dead Sea
SIMEON
Kir-haroseth (Kir-Moab)

0   25   50 km

mean a freeman. In the feudal system under the princes of the city-states all the drudgery was done by slaves. In the case of Israel the work of the farm was done by the freeborn sons of the family. At their head stood the father, the patriarch. Numerous new settlements sprang into being. Archaeologists have found traces of them throughout the highlands. But there is very little of them left. For the first building material they used was sun-dried mud bricks, and the buildings they put up in this way did not last.

Real pioneer work was done by the Israelites in the mountains. Uninhabitable areas, districts without springs or streams were opened up. Although it sounds unbelievable, what remains of a new technique used by their ancestors has been partly taken over and put into commission again by the state of Israel today. They dug cisterns in the ground to collect the rainfall, and lined the insides with a type of limestone plaster which was hitherto unknown. These fixtures were so solidly built that they have been able to withstand the ravages of time for thousands of years.

As the Book of Judges tells us, and investigation confirms, the Israelites struck roots in their home as settlers and farmers. In continuous fighting with their neighbours and feuds among themselves they gradually gained in military power and experience. The Bible mentions disputes with Moabites, Ammonites and Aramaean tribes from the Syrian desert. It speaks of bloody civil war, when the tribes fought against Benjamin (Judges 20). Bethel lay in the territory of Benjamin, and Albright, digging there, found strata which showed that the place had been destroyed four times between 1200 and 1000BC.

I t was around this time too that *All that day Abimelech pressed his attack against the city until he had captured it and killed its people. Then he destroyed the city and scattered salt over it* (Judges 9:45). So runs the description in the Book of Judges of the conquest of Shechem by Abimelech, the ambitious and vindictive son of Jerubbaal who murdered all his brothers.

In 1959 at Tell el Balata, on the site of this biblical city, the first place mentioned after Abraham's arrival in Canaan, excavations by American archaeologists from Drew University and McCormick Theological Seminary led by Professor G.

The Canaanite city of Ashkelon, in the course of its long history, has endured numerous sieges and conquests. From 1900BC there were conflicts with Egypt; later Ashkelon was a Philistine city. Scholars disagree over a suggested temporary occupation by Judah. Tiglath-Pileser II made the city Assyrian, while under the Persians it belonged to Tyre, then it passed to the Ptolemies, from whom it was snatched by the Seleucids, and finally it paid tribute to the Maccabees. In 104BC Ashkelon, with the permission of the Romans, became independent, and for a time it even introduced its own chronology. This golden age has left its stamp on the ruins of the town, which are not yet fully explored.

One of the conquests of Ashkelon was the work of Rameses II in about 1280BC, as part of his campaign against the Hittites. It is recorded in the temple of Amun at Karnak. While battle still rages on the slopes of the strongly fortified hill town, siege ladders are put in place, and an Egyptian is already battering at one of the gates with his battle-axe. The defenders on top of the walls, depicted with typically Semitic features, are ready to surrender their town; they have raised their hands in a plea for mercy. In spite of the lifelikeness of the portrayal, we should not forget that by this time Egyptian artists had long developed a standard formula for depicting such events, which they needed to vary only in small details according to the occasion.

Ernest Wright, who was following the earlier investigations of Professor Ernst Sellin of Germany, were able to confirm what the Bible has to say about the fate of Shechem. Fragments of clay jars which were scattered about among the ruins and could be identified as typical Israelite pottery put the date of the destruction of Shechem towards the end of the twelfth century BC, that is, about the period of Abimelech. At the same time the remains of the 'tower of Shechem' were identified, as well as the 'stronghold of the temple of El Berith' and 'Beth Millo' the 'house of Millo', which are mentioned in Judges 9:20, 46. It does seem, however, that all of these were part of a single building which towered above the city and which had been built upon the ruins of an earlier temple of the Hyksos period.

These troubled years of the first colonists have found an imperishable memorial in three narratives of the Book of Judges: in

The 'high place' of Gezer with ten stone pillars, some of which are more than three metres tall, dates from the middle of the second millennium BC. The Canaanite city lay on the northern ridge of the Shefela, about twelve kilometres away from the main road between Egypt and Mesopotamia. Its strong defences were destroyed in 1468BC by Pharaoh Thutmosis III. From that point on it was under the control of Egypt. During the Israelite invasion Horam, the Canaanite king of Gezer, tried to help Lachish, but was defeated (Joshua 10:33; 12:12); however the town was not taken.

the Song of Deborah, in the story of Gideon and in the doughty deeds of Samson.

The background of these 'pious tales' is made up of facts, contemporary events which as a result of the latest research can be dated with considerable accuracy. When Israel entered Canaan about 1230BC it had to be content with the mountains . . . for *they were unable to drive the people from the plains, because they had iron chariots* (Judges 1:19). It was not until a century later that the tide turned. It would seem that among the mountains of Galilee tribes which had settled there had to render bond-service to the Canaanites. Among them was the tribe of Issachar which is ridiculed in the Bible as a scrawny donkey. It is accused of lying down between two saddlebags and of submitting to forced labour (Genesis 49:14, 15).

Revolt broke out in Galilee in protest against this oppression. The impetus was supplied by a woman, Deborah. She summoned the tribes of Israel to fight for their freedom. Judges 5 tells us the story in the form of a song which is one of the oldest texts in the Old Testament.

Barak, one of the tribe of Issachar, became the leader. Other tribes joined in and a great army was

formed. Then Barak took a decisive step. He dared to do what Israel had never previously risked, he came to grips with the dreaded enemy on the plain: *So Barak went down Mount Tabor, followed by ten thousand men* (Judges 4:14). The scene of the encounter was the broad and fertile plain of Jezreel between the mountains of Galilee in the north and Samaria in the south—absolute and sovereign domain of the Canaanite city princes and feudal barons. Here they awaited the dangerous fighting forces of the Canaanites . . . The kings of Canaan fought at Taanach by the waters of Megiddo (Judges 5:19). The incredible happened—Israel won. For the first time they had succeeded in smashing and routing a force of chariots in open battle. The spell was broken: Israel had shown that it had the measure of the military technique of the Canaanites and could beat them at their own game.

Two mounds of rubble in the plain of Jezreel preserve all that is left of Taanach and Megiddo, lying about 5 miles apart. Both cities changed places several times in order of importance. About 1450BC Taanach was a large city-state while Megiddo was only a small Egyptian garrison. About 1150BC Megiddo was destroyed and deser-

ted by its inhabitants. For half a century it lay in ruins, and was not rebuilt and inhabited until 1100BC. The pottery of the new settlers there is striking. It consists of large clay preserving jars of exactly the same type as were used at this time by the Israelites. Archaeologists found them in all the other settlements in the mountains of Samaria and Judea. Taanach is specifically mentioned in the Song of Deborah as the site of the battle. The reference to its being 'by the waters of Megiddo' is presumably a more precise description of its situation. Megiddo itself, whose 'water' is the river Kishon, cannot at that time have been in existence.

Archaeological discoveries and biblical references make it possible to date the first battle against the Canaanite chariots in the period between the destruction and rebuilding of Megiddo, about 1125BC. If Judges 5:20 is interpreted as an eclipse of the sun, 30 September 1131BC is a possibility.

T he Gideon story tells of the second triumph of Israel. Suddenly out of the East came a new, unfamiliar and sinister threat to Israel's safety. Hordes of Midianite nomads, mounted on camels, attacked the country, plundering, burning and massacring... *They came up... like swarms of locusts. It was impossible to count the men and their camels; they invaded the land to ravage it.* (Judges 6:5). For years Israel was at the mercy of these Midianite attacks. Then Gideon appeared as their deliverer. He adopted successfully, as the Bible describes in detail (Judges 7:20ff), a new kind of surprise tactics which routed the Midianites and apparently persuaded them to leave the Israelites in peace from then on.

It is often the lot of peaceful inventions to be used first of all in time of war. The new 'invention' which made it possible for the Midianites to terrorize Israel was the taming of the camel!

Tame camels are likely to have been something quite new in the ancient world. The people

Megiddo, on the south-western edge of the plain of Jezreel, was already an important town in the third millennium BC. A circular platform with steps leading up to it dates from this time; it was probably one of the Canaanite bama **'high places', since its surface was strewn with animal bones and potsherds. In the first half of the second millennium BC, three temples were built around the platform in the shape of the** megaron, **or Greek open hall.**

169

Above From the end of the thirteenth century BC a great migration of peoples disturbed the eastern Mediterranean and its inhabitants. The Egyptians called the invaders 'the Sea Peoples', since they came across the sea in ships and forced their way into the Nile Delta. King Rameses III defeated them in a bloody battle about 1190BC and had the event recorded in large-scale reliefs on his temple of the dead at Medinet Habu. This detail shows the mustering of Egyptian troops.

Previous pages Nomads mounted on camels were a scourge to the Israelites for years, until Gideon could announce to Israel: 'Get up! The Lord has given the Midianite camp into your hands' (Judges 7:15). Assyrian artists, on a relief at the northern palace at Nineveh, have portrayed the turmoil and the various phases of a battle between Ashurbanipal and Arab camel-riders, with such gripping lifelikeness that we can follow it almost as if we were eyewitnesses. It must be remembered though that the Israelites under Gideon fought without cavalry or chariots.

of the Bronze Age probably knew nothing of them. Egyptian texts never mention them. Even in Mari, next door to the great Arabian desert, there is no single reference to them in any of that vast collection of documents. We must eliminate the camel from our conception of life in the ancient world of the orient. References to them in the book of Genesis must have crept in at a later date. The attractive scene, for example, where we meet Rebecca for the first time in her native city of Nahor, must make do with a change of stage props. The 'camels' belonging to her future father-in-law Abraham which she watered at the well were donkeys (Genesis 24:10ff). Similarly it was donkeys that for thousands of years carried on their backs all kinds of burdens and costly merchandise along the great trade routes of the ancient world until the tame camel saved them.

It is not quite certain when exactly the taming of the camel took place but there are some facts which point to a general conclusion. In the eleventh century BC the camel appears in cuneiform texts and reliefs and from then on is more and more frequently mentioned. This must be about the time of the Gideon story. Doubtless such marauding attacks with animals that had until then been regarded as wild must have come as a frightful shock.

The third challenge held the greatest and deadliest danger for Israel and threatened its very existence: the clash with the Philistines.

THE WARRIORS FROM CAPHTOR

Did I not bring Israel up from Egypt, the Philistines from Caphtor . . . ?

AMOS 9:7

The fabulous tales of the redoubtable Samson, that great bear of a man full of pranks and derring-do, herald the beginning of the great tussle.

Philistines!—This name has become common currency in so many ways. We talk of someone being 'a proper Philistine', or of someone else as a veritable 'Goliath'. He also was one of them. Who does not know the tragic love story of Samson and Delilah, the woman who betrayed him to the Philistines? Who does not remember the superhuman strength of Samson, who could strangle lions with his bare hands, who slew 1,000 Philistines with the jawbone of an ass, and in the end, blind

and deserted by the woman he loved, brought a Philistine temple crashing down about his head in the fury of his anger. Yet very few of us ever really think how little we know of these Philistines whom we talk so much about.

The Philistine people, who played a decisive role in the life of Israel, were for a long time wrapped in mystery. It is only quite recently that it has been possible to find out something about them. Bit by bit, as a result of careful examination of the fruits of scientific research, the picture has become clearer. Finds of pottery, inscriptions in temples and traces of burnt-out cities give us a mosaic depicting the first appearance of these Philistines, which is unrivalled in its dramatic effect.

Terrifying reports heralded the approach of these alien people. Messengers brought evil tidings of these unknown strangers who appeared on the edge of the civilized ancient world, on the coast of Greece. Ox-waggons, heavy carts with solid wheels, drawn by hump-backed bullocks, piled high with household utensils and furniture, accompanied by women and children, made their steady advance. In front marched armed men. They carried round shields and bronze swords. A thick cloud of dust enveloped them, for there were masses of them. Nobody knew where they came from. The enormous trek was first sighted at the Sea of Marmora. From there it made its way southwards along the Mediterranean coast. On its green waters sailed a proud fleet in the same direction, a host of ships with high prows and a cargo of armed men.

Wherever this terrifying procession halted it left behind a trail of burning houses, ruined cities and devastated crops. No man could stop these foreigners; they smashed all resistance. In Asia Minor towns and settlements fell before them. The mighty fortress of Chattusas on the Halys was destroyed. The magnificent stud horses of Cilicia were seized as plunder. The treasures of the silver mines of Tarsus were looted. The carefully guarded secret of the manufacture of iron, the most valuable metal of the times, was wrested from the foundries beside the ore deposits. Under the impact of these shocks one of the three great powers of the second millennium BC collapsed. The Hittite Empire was obliterated.

A fleet of the foreign conquerors arrived off Cyprus and occupied the island. By land the trek continued, pressed on into northern Syria, reached Carchemish on the Euphrates and moved on up the valley of the Orontes. Caught in a pincer movement from sea and land the rich seaports of

the Phoenicians fell before them. First Ugarit, then Byblos, Tyre and Sidon. Flames leapt from the cities of the fertile coastal plain of Palestine. The Israelites must have seen this wave of destruction, as they looked down from their highland fields and pastures, although the Bible tells us nothing about that. For Israel was not affected. What went up in flames down there in the plains was the strongholds of the hated Canaanites.

On and on rolled this human avalanche by sea and by land, forcing its way all the time towards the Nile, towards Egypt....

I n Medinet Habu west of Thebes on the Nile stands the imposing ruin of the splendid temple of Amun, dating from the reign of Rameses III (1195–1164BC). Its turreted gateway, its lofty columns, and the walls of its halls and courts are crammed with carved reliefs and inscriptions. Thousands upon thousands of square feet are filled with historical documents carved in stone. The temple is one vast literary and pictorial record of the campaigns of the Pharaohs and is the principal witness to events on the Nile at that time.

It is more than plain from these records that Egypt was then in a state of acute panic and only too conscious of the danger in which it stood. One of the texts rings with a note of anxious foreboding: *In the eighth year of the reign of Rameses III . . . No country has been able to withstand their might. The land of the Hittites, Kode, Carchemish . . . and Cyprus have been destroyed at one stroke . . . They have crushed their peoples, and their lands are as if*

Detail from the relief of the 'battle of the Sea Peoples' on the temple of the dead of Rameses III at Medinet Habu. The various tribes of the 'Sea Peoples' are not only pictorially displayed here, but also labelled by name, though of course to us most of the names are incomprehensible. However, we can safely identify the Philistines (Peleset), a people of Aryan appearance with horned or feathered helmets. It is possible that these are the north Aegean Pelasgians who were swept along by the wave of migrating peoples.

173

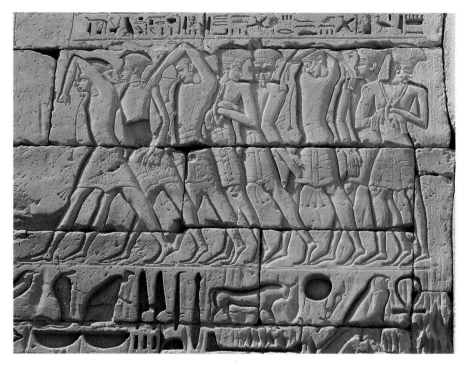

they had never been. They marched against Egypt . . . They laid hands on every land to the farthest ends of the earth. Their hearts were high and their confidence in themselves was supreme: 'Our plans will succeed.'

Rameses III made feverish preparations for battle and decreed a general mobilization: *I manned my borders . . . and drew up my armies before them: princes, garrison commanders and warriors. I turned the river mouths into a strong defensive wall, with warships, galleys and coastal vessels . . . fully manned from stem to stern with brave warriors armed to the teeth. The troops were the best that Egypt could muster. They were as ready for battle as lions roaring on the mountains. The chariot detachments consisted of the swiftest runners, and every first class charioteer available. The horses flew like the wind ready to crush foreign lands under their feet . . .*

With an enormous fighting force and every able bodied warrior that Egypt could call on, Rameses III advanced to engage in a great battle on land against the foreign hordes. The inscriptions have nothing very definite to say about this battle. As usual, the Egyptian war reports confine themselves in this case to singing the praises of the victor. *His troops,* it is recorded of Rameses III, *were like bulls ready for battle: his horses were like falcons amid a flock of tiny birds . . .* But a huge relief still portrays this terrible battle after 3,000 years: the Egyptian chariot commandos have scurried in among the armed enemy trekkers. Fearful slaughter rages among the ponderous ox-waggons

Although the Philistines only comprised part of the total military might of the 'Sea Peoples', they are depicted in particular detail on the temple of the dead of Rameses III. The file of Philistine prisoners (above) shows their typical featherlike headdress worn over a patterned headband, possibly a common hairstyle. The Egyptian king bloodily turned back the forces invading the Nile Delta in 1190BC (opposite: the symbolic 'slaying of the enemy' before the god Amun; above: the counting of chopped-off hands, probably equally symbolic). After that, the Philistines were probably settled by the Egyptians as a military column in Palestine. Their city-states of Gaza, Ashkelon, Ashdod, Ekron and Gath formed an alliance of five states which caused Israel no small amount of trouble.

carrying the women and children. Under the hooves of the bullocks and horses the bodies of the slain lie in heaps. Victory seems to have been won already, since Egyptian soldiers are seen plundering the ox-waggons.

Egypt had won a battle of prime significance in world history. The enemy land forces had been annihilated. Rameses III hastened to the coast in a swift chariot, since they had entered the mouths of the river with their ships.

This great naval battle is likewise perpetuated on a stone relief in the temple at Medinet Habu: the fleets of the two opposing forces have approached each other. Shortly before their encounter the wind must have suddenly died down, since the sails are reefed. That meant a severe handicap for the foreigners. Their ships could no longer be manoeuvred. The warriors are standing there, ready for the fray but helpless. Their swords and spears were useless except in hand to hand fighting when the ships were close enough together. The calm let the Egyptians have it all their own way. Their vessels, manned by oarsmen, approach the enemy ships at a safe distance, then the archers are given the order to fire. A murderous hail of arrows pours down upon the foreigners who provide a mass target and fall overboard in vast numbers. The bodies of badly wounded and dead men cover the water. When the enemy had been decimated and was in complete disorder, the Egyptians rowed towards them and capsized their boats. Those who escaped death by the hail of arrows or by drowning were killed or captured by Egyptian soldiers on the nearby shore.

Rameses III had been able to ward off this deadly threat to Egypt on land and sea in these two decisive battles. There had been no victory like it in all the past history of the Nile.

After the victory a gruesome reckoning was made of dead and wounded by hacking off their hands and piling them in heaps. This was the method of counting the numbers of a defeated enemy. About what happened to the women and children of the foreigners the inscriptions tell us nothing. The reliefs also show the prisoner of war camps in which the defeated soldiers were herded together. The treatment which the mass of prisoners received was in principle the same as happens today. Drawn up in rank and file they squat on the ground awaiting checking. Even the much maligned questionnaire was included: Egyptian offi-

Left **No truly independent Philistine culture can be shown to have existed. While the migratory peoples had their own customs and religious practices, they hardly had an established canon of artistic forms; and so their culture quickly succumbed to the influences of the ancient cultural landscape in which they settled. The most we can say is that the 'archaic' stage of civilization, to which this seated goddess from Ashdod belongs, was typical of the Philistines.**

cers dictate to scribes the statements made by the prisoners. Only one matter was differently dealt with in those days. Nowadays prisoners of war have P.O.W. or K.G. painted on their tunics, the Egyptians branded Pharaoh's name on their prisoners' skins. It lasted longer. It is to the hieroglyphics of these oldest questionnaires in the world that we owe the first historical information about the famous Philistines in the Bible.

Among these 'Sea Peoples' as the Egyptians called the foreign conquerors, one racial group assumed special importance, the Peleste or PRST. These are the Philistines of the Old Testament. Egyptian artists were masters at depicting the physiognomy of foreign races and had an extraordinary ability to distinguish characteristic features. The reliefs at Medinet Habu indicate with

It was in 1188BC that the Philistines suffered their severe defeat at the hands of Rameses III. Thirteen years later they were firmly settled on the coastal plain of southern Canaan, the fertile brown plain between the mountains of Judah and the sea. The Bible lists the five cities which they possessed: Askelon, Ashdod, Ekron, Gaza and Gath (1 Samuel 6:17). Each of these cities, and the land adjoining, which was cultivated by soldiers under the command of paid leaders, was ruled over by a 'lord' who was independent and free. For all political and military purposes however the

this wonted accuracy the faces of the biblical Philistines. They look like photographs carved in stone 3,000 years ago. The tall slim figures are about a head higher than the Egyptians. We can recognize the special type of dress, and weapons, and their tactics in battle. If we substitute the men of Israel for the Egyptian mercenaries we have a true-to-life picture of the battles which took place years later in Palestine and which reached the height of their fury in the reigns of Saul and David about 1000BC.

UNDER THE YOKE OF THE PHILISTINES

The Lord delivered them into the hands of the Philistines for forty years. JUDGES 13:1

Opposite and above left **Clay sarcophagi in quasi-human forms are typically Philistine; in fact the headband and hairstyle (above) are similar to those in Egyptian portrayals of Philistines at Medinet Habu. However the stylization of the face recalls Mycenaean death masks, which the Philistines also imitated in gold foil.**

Right **Philistine ceramics, too, echo Mycenaean ware in their form and decoration. Stylized birds enjoyed a special popularity.**

five city rulers always worked hand in hand. In contrast to the tribes of Israel the Philistines acted as a unit in all matters of importance. That was what made them so strong.

The biblical narrator tells of other groups of these 'Peoples of the Sea' who had arrived with the Philistines and had settled down on the coast of Canaan: *I am about to stretch out my hand against the Philistines, and I will cut off the Kerethites (Cretans) and destroy those remaining along the coast* (Ezekiel 25:16). Crete is an island in the Mediterranean which lies far removed from Israel. Since we have learned of the historical attack of the 'Sea Peoples' on Canaan the otherwise obscure meaning of these words has become clear. They fit exactly the situation at that time.

When the Philistines appeared in Canaan a

new and distinctive type of pottery also made its appearance. It is easily recognizable as different from the pottery which had previously been in use both in the cities of the Canaanites and in the hill settlements of the Israelites. Throughout the area occupied by the five Philistine cities excavations unearthed this type of ceramic ware, which was for this reason at first regarded as a product of the Philistines.

The first find of these 'Philistine ceramics' astonished the archaeologists. They had seen these shapes and colours and patterns before. The leather coloured drinking cups and jars, painted with red and black designs and bird motifs, were already known as coming from Mycenae. From 1400BC onwards the wonderful pottery made by Mycenaean manufacturers was greatly sought after in the ancient world and their export trade had flooded every country with them. Shortly before 1200BC with the destruction of Mycenae this import from Greece suddenly stopped. The reappearance of this type of pottery in Canaan was explained by the theory that the Philistines who came from Caphtor (Amos 9:7), that is from Crete, had acquired this style of ceramic manufacture in Greece and brought it to their new country. Since then this supposition has been abandoned. Rather it is now believed that the 'Palestinian sub-Mycenaean ceramic ware' was made by potters who emigrated from Cyprus to the southern coastal plain of Palestine.

But the pottery used by the Philistines illustrates another interesting fact, which is also hinted at in the Bible. Many of their handsome mugs are fitted with a filter, and there can be no doubt about what it was used for. They are typical beer mugs. The filter served to keep back the barley husks: they floated about in the home-brewed ale and would tend to lodge in the throat. Large numbers of wine cups and beer mugs have been found in the Philistine settlements. They must have been powerful drinkers. Carouses are mentioned in the Samson stories (Judges 14:10; 16:25), where the fact is emphasized that the strong man himself drank no alcohol.

Beer is however no Philistine invention. The first great breweries flourished in the ancient east. In the hostelries of Babylon there were in fact five kinds of beer: mild, bitter, fresh, lager, and a special mixed beer for export and carrying, which was also called honey beer. This was a condensed extract of roots which would keep for a long time. All that had to be done was to mix it with water and the beer was ready—an ancient prototype of our modern dry beer for use in tropical countries.

In the oasis of En Gedi on the western bank of the Dead Sea (above) life is made possible by a spring which rises 670 metres above the Dead Sea. Here the young David is supposed to have hidden from Saul (1 Samuel 24:1). On the terrace above the spring a Chalcolithic settlement has been excavated (opposite page, above). In the area around it a herd of ibex grazes (opposite, below).

But another discovery was much more important: that the Philistines had mastered the art of processing iron. Their graves contain armour, implements and ornaments made of this rare and costly metal, as it then was. As in the case of the Mycenaean jars they manufactured their own iron. The first iron foundries in Canaan must have been built in Philistine territory. The secret of smelting iron was brought back as part of their booty as they drove through Asia Minor, where the Hittites had been the first iron-founders in the world until 1200BC.

This formula which they had acquired was guarded by the Philistine princes like the apple of their eye. It was their monopoly and they traded in it. Israel during this first period of settlement up on the mountains, was far too poor to be able to afford iron. The lack of iron farm implements, of iron nails for building houses and of iron weapons was a severe handicap. When the Philistines had occupied the mountains as well as the plains, they tried to prevent the making of new weapons by prohibiting the trade of smiths. *Not a blacksmith could be found in the whole land of Israel, because the Philistines had said, 'Otherwise the Hebrews will make swords or spears!' So all Israel went down to the Philistines to have their ploughshares, mattocks, axes and sickles sharpened* (1 Samuel 13:19–20).

Equipped with the most up to date weapons, tested and tried in their long experience of military campaigns, organized into a first class political system, there stood the Philistines about 1200BC on the west coast hungry for conquest. They had their eye on the same goal as Israel: Canaan.

Samson's mighty deeds and his pranks are legends with some of the characteristics of fairy tales and sun myths (Judges 14–16). But there are hard facts behind them. The Philistines were beginning to push forward and extend their territory eastwards. To escape from their shadow the tribe of Dan moved a long way north from their original area of settlement on the north-western slopes of the Judean hills.

Separated from each other by long valleys, lines of hills sweep up from the coastal plain to the mountains of Judah. One of these long valleys is the valley of Sorek. Samson lived in Zorah (Judges 13:2) and in Timnath, not far from it, he married a young Philistine woman (Judges 14:1). Delilah too lived there (Judges 16:4). It was along this valley that the Philistines later on sent back the Ark of the Covenant which they had captured (1 Samuel 6:12ff). This penetration of the Philistines into the hill country below the

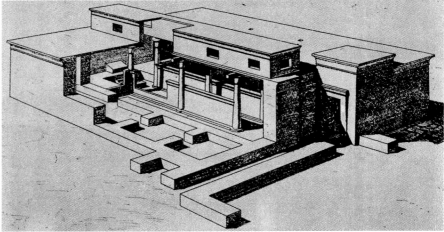

mountains of Judah was only the prelude to the great clash with Israel which followed years later.

Aphek lay on the northern rim of the Philistine domains. A mound of ruins, Tell el-Muchmar, conceals all that is left of this place which lay on the upper reaches of a river which flows into the sea to the north of Jaffa. From a strategic point of view Aphek was extremely favourably situated. Eastward lay the road to the mountains of central Palestine where Israel had settled. On the edge of the mountain range lay Eben-Ezer where the opposing forces met. At the first encounter the Philistines were victorious. The Israelites in dire straits sent to Shiloh for the Ark of the Covenant, their sacred talisman. In a second encounter they were completely beaten by the vastly superior force of the Philistines. The Israelite army was routed and the victors carried off the sacred Ark as the spoils of war (1 Samuel 4:2–11).

The hill country was occupied, Israel was disarmed, and garrisons were located in the tribal territories. At their first assault the Philistines had achieved their purpose, central Palestine was in their hands.

This advance of the Philistines must have gone hard with Israel, as can be judged from the contemporary evidence which has been discovered. The temple at Shiloh which Israel had built for the Ark of the Covenant was burnt to the ground. Fifteen miles south of Shechem lies Seilun which was once the flourishing town of Shiloh. On a neighbouring hill lay the sacred precincts, Israel's sanctuary and place of pilgrimage (Joshua 18:1; Judges 21:19ff; 1 Samuel 3:21). After the Old Testament period early Christian and Mohammedan memorials were erected on the site.

Between 1926 and 1929 a Danish expedition carried out excavations at this spot, under the direction of H. Kjaers. The remains of Shiloh clearly indicate that the city was destroyed about 1050BC at the time of the Philistine victory over Israel. Shiloh must have stood in ruins for a long

Above left **North of Jerusalem a massive construction of rough stone walling rises on the flat-topped hill of Tell el-Ful. Here excavators have uncovered Gibeah, the royal seat of King Saul.**

Right, above and below **At Beth-Shan the foundations of four shrines were found. One of them may have been the temple of Astarte, in which the Philistines laid the armour of the dead Saul; another (see reconstruction) is believed to have been the 'House of Dagon', the Canaanite god of grain, where they hung up Saul's head (1 Chronicles 10:10).**

time. For 400 years after its fall the prophet Jeremiah refers to it: *Go now to the place in Shiloh where I first made a dwelling for my Name, and see what I did to it because of the wickedness of my people Israel* (Jeremiah 7:12). Other places in the mountains of Judah shared the same fate as Shiloh. Archaeologists found tell-tale traces of ashes in Tell Beit Mirsim near Hebron, the Debir of the Bible, and in Beth-zur, south of Jerusalem.

About 1050BC Israel's very existence was threatened. It saw itself to be on the point of losing all the fruits of its conquests and all its work of colonization lasting almost 200 years. It was on the verge of falling under the yoke of the Philistines and facing an existence of hopeless slavery. The only way to meet this frightful peril would be to amalgamate the loosely federated tribes and form a solid united front. It was in face of this pressure from without that Israel

became a nation. In those days there was only one possible form of government, a monarchy. The choice fell upon Saul, a Benjamite, a man renowned for his bravery and his great height (1 Samuel 9:2). It was a wise choice, for Saul belonged to the weakest tribe (1 Samuel 9:21) and the remaining tribes would therefore have no cause to be jealous.

Saul constituted his native town Gibeah as the capital (1 Samuel 10:26; 11:4), collected round him a small standing army and began guerrilla warfare (1 Samuel 13:1ff). By surprise attacks he hunted the Philistine occupation troops out of the tribal territory.

That Saul was a tactician of a high order has recently, after 3,000 years, been demonstrated anew. One example, unique in its way, shows how accurate the Bible can be even in the smallest details and how reliable its dates and information.

We owe to Major Vivian Gilbert, a British army officer, this description of a truly remarkable occurrence. Writing in his reminiscences, entitled *The Romance of the Last Crusade*, he says:

'In the First World War a brigade major in Allenby's army in Palestine was on one occasion searching his Bible with the light of a candle, looking for a certain name. His brigade had received orders to take a village that stood on a rocky prominence on the other side of a deep valley. It was called Michmash and the name seemed somehow familiar. Eventually he found it in 1 Samuel 13 and read there: *Saul and Jonathan his son, and the people that were present with them, abode in Gibeah of Benjamin, but the Philistines encamped in Michmash.* It then went on to tell how Jonathan and his armour-bearer crossed over during the night *to the Philistines' garrison* on the other side, and how they passed two sharp rocks: *here was a sharp rock on the one side, and a sharp rock on the other side: and the name of the one was Bozez and the name of the other Seneh* (1 Samuel 14:4, AV). They clambered up the cliff and overpowered the garrison, *within as it were an half acre of land, which a yoke of oxen might plough*. The main body of the enemy awakened by the mêlée thought they were surrounded by Saul's troops and *melted away and they went on beating down one another* (1 Samuel 14:14–16, AV). Thereupon Saul attacked with his whole force and beat the enemy. *So the Lord saved Israel that day.*

'The brigade major reflected that there must still be this narrow passage through the rocks, between the two spurs, and at the end of it the "half acre of land". He woke the commander and they read the passage through together once more. Patrols were sent out. They found the pass, which

When the Philistines advanced against Israel, they camped by Michmash, and 'a detachment of Philistines went out to the pass at Michmash' (1 Samuel 13:23). This place is thought to have been discovered above a small deep valley about twelve kilometres north of Jerusalem. Here Jonathan and his armour-bearer attacked the Philistine detachment by night.

was thinly held by the Turks, and which led past two jagged rocks—obviously Bozez and Seneh. Up on top, beside Michmash, they could see by the light of the moon a small flat field. The brigadier altered his plan of attack. Instead of deploying the whole brigade he sent one company through the pass under cover of darkness. The few Turks whom they met were overpowered without a sound, the cliffs were scaled and shortly before daybreak the company had taken up a position on "the half acre of land".

'The Turks woke up and took to their heels in disorder since they thought that they were being surrounded by Allenby's army. They were all killed or taken prisoner.

'And so', concludes Major Gilbert, 'after thousands of years British troops successfully copied the tactics of Saul and Jonathan.'

Saul's successes gave Israel new heart. The pressure of the occupying power on the highlands had certainly been eased, but it was only a short respite. In the following spring the Philistines launched their counter attack.

Towards the end of the winter rainy season they gathered their fighting forces once again in Aphek (1 Samuel 29:1). But this time they had a different plan of action. They avoided an engagement in the mountains since Israel knew that country far too well. The Philistine princes chose rather to advance northwards across the coastal plain to the Plain of Jezreel (1 Samuel 29:11), the scene of Deborah's battle at Taanach by the waters of Megiddo, and then eastwards almost to the banks of the Jordan.

By the spring in Jezreel (1 Samuel 29:1)—the spring of Harod at the foot of the mountains of Gilboa—King Saul and his army ventured to meet the Philistines on the plain. The result was fatal. At the very first attack the army was scattered, the retreating troops were pursued and struck down. Saul himself committed suicide, after his own sons had been killed.

The triumph of the Philistines was complete. The whole of Israel was now occupied—the central uplands, Galilee and Transjordan (1 Samuel 31:7). Saul's body and the bodies of his sons were impaled and exposed on the city walls of Beth-Shan not far from the battlefield. *They put his armour in the temple of the Ashtoreths* (1 Samuel 31:10), the goddess of fertility. Israel's last hour appeared to have struck. It seemed doomed to extinction. The first kingdom which began so hopefully had come to a fearful end. A free people had sunk into slavery and its Promised Land had

The imposing mound of Tell el-Husn, ancient Beth-Shan, rises 80 metres above the fruitful plain of Harod, where water flows all year round. In its eighteen levels of occupation more than 5,000 years of occupation are documented. The first settlement must have been established about 3500BC; about 500 years later it grew into a town, which profited from its position on one of the busiest trade routes. Egyptian influence increased as after the battle of Megiddo (1479BC) Beth-Shan became for three hundred years a garrison town of the kingdom of the Pharaohs. The temples of Astarte, Mekal-Resef and Dagon originate from this period, commissioned by Kings Thutmosis III, Sethos I and Rameses III.

The solidly fortified town successfully withstood the Israelite invasion, but in the eleventh century BC it fell to the Philistines, who hung up Saul's body on its walls. It seems that King David was the first to conquer the town; at least Beth-Shan is counted among the twelve administrative districts of Solomon. After being plundered by Pharaoh Sheshonk, the town became insignificant until the coming of the Greek period when it flourished once more under the name of Scythopolis. Ptolemy II had probably settled veteran Scythian bowmen here. The impressive buildings of the forum (left) and the theatre (right) are more recent, having been erected in Roman times.

fallen into the hands of foreigners.

The spades of the archaeologists have unearthed from among the masses of heavy black rubble silent evidence of this fateful period, and laid bare the walls which witnessed Saul's happiest hours as a young king and also his shameful end.

A few miles north of Jerusalem, near the ancient road which leads to Samaria, lies Tell el-Ful, which means, literally, 'hill of beans'. This was once Gibeah.

In 1922 a team from the American Schools of Oriental Research began digging there. Professor W.F. Albright, who promoted the expedition, directed the operations. Remnants of walls came to light. After a long interval Albright continued

his work at Tell el-Ful in 1933. A log-shaped corner turret was exposed, and then three more. They are joined by a double wall. An open courtyard forms the interior. The total area is about 40 x 25 yards. The uncouth looking structure of dressed stone gives an impression of rustic defiance.

Albright examined the clay sherds which were scattered among the ruins. They came from jars which had been in use about 1020 to 1000BC. Albright had discovered Saul's citadel, the first royal castle in Israel, where he sat in his customary place by the wall (1 Samuel 20:25). It was here that Saul reigned as king, surrounded by his closest friends, with Jonathan his son, with Abner, his cousin and commander of his army, and with David, his young armour-bearer. Here he forged his plan to set Israel free and from here he led his partisans against the hated Philistines.

When Israel was an Empire

When all the elders of Israel had come to King David at Hebron, the king made a compact with them at Hebron before the Lord, and they anointed David king over Israel . . . and he reigned for forty years.

2 Samuel 5:3, 4

DAVID, A GREAT KING

The new king was so versatile that it is difficult to decide which of his qualities deserves most admiration. It would be just as difficult to find as gifted and rounded a personality within the last few centuries of our own times. Where is the man who could claim equal fame as soldier, statesman, poet and musician?

Certain it is, in any case that no people were more devoted to music than the inhabitants of Canaan. Palestine and Syria were renowned for their music as we learn from Egyptian and Mediterranean sources. Part of the essential goods and chattels which the group of members of the caravan, depicted in the wall painting at Beni-Hasan, took with them on their journey to Egypt, were musical instruments. The ordinary household instrument was the eight-stringed lyre. An ivory carving excavated in Megiddo shows a courtly scene with a musician playing a lyre of this

kind to the king, who is seated on the throne. The lyre travelled from Canaan to Egypt and Greece.

In the New Kingdom of Egypt (1580–1085BC) inscriptions and reliefs deal with a series of themes connected with Canaanite musicians and instruments. Canaan was an inexhaustible treasure house of musicians, from which court chamberlains and seneschals obtained singers and even orchestras to provide entertainment for their masters on the Nile, the Euphrates and the Tigris. Above all Ladies' Bands and ballerinas were in great demand. Artists with international engagements were by no means a rarity. And King Hezekiah of Judah knew very well what he was doing in 701BC when he sent men and women singers to Sennacherib the formidable king of Assyria.

'They made the lampstand of pure gold and hammered it out, base and shaft; its flowerlike cups, buds and blossoms were of one piece with it' (Exodus 37:17). Seen here are Menorah (seven-branched candelabra) from the synagogue at Tiberias (Israel Museum, Jerusalem).

In ancient Egypt, as with its Near Eastern neighbours, music played an important role: at great religious feasts, at festive banquets and also in private life. Of course we do not know any melodies from this era, but we can at least guess at the general sound from the many pictorial records.

From earliest times the harp was among the best loved instruments. It was used both for music for pleasure at home, and by professional harpists who sang to their instruments at banquets—most of these are depicted as blind. Inherchaui and his wife, painted on their tomb at Deir el-Medina, are also being entertained by a harpist. The harp was often accompanied by the 'double flute', which must have been more like a kind of oboe, and the lute, as in the female band portrayed on the famous 'Tomb of Nacht' (opposite page, below). From the New Kingdom on, the lyre, as played by one of the female musicians in the tomb of Wah (opposite, above) was imported from Asia; the nine-stringed variety was the most common. This instrument is the kinnor of the Bible.

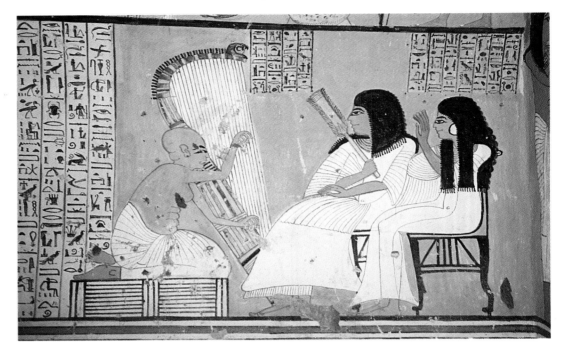

From the depths of despair, from their hopeless situation under the yoke of the Philistines, Israel climbed within a few decades to a position of power, esteem and greatness. All of that was the work of David the poet and singer of psalms. He first appears, completely unknown, as Saul's armour-bearer, becomes the leader of a troop of mercenaries, then fierce guerrilla fighter at war with the Philistines, then unexpectedly goes into the service of the Philistine King Achish of Gath—and misses by a hair having to take part in the decisive battle against Saul, only the suspicion of the other Philistine leaders prevents him from doing so and spares him the name of a collaborator with the arch-enemy. After Saul's death he becomes king of Judah and then of all Israel, which under his rule of more than thirty years' duration rises to become a great power.

As happened two centuries earlier at the time of the conquest of Canaan under Joshua, David's efforts were assisted by favourable external circumstances. Just after the beginning of the last millennium BC there was no state in Mesopotamia or Asia Minor, Syria or Egypt, which was in a position to stop an expansion of Canaanite territory.

After the death of Rameses XI, the last of the Ramessid dynasty, in 1085BC Egypt fell into the greedy hands of a priestly clique who ruled the land from Thebes. Vast wealth had come into the possession of the Temple.

A hundred years earlier, as the Harris Papyrus informs us, 2 per cent of the population was employed as temple slaves and 15 per cent of agricultural land was temple property. Their herds of cattle amounted to half a million head. The priests had at their disposal a fleet of eighty-eight vessels, fifty-three workshops and wharves, 169 villages and towns. The pomp with which the daily ritual of the great deities was carried out beggared all description. To make the temple scales alone, on which the sacrifices at Heliopolis were weighed, 212 pounds of gold and 461 pounds of silver were used. To look after the luxury gardens of Amun in the old royal city of Per-Rameses in the delta 8,000 slaves were employed.

We get some idea of Egypt's status in the eyes of the outside world during this priestly regime from a unique document, the travel diary of Wen-Amun, an Egyptian envoy, dating from 1080BC Wen-Amun's mission was to get cedar wood from Phoenicia for the sacred barge of the god Amun in Thebes. Herihor, the high priest, furnished him with only a small amount of gold and silver but with a picture of Amun, which he obviously expected to be more effective.

The frightful experiences which Wen-Amun had to go through on his journey have left their mark in his report. In the seaports he was treated like a beggar and an outlaw, robbed, insulted and almost murdered. He, an ambassador of Egypt, whose predecessors had always been received with the greatest pomp and the utmost deference.

At last Wen-Amun, having had his money

stolen on the way, reached the end of his journey. *I came to the port of Byblos. The prince of Byblos sent to me to tell me: 'Get out of my harbour.'*

This went on for nineteen days. Wen-Amun in desperation was on the point of returning to Egypt when, *The harbour master came to me and said: 'The prince will see you tomorrow!' When tomorrow came he sent for me and I was brought into his presence . . . I found him seated in his upper room, with his back leaning against a window . . . He said to me: 'What have you come here for?' I replied: 'I have come to get timber for the splendid great barge of Amun-Re, the king of the gods. Your father gave it, your grandfather gave it, and you must also give it.' He said to me: 'It is true that they gave it . . . Yes, my family supplied this material, but then Pharaoh sent six ships here laden with the produce of Egypt. . . . As far as I am concerned I am not your servant, nor the servant of him who sent you . . . What kind of beggar's journey is this that you have been sent on!' I replied: 'Don't talk nonsense! This is no beggar's errand on which I have been sent.'*

In vain Wen-Amun insisted on Egypt's power and fame, and tried to beat down the prince's price for the timber. For lack of hard cash he had to bargain with oracles and a picture of the god which was supposed to guarantee long life and good health. It was only when a messenger sent by Wen-Amun arrived from Egypt with silver and gold vessels, fine linen, rolls of papyrus, cow hides, ropes, as well as twenty sacks of lentils and thirty baskets of fish, that the prince permitted the required quantity of cedars to be felled.

In the third month of summer they dragged them down to the sea shore. The prince came out and said to me: 'Now, there is the last of your timber and it is all ready for you. Be so good as to get it loaded up and that will not really take very long. See that you get on your way and do not make the bad time of year an excuse for remaining here.'

David had nothing to fear from a country whose ambassador had to put up with disrespect of this sort. He advanced far into the south and conquered the kingdom of Edom, which had once refused Moses permission to pass through it on the 'King's Highway' (2 Samuel 8:14). This meant for David an accession of territory of considerable economic significance. The Arabah desert, which stretches from the south end of the Dead Sea to the Gulf of Aqabah, is rich in copper and iron, and what David needed most of all was iron ore. His most dangerous opponents, the Philistines, had a monopoly of

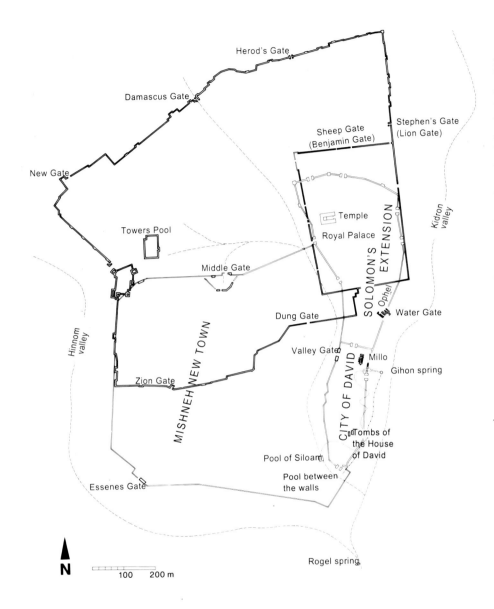

Herod's Gate

Damascus Gate

Sheep Gate
(Benjamin Gate)

Stephen's Gate
(Lion Gate)

New Gate

Temple

Royal Palace

Kidron valley

Towers Pool

Middle Gate

SOLOMON'S EXTENSION

Ophel

Dung Gate

Water Gate

Hinnom valley

MISHNEH NEW TOWN

Valley Gate

Millo

CITY OF DAVID

Gihon spring

Zion Gate

Tombs of
the House
of David

Pool of Siloam

Pool between
the walls

Essenes Gate

N
100   200 m

Rogel spring

Above **Plan of Jerusalem before the Babylonian exile.**

Opposite **Excavations in the City of David.**

Previous pages **View of Jerusalem from the Mount of Olives. Across the Kidron valley rises the Temple Mount with the Dome of the Rock and the Al-Aqsa Mosque.**

iron in their clutches (1 Samuel 13:19–20). Whoever controlled Edom could break the Philistine monopoly. David wasted no time: *He provided a large amount of iron to make nails for the doors of the gateways and for the fittings, and more bronze than could be weighed* (1 Chronicles 22:3).

The most important caravan route from South Arabia, the famous 'Incense Road', likewise terminated in the south of Edom. By pressing forward to the shore of the Gulf of Aqabah the sea route lay open to him across the Red Sea to the remote shores of South Arabia and East Africa.

The situation was also favourable for a northward advance.

In the broad plains at the foot of Hermon and in the fertile valleys which lay in front of Antileba-

non, Arab desert tribes had settled down and become static. They belonged to a race which was destined to play an important role in Israel's life, the Aramaeans, called simply Syrians in our Bible translations. They had founded city-states and smallish kingdoms as far down as the river Yarmuk, south of the Lake of Galilee over in Transjordan.

About 1000BC they were in the process of reaching out eastward into Mesopotamia. In the course of it they came up against the Assyrians, who were within the next few centuries to become the strongest power in the ancient world. After the downfall of Babylonia, the Assyrians had subjugated Mesopotamia as far as the upper reaches of the Euphrates. Cuneiform texts recovered from palaces on the Tigris and dating from this period, mention Assyria as being threatened by danger from the west. These were the Aramaeans whose thrusting attacks were made with ever increasing force.

In face of this situation David pushed north through Transjordan right up to the Orontes. The Bible says: *David fought Hadadezer king of Zobah, as far as Hamath, when he went to establish his control along the Euphrates River* (1 Chronicles 18:3). Reference to contemporary Assyrian texts shows how accurately these words in the Bible describe the historical situation. King David attacked the Aramaean king as he was on his way to conquer Assyrian territory on the Euphrates.

Without being aware of it David was aiding those same Assyrians who later wiped out the kingdom of Israel.

The boundaries of Israel's sphere of power were moved forward by David to the fertile valley of the Orontes. His most northerly sentries patrolled Lake Homs at the foot of the Lebanon. From this point it was 400 miles as the crow flies to Ezion-Geber on the Red Sea, the most southerly point in the kingdom.

Nevertheless, David captured the fortress of Zion, the City of David (2 Samuel 5:7). The romantic manner in which the stoutly guarded stronghold of Jerusalem fell into David's hands was brought to light last century partly by chance and partly by the scouting proclivities of a British army captain.

On the east side of Jerusalem where the rock slopes down into the Kidron valley lies the 'Ain Sitti Maryam', the 'Fountain of the Virgin Mary'. In the Old Testament it is called 'Gihon', 'bubbler', and it has always been the main water supply for the inhabitants of the city. The road to it goes past the remains of a small mosque and into a vault. Thirty steps lead down to a little basin in which the pure water from the heart of the rock is gathered.

In 1867 Captain Warren, in company with a crowd of pilgrims, visited the famous spring, which, according to the legend, is the place where Mary washed the swaddling clothes of her little Son. Despite the semi-darkness Warren noticed on this visit a dark cavity in the roof, a few yards above the spot where the water flowed out of the rock. Apparently no one had ever noticed this before because when Warren asked about it nobody could tell him anything.

Filled with curiosity he went back to the Virgin Fountain next day equipped with a ladder and a long rope. He had no idea that an adventurous and somewhat perilous quest lay ahead of him.

Behind the spring a narrow shaft led off at first horizontally and then straight up into the rock. Warren was an alpine expert and well acquainted with this type of chimney climbing. Carefully, hand over hand, he made his way upwards. After about 40 feet the shaft suddenly came to an end. Feeling his way in the darkness Warren eventually found a narrow passage. Crawling on all fours he followed it. A number of steps had been cut in the rock. After some time he saw ahead of him a glimmering of light. He reached a vaulted chamber which contained nothing but old jars and glass bottles covered in dust. He forced himself through a chink in the rock and found himself in broad daylight in the middle of the city, with the Fountain of the Virgin lying far below him.

Closer investigation by Parker, who in 1910 went from the United Kingdom under the auspices of the Palestine Exploration Fund, showed that this remarkable arrangement dated from the second millennium BC. The inhabitants of old Jerusalem had been at pains to cut a corridor through the rock in order that in time of siege they could reach in safety the spring that meant life or death to them.

Warren's curiosity had discovered the way which 3,000 years earlier David had used to take the fortress of Jerusalem by surprise. David's scouts must have known about this secret passage, as we can now see from a biblical reference which was previously obscure. David says: *Whosoever getteth up to the gutter and smiteth the Jebusites...* (2 Samuel 5:8, AV). The Authorized Version translated as 'gutter' the Hebrew word 'sinnor', which means a 'shaft' or a 'channel'.

Warren solved only half the problem, however, for the opening of the shaft lay outside the

Excavation of the wine cellar of Gibeon in 1959. The cistern-like containers, around two metres deep, were dug out of the rock and had a small round opening at the top, which could be closed with stone stoppers.

walls which in his day were thought to be those of the old Jebusite Jerusalem dating from before David's time. Anybody who had climbed through the shaft would still have found himself facing the Jebusite wall. It was not until the sixties of this century that the extensive excavations of Kathleen M. Kenyon cleared the matter up. The wall of what had been considered the most ancient Jerusalem was, in fact, not so old as had been thought. A much older wall was revealed which dated from before David's day and this wall ran along the slope below the opening to the entrance to the spring. David's men, who had climbed through the shaft, consequently emerged not *in front of* but a good distance *behind* what was actually Jerusalem's oldest wall; they were *right inside* the town which they were aiming to capture. This confirms the Second Book of Samuel 5:8 and thus removes much of the puzzling nature of this passage.

Seven miles north of Jerusalem, American excavations in 1956 brought to light not only traces of the walls of the town of Gibeah, which is so frequently mentioned in the Bible, but also uncovered the scene of a bloody encounter in these olden days. As we are told in 2 Samuel, once upon a time on this spot there took place a murderous hand-to-hand combat between supporters of the rival generals Joab and Abner—twelve on each side, the one lot on the side of David, the other owing allegiance to the surviving son of Saul. According to 2 Samuel 2:13, they met together by the pool of Gibeon. Beneath a field of tomatoes in el-Jib, as the place is now called, Professor J.B. Pritchard, of Columbia University, discovered the 'Pool of Gibeon', apparently in its day a well known spot. He found a circular shaft, over thirty feet in diameter and thirty feet deep, which had been driven vertically into bed rock. A spiral path led down a ramp cut into the inside wall. Below that a winding staircase, with two openings for light and air, descended for a further forty-five feet to the reservoir itself, chiselled out

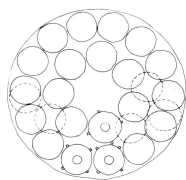

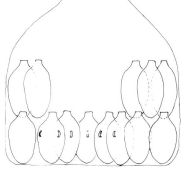

of solid limestone. When the rubble which covered the whole lay-out had been cleared away, the great cistern began to fill slowly again with water from the fissures in the rock as it had done 3,000 years ago. This biblical 'Pool of Gibeon' had also provided the town with an ample supply of fresh drinking water during an emergency or in time of siege.

Valuable evidence as to the celebrated wealth of the place—because Gibeon was an important city, like one of the royal cities (Joshua 10:2)—was collected by the American scholars from among the rubble of the vast cistern. It is now clear that the source of Gibeon's prosperity was a flourishing and well organized wine trade. Sixty handles belonging to clay wine-pitchers, together with the appropriate clay stoppers and fillers, were stamped in ancient Hebrew characters with firms' trade marks—among them vintners with genuine biblical names. Repeatedly the stamp of 'Gibeon' cropped up and a word that probably means 'walled vineyard' and might indicate a wine of special quality. Other handles again bore the names of towns in Judah, like Jericho, Succoth and Ziph (Joshua 15:24) to which the various consignments were to be delivered.

Quite near the reservoir, further diggings in the winter season of 1959–60 led to the discovery of extensive wine cellars. Sixty-six almost circular cavities about six feet deep and the same in diameter had been carved out of the rock and sealed with round stone bungs. Some of these cellars had obviously been used as wine presses for trampling out the grapes; other cavities, pro-tected by a waterproof cover, could be identified as fermentation vats. The total storage capacity so far discovered approaches 50,000 gallons.

In view of this new evidence of what was at one time a flourishing wine industry at Gibeon, a hitherto apparently insignificant point in the biblical narrative acquires fresh significance. It concerns an incident which took place while the Israelites were bent on the conquest of Canaan. We are told in Joshua 9:3–5 that *when the people of Gibeon heard what Joshua had done to Jericho and Ai they resorted to a ruse. They went as a delegation whose donkeys were loaded with worn-out sacks and old wineskins, cracked and mended. The men put worn and patched sandals on their feet and wore old clothes.* In this guise they appeared before Joshua and succeeded in hiding from him both where they came from and what a prosperous place it was.

Even if the poetic veil of legend clouds our view of David's life, especially his youth, it is with this great king that the period which can truly be called 'historical' and with it the written record of history begins.

The increasing clarity and lucidity of contemporary records is closely associated with the gradual creation of a political system which was David's great achievement and something new for Israel. A loose federation of clans had become a nation: a settlers' colony grew into an empire which filled Palestine and Syria.

For this extensive territory David created a

Above right **Ground plan and section of one of the cellars of Gibeon. The jars stacked up inside it each held about forty-five litres. In the cellars, sixty-six in all, over 100,000 litres of wine could be stored, and even kept at a constant temperature of about 18 degrees Celsius.**

Above left **Among the rubble which filled the pool of Gibeon, excavators discovered numerous jug handles. Each is inscribed with 'Gibeon' or 'Vineyard of Gibeon' in the archaic script of the seventh century BC, and some also bear personal names.**

Civil Service, at the head of which, next to the Chancellor, stood the Sopher. 'Sopher' means 'writer of chronicles' (2 Samuel 8:16, 17). A writer in the second highest position in the state!

In face of the millions of secretaries and typists in the modern world, and the thousands of tons of paper that they put into their machines and cover with type every day, the legendary glory of the 'scribe' has long since departed. Not even the enviable post of chief secretary to an oil magnate can be compared with that of her ancient colleague either in salary or still less in influence. It was only on the stage of the ancient orient that the scribes played the role of their profession incomparably and uniquely. And little wonder, considering how much depended on them. Mighty conquerors and rulers of great empires were their employers and they could neither read nor write!

This can clearly be seen from the style of the letters. It is not the person to whom the letter or message is sent who is addressed in the first instance. Greetings and good wishes from scribe to scribe take precedence. There is also a request to read out the contents of the letter distinctly, and most important, correctly and under no circumstances to suppress any of it. How things were managed within this scribal sphere of authority is indicated by numerous Egyptian reliefs and paintings, such as a vivid scene in the Foreign Office of Pharaoh Merenptah. The scribes' department is divided into three sections. In each of the two side aisles about ten secretaries sit tightly packed together. Some of them have one foot on a stool, great rolls of papyrus lie across their knees. The spacious middle section is reserved for the chief. A zealous slave keeps the troublesome flies off him with a fan. At the entrance stand two commissionaires. One is telling the other *Spray some water and keep the office cool. The chief is busy writing.*

No doubt the administrative office at the court of Jerusalem was considerably less impressive. The young state of Israel was still too rustic and too poor for that. Yet David's 'recorder' must have been an important and awe-inspiring official. It was his job to compile the 'Imperial Annals', which doubtless were the basis of all the factual biblical references to the administrative system and social structure under David. Among these are the great national census conducted on the approved Mari-plan (2 Samuel 24) as well as the information about his bodyguard of 'Kerethites and Pelethites', a kind of Swiss guard, which consisted of Cretans and Philistines (2 Samuel 8:18, 15:18; 20:7).

Undoubtedly the 'Sopher' would also be the

first to write down the new name of his sovereign.

This question of 'writing' conjures up one of the arguments levelled by critics of the Bible. In Egypt waggon loads of papyrus have been found, similarly in Babylonia and Assyria mountains of cuneiform tablets—where then are the literary documents of Palestine?

Archaeologists and meteorologists may be permitted to answer this question.

About the beginning of the last millennium BC Canaan deserted its angular cuneiform script and the use of clumsy clay tablets in favour of a less cumbersome method of writing. Until then the text of the document had to be scratched in soft clay with a stylus. The clay had then to be baked or dried in the sun, a timewasting procedure, before the bulky letters were ready for despatch. A new type of writing, with wavy lines, became more and more fashionable. This was the alphabet which we have already encountered in the attempts at writing made by the Semitic miners at Sinai. Stylus and clay were clearly unsuited for these new smoothly rounded letters. So they looked for new writing utensils and found them in broken pieces of thin baked clay pots and in inkpots and ink. Archaeologists call these pottery fragments with their writing 'Ostraca'. They were replaced in special cases by papyrus, the most elegant writing material of the ancient world. The Wen-Amun report shows how greatly this Egyptian export was in demand.

Above **3,000 tons of limestone had to be hacked out of the living rock to create the pool of Gibeon. A spiral staircase leads to the reservoir, twenty-seven metres below the earth's surface. It is thought that the pool was constructed in the ninth century BC at the earliest.**

Opposite page **The cellars of Gibeon, too, were dug out of the rock. Blocks of stone were used to seal the round openings of the two-metre-deep containers.**

In the cultures of the ancient East the art of writing was not common property, but the privilege of a small elite class of high-ranking officials. The invention of writing resulted from the founding of states around 3000BC, for neither the rapid growth of administrative activity nor a system of economic accounting would have been possible without it. The 'scribe' in the Cairo Museum (opposite) demonstrates that members of his profession were no scribbling underlings, but highly-placed personages. He sits proudly upright, looking neither at the papyrus in his lap nor at anything opposite him, but into space as though listening for inspiration from a higher plane. Writing implements consisted of paintbrush-like frayed rush stalks; black and red ink were taken from a palette with two wells (above).

The prince of Byblos received in return for his cedars 500 rolls of it: well over a mile of writing paper!

Palestine has a damp climate in winter on account of its rainfall. In such a climate ink is very quickly washed off hard clay, and papyrus soon disintegrates. Greatly to the distress of archaeologists, scientists and historians, all of them thirsting for knowledge, practically the sum total of Canaan's records and documents has been lost to posterity for this reason. The fact that the archaeologists were able to produce such an impressive haul from Egypt is simply the result of its proximity to the desert and the unusually dry climate.

SOLOMON THE 'COPPER-KING'

So King Solomon ruled over all Israel.

1 KINGS 4:1

And Solomon had four thousand stalls for chariot horses, and twelve thousand horses.

1 KINGS 4:26

And Solomon rebuilt . . . all his store cities and the towns for his chariots and for his horses.

1 KINGS 9:17, 19

King Solomon also built ships at Ezion-Geber which is near Elath . . . and they sailed to Ophir.

1 KINGS 9:26, 28

All King Solomon's goblets were gold . . . Nothing was made of silver, because silver was considered of little value in Solomon's days. The king had a fleet of trading ships . . . carrying gold, silver and ivory, and apes and baboons.

1 KINGS 10:21, 22

And the temple that King Solomon built for the Lord . . . was . . . overlaid with gold.

1 KINGS 6:2, 22

And Solomon had horses brought out of Egypt and linen yarn . . . and so for all the kings of the Hittites, and for the kings of Syria, did they bring them out by their means.

1 KINGS 10:28, 29

The weight of the gold that Solomon received yearly was 666 talents.

1 KINGS 10:14

Doesn't it sound like a fairy-tale? Any man, even a king, about whom so much is told, is hard put to it to escape the charge of boasting. And any chronicler, telling such a story, easily gets a reputation for exaggeration. There are certainly stories in the Bible which are regarded by scholars as legends, such as the tale of Balaam the sorcerer and his talking ass (Numbers 22) or the tale of Samson whose long hair gave him strength (Judges 13-16). But this most fabulous of all stories is really no fairy tale at all.

The archaeologists dug their way to the heart of the trustworthiness of these Solomon stories—and lo and behold Solomon became their unique showpiece.

When the 'fairy-tale' of King Solomon—as many still believe it to be—has been stripped of its frills, there remains a framework of sober historical facts. That is one of the most exciting discoveries of very recent times. It was only in 1937 that a wealth of surprising finds during excavations by two American expeditions produced proof of the truth of this biblical story.

Packed high with the latest equipment with drills, spades and picks and accompanied by geologists, historians, architects, excavators and the photographer who is now indispensable on a modern expedition, a caravan of camels is leaving Jerusalem. Its leader is Nelson Glueck, who like the others is a member of the famous American Schools of Oriental Research.

Soon they have left the brown mountains of Judah behind. They head south through the dreary Negev. Then the caravan enters Wadi el-Arabah, the 'Valley of the Desert'. The men feel as if they had been transported into some scene from a primeval world, where some Titanic power out of the depths had left its mark when it formed the earth. The 'Valley of the Desert' is part of the mighty fissure which begins in Asia Minor and ends in Africa.

The scientists pay their respects to this impressive vista and then turn to the task which awaits them. Their questing eyes roam over the steep rock-face. Light and shade vary with the sun, and here and there the stone is hacked away and dented. They find that it consists of muddy yellow felspar, silvery white mica, and, where the stone shows up reddish black, iron ore and a green mineral—malachite, copper spar.

Along the whole length of the wadi the American scientists come upon deposits of iron ore and copper. Wherever their tests indicate the presence of ore they find galleries let into the rock, all that remains of mines long since deserted.

At last the caravan reaches the shores of the Gulf. However invitingly the white houses of Aqabah, the Eloth of the Bible, seem to beckon them in the glaring sun, however tempting are the

sounds of this busy eastern seaport after their trek through the desolate wadi, nevertheless the scientists turn their backs on this intersection of three words. Their goal is 'Tell el-Kheleifeh'. This lonely mound, which seems no more than a pile of rubble, rises inland out of the shadeless plain.

Careful probing with spades launches the first stage of the excavation and produces unexpectedly quick results. Fish hooks come out; they are made of copper. Then tiles and remnants of walls. Some coarse looking lumps of some material in the vicinity of the Tell show traces of green. They turn out to be slag. Everywhere around them the scientists meet this sandstone with the distinctive green colour.

In his tent one evening Glueck reflects on the results of the work up to date. It has produced nothing remarkable. Meantime the whole of Transjordan is still on the programme. Glueck wants to track down the past in Edom, Moab, Ammon, even as far as Damascus. Looking through his notes, he stops and ponders. Iron-ore and malachite in the Arabah—and, in his mound of debris in front of his tent, remains of walls, slag, and copper fishhooks—and all of it in the immediate neighbourhood of the Gulf which the Bible calls the 'Red Sea'. Thoughtfully Glueck turns up the Bible passage which mentions the Red Sea in

The relief on the sarcophagus of King Ahiram of Byblos, in the Beirut Museum, shows the ruler on a throne flanked by winged sphinxes. For centuries this symbolic decoration, which also appears on the stone throne of a later prince of this area (left), was a sign of majesty used by Phoenician and Canaanite local kings. The features, hairstyle and beard of Ahiram, who lived in the tenth century BC, are Semitic-Amorite. We can imagine King Hiram of Tyre, Solomon's ally, looking similar in his appearance and clothing.

connection with a great king: *King Solomon also built ships at Ezion Geber, which is near Elath in Edom, on the shore of the Red Sea.* (1 Kings 9:26). In biblical times Edom came right down to the gulf of the Red Sea. Could this mound be . . .

It is decided to make a thorough investigation of Tell el-Kheleifeh next day. As they dig up the material from the testshafts they find that at several points they came upon wall foundations at the same level. Below that is virgin soil. Sherds give them an indication of the date of construction of the masonry. Glueck is convinced that it originates from the period of Solomon's reign, after 1000BC.

The time factor compelled Glueck to stop operations. This particular expedition had other tasks ahead. But in the following years the Americans continued the excavations in three stages, which ended in 1940 and confirmed Glueck's theory. It appeared that the first ruins that came to light had once been workers' dwellings. Then

The inscription on the sarcophagus of King Ahiram of Byblos is already written in the 'modern' Phoenician alphabet, of which the rock inscriptions on the Sinai Peninsula are forerunners.

came ramparts of the casemated type, the unmistakable building style of the first Iron Age. After that remains of an extensive settlement were excavated. The most interesting things were casting-moulds and a vast quantity of copper slag.

Casting-moulds and copper slag in the middle of the scorching pitilessly hot plain?

Glueck tried to find an explanation for this strange fact. Why did the workshops have to be located right in the path of the sandstorms which almost incessantly sweep down the wadi from the North? Why were they not a few hundred yards further on in the shelter of the hills, where there were also fresh water springs? The astonishing answer to these questions was not forthcoming until the last excavation period.

In the middle of a square walled enclosure an extensive building came into view. The green discoloration on the walls allowed Glueck to conclude that he was dealing with a blast furnace. The mud-brick walls had two rows of openings. He took them to be flues: a skilful system of air passages. The whole thing was, as he saw it, a proper up-to-date blast furnace, built in accordance with a principle that celebrated its resurrection in modern industry a century ago as the Bessemer-system. Flues and chimneys both lay along a north to south axis. For the incessant winds and storms from the Wadi el-Arabah had to take over the role of bellows. That was 3,000 years ago: today compressed air is forced through the forge.

One question alone still remained unanswered: how was the copper refined in this ancient apparatus? Smelting experts of today cannot solve the mystery.

Earthenware smelting-pots still lie about in the vicinity: many of them have the remarkable capacity of 14 cubic feet. In the surrounding hill-slopes the multiplicity of caves hewn out of the rock indicate the entrance to the galleries. Fragments of copper sulphate testify to the busy hands that worked these mines thousands of years ago. In the course of fact-finding excursions into the surrounding country the members of the expedition succeeded in identifying numerous copper and iron mines in the wadis of the Arabah desert.

Eventually Nelson Glueck discovered in the casemated wall of the mound of rubble a stout gateway with a triple lockfast entrance. He was no longer in any doubt. Tell el-Kheleifeh was once Ezion-Geber, the long-sought vanished seaport of King Solomon: *King Solomon also built ships at Ezion Geber, which is near Elath in Edom . . .*

Ezion-Geber was however not only a seaport. In its dockyards ships for ocean travel were also built. But above all Ezion-Geber was the centre of the copper-industry. Nowhere else in the 'Fertile Crescent,' neither in Babylonia nor in Egypt, was such a great furnace to be found. It was here, then, that they produced the metal for the ritual furnishings of the Temple at Jerusalem—for the 'altar of brass', the 'sea', as a great copper basin was called, for the 'ten bases of brass', for the 'pots, shovels, basins' and for the two great pillars 'Jachin and Boaz' in the porch of the Temple (1 Kings 7:15ff; 2 Chronicles 4, AV). For *the king had them cast in clay moulds in the plain of the Jordan between Succoth and Zarethan* (1 Kings 7:46). One of the most recent finds in biblical archaeology fell to the lot of a Dutch expedition which has now established the site of the former of these two places. At Tell deir Alla in Transjordan, where the river Jabbok leaves the hills six miles before it joins the Jordan, the expedition discovered traces of Succoth, the Israelite city dating from the days of Joshua.

Glueck's delight at his discovery can still be detected in the official report which gathered together the results of the researches at the Gulf of Aqabah: 'Ezion-Geber was the result of careful planning and was built as a model installation with remarkable architectural and technical skill. In fact practically the whole town of Ezion-Geber, taking into consideration place and time, was a phenomenal industrial site, without anything to compare with it in the entire history of the ancient

Since about 3000BC copper ore has been mined at Wadi Timna, twenty-five kilometres north of Ei-lat. The modern quarries lie some-what west of the ancient workings.

in Wadi Ghazze. The furnaces are like those at Tell el-Kheleifeh but smaller. David had disputed the Philistines' right to their monopoly of iron and he had extracted their secret smelting process as one of the prices of their defeat. What would be easier to assume than that Solomon then went on to mine iron and copper on a large scale?

For the Lord your God is bringing you into a good land . . . a land where the rocks are iron and you can dig copper out of the hills. (Deuteronomy 8:7–9)

So runs part of the detailed description of the Promised Land which Moses gives the children of Israel. Copper and iron in Palestine? The work of the archaeologists has now produced evidence showing how true is this description which the Bible gives, and introduces a new factor into our picture of Old Palestine which we shall in future have to take into account, namely its remarkable industrial development.

Solomon was a thoroughly progressive ruler. He had a flair for exploiting foreign brains and foreign skills and turning them to his own advantage. That is the secret, otherwise scarcely understandable, of how the simple peasant regime of his father David developed by leaps and bounds into a first class economic organism. Here also is to be found the secret of his wealth which the Bible emphasises. Solomon imported smelting technicians from Phoenicia. *Huram-Abhi, a craftsman from Tyre, was entrusted with the casting of the Temple furnishings* (1 Kings 7:13, 14). In Ezion-Geber Solomon founded an important enterprise for overseas trade. The Israelites had never been sailors and knew nothing about shipbuilding. But the Phoenicians had behind them practical experience accumulated over many centuries. Solomon therefore sent to Tyre for specialists for his dockyards and sailors for his ships: *And Hiram sent his men—sailors who knew the sea . . .* (1 Kings 9:27).

Ezion-Geber was the well-equipped and heavily defended export centre for the new foreign trade. From Ezion-Geber the ships set sail on their mysterious voyages to distant and unfamiliar shores. Ophir?—where was the legendary land of Ophir, the 'warehouse' in which the ancient orient purchased the costliest and choicest commodities?

Many a scholarly quarrel has broken out about Ophir. Someone was always claiming to have found it. In 1871 the geologist Carl Mauch came across a large area covered with ruins in Zimbabwe. Fifteen years later Steinberg of South

orient. Ezion-Geber was the Pittsburgh of old Palestine and at the same time its most important seaport.'

King Solomon, whom Glueck describes as the 'great copper king', was reckoned by him to be among the greatest exporters of copper in the ancient world. However, since then his research findings have of course been questioned. Investigations by Israeli achaeologists revealed that no copper mining was done in the mines of Wadi Timnah, north of Ezion-Geber, between the twelfth century BC and the Roman period, which means none was done in Solomon's time, and the installations at Tell el-Kheleifeh have been interpreted by some scholars as warehouses or grain silos. South of the old Philistine city of Gaza, Flinders Petrie dug up iron-smelting installations

Above **Ancient copper smelting oven at Timna.**

Left **This mushroom-shaped rock formation became a distinguishing feature of the mining district of Timna.**

Overleaf **The fifty-metre-high rock towers in the south of the Wadi Arabah are known as 'King Solomon's Pillars'. Sir Henry Rider Haggard's nineteenth-century adventure story** King Solomon's Mines **first linked the area of Timna with King Solomon.**

Africa dug up, a few miles to the south, mining installations which he took to be pre-Christian and to have been connected with the temple city, which today is dated to the eleventh to fifteenth century AD. Rock-tests were supposed to show that gold and silver had at one time been quarried there. In 1910 the famous African explorer, Dr. Karl Peters of Germany, photographed carvings on this site in which experts claimed that they detected odd Phoenician characteristics.

This mysterious land of Ophir has however so far eluded the grasp of the scientists. Many indications nevertheless point to East Africa. Experts like Prof. Albright suggest that it was located in Somaliland. That would tie up very well with what the Bible says about the length of time it took to get there.

Once in three years came the navy ... (1 Kings 10:22, AV). 'The fleet may have sailed from Ezion-Geber in November or December of the first year,' suggested Albright, 'and returned in May or June of the third year. In this way the hot weather in summer would be avoided as much as possible. The journey in this case need have taken no more than eighteen months.' Further, the nature of the merchandise gold, silver and ivory, and apes and baboons (1 Kings 10:22) points to Africa as the obvious place of origin.

The Egyptians were well informed about 'Punt', which may be identifiable with Ophir. They must have been on the spot and kept their eyes open. How otherwise could these impressive pictorial representations of 'Punt' have originated, which light up the walls of the terraced temple of

From the Old Kingdom on, the Egyptians undertook expeditions to faraway lands to bargain for exotic wares. In most cases these were not hostile incursions; the military presence in them was purely a defence against attack. The journey to the incense country of Punt was popular, but also particularly expensive, since ships had to be transported overland from the Nile to the Red Sea. (Punt has sometimes been linked with the biblical Ophir.)

It was only after a long break that Queen Hatshepsut once more equipped an expedition to Punt. This trip was apparently accompanied by scientists who meticulously recorded their observations in drawings, so that the account of the enterprise in the Queen's temple of the dead could be based on authentic models. On the banks of the Red Sea, whose fauna is reproduced in detail, the leader of the Egyptian expedition is greeted by the inhabitants of Punt. He has brought with him, as objects of barter, manufactured goods, including weapons.

Deir el-Bahri? Wonderful coloured reliefs adorn this temple on the west side of Thebes, lending splendour and charm to a dusky lady—the queen of Punt—and her retinue. As usual the Egyptian artists have here too lavished devoted attention to the details of the costumes, the round huts, the animals and plants of 'Punt'. Anyone looking at them has a clear picture in his mind's eye of what this legendary Ophir looked like.

Inscriptions adjoining the reliefs give an account of the sensational expedition which a woman ordered to be equipped and to set out for 'Punt' in 1500BC. On the throne of the Pharaohs at that time sat the famous Queen Hatshepsut, 'the first great woman in history' as James H. Breasted the Egyptologist calls her. In response to an oracle of the god Amun, which enjoined that the routes to 'Punt' should be explored and that trade relations with the Red Sea ports which had been interrupted by the Hyksos wars should be resumed, the queen sent out a flotilla of five sea-going vessels in the ninth year of her reign. They were to bring back myrrh trees for the temple terraces. The fleet sailed from the Nile along a canal in the eastern part of the delta into the Red Sea and 'arrived safely in Punt', where it exchanged Egyptian produce for a precious cargo of myrrh trees, ebony, gold, as well as all sorts of sweet smelling wood and other exotic articles like sandalwood, panther skins, and apes.

A display such as they had never seen before met the gaze of the Thebans as at the close of a successful trip the strange collection of dark-skinned natives of Punt made their way to the queen's palace with the marvellous products of their country. *I have made his garden into another Punt, as he commanded me . . .* says Hatshepsut exultingly, referring to the myrrh trees on the temple terraces. Egyptologists found dried up roots of myrrh in the hot yellow sand in front of the temple of Deir el-Bahri.

Like the Thebans, men and women of Israel must also have stood in wonder and amazement on the quayside of Ezion-Geber when their King Solomon's fleet returned from distant Ophir and discharged its cargo of sandalwood and precious stones, gold, silver, ivory, apes and peacocks (1 Kings 10:11,22, AV).

Archaeological work can normally only be started when permission to excavate has been given by the landowner or by the government of the country. This is not always easy to obtain, quite apart from the fact that in the course of the operations protests or restrictions can make life difficult for the investigators. In 1925 the Americans hit upon an unusual way of ensuring that they would be left in peace to get on with the work. They bought without a moment's hesitation the mound of rubble called Tell el-Mutesellim in the Plain of Jezreel from ninety

Left **As well as incense for sacrifices to the gods, the expedition to Punt brought Queen Hatshepsut saplings of incense trees, which were shipped to Egypt complete with root balls. However, the Egyptians had no success in making the incense tree indigenous to their country.**

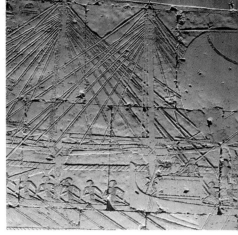

Above **The inhabitants of Punt lived in round huts resting on stilts and accessible only by ladders.**

Top **Laden with incense and other exotic wares such as ebony, elephant's tusks, panther skins, ostrich eggs and feathers, the ships of the Punt expedition once more breast the waves. On board they also carry living animals: apes, panthers and even a giraffe.**

native proprietors, peasants and shepherds, lock, stock and barrel. For the Oriental Institute of the University of Chicago had in mind a model excavation for the whole of the Middle East, the most comprehensive, most painstaking, and most accurate investigation that had ever been started in Palestine.

Tell el-Mutesellim covers the site of the Megiddo of the Bible. This discovery is based on the first large-scale excavation which was undertaken on this spot by the German Oriental Society under Dr. J. Schumacher between 1903 and 1905.

Like a small edition of Table Mountain, Tell el-Mutesellim lies in the heart of a unique scenic setting. Looking down from the plateau is like looking down on a vast green lake. Into the far distance stretches the great plain, the 'valley of Jezreel' (Joshua 17:16), in which the green meadows of the fenland and well-stocked fields of grain alternate with one another. Flocks of cranes and storks frequent the spot. Where the plain ends, the wooded hump of Carmel stands guard over the Mediterranean shore. To the north the hills of Galilee with the little village of Nazareth sweep upwards, tinted a delicate blue, and far to the right the sombre summit of Mt. Tabor bars the view into the deep cleft of the Jordan valley.

Nothing in this fertile triangle, this friendly countryside girt with gentle lines of hills, suggests that this tiny bit of land was for many thousands of years the scene of mighty battles and of momentous and decisive history.

About 1500BC Pharaoh Thutmose III, riding in a 'golden chariot', led his army through a narrow pass into the plain and attacked the Canaanites, who fled in terror and complete disorder to Megiddo. On the same plain the Israelites, incited by the heroic Deborah, smashed the supremacy of the Canaanite charioteers, Gideon surprised the plundering camel-borne nomads from Midian, Saul lost the battle against the Philistines, and King Josiah of Judah died about 600BC as he and his men threw themselves in vain against the armed might of Egypt under Pharaoh Necho. Ruins mark the site of the Frankish castle of Faba, which the knights of St. John and the Templars occupied during the Crusades, until Saladin drove them off the plain after a frightful massacre. On the sixteenth of April 1799 there was a battle here between the Turks and the French. With only 1,500 men Kleber, the French general, held 25,000 of the enemy at bay. The French fought like heroes from sunrise till noon. Then over a ridge to the rescue charged a troop of 600 mounted men. The officer at their head was called Napoleon Bonaparte. After the victorious 'Battle of Tabor' Napoleon rode up into the hills of Galilee and ate his supper in Nazareth. In 1918 British

Above **View over the plain of Jezreel from Megiddo. The plain of Jezreel lies between the hill countries of Samaria, Carmel and Galilee, bordered by the mountains of Gilboa in the east and Mount Tabor in the north-east. Its volcanic soils are very fertile, but were waterlogged for a long time. The soil treatment begun in 1920 has created a flourishing agriculture. The plain takes its name from the town of Jezreel, which lay in the foothills of the Gilboa range and was for a time the royal seat of King Ahab. From earliest times it was ruled by Megiddo; possession of Megiddo was the key to control of the area, through which ran one of the most important trade routes.**

Opposite **The tell of Megiddo rises twenty-one metres from the plain of Jezreel. Its twenty strata of occupation reach from the fourth millennium BC to nearly 350BC.**

cavalry under Lord Allenby swept through the same pass as Thutmose III and destroyed the Turkish army which was encamped on the plain.

A silent witness of all these events was Tell el-Mutesellim, where Clarence S. Fisher began operations on the model excavation in the spring of 1925.

The hill was literally cut into slices inch by inch—like cutting a cake except that the slices were horizontal ones. The centuries flashed past like a kaleidoscope. Every layer that was removed signified a chapter of world history from the fourth to the tenth century BC.

Of the four top layers Stratum I contained ruins from the time of the Persian and Babylonian empires. Cyrus, king of Persia, destroyed the power of Babylon in 539BC. King Nebuchadnezzar of Babylon had conquered Syria and Palestine fifty years earlier in 597BC. The walls of an unusually solidly built palace still remain from that period. Stratum II provided evidence of Assyrian rule with ruins of a palace dating from the eighth century BC. Tiglath-Pileser III subdued Palestine in 733BC. Stratum III and Stratum IV incorporated the Israelite period.

The most important find in this case was two seals with old Hebrew letters on them. One of them bore the inscription, 'Shema, servant of Jeroboam'. Jeroboam I was the first ruler of Israel after the kingdom had been divided (926–907BC). A stone preserved another familiar name:

Pharaoh Sheshonk I, of Egypt. The Bible calls him Pharaoh Shishak. In 922BC, the fifth year of King Jeroboam's reign, he attacked Palestine.

After almost ten years of toil, picks and spades had reached the layers dating from the time of King Solomon, who had died four years before the attack of Sheshonk in 926BC. The lowest level of rubble in Stratum IV then produced sensational surprises for the archaeologists, Gordon Loud and P.L.O. Guy.

In Solomon's day a new method of construction was adopted in the case of public buildings, defence walls, etc. Instead of the previous style of building this new type involved the introduction of smooth dressed stones at the corners and at intervals along the walls. On the lowest level of the rubble of Stratum IV ruins of a palace were exposed which displayed this characteristic feature. They are enclosed by a square wall whose sides are about 60 yards long. Additional protection was afforded by the handsome entrance gateway flanked by three pairs of close-set pillars. Archaeologists came across similar town gates with this threefold security in Ezion-Geber and in Lachish. A building with massive walls that was excavated almost at the same time turned out to be a granary, one of the store cities Solomon had (1 Kings 9:19). Storehouses of this kind were also found at Beth-Shan and Lachish. Megiddo was the administrative centre of the 5th District in the Israel of Solomon's day. Solomon's representative in the palace, who was also responsible for the deliveries of taxes in kind to the store city was Baana son of Ahilud (1 Kings 4:12).

Although these finds were remarkable they were not sensational. The sensation was still lying untouched in the heart of Tell el-Mutesellim as if the old mound had been keeping the best to the last. In the course of the excavations there appeared among the rubble on the edge of the Tell a flat stone surface, studded with stone stumps, ranged one behind the other in long rows and square in shape.

Loud and Guy had at first no idea what it could have been. There seemed to be no end to this remarkable series of flat surfaces which emerged yard by yard out of the rubble. It occurred to Guy that they might be the remains of stables. Did the Bible not speak of the untold horses of King Solomon?

Amid the generally monotonous sameness of a dig that had lasted several years with its daily stint of carrying away, emptying out, sifting and arranging every fragment worth considering, Guy's idea gave at once a new fillip to the excavations, which even the digging gangs shared.

The archaeologists' astonishment grew with every new structure which came to light. They found that several large stables were always grouped round a courtyard, which was laid with beaten limestone mortar. A 10-foot wide passage ran down the middle of each stable. It was roughly paved to prevent the horses from slipping. On each side, behind the stone stumps, lay roomy stalls, each of which was exactly 10 feet wide. Many of them had still remains of feeding troughs and parts of the watering arrangements were still recognizable. Even for present day circumstances they were veritable luxury stables. Judging by the extraordinary care which had been lavished on buildings and services, horses in those days were at a premium. At all events they were better looked after than were human beings.

When the whole establishment was uncovered, Guy counted single stalls for at least 450 horses and sheds for 150 chariots. A gigantic royal stable indeed! *Here is the account of the forced labour King Solomon conscripted to build the Lord's temple, his own palace, the supporting terraces, the wall of Jerusalem, and Hazor, Megiddo and Gezer* (1 Kings 9:15). *Solomon accumulated chariots and horses; he had fourteen hundred chariots and twelve thousand horses, which he kept in the chariot cities . . .* (1 Kings 10:26). In view of the size of the royal stable at Megiddo and the stables and chariot sheds of similar type which have been found at

Above right **Plan of Megiddo at the time of King Solomon.**

1 South palace
2 North palace
3 Administrative buildings
4 City gate
5 Approach to the spring
6 Private houses

Below right **Plan of Megiddo at the time of King Ahab.**

1 Stables or storehouses
2 Stables or storehouses with adjacent courtyard
3 Water supply installations
4 City gate
5 City wall
6 Private houses

Far right **The strongest defensive walls are useless if the besieged city runs out of supplies and water. The spring supplying Megiddo lay at the foot of the tell outside the city walls. This is probably the reason why the Canaanite rulers of the town had already bored a channel to the watering-place. The sixty-four-metre-long tunnel, which leads under the town up a gently rising slope from the spring and then reaches the surface via a twenty-two-metre-deep shaft, was installed under King Ahab. Evidently tunnelling was begun from both ends at once, and it does credit to the surveyors of the time that the tunnellers were only out by sixty centimetres.**

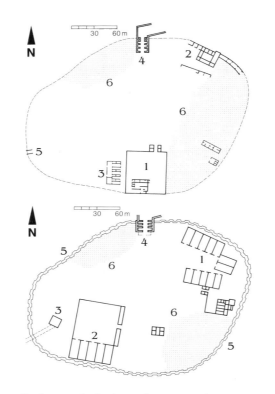

Tell el-Hesi (Eglon), and at Taanach, it is not surprising that the excavators thought of these Bible passages and were convinced by them that they had discovered one of the garrisons of the chariot corps which Solomon set up. Of course since then most scholars have come to the conclusion that Stratum IV of Megiddo should be dated to the ninth century BC, while Stratum V comes from the time of Solomon. Solomon's stables, which some scholars take to be storehouses or barracks, were probably only erected in the time of King Ahab of Israel. Be that as it may, horses and chariots alike were considered in Solomon's day to be worth-while trading commodities. Israel had indeed in this matter a complete monopoly (1 Kings 10:28,29).

All the important caravan routes between Egypt, Syria and Asia Minor went through Solomon's kingdom. Egypt was the chief exporter of war-chariots . . . the king's merchants received the linen yarn at a price. And a chariot came up and went out of Egypt for six hundred shekels of silver. Egyptian wheelwrights were unsurpassed craftsmen in building swift two-wheeled chariots for war and hunting. The hardwood for them had to be imported from Syria. This explains the high rate of exchange. According to the Bible one chariot was worth four horses (1 Kings 10:29). In this connection it will not be necessary to insist on the fact that the 'shekels of silver' mentioned by the

Bible are an anachronism since minted coins were still unknown in King Solomon's day.

The horses came from Egypt, 'and from Koa' as another tradition tells us. 'Koa' was the name of a state in Cilicia which lay in the fertile plain between the Taurus Mountains and the Mediterranean. After the destruction of the kingdom of Mitanni by the Hittites, Cilicia became the land of horse breeders and the livery stables of the ancient world. Herodotus mentions that later on the Persians fetched the best horses for their Imperial Messenger Service from Cilicia.

Israel's trading partners in the north were the 'Kings of Syria and the Kings of the Hittites' (1 Kings, 10:29, AV). This too is historically accurate. The kingdom of the Hittites had long been extinct by Solomon's day but some smaller successor states had taken its place. One of them was discovered in 1945 by the archaeologist H.T. Bossart of Germany, although it is a century younger than Solomon. This was the royal castle in the forest of Mt. Karatepe, not far from Adana in the south-east of Turkey. Asitawanda, who built it in the ninth century BC, was one of these 'Kings of the Hittites'.

Other late Hittite centres in the border region between Syria and Anatolia were Carchemish, Malatya and Marash. Until the end of the seventh century BC, these small states with their Hittite kings managed more or less to survive. Then, like

all the other nations of the Near East, they succumbed to the advancing Assyrians.

THE QUEEN OF SHEBA AS A BUSINESS PARTNER

When the queen of Sheba heard of Solomon's fame, she came to Jerusalem to test him with hard questions. Arriving with a very great caravan—with camels carrying spices, large quantities of gold, and precious stone. . .

2 CHRONICLES 9:1

For thousands of years richly laden caravans have made their way from *Arabia Felix*, 'fortunate Arabia', to the north. They were well known in Egypt, in Greece and in the Roman Empire. With them came tales of fabulous cities, of tombs filled with gold, tales which persisted through the centuries. The Roman Emperor Augustus, determined to find out the truth about what camel drivers continually extolled in their remote country. He instructed Aelius Gallus to fit out a military expedition and to satisfy himself on the spot as to the truth incredible tales about south Arabia. With an army of 10,000 legionaries Gallus marched south from Egypt and proceeded along

the desolate shores of the Red Sea. Marib, the legendary capital city, was his goal. But he was never to reach it. For in the pitiless heat of the desert, after endless clashes with wild tribes, decimated by treacherous diseases, his army went to pieces. The few survivors who reached their native land again had no reliable factual details to add to the legendary stories of 'Arabia Felix'.

In fortunate Arabia, writes Dionysius the Greek in A.D. 90, *you can always smell the sweet perfume of marvellous spices, whether it be incense or wonderful myrrh. Its inhabitants have great flocks of sheep in the meadows, and birds fly in from distant isles bringing leaves of pure cinnamon.*

South Arabia was even in the ancient world export country Number One for spices and it is still so today. Yet it seemed to be shrouded in dark mystery. No man had ever seen it with his own eyes. 'Arabia Felix' remained a book with seven seals. The first man in recent times to embark upon this dangerous adventure was Carsten Niebuhr, a German, who led a Danish expedition to south Arabia in the eighteenth century. Even he only got as far as Sana. He was still 60 miles from the ruined city of Marib when he had to turn back.

A Frenchman, J. Halevy, and an Austrian, Dr. Eduard Glaser, were the first white men actually to reach this ancient goal about a century ago. Since no foreigner, far less a European, was allowed to cross the frontier of the Yemen, and no permit

This wooden scale model of Megiddo shows the condition of the fortified town, mainly during the period of the Israelite kings. In the foreground a street climbs to the northern city gate with its outworks. The remains below it belong to the gatehouses of the eighteenth and fifteenth centuries BC. On the left, behind the north wall, where Solomon's 'North Palace' and the office of the commander once stood, King Ahab erected a long row of stables or storehouses. In the background can be seen the southern gatehouses, and right of them more stabling or perhaps storerooms, with a large adjoining courtyard. From the western promontory of the tell (right) the shaft to the water supply leads down into the depths.

By far the strongest fortified gate of Solomon's Megiddo lies in the north of the town. The remains which have survived show us a roomy, bastion-like outwork. From here the way into the town leads through a twin-towered ornamental gate, each tower having three side-rooms for the staff of watchmen.

could be obtained, Halevy and Glaser embarked on an enterprise which might have cost them their lives. They chartered a sailing boat and landed secretly in the Gulf of Aden disguised as Bedouins. After an arduous journey of over 200 miles through parched and desolate mountain country they eventually reached Marib. Greatly impressed by what they saw they threw caution to the winds and clambered around the ruins.

Suspicious natives came towards them. The two scholars knew that it would cost them their

lives if their disguise was discovered and took to their heels. At last after many adventures they reached Aden by a circuitous route. However they had been able to smuggle out copies and rubbings of inscriptions, concealed under their burnous, on the strength of which they were able to prove that Marib really existed.

Travelling merchants likewise brought inscriptions with them later on. Up to the present day their number reaches a total of several thousand. Scholars have examined and sifted the mate-

rial. The script is alphabetic and therefore originated in Palestine. Dedicatory inscriptions give us information about gods, tribes and cities of a million inhabitants. And the names of four countries—'The Spice Kingdoms'—which are mentioned are: Minaea, Kataban, Hadhramaut and—Sheba.

The kingdom of Minaea lay in the northern part of Yemen and is referred to up to the twelfth century BC. Writings of the ninth century BC mention its southern neighbour, the land of the Shebans. Assyrian documents of the eighth century BC likewise speak of Sheba and of close trade relations with this country whose kings were called 'Mukarrib', 'priest-princes'.

Gradually, with the discovery of documentary evidence, this fairy-tale country of Sheba began to take definite shape.

A gigantic dam blocked the river Adhanat in Sheba, collecting the rainfall from a wide area. The water was then led off in canals for irrigation purposes, which was what gave the land its fertility. Remains of this technical marvel in the shape of walls over 60 feet high still defy the sand-dunes of the desert. Just as Holland is in modern times the Land of Tulips, so Sheba was then the Land of Spices, one vast fairy-like scented garden of the costliest spices in the world. In the midst of it lay the capital, which was called Marib. For 1,500 years this garden of spices bloomed around Marib. That was until 542BC—then the dam burst. The importunate desert crept over the fertile lands and destroyed them. *The people of Sheba*, says the Koran, *had beautiful gardens in which the most*

The famous 'Solomon's stables' in Megiddo were large halls whose roofs were borne by strong stone pillars (above). It has been calculated that around 450 horses could be kept here, and the stone feeding troughs are also claimed as evidence (right). Recently the date of origin and the purpose of these buildings have been a matter of fierce dispute. Most experts believe that they were only erected under King Ahab in the ninth century BC and served as storehouses for food. Yet the idea that animals were kept there is not entirely ruled out, since fresh meat is best kept live!

costly fruits ripened. But then the people turned their backs upon God, wherefore he punished them by causing the dam to burst. Thereafter nothing but bitter fruit grew in the gardens of Sheba.

In 1928 German scholars Carl Rathjens and H. von Wissmann uncovered the site of a temple near Sana which had been first seen by their countryman Niebuhr. It was a significant start but almost another quarter of a century was to elapse before the greatest team of experts so far set out on an expedition at the end of 1951 to solve the archaeological riddle of Sheba. 'The American Foundation for the Study of Man' provided the expedition with unusually large financial resources. The organizer of the enterprise was an extremely versatile palaeontologist from the University of California, Wendell Phillips, then only twenty-nine years old. After long drawn-out negotiations they succeeded in getting permission from King Imam Achmed to excavate at Marib. Marib lies at the southern tip of the Arabian peninsula about 6,000 feet up on the eastern spurs of the mountain range that skirts the Red Sea. The archaeologists

Chariots for battle and for racing, imported from the Near East, were a treasured possession in Egypt. On a wall painting in the tomb of the officer Haremhab, servants carry the vehicle carefully on their shoulders. But Egypt soon began to manufacture such chariots for themselves—albeit of a type with eight- or six-spoked wheels—and even exported them. King Solomon too ordered chariots and horses from Egypt.

started with high expectations.

A long column of jeeps and trucks rolled northwards in a cloud of dust through barren mountain country with neither roads nor paths. Suddenly like a phantom out of the shimmering yellow sand dunes there appeared before them massive ruins and columns—what the Arabs called Mahram Bilqis, the 'throne of the Queen of Sheba'. It was the ancient Ilumquh temple of Awwam, a centre of worship wrapped in legend, in the neighbourhood of Marib, the capital of the old Arabian kingdom of Sheba. Although partly covered by sand dunes as high as houses the lines of

this oval-shaped temple over 300 feet long were clearly recognizable. The sanctuary was of the same type as the ruins of Mozambique in the East African jungle, discovered during the quest for Ophir. The ground plans of the two temples were remarkably alike.

According to an inscription on the wall, Ilumquh, god of the moon, was worshipped at Mahram Bilqis. Masses of sand covered the temple which stood in the middle of the oval. Digging therefore began on the entrance to the great circle. The archaeologists wanted to try to approach the temple gradually from that point.

Under a boiling sun a gatehouse of surprising splendour and beauty was exposed amid understandable excitement. Wide steps covered with bronze led inside. The inner court was surrounded by a pillared hall. Stone columns 15 feet high once bore a roof which shielded it from the sun. Flanked by pillars on each side the processional way led from this point to the sanctuary of the moon god. An unusual ornamental fixture caused astonishment. From a height of 15 feet glittering fountains of water must in those days have played into this quiet courtyard. As it descended the water was caught in a narrow channel which then wound its way through the whole pillared court.

What must have been the feelings of pilgrims who made their way past these splashing sparkling fountains, fanned by the drowsy fragrance of incense and myrrh, through the pillared courts of this most marvellous edifice in old Arabia?

The digging went steadily forward until they were within a few yards of the temple. The archaeologists could see in front of them the wonderful temple gate, flanked by two slender columns—but at this point the excavation had to be precipitately abandoned. The chicanery of the governor of Marib which had been going on for weeks had

Haremhab, who was employed as a recruiting officer in the time of Tutmosis III, evidently had a preference for cavalry, for in the paintings in his grave not only chariots but also noble horses are being presented to him. At this time the Egyptians had to import horses from the Near East. But during the Eighteenth Dynasty they had great success in breeding, so that they themselves could export horses.

now reached a dangerous point and the members of the expedition were no longer sure of their safety. They had to rise and run, leaving everything behind them. Fortunately they had some photographs among the few things they had been able to salvage on their hasty escape.

Nearby in the Hadhramaut three digs were carried out in the following few years which were crowned with more success.

Soon after the experts had begun to evaluate the results of these four brief and somewhat dramatic expeditions, Professor William. F. Albright could say: 'They are in process of revolutionising our knowledge of Southern Arabia's cultural history and chronology. Up to now the results to hand demonstrate the political and cultural primacy of Sheba in the first centuries after 1000BC.'

Above **Fragment of a Sabaean inscribed tablet written in the decorative consonantal script of ancient Southern Arabia.**

Right **A stylized, stumpy shape is typical of Sabaean representational art. The eyes of this alabaster statuette are inlaid with mussel shells and a copper sulphate mixture. On the hem of its robe an inscription names the person portrayed and the god to whom the votive offering was dedicated.**

Just as King Solomon's ships made long sea voyages through the Red Sea to Arabia and Africa, so long distance travel began on the Red Sea coast route through the southern Sea of Sand. The new form of transport called, not unjustly, 'Ships of the Desert,' consisted of camels. They were able to compass distances which were hitherto reckoned impossible. An unsuspected development both in trade and transport through these vast desolate territories took place about 1000BC thanks to the taming and training of these desert animals. South Arabia, which had for so long been almost as far away as the clouds, was suddenly brought into the Mediterranean world and into closer contact with the other kingdoms of the Old World.

Previously it was by the employment of donkeys, plodding endlessly and painfully month after month, each short day's journey governed by the distance from water hole to water hole, and always in danger of attack, that the treasures of Arabia trickled northwards along the ancient Incense Road through 1,250 miles of desert. With the arrival of the new type of long-distance transport, however, a wide range of goods began to flow our of 'fortunate Arabia'. The new method was quicker, almost independent of water holes and therefore not tied to the old traffic routes which zig-zagged from well to well. It has also a greater capacity. The camel could bear many times the burden which an ass could carry.

The terminus of the Incense Road was Palestine. Solomon's official agents, the 'king's merchants', took delivery of the costly wares. It also depended on them whether the caravans would be

allowed to proceed on their journey through Solomon's kingdom to Egypt, Phoenicia and Syria.

No wonder that 'Solomon's fame' came to the knowledge of the queen of Sheba (1 Kings 10:1). Bearing all this in mind, if we read carefully the tenth chapter of the first book of Kings, we shall think of it no longer as a 'pious story' or a fairy tale. Of course we cannot prove there was a Queen of Sheba in Solomon's time. However, in the eighth century BC women do appear on the Sabaean throne in Assyrian royal inscriptions. *Arriving at Jerusalem with a very great caravan... she came to Solomon and talked with him about all that she had on her mind.* (1 Kings 10:2) The queen of Sheba had assuredly quite a number of things she wanted to talk about. The head of a state whose chief export trade could only be with and through Israel, and that for unavoidable geographical reasons, would certainly have plenty to discuss with the king of that country. We should nowadays describe the affair more concretely as trade talks and should send experts minus crowns to other countries for discussions. They too would carry

with them in their diplomatic bags presents which would show the respect due to the head of the state, like the queen of Sheba.

ISRAEL'S COLOURFUL DAILY LIFE

Amid these revelations of Egyptian, Babylonian or Assyrian splendour to which archaeology has borne witness, we have been inclined to forget until now the grey and apparently monotonous daily life of Israel. Certainly there has been nothing to record which could compare with the golden treasure of Troy, no Tutankhamun, no charming Nofretete. But was the daily life of Israel really so drab, with no colour and no sparkle?

The Israelites loved bright colours. They coloured their dress, the walls of their houses and the faces of their women. Even in the days of the patriarchs their delight in colour was apparent:

Above **The Awwam temple at Marib, consecrated to the national god Ilmuqah, was probably built in the eight century before Christ. Out of the sand-dunes, which have partially covered the remains excavated by Wendell Philips, a row of columns rears up. This is Marib's propylon, or monumental gateway.**

Overleaf **The southern sluices of the great coffer dam at Marib.**

215

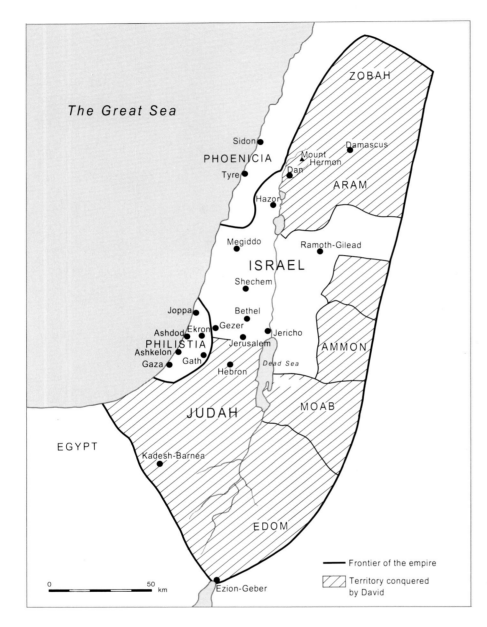

The Great Sea

ZOBAH

Sidon

Damascus

PHOENICIA

Mount
Hermon

Tyre

Dan

ARAM

Hazor

Megiddo

Ramoth-Gilead

ISRAEL

Shechem

Joppa

Bethel

Ashdod

Ekron

Gezer

Jericho

PHILISTIA

Jerusalem

AMMON

Ashkelon

Gaza

Gath

Dead Sea

Hebron

JUDAH

MOAB

EGYPT

Kadesh-Barnea

EDOM

0   50 km

Ezion-Geber

—— Frontier of the empire

/// Territory conquered
     by David

The kingdom of David and Solomon.

Now Israel loved Joseph more than any of his other sons . . . and he made a richly ornamented robe for him (Genesis 37:3). One of the pictures in the tomb at Beni-Hasan shows this type of coat with a wonderful red and blue pattern. Red and blue were the colours for men's wear, green seems to have been reserved for women. During the desert days mention is made of *blue, purple and scarlet* (Exodus 25:4). *O daughters of Israel, weep over Saul, who clothed you in scarlet . . .* (2 Samuel 1:24), cries David in his grief after the death of the first king. *She was wearing a richly ornamented robe,* it is recorded of Tamar, daughter of David, *for this was the kind of garment the virgin daughters of the king*

wore (2 Samuel 13:18).

Nature had given the land of Canaan one of the most wonderful painters' palettes. The children of Israel only needed to stretch out their hands. Pomegranates and saffron yielded a lovely yellow, madder-root and safflower a fiery red, woad a heavenly blue: there was also ochre and red chalk. The sea donated the queen of all dye merchants, the murex snail. Its soft colourless body turned purple in the sunlight. That was its undoing. Vast mountains of empty snail shells have been found at Tyre and Sidon, which leads us to the conclusion that this was the centre for the extraction of purple. The Phoenicians were the first to create a proper industry for the extraction of purple in their seaports, but later Palestine too devoted itself to the profitable business of snail catching.

The textile town of Beth-Asbea in south Judah was famous for byssus, the finest kind of bleached linen. Ten shirts of byssus are actually mentioned in an inscription of Esarhaddon, the mighty king of Assyria. Hebron and Kirjath-Sepher had the reputation of being important centres of the dye industry. Great stone basins and things like cauldrons with inflow and outflow pipes, which were dug up in these places turned out to be dyeing vats. In Tell Beit Mirsim, the ancient Debir, they were au fait even with the technique of cold dyes. He says, *'I will build myself a great palace,'* says Jeremiah (22:14), . . . *So he makes large windows in it, panels it with cedar and decorates it red.* Walls were varnished, mosaic chips and fabrics, leather and wood were dyed, as also were the lips, cheeks, eyelids of beautiful women. *Your lips are like a scarlet ribbon . . . Your temples behind your veil are like the halves of a pomegranate . . . Your hair is like royal tapestry . . . How much more pleasing is . . . the fragrance of your perfume than any spice!* (Song of Songs 4:3; 6:7, 5; 4:10), sings King Solomon himself in his Song of Songs, one of the most beautiful love songs in the world.

In highly poetic language it refers to Israel's delight in adornment and discreetly deals with the secrets of the beauty-parlour. These perfumes and paints, ointments and hair dyes, choice and expensive, manufactured with the best ingredients that the world could provide would still do credit to the much lauded cosmetics industry of Europe and overseas.

Sweet smelling perfumes have always been highly prized; aromatic resins were not only primarily esteemed as incense in the ritual of the temple, but they had also their place in everyday life, in the home, in clothing, on the hair and in divans and beds.

I have covered my bed with coloured linens from Egypt. I have perfumed my bed with myrrh, aloes and cinnamon (Proverbs 7:16f) runs the warning against the artful wiles of the adulteress. *All your robes are fragrant with myrrh and aloes and cassia; from palaces adorned with ivory the music of the strings makes you glad* is the song of praise in Psalm 45:8.

Botanists have investigated these stories that often sound like fairy tales, and have hunted up the ingredients of perfumes and the supplies of dyes. They found them among delicate flowers and herbs, in the sap of shrubs and blossoms. Many came from foreign lands, but many still grow in Palestine today.

From India came cassia (*Cinnamomum Cassia*), a tree with a cinnamon-like bark, and calamus (*Andropogon Aromaticus*). They came across the Indian Ocean to the packing stations for spices in South Arabia and made their way from there by caravan to the Mediterranean countries.

Cinnamon had a world tour behind it. Originally it came from China, then on to Persia, thence to India, where it became indigenous and was exported to Arabia.

Incense was obtained from the *Boswellia* bush. Its home is in Arabia and Somaliland, like the *Commiphora Myrrha*, the myrrh tree. The cradle of the aloe is the island of Socotra at the lower end of the Red Sea, whence comes its name *Aloe Succotrina*.

There was many a dispute about the origin of balsam. The Bible seemed to be really in error, for botanists know very well that the balsam bush (Commiphora Opobalsamum) grows only in Arabia. How could Ezekiel (27:17) claim that Judah and Israel had sent to Tyre *wax, honey, oil and balsam* (Moffatt)?

The botanists and Ezekiel are both right. The botanists had merely forgotten to look up Josephus, the great Jewish historian, where he tells us that there has been balsam in Palestine since the time of Solomon. The bushes were cultivated principally in the neighbourhood of Jericho. Josephus also answers the question as to how they got there. They were reared from seeds which had been found among the spices which the queen of Sheba brought as gifts.

That seems a daring assertion.

But there is a further bit of evidence. When the Romans entered Palestine, they actually found balsam plantations in the plain of Jericho. The conquerors prized the rare shrub so highly that they sent twigs of it to Rome as a sign of their victory over the Jews. In AD70 Titus Vespasian put

an imperial guard in charge of the plantings to protect them from destruction. A thousand years later the Crusaders found no trace of the precious bushes.

Mastic, which Ezekiel also mentions, is still found in Palestine. These are the yellowish-white transparent globules from a pistachio-bush (*Pistacia Lentiscus*). They are greatly valued for their perfume and are used medicinally. Children gladly surrender their last baksheesh for a few drops of this native chewing-gum, which was wisely extolled in ancient times as being good for teeth and gums.

In the Promised Land the following aromatic resins are indigenous: Galbanum from a parsley-shaped plant (Exodus 30:34), Stacte from the Storax bush (Exodus 30:34), Ladanum from the rock-rose and Tragacanth (Genesis 37:25) from a shrub of the clover family. Botanists found all the biblical spices.

The receptacles for these often expensive

To gain a picture of what Solomon's temple in Jerusalem looked like is exceptionally difficult, since excavations on the Temple Mount are impossible. No one knows what remains of this famous building may still lie under the huge temple platform of Herod the Great and the Dome of the Rock of Khalif Omar's successors. So in attempting to reconstruct it (above) we are dependent on the descriptions in 1 Kings chapters 5 to 8 and 2 Chronicles chapters 3 to 6, and also on deductions from similar buildings.

According to these the shrine stood on a pedestal, its entrance flanked by the two pillars of Jakin and Boaz. The building itself consisted of three rooms, one behind the other: the 'antechamber' (ulam), the 'hall' (hekal) and the 'Holy of Holies' (debir). Daylight came mainly through windows in the roof, since the temple was surrounded by vestry-like chambers. For the architecture as for the furnishings we have to look for models in the Canaanite/Phoenician culture. The bronze basins in the temple courts, which served to clean the sacrificial meat, cannot have looked very different from the sacrificial bowl on wheels which was found in a roughly contemporary grave on Cyprus (left).

items have been found by archaeologists under the debris of walls, among the ruins of patrician houses, and in royal palaces. Bowls of limestone, of ivory and sometimes of costly alabaster, with little pestles, were used for mixing the aromatic ingredients of the finest unguents. The recipes of experts in ointments were greatly sought after. Tiny bottles of burnt clay were used for keeping perfumes. In larger jars and jugs the scented spices were replaced with olive oil. Oil was well known for keeping hair and skin in good condition. Even poor folk rubbed it into their hair and skin, without the scented and generally very expensive ingredients. They got plenty of oil from their olive groves.

Washing in water was a daily necessity and was done as a matter of course. People washed before and after meals, washed the feet of their guests and washed themselves each evening. Stone basins, foot baths and clay bowls found throughout the whole country during excavations, confirm the numerous biblical references to this practice. (Genesis 18:4; 19:2; 24:32; Song of Songs 5:3; Job 9:30). Lyes from plants and minerals provided lotions and soap (Jeremiah 2:22; Job 9:30).

My lover is to me a sachet of myrrh resting between my breasts (Song of Songs 1:13). This is a transference of ideas referring to the discreet practice whereby women carried a small bag containing myrrh under their dresses. Neither curling pins, nor hair pins, nor mirrors—brightly polished metal discs—failed to find a place on the dressing table. These important items of beauty culture counted as luxury imports from the Nile, where they had been regarded as indispensable by the wives of the Pharaohs for many centuries.

However much the prophets railed against it they were never able to drive the ancient equivalents of rouge and mascara completely out of the boudoirs of the wealthy.

Women were fond of decorating their hair with delicate yellow sprays of the lovely Loosestrife bush. But they were even more fond of a yellowish red powder which was extracted from the bark and from the leaves of the same shrub. The Arabs call it Henna. With this henna they dyed their hair, their toe nails and their finger nails. Astonished archaeologists found nail varnish of this bright red hue on the hands and feet of Egyptian mummies. Cosmetic laboratories and factories still use henna despite all recent developments. Eyebrows and eyelashes were tinted with Galena, powdered Lapis-lazuli gave the desired shadows on the eyelids. Dried insects provided, as in the modern lipstick, the necessary carmine for a seductive mouth.

In view of the dainty perfume flasks, the ivory ointment boxes, the mixing jars and rouge pots, which have been salvaged from the ruins of Israelite cities, we can well imagine how harsh the threats of the prophet Isaiah sounded in this world which cared so much for colour, cosmetics and perfume: *Instead of fragrance there will be a stench; instead of a sash, a rope; instead of well-dressed hair, baldness; instead of fine clothing, sackcloth; instead of beauty, branding* (Isaiah 3:24).

In the Old Testament there is certainly mention of sitting at table on couches but no one goes to bed in our sense. The bed is a rare de luxe item of furniture.

The question whether the bed was invented in the Nile region is one that we cannot answer with certainty. Naturally beds were to be found in all the countries of the Ancient East and one has even been found in a middle Bronze Age grave (grave H 18) at Jericho. Together with other items this grave also contained a table. It can nevertheless be stated without fear of contradiction that beds were more common in Egypt than elsewhere. With great delight Sinuhe on his return observes: *I slept on a bed once more.* But even 500 years later a bed was still a novelty. For when the Princess of Mitanni, Taduchepa, presumably afterwards Queen Nofretete, was married into the Egyptian royal family, she brought bedspreads as her dowry, admittedly expensively woven, but only bedspreads. The royal palace in her home country did not know what a bed was—everybody slept on the floor.

In Israel too only court circles and the well-to-do possessed so expensive an item. The plain man's bed was his cloak. At night he wrapped himself in it (Exodus 22:27). The law made allowance for this in that while it declared that a man's 'bed' could be taken in pledge, that was only permissible during the day. At night he had to have it back again (Exodus 22:26). A lucky chance led to the discovery in 1959 among the ruins of Yavne Yam, eight miles south of Tel Aviv, of a unique document which records an actual case of a cloak being taken in pledge. In a letter of the seventh century BC, the text of which is clearly written in ink on a fragment of pottery, an 'ostracon', a peasant from whom such a cloak had been taken in pledge, defends himself against the charge of being in debt. The archaeologists could make out distinctly... *And he took thy servant's cloak after I had brought in the harvest... and all my brothers will testify truthfully on my behalf that I am not in his debt.* The 'cloak' was in reality only a woollen cover and seems to have been designed for any emergency. As well as keeping out the cold in our sense and serving as a bed it was also used as a carpet (2 Kings 9:13; Matthew 21:7, 8).

The bed was never regarded as the ideal place to rest either in Israel or in the ancient East in general. It was a foreign institution and always remained so. Its cousin the divan, however, likewise a product of the 'Fertile Crescent', became famous for its comfort and its cushions. With its arrangement of pillows during the day, which were spread out at night, it was the prototype of our modern variety. What even bombed-out Central Europe and the smallest twentieth-century households have been able to afford was the last word in furniture 3,000 years ago. The divan was also known in Israel. *You sat on an elegant couch, with a table spread before it...* (Ezekiel 23:41).

We are prone to thunder against the nerve shattering noise of our machine age and often wish the good old days of peace and quiet would come back again. Was Israel any better off?

Instead of the blaring of loudspeakers, from daybreak onwards houses and tents echoed to the sound of stone hand-mills. At crack of dawn began the grinding of the corn and pounding it into flour. This was as much the women's job as grinding coffee is in that part of the world today. Only grinding flour with a millstone was incomparably harder and heavier work.

The threat of a thorough-going anti-noise campaign which is often talked about nowadays would have meant something frightful in those circumstances. If the noise of the mill stopped, hunger crept over the land. Jeremiah had a vision of this as he foretold what would happen during the Exile in Babylon: *I will banish from them the sounds of joy and gladness... the sound of the millstones and the light of the lamp. This whole country will become a desolate wasteland...* (Jeremiah 25:10, 11).

Below **In the ancient Orient, cosmetic palettes often served both male and female beauty. While ordinary people used simple mussel shells in which to grind the colours for their make-up and mix them with oil, more elevated society could afford stone palettes. This example from the Amman Museum, made of veined alabaster and decorated with a head, originates from the seventh century BC.**

Opposite **Work at home as well as in workshops must have been the same everywhere in the ancient Orient. We owe the most lifelike portrayals to the Egyptian wooden models from the tombs of the Eleventh Dynasty. Daily bread was normally baked by the housewife herself, and grinding flour was also one of her duties (above). Millstones have been found in their thousands in residential areas. However, the production of fine linen and colourful woven woollen material, as shown in many wall paintings, demanded businesses employing qualified craftspeople.**

Two Kings, Two Kingdoms: Judah and Israel

> *When all Israel saw that the king refused to listen to them, they answered the king: What share do we have in David, what part in Jesse's son? To your tents, O Israel! Look after your own house, O David! ... So Israel has been in rebellion against the house of David to this day.*
>
> 1 Kings 12:16, 19–20

THE SHADOW OF A NEW WORLD POWER

Solomon the Great died in 926BC. The dream of Israel as a great power was buried with him for ever. Under the leadership of two unusually gifted men—David and Solomon—this ambitious dream had been built up stone by stone for two generations. But at the very moment of Solomon's passing, the old tribal dissensions broke out again and the empire of Syria and Palestine was shattered as the inevitable end of the quarrel. Two kingdoms took its place—the kingdom of Israel in the north, the kingdom of Judah in the south. A new chapter in the history of the people of the Bible had begun.

It was the Israelite people themselves that gnawed away their own foundations and destroyed their empire. It became only too plain what road they proposed to follow slowly until the bitter end when the inhabitants of Israel fell a prey to the Assyrians, and the inhabitants of Judah a prey to the Babylonians. Divided among themselves, what happened to them was worse than simply sinking back into obscurity. They were caught between the millstones of the great powers which were in the following centuries to dominate the world stage. Israel and Judah collapsed amid a welter of dispute and barely 350 years after Solomon's death both kingdoms were no more.

Solomon's last wish was certainly carried out: his son Rehoboam sat on the throne at Jerusalem for a short spell as ruler of all the tribes. The endless quarrelling of the tribes among themselves hastened the end of the empire, since this resulted in civil war. Ten tribes in the north insisted on their right to elect a ruler, and chose Jeroboam, who was not descended from David. He had lived as an exile in Egypt, from where he returned in 926BC to become king of Israel. The remainder stayed faithful to Rehoboam, and formed Judah in the south with its capital Jerusalem (1 Kings 12:19, 20).

There was no harmony between Judah and Israel. They shed each other's blood in feud after

The storming of the Elamite royal town of Chamanu by the troops of the Assyrian king Ashurbanipal. Alabaster relief from Ashurbanipal's northern palace at Nineveh (British Museum, London).

feud. Time and again fighting broke out on the question of frontiers. *There was continual warfare between Rehoboam and Jeroboam* (1 Kings 14:30). It was no different under their successors. *There was war between Asa and Baasha king of Israel throughout their reigns* (1 Kings 15:16). Judah built the fortress of Mizpah on the main strategic route from Jerusalem to the north, further to the east they strengthened Geba ... *With them King Asa built up Geba in Benjamin, and also Mizpah* (1 Kings 15:22). That was the final frontier.

From 1927–35 an American expedition from the Pacific School of Religion, under the direction of William Frederick Bade, excavated abnormally massive stonework at Tell en-Nasbe, 7 miles north of Jerusalem. It was the remains of the old frontier fortress of Mizpah. The enclosing wall was 26 feet thick. This tremendous defensive wall shows how hard and bitter was the civil war that raged between north and south.

Israel was hemmed in on both sides: by Judah on the south, and in the north by the kingdom of the Aramaeans, whose powerful aid had been secured by Judah through an alliance (1 Kings 15:18ff).

The conflict with this deadly enemy, vastly superior in power, lasted half a century, and the continuous sequence of wars did not end until the new world power Assyria had crushed the Aramaeans. But with the emergence of Assyria Israel's days, indeed the days of both kingdoms, were numbered.

Over and above all this, just after the civil was had started the country suffered unexpectedly the first foreign invasion for generations. In the year 918 Pharaoh Sheshonk of Egypt, known in the Bible as Shishak, attacked with his armies and marched through the country, plundering as he went. His greatest haul was from the old capital Jerusalem ... *Shishak king of Egypt attacked Jerusalem. He carried off the treasures of the temple of the Lord and the treasures of the royal palace. He took everything, including all the gold shields Solomon had made* (1 Kings 14:25, 26). The Temple and the House of Lebanon, as the Bible calls the royal palace, had hardly been standing twenty years, and already these proud tokens of Solomon's greatness were robbed of their glory. Instead of the golden shields which had been plundered *King Rehoboam made bronze shields to replace them* (1 Kings 14:27). It was an ill-omened act.

The first European of note to stand in front of a large document of the Pharaoh whom the Bible calls Shishak was Napoleon Bo-

naparte. He was not aware of it however since at that time no one had as yet deciphered hieroglyphics. It was in 1799 that he wandered, deeply impressed, with a company of French scholars, through a vast Egyptian temple area at Karnak on the east side of Thebes. In the middle of this, the greatest temple area ever constructed by human hands, 134 columns up to 75 feet high support the ceiling of a colossal court. On the outer wall, on the south side, an imposing relief which perpetuates the marauding expedition of this Pharaoh stands out boldly in the bright sunshine of the Nile.

The god Amun, holding in his right hand a sickle-shaped sword, brings to Pharaoh Sheshonk I 156 manacled Palestinian prisoners who are attached by cords to his left hand. Every prisoner represents a city or a village. Some of them have biblical names such as *the king of Arad* (Joshua

One hundred and thirty-eight conquered towns in Palestine are listed in a victory document of Egyptian Pharaoh Sheshonk in the temple of Karnak (above). The goal of his campaign was to restore Egyptian supremacy in this area, but the enterprise only succeeded in being a plundering expedition, in which the Pharaoh overran even Jerusalem and 'carried off the treasures of the temple of the Lord and the treasures of the royal palace' and 'took everything' (1 Kings 14:26). For centuries the booty of Egyptian military campaigns went to the imperial god Amun. From it Sethos I and Rameses II built the 'great hall of pillars' at Karnak (opposite).

In addition to its frieze of military exploits, the throne room of the Assyrian king Ashurnasirpal was decorated with hunting scenes.

Hunting of wild bulls and lions was more than a royal privilege and entertainment; it also symbolized the defeat of enemies. The cultic character of the royal hunt is underlined by the accompanying festival with sacrifices to the gods. Behind this custom, in the last analysis, stands the Bible's reference to Nimrod, the 'mighty hunter before the Lord'. This legendary ruler and founder of Nineveh and Calah was linked to the Assyrian and Babylonian god of war and hunting, Ninurta, and it was with him that Ashurnasirpal identified himself.

12:14; Judges 1:16) and *the Field of Abraham*. The fortified city of Megiddo is among those represented, and in the ruins of Megiddo the name of Sheshonk I has been found.

Sheshonk's campaign was for a long time the last. Not for more than 300 years was Egypt again in a position to enforce its ancient claim to the suzerainty of the Syrian-Palestine territories.

The deadly danger that faced Israel came from the north—Assyria. During the reign of King Omri (882–871BC) Assyria prepared to pounce. As if in a practice manoeuvre for the real thing it tried a thrust westwards from Mesopotamia.

From Aleppo I launched the attack and crossed the Orontes. This sentence from a cuneiform inscription of Ashurnasirpal II rings out like an opening fanfare of trumpets. It had taken Assyria over 200 years to dispose of its enemies inside and outside Mesopotamia. From the ancient city of Ashur on the Tigris, which bore the name of their chief god, the Semitic race of Assyrians, eager for conquest and skilled in administration, had extended their dominion over all the peoples of Mesopotamia. Now their eyes were fixed on the conquest of the world. The prelude to that had to be the possession of the narrow coastal strip of Syria and Palestine which barred the way to the Mediterranean, as well as the occupation of the important seaports, the control of the chief caravan routes and of the only military road into Egypt.

When Assyria set itself this target the fate of Syria and Palestine was sealed.

The report of Ashurnasirpal indicates briefly what was also in store for Israel and Judah. *I marched from the Orontes... I conquered the cities... I caused great slaughter, I destroyed, I demolished, I burned. I took their warriors prisoner and impaled them on stakes before their cities. I settled Assyrians in their place. ... I washed my weapons in the Great Sea.*

As unexpectedly as the Assyrians had appeared, so with equal abruptness they departed, laden with *silver, gold, lead, copper*, the tribute of the Phoenician cities of Tyre, Sidon and Byblos.

King Omri of Israel heard of all this with dark foreboding. This former army officer however still showed his outstanding flair for soldiering now that he had become king. In the heart of the Samarian highlands he bought a hill on which he built a new capital for Israel, the stronghold of Samaria (1 Kings 16:24).

The choice of a site revealed the expert who was guided by strategic considerations. Samaria lies on a solitary hill, about 300 feet high, which

rises gently out of a broad and fertile valley and is surrounded by a semi-circle of higher mountains. The view westwards from the summit extends as far as the Mediterranean.

King Omri made an impression on the Assyrians. A century after his dynasty had crashed Israel was still officially called *The House of Omri* in cuneiform texts.

Eighteen years after Omri's death what they had dreaded actually happened. Shalmaneser III fell upon Carchemish on the Euphrates and was on his way to Palestine.

Ahab, Omri's son who succeeded him on the throne, guessed what a violent clash with the rising world-power of Assyria would mean and did the only proper thing in the circumstances. He had recently beaten his old enemy Ben-Hadad of Damascus, king of the Aramaeans. Instead of letting him taste to the full the victor's power, he handled him with unwonted magnanimity, he *had him come up into his chariot*, called him *my brother*, made *a treaty with him, and let him go* (1 Kings 20:33, 32, 34). So he made an ally out of an enemy. His people misunderstood his policy and one of the prophets took him to task. Only the future would show how well he had known what he was doing. War on two fronts had been avoided.

In sheepskin boats I crossed the Euphrates in flood, runs the cuneiform report of Shalmaneser III, King of Assyria.

In Syria he was met by an opposing coalition, and he took careful note of how the army was made up. Apart from the troops of the biblical Ben-Hadad on Damascus and another Syrian prince, there were *2,000 chariots and 10,000 horses belonging to Ahabbu the Sirilaean*. Ahabbu the Sirilaean, who provided the third strongest army, was king of Israel.

The alliance between Israel and Damascus did not last long. Hardly had the Assyrians left the country when the old enmities broke out again and Ahab lost his life fighting the Aramaeans. (1 Kings 22:34–38)

The Bible devotes six chapters to the life of this king. Much of it has been dismissed as legend, such as *the palace he built and inlaid with ivory* (1 Kings 22:39), or his marriage to a Phoenician princess, who brought with her a strange religion, *... he married Jezebel daughter of Ethbaal king of the Sidonians, and began to serve Baal and worship him... Ahab also made an Asherah pole...* (1 Kings 16:31, 33—RV) or the great drought in the land,

Elijah ... said to Ahab, 'As the Lord, the God of Israel, lives, whom I serve, there will be neither dew nor rain in the next few years except at my word' (1 Kings 17:1).

None the less they are historical facts.

Two great assaults have been made on the old ruined mound of Samaria. The first campaign was led by George A. Reisner, Clarence S. Fisher, and D.G. Lyon of the University of Harvard from 1908-10, the second excavation by an Anglo-American team under the British archaeologist J.W. Crowfoot from 1931-35.

The foundations of Israel's capital rest on virgin soil. Omri had in fact acquired new land.

During the six years when he reigned there this otherwise peaceful and lonely hill must have been one great bustling building site. The huge blocks of the strong fortifications make the strategic intention of the builder plain. The walls are 15 feet thick. On the acropolis on the west side of the hill foundations and walls of a building were exposed. This enclosed a wide courtyard and was the royal palace of the northern kingdom of Israel.

After Omri, Ahab his son, the new king, lived here. He continued building in accordance with his father's plans. The construction was carried out with remarkable skill, nothing but these huge carefully dressed limestone blocks being used.

As the rubble was being carted off the diggers very quickly noticed the innumerable splinters of ivory that it contained. Finds of ivory itself are nothing unusual in Palestinian excavation. On almost every site this expensive material is encountered, but always in isolated pieces, yet in Samaria the ground is literally covered with them. At every step, every square yard, they came across these yellowish brown chips and flakes, as well as fragments which still showed the marvellous

A long frieze of alabaster reliefs from the palace of Ashurnasirpal II in Calah portrays the military exploits of the king (British Museum, London). One particularly impressive scene shows the siege of a town, which is still trying to fend off the attackers, but is not going to be a match for their armoured battering rams (above). The siege tower, equally mobile, rears up right to the top of the city walls. It serves both as an artillery tower and as a means for the attackers to scale the fortifications. It is not long before the king receives the report of victory (below).

Ivory carvings adorn furniture, jewellery boxes, cosmetic implements, and, though more rarely, even walls. In most cases the wooden object which they once decorated has not survived. These ivories were almost never found in the place where they were made, indeed rarely even at the court which first acquired them, since precious items of this kind were often carried off as plunder or extorted as tribute several times. This work has mostly been classified as 'Phoenician'. The raw material must have been acquired in large measure from Egypt, though some of it could also have come from Syrian elephants. It was in the 'Ivory House' of Samaria that this attractive edging patterned with palm leaf motifs (above left) was found; the Egyptian-looking woman's head in a window (above right) came from Nimrud.

craftsmanship of these elegant reliefs carved by Phoenician masters.

There was only one explanation of these finds: this palace was the famous 'ivory palace' of King Ahab (1 Kings 22:39). Ahab and his successors had the rooms of the palace decorated with this wonderful material and filled them with ivory furniture.

The proofs of the historical basis for the drought and for Ahab's father-in-law Ethbaal were provided by Menander of Ephesus, a Phoenician historian. The Ethbaal of the Bible was called Ittobaal by the Phoenicians and in Ahab's day he was king of the port of Tyre. Menander records the catastrophic drought which set in throughout Palestine and Syria during the reign of Ittobaal and lasted a whole year.

U nder King Jehoram, Ahab's son, Israel suffered an invasion which had terrible consequences and resulted in a considerable loss of territory.

The Aramaeans attacked them and besieged Samaria. A frightful famine racked the inhabitants. Jehoram, who held the prophet Elisha responsible for it, wanted to have him put to death. Elisha however prophesied that the famine would end on the following day. As the Bible records, the officer on whose arm the king was leaning (2 Kings 7:2), doubted this prophecy.

This 'officer' has given rise to great discussions. Nothing was known of any office of this sort. Biblical commentators sought in vain for some explanation. Eventually philologists found a slight clue. The Hebrew word shalish, which has been translated as 'officer', comes from the word

for 'three'. But there was never a third-class officer. When Assyrian reliefs were examined more closely the true explanation was found.

Every chariot was manned by three men: the driver, the fighter, and a man who stood behind them. With outstretched arms he held on to two short straps which were fastened to the right and left sides of the chariot. In this way he protected the warrior and the driver in the rear and prevented them from being thrown out during those furious sallies in battle when the open car passed over dead and wounded men. This then was the 'third man'. The inexplicable officer on whose arm the king was leaning was the strap-hanger in King Jehoram's chariot.

Under Jehoram Israel lost a large slice of territory east of the Jordan. Moab in Transjordan was a tributary of Israel. There is a detailed account of a campaign against Mesha, the rebellious 'Mutton-King': Now Mesha king of Moab raised sheep, and he had to supply the king of Israel with a hundred thousand rams. But after Ahab died, the king of Moab rebelled against the king of Israel (2 Kings 3:4, 5). Israel summoned to her aid the southern kingdom, Judah, and the land of Edom.

They decided to make a joint attack on Moab from the south. This meant going round the Dead Sea. Relying on the prophecy: You will neither see wind nor rain, yet this valley will be filled with water, and you, your cattle and your other animals will drink (2 Kings 3:17), the allies venture to march through that desolate country. After a roundabout march of seven days, the army had no more water for themselves or for the animals with them. On the advice of the prophet Elisha they made the valley full of ditches. The next morning . . . there it was— water flowing from the direction of Edom! And the land was filled with water. This was seen by spies from Moab, to whom the water looked red—like blood (2 Kings 3:9, 16, 20, 22) and thought that the enemy were fighting among themselves.

The allied forces were successful in Moab, they laid waste the land, They destroyed the towns, and each man threw a stone on every good field until it was covered. They stopped up all the springs and cut down every good tree. Only Kir Hareseth was left with its stones in place (2 Kings 3:25).

Oddly enough the end of this successful campaign was that they withdrew and returned to their own land (2 Kings 3:27).

It seemed impossible to check up on the accuracy of this biblical story.

In 1868, F.A. Klein, a missionary from Alsace, was visiting biblical sites in Palestine. The route he followed took him, among other places, through

Transjordan, through Edom and eventually to Moab. As he was riding in the neighbourhood of Diban, the ancient Dibon on the middle reaches of the Arnon, his attention was particularly aroused by a large smooth stone. The yellow sand had almost completely drifted over it. Klein jumped from his horse and bent over the stone curiously. It bore unmistakably ancient Hebrew writing. He could hardly believe his eyes. It was as much as he could do in the heat of the mid-day sun to stand the heavy basalt stone upright. It was three feet high and rounded on top. Klein cleaned it carefully with a knife and a handkerchief. Thirty-four lines of writing appeared.

He would have preferred to take the stone document away with him there and then, but it was far too heavy. Besides, in no time a mob of armed Arabs was on the spot. With wild gesticulations they surrounded the missionary, maintaining that the stone was their property and demanding from him a fantastic price for it.

Klein guessed that his discovery was an important one and was in despair. He tried in vain to

An ivory cow with her little calf was among the forced tribute which King Ben-Hadad of Damascus had to pay to Assyria (above). The winged sphinx (left) from the 'Ivory House' of Samaria corresponds to the emblem of majesty of the throne of the Phoenician kings. Vastly inflated prices must have been paid for luxury objects decorated with ivory. It was in vain that the prophet Amos thundered against such indulgence at the royal court in Samaria.

make the natives change their minds. There was nothing for it but to mark the site carefully on his map. He then gave up the idea of continuing his journey, hurried back to Jerusalem and from there straight home to Germany to try to collect the

Since the time of David, the Moabites had to pay tribute to Israel. Apparently Moab had to deliver 100,000 lambs and the wool of 100,000 rams. After the collapse of David's kingdom the tribute to the northern kingdom of Israel remained in force. Towards 850BC, Israel was increasingly threatened by the Aramaeans and a joint campaign by the kings of Israel and Judah —Jehoram and Jehoshaphat. This was repelled by the Moabites, and only then was Moab able to free itself from its vassal status, shake off the obligation of tribute and even win back some towns.

The stela of the Moabite king Mesha in the Louvre museum provides a record of this development. It was set up in a 'high place' at Diban, probably towards the end of the ninth century BC, and was discovered there in 1868. Fortunately an impression of the inscription was taken before the stela was smashed to pieces by Arab traders. As was customary in the ancient Orient, King Mesha is not backward in coming forward about his accomplishments. First he complains of the oppression of his country by Omri and his successors, but then 'I gained the upper hand over him and over his house; and Israel was destroyed for ever'. There follows a long list of towns which have been won back and rebuilt. Unfortunately the last lines of the basalt block, with Mesha's concluding hymn of praise to himself, are missing.

necessary money for the Arabs.

But in the meantime other people got busy, which was a good thing. Otherwise an extremely valuable piece of evidence for biblical history might well have been lost for ever.

A French scholar, Clermont-Ganneau, who was working in Jerusalem, had heard of the German missionary's discovery and had at once set out for Diban. It needed all his powers of persuasion to get the suspicious Arabs even to allow him to examine the writing on the basalt stone. Surrounded by the hostile eyes of the natives, Clermont-Ganneau took a squeeze of the surface. Months later, when Parisian scholars had translated the text, the French government sanctioned the purchase without hesitation. But judge the Frenchman's disappointment when he reached Diban, equipped with a caravan and the necessary sum of money, and found that the stone had disappeared. Only a patch of soot indicated the spot where it had been. The Arabs had blown it to pieces with gunpowder—for they hoped to do a more profitable trade with Europeans whose obsession with antiquity would

make them willing to buy individual pieces.

What could Clermont-Ganneau do but set out on the trail of the individual pieces of the valuable document. After a great deal of trouble and searching, and after endless haggling, he was successful in retrieving some of the broken fragments. Two larger blocks and eighteen smaller pieces were reassembled and completed in accordance with the squeeze, and before Klein had even collected the necessary money, the impressive stone from Diban was standing among the valuable recent acquisitions in the Louvre in Paris.

This is what it says: *I am Mesha, son of Chemosh, king of Moab . . . My father was king of Moab for thirty years and I became king after my father: and I built this sanctuary to Chemosh in Qerihoh, a sanctuary of refuge: for he saved me from all my oppressors and gave me dominion over all my enemies. Omri was king of Isrel and oppressed Moab many days, for Chemosh was angry with his land. And his son succeeded him and he also said, I will oppress Moab. In my days he said this: but I got the upperhand of him and his house: and Israel perished for ever . . . I have had the ditches of Qerihoh dug by Israelite prisoners . . .*

This Moabite victory message aroused considerable interest in learned circles. Many scholars did not conceal their suspicion that it was a forgery. International experts scrutinized the stone and its inscription. All the tests made it plain beyond doubt that this was in fact a historical document, a contemporary record of the King. Mesha of Moab who is mentioned in the Bible.

It is also Palestine's oldest written document, dating from about 840BC in Moabite dialect, which is closely related to biblical Hebrew. That caused a real sensation.

If we want an objective picture it is always advisable to study the war-diaries of both opponents. There is more likelihood of getting a clearer picture of the real situation. In this particular case, as it happens, the biblical description and the text of the stela supplement each other admirably. The Mesha-stela adds the necessary colour to the biblical narrative and illumines its obscurity. The stela and the Bible agree on the decisive point, namely that the campaign ended with the defeat of the Israelite king. The Bible describes at length the initial success of Israel, which King Mesha passes over in silence. The unfortunate outcome of the campaign is only briefly hinted at in the Bible, whereas the Moabite king revels in his victory. Both are telling the truth.

As far as the 'blood-red water' is concerned, which saved the allies from dying of thirst on their

march through this barren country, a geologist found a natural explanation. If trenches are dug in the tufa beside the Dead Sea, they fill up with water at once, which seeps through from the high plateau and owes its reddish colour to the character of the soil. To this day shepherds in Transjordan often manufacture water-holes in exactly the same manner.

And Israel perished for ever, says the Mesha-stela triumphantly. By this is meant the bloody extirpation of the dynasty of Omri from the throne of Israel. Jehoram was killed. Not one member was spared of the ruling house which had propagated the worship of Baal in Israel through King Ahab's marriage to the Phoenician princess Jezebel (2 Kings 9:24ff: 10:11ff).

The prophets Elijah and Elisha stirred up the overthrow of the dynasty, and in 841BC the commander of the army, Jehu, who was loyal to Yahweh, was raised to the throne (2 Kings 9:1ff). The priests of Baal shared the fate of Omri's family; they were mercilessly slaughtered (2 Kings 10:25ff). This resulted in a break with the Phoenicians.

Information about King Jehu's reign is scanty: *In those days the Lord began to reduce the size of Israel. Hazael overpowered the Israelites throughout their territory* (2 Kings 10:32). The total extent of the losses in men and material first becomes plain in a passage about the reign of Jehoahaz, son of Jehu: *Nothing had been left of the army of Jehoahaz except fifty horsemen, ten chariots and ten thousand foot soldiers, for the king of Aram had destroyed the rest and made them like the dust at threshing time* (2

Kings 13:7). Ahab's proud chariot-corps was reduced from 2,000 to ten. How could that have happened?

A young Englishman, Henry Layard, a lawyer by profession and attaché-elect at Constantinople, had an incredible stroke of luck as a novice in archaeology in 1845. With literally only £50 in his pocket he had set out to excavate an old mound on the Tigris, Tell Nimrud. On the third day he came upon remains of a palace. He dug a trench, but nothing but masses and masses and sand came out of it. When the trench was 20 feet deep Layard had to stop work, to his great disappointment, as his money had run out.

He was feeling depressed as he loaded his few tools on to the pack-mules, when excited cries from the natives made him pause. One of them ran up to him and got him to go and look at the end of the trench where something dark was showing up against the golden yellow sand. Digging was hastily resumed and produced a huge pure black stone in the shape of an obelisk. Layard tenderly cleaned the ancient dust and dirt off his find. And now he could see reliefs, pictures and inscriptions in cuneiform writing on all four sides.

Well wrapped up and guarded like the apple of his eye the black stone sailed up the Tigris in one of the river-boats to be presented to the more than somewhat astonished officials of the British Embassy in Constantinople.

Proudly the technicians cleared a fitting site

Above left **The tribal area of the Moabites lay to the east of the Jordan between the lands of the Ammonites in the north and Edom in the south. Here the Wadi el-Hesa served as a border.**

Above right **Basalt fragment showing a Moabite warrior (Louvre, Paris).**

for the stone in the British Museum. Thousands of Londoners and European scholars marvelled at this ancient piece of evidence from the distant east. The tip of the 6 foot obelisk of black basalt is in the shape of a three-tiered temple tower. Visitors gazed in astonishment at the wonderful reliefs displayed in the five rows round the column.

Magnificently attired royal personages are chiseled out as in real life: some of them prostrate themselves with their faces to the ground in front of a commanding figure. Long columns of bearers are laden with costly treasures, such as ivory tusks, bales of fringed fabrics borne on poles, pitchers and baskets full to the brim. Among the animals included can be observed an elephant

with remarkably small ears: there are camels with two humps, apes, antelopes, even a wild bull and a mysterious unicorn.

Anyone trying to interpret the meaning of the reliefs was thrown back on pure conjecture. For at that time no one could read cuneiform script. The stone remained dumb. Even the scholars learned no more about the Assyrians than the Bible told them. At the beginning of the nineteenth century even the names Sumerian and Akkadian meant nothing. 'One box, not more then three feet square,' wrote Layard, 'fitted with little inscribed cylinders, seals and textual fragments, which could not even be systematically arranged, were at that time all that London knew of the early period

These bronze strips of relief covered a double gate almost four metres high at Imgur Elil (Balawat), which was presented to the city by the Assyrian King Shalmaneser II (British Museum, London). They depict in long rows the king's military campaigns to the Mediterranean and against Urartu: sieges, victories, conquests, prisoners in endless lines, booty of great value. One exception is the Phoenician island city of Tyre (second row, left). It was indeed besieged by the Assyrians, frequently and for long periods, but never overcome. But Shalmaneser II did succeed in ex-

tracting a tribute from the rich seaport, which was probably still cheaper for the Tyrians than years of blockade of their lucrative trade. So the Tyrians ferry over to the mainland and bring the king the requested ransom money.

of Mesopotamian history.'

It was only later, when the text had been translated, that it transpired that the black obelisk was a victory monument by the Assyrian king, Shalmaneser III contemporary and adversary of King Ahab of Israel. It celebrates an endless succession of bloody campaigns.

The enumeration of them contains an extremely interesting cross-reference to the biblical tradition dealing with the period.

Three times, in the sixth, eleventh, and fourteenth year of his reign, the Assyrian came up against a coalition of kings of Syria and Palestine during his victorious incursions into the West. In the campaign in the eighteenth year of his reign

however only one king opposed him in this territory. The Assyrian texts name as the adversary only King Hazael of Damascus, whom the Bible also mentions.

But the victory monument gives ample information about the former ally of the king of Damascus, Jehu of Israel.

The second row of the relief shows a long queue of heavily laden envoys in richly ornamented tunics and peaked caps. The relevant text reads: *Tribute of Jaua of Bit-Humri: Silver, gold, a golden bowl, a golden tankard, golden beakers, golden pitchers, tin, a staff for the king and a wooden object.*

Jaua of Bit-Humri is none other than King Jehu

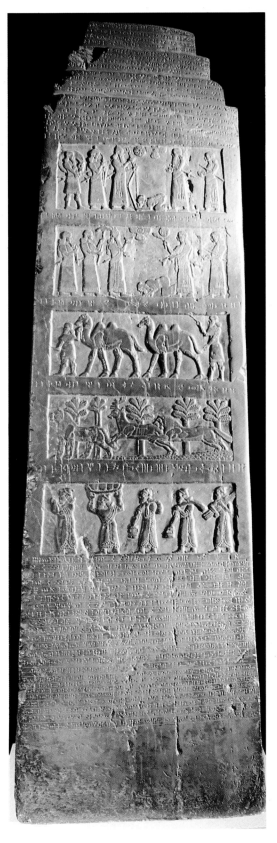

From Tell Nimrud (Calah) English-man Henry Layard, one of the first and most important Assyriologists of the nineteenth century, excava-ted the world-famous Black Obe-lisk, now in the British Museum. This monument, two metres high and carved out of black alabaster, glorifies the deeds of the Assyrian king Shalmaneser III, who reigned from 858 to 824BC. Its top and its lower section are covered with a long inscription chronicling events. In between, each of the four sides bears five relief friezes. From the commentary above the bands of relief, we learn that friezes on the same level belong together. The top two series of pictures contain scenes of homage paid by King Sua of Gilzan (west of the Sea of Urmia) and King Jehu of Israel (detail, opposite). Both have prostrated themselves before the Assyrian king, while their follow-ers bring the tribute. According to the inscriptions, the Gilzanites brought 'silver, gold, lead, copper vessels, staffs for the hand of the king, horses and two-humped camels', and the Israelites 'silver, gold, a golden bowl, a golden tan-kard, golden beakers, golden jugs, tin, a staff for the king and a wooden object'.

Below this follow the gifts from the land of Musri (which may mean India): 'Bactrian camels, water buffalo, gayal (East Indian oxen), black buck, elephants and apes', the tribute of Marduk-pla'usur of Suchi (on the middle Euphrates): 'silver, gold, golden tankards, ivory, spears and robes', and that of Karparunda of Hattina (northern Syria): 'silver, gold, lead, copper, copper vessels, ivory and cypress wood'.

The Israelite tribute carriers, thirteen in all, are all bearded. Pointed, 'nightcap-style' caps and headbands decorate their heads. Their costume is composed of a long chemise with a belt and frin-ges on the hem, a long cloak, also edged with fringes, slung over one shoulder, and pointed shoes.

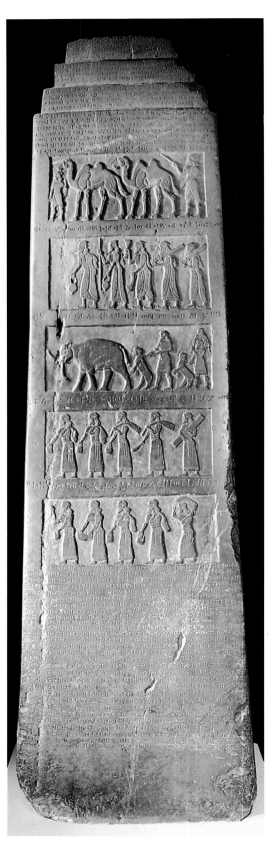

Above **Detail of the reliefs on the Black Obelisk. Jehu, son of Omri, pays homage to Shalmaneser III. The king of Israel lies in the dust before the Assyrian king, who is pouring an offering out of a bowl to the god Ashur, symbolized by the winged sun. Four servants assist the ruler. The one standing behind him holds a sunshade, the one in front of him is waving a fan.**

of Israel. The Assyrians called Israel *Bit-Humri*, which means 'House of Omri'.

This hint from the royal palace on the Tigris provides the key to our understanding of the losses which the northern kingdom of Israel sustained during the reign of Jehu.

Tribute is only paid by those who voluntarily surrender: a vanquished enemy supplies loot. Jehu had been disloyal to Damascus and had brought gifts to the Assyrians. For his faithlessness towards an old ally, for deserting Damascus, Jehu and his son Jehoahaz and most of all the people of Israel had to pay a bitter price. Hardly had the Assyrians turned their backs on Syria then Hazael of Damascus began to make a destructive onslaught on Israel in revenge. The result of it is described in the Bible: *In those days the Lord began to reduce the size of Israel. Hazael overpowered the Israelites throughout their territory.*

The fact that Assyria had, after Shalmaneser III, a succession of weak kings, allowed both kingdoms, Israel and Judah, another respite, which however meant only a postponement. Since Assyria was occupied with unrest in its own territory, Israel and Judah were able to enjoy a spell of peace in the first half of the eighth century BC.

For forty years Uzziah, the leper, reigned as king of Judah. Israel was governed by Jeroboam II. Under his long rule Israel flourished again, became rich, wallowed in luxury, and the aristocracy lived for themselves and for the moment, effete, corrupt and vicious. The prophet Amos raised his voice in warning. He lashed out at their unbridled love of pleasure.

Archaeological reports and dry accounts of expeditions shed a powerful light upon these prophetic warnings. In Israel, in and around the old mound of ruins that represented ancient Samaria, evidence was laying dormant which would indicate this materialism and luxury in the soil strata from the decades in the reign of Jeroboam II. The royal palace of Samaria contained a considerable number of elegant clay tablets inscribed with ink and paint. On sixty-three of these invoices for wine and oil which had been delivered at the Court the senders are the managers of the crown lands of Jeroboam II.

From the same period comes a number of beautifully carved ivories, some of which are expensively embellished with gold and semi-precious stones and ornamented with colourful powdered glass. They show motifs borrowed from Egypt, like Harpocrates on the lotus flower or figures of gods like Isis and Horus or cherubs. At

235

In the excavations at Arslan Tash (Hadatu) in Syria a whole treasure-house of ivory carvings came to light, which had once served as decorative mountings for beds and other furniture. Phoenician and Syrian work of this kind was coveted in the whole of the Near East and there was a lively trade. It seems certain that the finds at Hadatu represent booty from Damascus, which was carried off by the Assyrian conquerors in 732BC. On the basis of their style the carvings must have been made at least a hundred years earlier, and anyway an inscribed fragment names Hazael, who was king of Damascus between 840 and 810BC.

This ivory figure of a ruler, acquired by the Louvre Museum, is thought to be a portrait of Hazael. The second Book of Kings tells us that the king of the Aramaeans fought successfully against Joram and Jehoahaz of Israel, and Jerusalem could turn away the threat of conquest by Hazael only by paying a tribute from the temple treasures.

that time all over Israel granaries and storehouses were being built to hold goods of all descriptions whose supply exceeded demand.

What was the reason for this sudden change? To what did they owe their new found riches?

A few decades previously things had looked black for Israel. A sentence from the record of the forty-one-year reign of Jeroboam II contains the clue to the problem: *He was the one who restored the boundaries of Israel from Lebo Hamath to the sea of Arabah* (2 Kings 14:25). The *sea of Arabah* is the Dead Sea. Once again the kingdom stretched into Transjordan and—as in David's and Solomon's time—up to Syria.

The conquest of Damascus by the Assyrians in 802BC had broken the power of the Aramaeans and thereby—it sounds as if fate were being ironical—cleared Israel's arch-enemy out of the way. Israel seized the opportunity to reconquer long-lost territory, exploited the situation to its own advantage and the tribute exacted from Transjordan proved a source of new wealth for Israel.

Evidence of a similar period of peace and prosperity in the southern kingdom of Judah has recently come to hand. Professor Michael Evenari, vice-president of the Hebrew University, discovered in 1958 traces of several Judean farms equipped with cisterns, irrigation systems, and fortifications, for south in the arid Negeb near Mizpeh Ramon. The finds date from the reign of Uzziah, king of Judah. We are specifically told in 2 Chronicles 26:10 that this king *built towers in the desert and dug many cisterns, because he had much livestock in the foothills and in the plain.*

In 1959 Professor Aharoni of the Hebrew University was the first to discover a Judean palace two miles south of Jerusalem. On Rachel's hill on the road to Bethlehem, at the spot where, according to tradition, Mary and Joseph on their way to Bethlehem 'to be taxed' refreshed themselves at the spring, the site of a large castle was excavated, 250 feet by 150 feet square, and dating from the eighth century BC. It had been surrounded by a casemated wall like that of King Ahab in Samaria and had a triple gate in the style of Solomon's day. Three sides of the courtyard were surrounded by buildings, two sides residential and the third for stores. When the excavators asked themselves the question as to who could have been the builder and first tenant of this lordly rural demesne they were given only one hint: *King Uzziah had leprosy until the day he died. He lived in a separate house—*

leprous, and excluded from the temple of the Lord (2 Chronicles 26:21).

Individual items removed from the palace rubble indicate how right the prophets were in their condemnation. Several symbols of Astarte witness to the 'idolatry' that went on in this princely home (2 Kings 15:4).

Harsh and full of foreboding in these days of pseudo-prosperity ring out the prophetic words of Amos: *Woe to you who are complacent in Zion, and to you who feel secure on Mount Samaria . . . You put off the evil day and bring near a reign of terror . . . Therefore you will be among the first to go into exile; your feasting and lounging will end* (Amos 6:1, 3, 7). But in vain—they fall upon deaf ears. Only King Jeroboam cannot have had much faith in the peace, perhaps because the words of the prophet found an echo in his heart. At all events he feverishly set about strengthening the defences of the royal city of Samaria, which were in any case sufficiently forbidding.

J.W. Crowfoot, the English archaeologist, found what Jeroboam in his wisdom and foresight had achieved. Samaria had been surrounded with a double wall and the existing walls which were already massive had been further strengthened. In the northern section of the acropolis, where Samaria must have been most vulnerable, Crowfoot exposed a titanesque bastion. He measured it and was certain he must have made a mistake. He

Also among the finds of Arslan Tash is this ivory furniture decoration composed of two sphinxes with the heads of rams, typical of the Phoenician/Egyptian mixed style (above). The motif of the birth of the sun-god from the lotus blossom, guarded by two winged and crowned gods, is purely Egyptian. Here the strong influence of the land of the Nile on the Phoenician coastal towns is in evidence. Like the others, these two reliefs, in the Aleppo Museum, can be dated to the end of the ninth century BC.

measured it carefully once more. No doubt about it, the wall—solid stone through and through—was 30 feet thick.

THE END OF THE NORTHERN KINGDOM

Then Pul king of Assyria invaded the land.
2 KINGS 15:19

Concise, sober and dispassionate, these words announce the end of the northern kingdom. The death of Jeroboam II introduced the last act. In the same year, 747BC, the

An alabaster relief from the central palace in Calah (Nimrud) depicts the attack by the troops of the Assyrian king Tiglath-Pileser III on the town of Gazru, which may be identical with Gezer. The Assyrian bowmen are fighting behind shields taller than a man's height. In front of them a battering ram on wheels is being driven up a ramp towards the walls, in which it has already made a breach. In the background three impaled defenders can be seen. On the left soldiers are storming the fortress up siege ladders, and the defenders in the towers are already giving signs of surrender.

leprous King Uzziah of Judah also died. In the short intervening period during which anarchy reigned Menahem made himself king at Samaria. In 745BC a former soldier by name Pulu had ascended the throne of Assyria, and from then on was known as Tiglath-Pileser III. He was the first of a succession of brutal tyrants who by their conquests set up the greatest empire the Ancient East had yet seen. Their goal was Syria, Palestine, and the last cornerstone of the old world, Egypt. That meant that both Israel and Judah were caught between the pitiless millstones of a military state, for which the word peace had a contemptible sound, whose despots and cohorts had only three values: marching, conquering, oppressing.

From North Syria Tiglath-Pileser III swept through the Mediterranean countries, and forced independent peoples to become provinces and tributaries of the Assyrian Empire. Israel at first submitted voluntarily: *Then Pul king of Assyria invaded the land, and Menahem gave him a thousand talents of silver to gain his support and strengthen his own hold on the kingdom. Menahem exacted this money from Israel. Every wealthy man had to contribut fifty shekels of silver to be given to the king of Assyria. So the king of Assyria withdrew and stayed in the land no longer.* (2 Kings 15:19, 20). *I received tribute from Menahem of Samaria*, notes Tiglath-Pileser III in his annals. One thousand talents correspond to 6 million gold sovereigns, 50 shekels per head from the wealthy men amounted to 100 gold sovereigns each. Economists and statisticians will gather that there must have been 60,000 well-to-do people in Israel.

King Menahem entertained the illusion that a pact with the tyrant and voluntary tribute would be the lesser of two evils. But the result was bad blood among his own people. Anger at the Assyrian taxes found an outlet in conspiracy and murder. Pekah, an army officer, murdered Menahem's son and heir and ascended the throne. From then on the anti-Assyrian party was the determining factor in the policy of the Northern Kingdom.

Rezin, king of Damascus, powerfully grasped the initiative. Under his leadership the defensive league of the Aramaean states against Assyria came to life again. Phoenician and Arab states, Philistine cities and Edomites joined the alliance. Israel too took its place in the federation. Only King Ahaz of Judah remained obstinately outside. Rezin and Pekah tried to force Judah into the league violently. *Then Rezin king of Aram and Pekah son of Remaliah king of Israel marched up to fight against Jerusalem and besieged Ahaz, but they could not overpower him* (2 Kings 16:5).

In dire straits the king of Judah sent out an SOS. *Ahaz sent messengers to say to Tiglath-Pileser king of Assyria, 'I am your servant and vassal. Come up and save me out of the hand of the king of Aram and of the king of Israel who are attacking me.' and Ahaz took the silver and gold found in the temple of the Lord and in the treasuries of the royal palace and sent it as a gift to the king of Assyria* (2 Kings 16:7,8).

I received tribute from Jauhazi (Ahaz) of Judah, observes the Assyrian once more.

Now events took their disastrous course. For our knowledge of further developments we are indebted to two great historical records. Firstly, the Bible and secondly the cuneiform tablets of stone and clay, on which—over 600 miles from where the terrible events took place—the military developments were officially recorded. For more than two and a half millennia these documents lay in the rubble of the magnificent palaces on the Tigris until scholars ran them to earth and translated them into our tongue.

The Bible and the Assyrian monuments are in entire agreement in their description of these events which were fatal for the Northern Kingdom. The Old Testament historian notes down the facts soberly, the Assyrian chronicler records every brutal detail:

The king of Assyria complied by attacking Damascus and capturing it. He deported its inhabitants to Kir and put Rezin to death. (2 Kings 16:9)
His noblemen I impaled alive and displayed this exhibition to his land. All his gardens and fruit orchards I destroyed. I besieged and captured

the native city of Reson (Rezin) of Damascus. Eight hundred people with their belongings I led away. Towns in sixteen districts of Damascus I laid waste like mounds after the Flood. (From: Western Campaign 734–735BC, Cuneiform Text of Tiglath-Pileser III)

In the days of Pekah king of Israel, Tiglath-Pileser king of Assyria came and took . . . Hazor. He took Gilead and Galilee, including the land of Naphtali, and deported the people to Assyria. (2 Kings 15:29) Bet-Omri (Israel) all of whose cities I had added to my territories on my former campaigns, and had left out only the city of Samaria . . . The whole of Naphtali I took for Assyria. I put my officials over them as governors. The land of Bet-Omri, all its people and their possessions I took away to Assyria. (From: Western Campaign and Gaza/Damascus campaign 734–733BC)

Hoshea . . . conspired against Pekah . . . and assassinated him, and then succeeded him as king. (2 Kings 15:30) They overthrew Pekah their king and I made Hoshea to be king over them. (From: Gaza/Damascus campaign)

Sombre evidence of the capture of Hazor by Tiglath-Pileser III, king of Assyria (2 Kings 15:29), has been supplied by a layer of rubble at Tell Qedach el-Ghul in Israel. In the course of the most recent excavations by archaeologists from the Hebrew University, traces came to light of the shattered Israelite fortress which had been rebuilt during the monarchy for defence purposes by Solomon and Ahab on the site of the old Canaanite fort which had been conquered by Joshua. The strength of the keep with its six-foot-thick walls was such that it was only surpassed by the royal palace at Samaria, now likewise rediscovered.

The apartments in the castle at Hazor were covered by a layer of ashes three feet thick, the stones were blackened with smoke, charred beams and fragments of what had been at one time panelled ceilings lay scattered about the ground. By exercising the utmost care the archaeologists were able to salvage from the piles of rubble some precious examples of the arts and crafts of northern Israel: a statuette of a young woman and a marble incense-spoon. The greatest thrill was to find among the fragments of broken pottery the name of King Pekah himself, written in old Semitic

Deportation and resettlement had long been proven ways of permanently weakening the defeated enemy, although the Assyrians were probably the first to use this policy on the grand scale. As a spin-off, this practice also provided labour for the extension of their spectacular palaces. Tiglath-Pileser III had this gruesome act depicted on the alabaster reliefs in his central palace at Calah (Nimrud). Women and children, with their scanty possessions, are loaded onto ox-carts, goats and fat-tailed sheep are driven along. A precise written record of the proceedings is being kept in two languages: in Akkadian on clay tablets, and in 'modern' Aramaic with a brush on 'paper'.

239

script. This was the first written evidence of an Israelite king in Galilee.

When the armed hordes of Assyrians withdrew from Palestine they left Israel mortally wounded, smashed to the ground, decimated by deportation, beaten back into a tiny corner of the northern kingdom. Most of its cities had been annexed and the country had been divided into provinces over which Assyrian governors and officials exercised strict control.

All that was left of Israel was a dwarf state: the mountain of Ephraim with the royal city of Samaria. There lived King Hoshea.

The southern kingdom of Judah still remained free from foreign domination—for the time being. But it had to pay tribute to Tiglath-Pileser III.

The warlike Assyrian colossus had enclosed in his mighty grip the whole of the 'Fertile Crescent' from the shores of the Persian Gulf, from the mountains of Persian to Asia Minor, from the Mesopotamian plain through Lebanon and Antilebanon as far as Palestine. Alone, away to the southwest, the 20 acre royal city of Samaria with its few square miles of hinterland, providing it with corn and barley, was unsubdued.

From this corner a gauntlet of defiance flew through the air to land at Assyria's feet.

After the death of Tiglath-Pileser III Hoshea conspired with Egypt. He refused to pay his annual tribute to Assyria. Shalmaneser V the successor of Tiglath-Pileser III at once struck back. For he *discovered Hoshea was a traitor, for he had sent envoys to So king of Egypt, and he no longer paid tribute to the king of Assyria, as he had done year by year. Therefore Shalmaneser seized him and put him in prison* (2 Kings 17:4).

With the fall of Samaria the last remnant of the Northern Kingdom of Israel suffered the fate of Damascus . . . *in the ninth year of Hoshea, the king of*

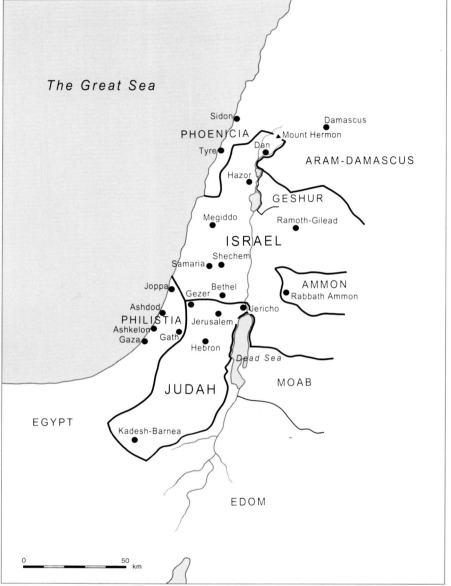

Above **The borders of Israel and Judah after the division of the kingdom.**

Above left **In the first excavations at Megiddo a jasper seal was found, with a roaring lion device. The inscription names its owner: 'Shema, servant of Jeroboam'. Without doubt it belonged, not to an ordinary servant, but to a higher administrative official in the king's service.**

Assyria captured Samaria and deported the Israelites to Assyria (2 Kings 17:6).

For three years the little mountain fortress withstood the deadly pressure of superior forces with the courage of a lion (2 Kings 17:5).

Cuneiform texts record that Shalmaneser V died unexpectedly during the siege of Samaria. His successor Sargon II nevertheless continued the attack. *In the first year of my reign,* boasts Sargon in his annals, *I besieged and conquered Samaria . . . I led away into captivity 27,290 people who lived there.*

fascinate him more. Admittedly they had nothing to do with the routine duties of consular agent, but M. Botta was a scholar. He had been carefully following an academic dispute which had broken out over the biblical name Nineveh. No one could say with any certainty where this city lay in olden times. It was a case of one surmise being as good as another. One suggestion pointed in the direction of Mosul. In the course of his wanderings among the yellow brown sandhills on the far side of the river Botta had repeatedly noticed fragments of bricks. They were only plain looking uncommunicative fragments. Nevertheless he mentioned them in a letter to Paris. In reply came a letter from M. Mohl, secretary of the Société Asiatique. It encouraged him to examine the terrain a little more closely.

Botta hired a bunch of natives out of his own

The discovery of the Sargon inscriptions over 100 years ago is like a romantic tale from the fabulous land of the caliphs. None the less it is a milestone in our knowledge of the ancient world. For it marked the birth of Assyriology, which by its sensational discoveries has for the first time given many biblical narratives a genuine historical content.

The motor car had not been invented: electric light was still unknown: no steel frames of derricks towered out of the sandflats by the Tigris: Mosul still wore the colourful variegated garb of a city from the Arabian Nights. Bazaars, harems, and a real live caliph were all there. It was the heart of the ancient orient and the year was 1840.

Summer lay like a red-hot breath over the city with its elegant white minarets and its narrow dirty muddy alleyways.

For a European the heat was enervating and unbearable. Paul Emile Botta, the new French consular agent, escaped from the incubator as often as he could to take a ride by the Tigris and breathe fresher air. But soon certain desolate mounds on the other side of the river begin to

In the Russian church on the Mount of Olives this stone plaque was found (Israel Museum, Jerusalem). It bears the tomb inscription of the leprous king Uzziah. It declares: 'To this place the bones of Uzziah, the king of Judah, were brought. Do not open' (left). From his son Jotham a severely weathered seal has come to us (far right). This beautiful carnelian seal in the form of a scarab belonged to an official of King Ahaz, the son and successor of Jotham. 'Ushna, servant of Ahaz', announces its inscription (right).

pocket. In the typical round Tigris-boats they headed up river towards the mounds and prepared to excavate.

This first attempt of a European to wrest its secrets from Nineveh failed to achieve the desired result. Botta ordered digging to begin on several slopes. Some weeks flashed past as the work went busily on. But the result was precisely nothing. Botta saw his money being expended to no purpose and brought his private expedition which had been started with such enthusiasm to a disappointing end.

Perhaps he might have kept his hands off any further researches in this area except that he heard something which spurred him to new activity. In the village of Khorsabad, 7 miles to the north, Arabs working in the fields were said to have found great pillars.

In the early part of March 1842 Botta and his workers were on the spot. They began to excavate, and on the same day they struck stonework, apparently the inner walls of a large building.

Botta was highly delighted although at the moment he had no idea that he was responsible for

From early times lions or mythical beasts were set up on either side of town gates, temple or palace doors as protective gods to ward off demons. Among the Assyrians these works of art acquired truly gigantic proportions. These gate-protecting spirits in the form of winged oxen with the bearded heads of gods were called Lamassu or Shedu. This alabaster winged ox, over three metres high (above), is now in the British Museum. It comes from the northern palace of King Ashurnasirpal at Calah (Nimrud). To make the transportation of such colossal statues easier, the excavators of the nineteenth century simply had them sawn up (opposite left).

a historic event of the greatest importance for scholarship. The stonework was part of the first of the gigantic Assyrian palaces which after lying dormant for thousands of years were now to come to light. It was the birth of Assyriology. And the first thing that this new science got itself involved in was an erroneous idea.

Once again French scholarship displayed in this case sound judgement. The Académie des Inscriptions, which Botta informed at once, saw to it that the government placed funds at his disposal. It was to begin with no vast amount of money but gold francs were still worth something in the East. The sultan gave the required permission for excavation.

But on the site itself Botta had to endure unimaginable difficulties due to the extremely underhand dealings of the local authorities in Mosul. At one moment the trenches came under suspicion as being military defences; at another the primitive shelters of the members of the excavations were suspected of being army bivouacs. It seemed that by every possible means the great excavation was to be thwarted. More than once Botta had to send an S.O.S. to Paris and invoke the aid of the French diplomatic service.

Despite all this, sections of a huge palace were liberated from the sand at Khorsabad.

Eugène N. Flandin, a well-known Paris artist who had specialized in antiquities, had been given the assignment by the Louvre which nowadays falls on the official photographer of any expedition. His pencil reproduced accurately on paper all that the ground yielded up. The drawings were collected into a handsome folio and the large volume was adorned with the proud title *Le Monument de Ninive*. For Botta was convinced that he had found the biblical city of Nineveh at Khorsabad. And that was where he was wrong.

If he had only dug a few inches deeper into the mounds opposite Mosul, where two years earlier he had given up the apparently hopeless task in disgust, he would in fact have made the discovery of his life. As it happened the credit for discovering Nineveh went to Henry Layard, who at the instigation of the British Government commenced digging in 1845 at the very spot where Botta had given up.

At the first spadeful, so to speak, Layard came upon the walls of one of the great palaces of Nineveh.

What Botta had excavated at Khorsabad was the great castle of Sargon, the home of Sargon II, king of Assyria. But that did not emerge until later. If Botta had been able to read the tablets which

were salvaged at Khorsabad he would never have made his mistake. *Dur-Sharrukin*, Castle of Sargon, was written there in cuneiform, which at that time, 1842, had not yet been completely deciphered. The key to its translation was not agreed on until fifteen years later.

In 1857 Rawlinson and Hincks in England and Oppert in France independently of each other produced translations of a piece of text which corresponded exactly. With that the correct interpretation of Assyrian script was assured.

In October 1844 the tablets salvaged by Botta containing reliefs and historical texts, as well as statues and sections of pillars, started out on an adventurous journey. From Khorsabad the precious cargo rocked its way down the Tigris on skiffs and rafts. At Basra on the Persian Gulf the valuable freight was transferred to the *Cormoran*, which conveyed it to Europe. It made a great sensation in Paris and evoked as lively an interest among the general public as among the scholars.

On the first of May 1847 in the splendid galleries of the Louvre designed by Percier and Fontaine, Louis Philippe, the bourgeois king, handed over to the public with impressive ceremony this collection, which contained the earliest evidence from the realm of biblical story. With that the first Assyrian museum in the world had been founded.

The mounds of old Nineveh provided the new world with its most extensive collection of information about ancient times.

The story of the discovery of this left a bitter taste in French mouths. When the British began their diggings, the French had also staked a claim on a section of the mounds.

In the British excavation area a vast palace had come to light which had been identified as the historic Nineveh of the Bible. But what might still be lying hidden over there in the French sector? Rassam, one of the members of the British party, decided to take time by the forelock. He took advantage of the absence of his chief, Rawlinson, leader of the expedition, and of the presence of a full moon to make a purposeful excursion into the French reservation. At the first stroke he came upon the palace of Ashurbanipal with the famous library belonging to that monarch, which was indeed the most famous in the whole of the ancient orient. Twenty-two thousand cuneiform tablets found their way into the British Museum.

They contained the historical and intellectual legacy of Mesopotamia, its peoples, its kingdoms

with their arts and crafts, cultures and religions. Among them were the Sumerian flood story and the epic of Gilgamesh.

What had been until then a mysterious sealed chapter of our world's history was suddenly opened and page after page was turned over. Rulers, cities, wars, and stories which people had only heard about through the Old Testament revealed themselves as facts.

We must include among these the city of Erech which is described in the tenth chapter of Genesis as part of the kingdom of Nimrod, the *mighty hunter before the Lord*. About fifty miles to the north-west of Ur of the Chaldees, Professor H.J. Lenzen has been directing excavations which have continued from 1928 to the time of writing. From a pile of ruins, which the Arabs call Warka, he has produced impressive evidence of the ancient city of Uruk, as Erech is styled in the cuneiform texts, including written tablets which go back to the fourth and third millennium BC. In the course of his investigations the German archaeologist came across the remains of walls which could be credited to the legendary king Gilgamesh. Over five miles in length they afforded their protection to this ancient biblical city.

Meantime the original starting point of all these exciting investigations and discoveries had long been forgotten. But if it had not been for the Bible perhaps the quest would never have begun.

Right **This limestone statue of Ashurnasirpal II from the temple of Ninurta in Calah gives us a model of what an Assyrian king looked like. The king wears the customary fringed 'shawl robe' and holds as a sign of his power a sceptre and a curved axe. His hair and beard are highly stylized according to Assyrian fashion. The eight lines of inscription on his breast give the name and title of the king and a brief summary of his most famous military deeds.**

About the middle of last century, Nineveh, Sargon's castle, and, at Tell Nimrud, the Calah of Genesis which Nimrod built (Genesis 10:11) were all discovered. But it was several decades before any great number of the cuneiform texts were deciphered, translated, and made available to a wider circle. It was not until the turn of the century that several comprehensive scholarly works appeared, containing translations of some of the texts, including the annals of Assyrian rulers well known to readers of the Old Testament, Tiglath-Pileser or Pul, Sargon, Sennacherib, and Esarhaddon.

The Assyrian documents contain a wealth of interesting and informative details which corroborate the historical truth of the Bible.

Botta found in Sargon's castle at Khorsabad his reports on his campaigns in Syria and Palestine, and his capture of Samaria in Israel.

... In the first year of my reign I besieged and conquered Samaria. Sargon II reigned from 721 to 705BC. According to that the northern kingdom of Israel collapsed in 721BC (2 Kings 17:6).

People of the lands, prisoners my hand had

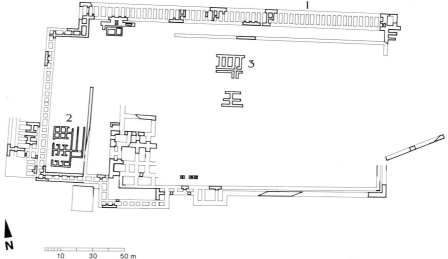

This plan of Samaria shows the town as it was in the ninth century BC, with the casemate wall which King Ahab had built (1), the 'House of Ostraca' (2) and the 'House of Ivory' (3).

captured, I settled there. My officials I placed over them as governors. I imposed tribute and tax upon them, as upon the Assyrians. So reads the account of the conquest of Samaria in the annals. The Old Testament describes the uprooting tactics employed in this case too by ruthless dictators, the

first large scale experiment of its kind in the world made by the Assyrians: *The king of Assyria brought people from Babylon, Cuthah, Avva, Hamath and Sepharvaim and settled them in the towns of Samaria to replace the Israelites* (2 Kings 17:24).

Tens of thousands of human beings were violently driven from their homeland, deported to foreign lands, and their placed filled by others dragged from different areas.

The aim of this was clear: national consciousness, and with it the will to resist, was to be broken. The 'Fertile Crescent' was ploughed up, its peoples tossed about hither and thither. Instead of a varied range of races and religions existing side by side the result was a jumble.

Samaria shared this fate. Its motley collection of inhabitants became known as 'Samaritans'. 'Samaritans' became in the Roman period a term of abuse, an expression of abhorrence. The Samaritans were despised as an ethnic group as well as on religious grounds: *For Jews do not associate with Samaritans* (John 4:9). It was only when Jesus told the story of the 'Good Samaritan' that he turned this term of abuse into a byword for practical Christian charity (Luke 10:30ff).

The people of the Northern Kingdom and their kings with them disappeared, were absorbed into the population of these foreign lands, and never emerged again in history. All investigation into what became of the ten tribes who had their home there has so far come to nothing.

JUDAH UNDER THE YOKE OF ASSYRIA

Because of this I will weep and wail; I will go barefoot and naked. I will howl like a jackal and moan like an owl. For her wound is incurable; it has come to Judah. It has reached the very gate of my people, even to Jerusalem itself.

MICAH 1:8–9

In Judah there may have been some who rejoiced at the downfall of their hostile brother. The prophet Micah however was

King Omri 'bought the hill of Samaria from Shemer for two talents of silver and built a city on the hill, calling it Samaria' (1 Kings 16:24–25). Omri placed his royal palace on a rectangular terrace and separated it from the residential town with a wall. His son Ahab, after 871BC, erected a strong casemate wall (above). Two buildings in the palace area are named after finds discovered there: in the 'House of Ostraca' inscribed pottery fragments were found, recording accounts of wine and oil, and in the 'House of Ivory' a wealth of ivory decorative mountings for furniture or implements. In 721BC Samaria was conquered by Sargon II. The impressive colonnaded streets (opposite, above) originate from the time of the Roman emperor Septimius Severus, when the town was called Sebaste.

he was successful in whatever he undertook (2 Kings 18:7).

In the Philistine city-state of Ashdod, which was oppressed in the same way, anti-Assyrian riots broke out. That brought into being a league against the tyrant on the Tigris. Hezekiah saw a chance to further his plan. He showed his sympathy but remained officially aloof, and intrigued behind the scenes.

Jerusalem had at this time visitors from overseas, tall personages from *along the rivers of Cush* (Isaiah 18:1). These were Ethiopian envoys. The king of Egypt at that point was Shabaka, a Pharaoh from Ethiopia. The Assyrians replied to the riots in Ashdod with armed force. A *turtanu*, a field-marshal, appeared on the scene with an army. *In the year that the supreme commander, sent by Sargon king of Assyria, came to Ashdod and attacked and captured it . . .'* (Isaiah 20:1).

On the walls of Sargon's castle the court chroniclers describe the carrying out of this punitive expedition as follows: *Ashdod . . . I besieged and conquered . . . its gods, its women, its sons, its daughters, its goods and chattels, the treasures of its palace, and all the people of its territory I counted as plunder. I settled those cities anew . . .*

The anti-Assyrian league had gone to pieces on the approach of the Assyrians. Ashdod's territory became an Assyrian province.

Nothing happened to Hezekiah, although his name was on the blacklist. Assyrian informers had seen through his game and had given Sargon II full details of Hezekiah's secret dealings with Egypt, as can be seen from the text of a fragment of a prism:

> Philistia, Judah, Edom and Moab, who planned hostilities, infamies without number . . . who, in order to prejudice him against me and make him my enemy, brought gifts in homage to Pharaoh, king of the land of Egypt . . . and begged him to form an alliance . . .

I n 705BC news spread like wildfire, raising at once fresh hopes of liberation from the Assyrian yoke: Sargon had been murdered! All over the 'Fertile Crescent,' in the Assyrian provinces and in the vassal states, conspiracies, discussions and intrigues began.

> *In those days Hezekiah became ill and was at the point of death. (2 Kings 20:1)*

Happening precisely at this moment of feverish political activity it was a grave handicap. The

Previous pages **This detail from the bronze gate of Shalmaneser III, from Imgur Enlil (Balawat), shows the Assyrian king receiving the tribute of the Phoenician city of Tyre (upper frieze) and a procession of prisoners of war, who are being led away naked and chained by Assyrian soldiers (lower frieze).**

overwhelmed with grief and filled with deep anxiety at the news. He guessed that the blow that had crushed Samaria would one day strike the people of Judah and the city of Jerusalem. At that time Hezekiah was king of Judah, *He did what was right in the eyes of the Lord* (2 Kings 18:3). Since the father of Hezekiah had voluntarily submitted to Tiglath-Pileser III in 733BC, Judah had been a dependent vassal-state, whose deliveries of tribute were carefully noted in Nineveh. Hezekiah was not prepared to follow in his father's footsteps. The reaction set in when he came to the throne.

Hezekiah was no hothead, but a clever, cool, calculating and far-sighted man. He knew very well that what he was about was a highly dangerous and risky business for himself and his people. Only 30 miles from Jerusalem the Assyrian governor of Samaria was sitting eyeing him with suspicion. One careless step, a nod to Nineveh, and Hezekiah would find himself off his throne and clapped in irons. He merely held the throne in fee. Hezekiah proceeded with the utmost caution, and

Opposite page and this page **Deported prisoners from the areas conquered by the Assyrians had to engage in forced labour of the hardest nature. Reliefs from the south-western palace of King Sennacherib at Nineveh depict the transportation of alabaster from a quarry (opposite). The men load the stones into baskets out of the pit; larger pieces are tied on their backs with ropes, while others return to the depths with empty baskets. Armed soldiers oversee the work and prevent the prisoners from escaping.**

The accompanying inscription reads: 'Sennacherib, the king of the world, king of Ashur. Alabaster, which by the command of God was found in the land of Balada for the building of my palace, and which I have employed the people of enemy cities and the inhabitants of obscure hill countries, the booty of my hand, to break by means of iron axes and mattocks—this I have made into great colossi of oxen for the gates of my palace'.

The transportation of an ox colossus of this type is portrayed in a frieze made up of several plaques. The strictly supervised forced labourers, on the word of command, pull the huge blocks of stone with strong cables which are attached to them by shoulder straps. The route looks long, leading over mountains, through valleys, and across watercourses, and the host of slave labourers is immense.

prophet Isaiah is said to have healed Hezekiah of his sickness: *Then Isaiah said, 'Prepare a poultice of figs.' They did so and applied it to the boil, and he recovered* (2 Kings 20:7).

French excavators stumbled on a parallel to this biblical therapy in the Phoenician seaport of Ugarit. In 1939 they discovered there fragments of an old book of veterinary science from about 1500BC, containing prescriptions for the treatment of sick horses. The captain of the household cavalry of the king of Ugarit entered in it well-tried remedies of this sort: *If a horse has a swollen head or a sore nose, prepare a salve from figs and raisins, mixed with oatmeal and liquid. The mixture should be poured into the horse's nostrils.*

For every kind of sickness there is a very detailed prescription. The chief medicaments are plants and fruit, like mustard and liquorice juice. Advice is even given on how to deal with horses that bite and neigh too much. Does any modern breeder or owner of horses know how to cure that? In those days a neighing horse could in certain circumstances be fatal. Horses were used exclusively for fighting and hunting. A troop of chariots, however well hidden in an ambush, could be betrayed by a sudden loud neighing. It was the same with hunting.

These recognized cures have been tried out

successfully from time immemorial by the peoples of the ancient orient. They are nature's remedies which can also be profitably used in the case of human beings. One of them, which is particularly commended in the veterinary manual, is *Debelah*, a sort of poultice of compressed figs. It was a *Debelah* that the prophet prescribed for Hezekiah's abscess. Within three days, the story goes, he was all right again.

Many of these tried remedies dating back to biblical times, and largely consisting of ingredients supplied by Mother Nature, have been either lost or forgotten in the whirligig of time. Many of them on the other hand have been quietly passed on from generation to generation. This prescription for figs is one of them. Swiss doctors still prescribe finely chopped up figs steamed in milk, for certain kinds of abscesses. An Arabic remedy reminds us of the *Debelah*. A thick sticky liquid made from grape-juice is called *Dibis* in the native tongue.

> *At that time Merodach-Baladan son of Baladan king of Babylon sent Hezekiah letters and a gift, because he had heard of Hezekiah's illness. (2 Kings 20:12)*

This was the traditional practice in court circles and was part of the royal etiquette in the ancient East. Presents were sent and enquiries made about the health of 'our brother'. The clay tablets of El-Amarna mention the habit frequently.

Merodach-Baladan, however, found Hezekiah's illness a convenient pretext for making

royal parks, but with an interest in such useful things as the vegetables and fruit of Mesopotamia. He described in the various types of plants and how to cultivate them, and was in fact the author of a practical handbook on vegetable gardens.

As a politician Merodach-Baladan was the most bitter and determined opponent of Nineveh. No other monarch in the 'Fertile Crescent' attached the Assyrians so vigorously over many years, engaged them in so many heated battles, or intrigued so unremittingly against the tyrants of the Tigris, as he did.

The assassination of Sargon brought Merodach-Baladan into the field. It was at this point that his ambassadors visited Hezekiah. What was in fact discussed on the occasion of the official visit during the convalescence of Hezekiah, can be read between the lines: *Hezekiah received the messengers and showed them all that was in his storehouses ... his armoury and everything found among his treasures* (2 Kings 20:13), Judah's arsenal. Secret armaments and feverish preparations for D-day, the great show-down with Assyria which they saw to be imminent, were in full swing. *Then he worked hard repairing all the broken sections of the wall and building towers on it. He built another wall outside that one and reinforced the supporting terraces of the City of David. He also made large numbers of weapons and shields* (2 Chronicles 32:5).

Jerusalem's defences were overhauled and strengthened for a long siege, the old perimeter wall was renewed, breaches repaired, and turrets erected. On the north side of the city, its most vulnerable point, a second outer wall was added. But that did not exhaust his precautions. *As for the other events of Hezekiah's reign, all his achievements and how he made the pool and the tunnel by which he brought water into the city, are they not written in the book of the annals of the kings of Judah?* (2 Kings 20:20).

The Chronicler completes the story: *It was Hezekiah who blocked the upper outlet of the Gihon spring and channelled the water down to the west side of the City of David* (2 Chronicles 32:30).

The pool of Siloam in ancient Jerusalem was the end of a tunnel through the rock under the city. It was fed by the Gihon spring, which lay underground outside the Israelite city wall.

contact with him. The real reason for his polite courtesies lay in the field of high level politics.

Merodach-Baladan, king of Babylon, was for a long time a mysterious personage both to readers of the Bible and to scholars. It is now quite certain that he was in his own day an extremely important person. We even know something about his private habits. He was for example a great gardener, not in the sense of being keen to lay out handsome

Jerusalem has many mysterious corners. Pilgrims from all over the world, travellers of three faiths, Christians, Jews, Muslims, come to pay homage at its holy places. Seldom does one of these endless visitors stumble upon the dark depressing spot outside the walls, far below the noisy streets of the city, which bears eloquent testimony to one of the most dire moments in its ancient story, to a time fraught with fear and

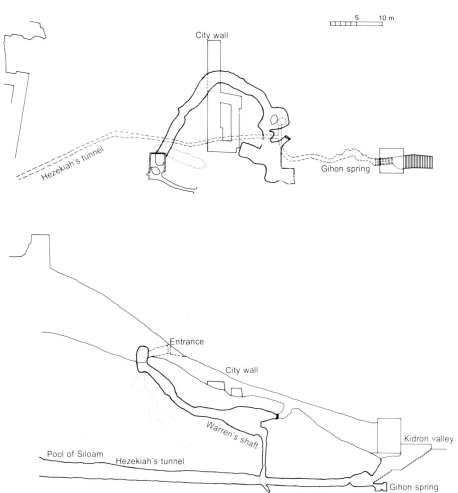

menace. This spot had sunk into oblivion. In 1880 it was discovered by a fluke. It still bears as plain as day all the marks of feverish haste.

Outside the city, where its south-eastern slopes sweep gently down to the Valley of the Kidron, lies a small still sheet of water, enclosed by walls, the Pool of Siloam. Two Arab boys were playing there—one of them fell in. Padding for all he was worth, he landed on the other side, where a rock wall rose above the pool. Suddenly it was pitch black all round him. He groped about anxiously and discovered a small passage.

The name of the Arab boy was forgotten but not his story. It was followed up and a long underground tunnel was discovered.

A narrow passage about 2 feet wide and barely 5 feet high had been cut through the limestone. For about 500 yards the passage winds imperceptibly uphill. It ends at the Virgin's fountain, Jerusalem's water supply since ancient times. In biblical days it was called the Fountain of Gihon.

As experts were examining the passage they noticed by the light of their torches old Hebrew letters on the wall.

The inscription, which was scratched on the rock only a few paces from the entrance at the Pool of Siloam, reads as follows: *The boring through is completed. And this is the story of the boring: while yet they plied the pick, each toward his fellow, and while yet there were cubits to be bored through, there was heard the voice of one calling to the other that there was a hole in the rock on the right hand and on the left hand. And on the day of the boring through the workers in the tunnel struck each to meet his fellow, pick upon pick. Then the water poured from the source to the pool twelve hundred cubits, and a hundred cubits was the height of the rock above the heads of the workers in the tunnel.*

It was Hezekiah's aqueduct.

During a siege the Number One problem is that of providing drinking water. The founders of Jerusalem, the Jebusites, had sunk a shaft down through the rock to the Fountain of Gihon. Hezekiah directed its water, which would otherwise

have flowed into the Kidron valley, through the mountain to the west side of the city. The pool of Siloam lies inside the second perimeter wall which he constructed.

Oddly enough the canal takes an S-shaped course through the rock. Why did the workmen not dig this underground tunnel the shortest way to meet each other, that is, in a straight line? The wretched job would have been finished quicker. Seven hundred feet of hard work would have been saved out of the total 1,700 feet.

Locally, there is an old story which has been handed down which claims to explain why they had to go the long way round. Deep in the rock, between the spring and the pool, are supposed to lie the graves of David and Solomon.

Archaeologists took this remarkable piece of folk-lore seriously and systematically tapped the walls of the narrow damp tunnel. They sank shafts into the rock from the summit and R. Weill actually came across cavities cut in the rock, which

Above **Ground plan and cross section of Warren's Shaft and Hezekiah's Tunnel. Jerusalem's water supply was fully guaranteed by the Gihon spring. Since the spring lay outside the city, the Jebusites had already dug a shaft, through which one could reach the spring from the city unobserved. Towards 700BC, under threat from the Assyrian king Sennacherib, King Hezekiah had a 512-metre-long tunnel bored from the spring to the Pool of Siloam. We know that the work was begun at both ends, from a Hebrew inscription which celebrates the meeting of the two groups of tunnel workers (above left).**

were perhaps graves, but which had obviously been despoiled in early times.

In the fourteenth year of King Hezekiah's reign, Sennacherib king of Assyria attacked all the fortified cities of Judah and captured them. (2 Kings 18:13)

The states of Syria and Palestine had four years left in which to take defensive measures. The Assyrian governors were expelled. A strong league was formed. The kings of Askelon and Ekron joined up with Hezekiah, and Egypt promised help in case of military developments.

Naturally the new Assyrian ruler Sennacherib was not unaware of all this. But at first his hands were tied. After the assassination of his predecessor Sargon, the eastern part of his empire revolted. The leading spirit in this was Merodach-Baladan. As soon as Sennacherib was once more in control of the situation in Mesopotamia, by the end of the year 702BC, he set out for the west and smashed the rebellious little countries in one single campaign. A similar fate overtook the Egyptian army which Shabaka, a pharaoh of the Ethiopian dynasty, had sent under the command of his nephew Taharka against the Assyrians. Judah was occupied by Sennacherib's troops, Hezekiah was shut

up in Jerusalem. Among the frontier fortresses Lachish alone still offered resistance. Sennacherib deployed his storm-troopers against this unusually strongly fortified city.

Anyone who wishes to relive the frightful battle of Lachish, vividly and dramatically to the smallest detail, must pay a visit to the British Museum. It is here that the massive reliefs, on which Sennacherib ordered the events to be recorded, have found a resting place. Sir Henry Layard salvaged this precious object from the ruins of Nineveh.

On the turrets and breastwork of the stronghold of Lachish with its stout high walls the Judahite defenders fought with clenched teeth. They showered a hail of arrows on the attackers, hurled stones down upon them, threw burning torches—the fire-bombs of the ancient world—

These reliefs from the palace of the Assyrian king Sennacherib in Nineveh depict the siege of Lachish in the year 701BC (below) and the deportation of prisoners (opposite page). The siege ramp, by which the attackers could scale the walls, is also shown. On a base of gravel, a pavement bonded with cement was laid. Archaelogists working outside Lachish believe they have found the remains of a ramp of this kind, and also a counter-ramp built by the defenders.

In 1938, on the outskirts of Lachish, the English archaeologist James Lesley Starkey stumbled upon a mass grave with almost 2000 human skeletons—perhaps the victims of the epidemic which broke out among the besieging Assyrian army.

among the enemy. The faces, curly hair, and short beards are easily recognizable. Only a few wear any protection for head or body.

At the foot of the wall the Assyrians are attacking with the utmost violence and with every type of weapon. Sennacherib had deployed the whole range of approved assault-tactics. Every Assyrian is armed to the teeth: each one wears shield and helmet. Their engineers have built sloping ramps of earth, stones and felled trees. Amoured siege-engines push forward up the ramps against the walls. They are equipped in front with a battering ram which sticks out like the barrel of a cannon. The crew consists of three men. The archer shoots his arrows from behind a sheltering canopy. A warrior guides the ram, and under its violent blows stones and bricks crash down from the walls. The third man douses the amoured vehicles with ladlefuls of water, extinguishing the smouldering torches. Several such siege engines are attacking at the same time. Tunnels are being driven into the rock beneath the foundations of the walls. Behind the amoured vehicles come the infantry, bowmen, some of them kneeling, some stooping, protected by a shield-bearer. The first captives, men and women, are being led off. Lifeless bodies are hanging on pointed stakes—impaled.

James Lesley Starkey, a British archaeologist, dug up the ruins of the walls of the fortress of Lachish. The holes and breaches made by the Assyrian battering rams can be seen to this day.

Amid the confusion of the battle and the din of the siege around the frontier fortress of Judah an order went out from Sennacherib: *The king of Assyria sent his supreme commander, his chief officer and his field commander with a large army, from Lachish to King Hezekiah at Jerusalem* (2 Kings 18:17).

That meant attack on Jerusalem.

The historians of the Assyrian king have preserved a record of what happened next. A hexagonal prism from the rubble heaps of Nineveh says: *And Hezekiah of Judah who had not submitted to my yoke . . . him I shut up in Jerusalem his royal city like a caged bird. Earthworks I threw up against him, and anyone coming out of his city gate I made to pay for his crime. His cities which I had plundered I cut off from his land . . .*

Surely now must come the announcement of the fall of Jerusalem and the seizing of the capital. But the text continues: *As for Hezekiah, the splendour of my majesty overwhelmed him . . . Thirty gold talents . . . valuable treasures as well as his daughters, the women of his harem, singers both men and women, he caused to be brought after me to Nineveh.*

To pay his tribute and to do me homage he sent his envoys.

It is simply a bragging account of the payment of tribute—nothing more.

The king of Assyria exacted from Hezekiah king of Judah three hundred talents of silver and thirty talents of gold. (2 Kings 18:14)

The Assyrian texts pass on immediately from the description of the battle of Jerusalem to the payment of Hezekiah's tribute. Just at the moment when the whole country had been subjugated and the siege of Jerusalem, the last point of resistance, was in full swing, the unexpected happened: Sennacherib broke off the attack at five minutes to twelve. Only something quite extraordinary could have induced him to stop the fighting. What might it have been?

Whilst the Assyrian records are enveloped in a veil of silence, the Bible says: *That night the angel of the Lord went out and put to death a hundred and eighty-five thousand men in the Assyrian camp. When the people got up the next morning—there were all the dead bodies! So Sennacherib king of Assyria broke camp and withdrew. He returned to Nineveh and stayed there* (2 Kings 19:35, 36).

Herodotus of Halicarnassus, the most famous traveller in the ancient world, historian and author of an early Baedeker, helped to solve the puzzle. This friend of Pericles and Sophocles, who was born about 500BC, had a definite flair for finding out strange facts about people and nations. Like a personified questionnaire he extracted from his contemporaries on his travels through the Ancient East information on all sorts of things which he thought were worth knowing or were unknown to him. In Egypt he had a long conversation with a temple priest who imparted a strange story to the inquisitive Greek.

It happened that at the very time that Sennacherib the Assyrian marched against Egypt with a large armed force, there was a priest-king on the throne of Egypt who treated the army as a contemptible profession. The Egyptian soldiers, who had been so disdainfully dealt with, refused to take the field. Thereupon the priest-king hurried to the temple in deep despair. There he was told that the god would help him. Relying upon this, the king, who had actually no soldiers behind him but only shopkeepers, tradesmen and market folk, went to meet Sennacherib. At the narrow entrances into the country *an army of field-mice swarmed over their opponents in the night . . . gnawed through their quivers and their bows, and the handles of their*

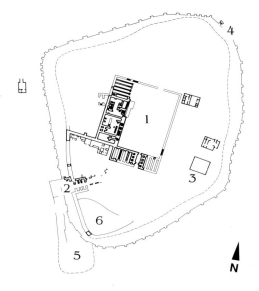

shields, *so that on the following day they fled minus their arms and a great number of them fell.* Hence, this king still stands in Hephaestus' temple with a mouse in his hand, and with the following inscription: *'Look on me and live in Safety.'*

However obscure the meaning of this religious legend may be, its core is historical.

For the peoples of the ancient world—as also for the Bible (1 Samuel 6:4)—the mouse was what the rat was for the people of the Middle Ages. It was the symbol of plague.

On the edge of the city of Lachish, Starkey, the archaeologist, found shocking proof of the story in 1948: A mass grave in the rock with 2,000 human skeletons, unmistakably thrown in with the utmost haste. If these were the remains of the victims of an epidemic, then its effects must have been devastating.

The drama of the campaign had been unfolded and once more Jerusalem had escaped. But all round it the land of Judah presented a pitiable spectacle: *The Daughter of Zion is left like a shelter in a vineyard,* laments the prophet Isaiah, *like a hut in a field of melons.* The *country is desolate,* the *cities burned with fire . . . laid waste as when overthrown by strangers* (Isaiah 1:8, 7).

Only the thought of the marvellous deliverance of the city of David gives the sorely tried people new hope and courage. Undaunted, they bend all their energies to rebuilding, which, without interference from Nineveh, goes quickly forward. Sennacherib never came back. For the next twenty years the tyrant devoted himself to campaigns and battles in Mesopotamia. Then Sennacherib fell by an assassin's hand. *One day,*

while he was worshipping in the temple of his god Nisroch, his sons Adrammelech and Sharezer cut him down with the sword, and they escaped to the land of Ararat. And Esarhaddon his son succeeded him as king (2 Kings 19:37). So runs the brief account of the event in the Bible.

Esarhaddon himself, the successor to the throne, describes in vivid detail these turbulent days in Nineveh: *Disloyal thoughts inspired my brothers . . . They rebelled. In order to exercise royal authority they killed Sennacherib. I became a raging lion, my mind was in a fury . . .*

Despite the intense cold and amid snow and ice he set out without delay to destroy his enemies in the eleventh month of the year 681BC. *These usurpers . . . fled to an unknown land. I reached the quay on the Tigris, sent my troops across the broad river as if it were a canal. In Addar . . . I reached Nineveh well pleased. I ascended my father's throne with joy. The south wind was blowing . . . whose breezes are propitious for royal authority . . . I am Esarhaddon king of the world, king of Assyria . . . son of Sennacherib.*

Above left **Plan of Lachish.**

1 **Judean fortified palace**
2 **City gate**
3 **Large shaft**
4 **Well**
5 **Siege ramp**
6 **Counter-ramp**

Above right **In the ruins of the defensive walls of Lachish, the holes and breaches made by the Assyrian battering rams can still be traced.**

This statuette of an enthroned divinity, made of bronze overlaid with gold, is now in the Aleppo Museum. It comes from Hama, the capital city of an Aramaean kingdom which was conquered and destroyed by Sargon II in 720BC. The god wears the long Syrian skirt decorated with patterned borders, and a horned crown; in his hand he once held a sceptre.

THE SEDUCTIVE RELIGIONS
OF CANAAN

Manasseh was twelve years old when he became king, and he reigned in Jerusalem for fifty-five years . . . following the detestable practices of the nations the Lord had driven out before the Israelites.

2 KINGS 21:1, 2

The official report speaks of *The detestable practices of the nations*. And Isaiah, the great prophet who was contemporary with King Manasseh, puts it more plainly when he complains bitterly: *See how the faithful city has become a harlot* (Isaiah 1:21).

All the other prophets through the centuries constantly utter the same harsh and unambiguous accusation, which seems too monstrous to readers of the Bible.

The charge runs like a red thread through many books of the Old Testament, accompanying the chances and changes of Israel's history.

It rings out from the time when Israel after its long desert wanderings reached the Jordan (Numbers 25:1, 3). We hear it in the time of the Judges (1 Samuel 2:22). It echoes through the two kingdoms, Judah (1 Kings 14:23, 24) as well as Israel (Hosea 4:13, 14). Even in the years of captivity by the waters of Babylon in the sixth century BC it is not silent (Ezekiel 16:15ff).

There is secular evidence for what the Bible calls *the detestable practices of the nations*. Philo of Byblos, a Phoenician scholar, who lived 100 years before Christ, had collected abundant material from his native land and had written a history of Phoenicia, the *Phoinikika*. It deals with historical events in the seaports and maritime republics of Canaan from earliest times, and describes the Phoenician gods, myths and religious practices. As a reliable source for his work Philo cites the Phoenician priest Sanchuniathon, who has been already referred to, and who lived in the sixth or seventh century BC. When, as the result of an earthquake, the inscribed pillars in the temple of Melkart at Tyre crashed to the ground, Sanchuniathon is said to have copied the ancient inscriptions.

Bishop Eusebius of Caesarea in Palestine discovered the writings of Philo in AD314 and gave an account of them. Much of what they recorded, particularly as regards mythology and religion, seemed quite incomprehensible.

At the head of the baals of Canaan was the god El. His wife was Asherah, a goddess who is also mentioned in the Bible. El married his three sisters, one of whom was Astarte. She too is frequently referred to in the Old Testament. El not only kills his brother but also his own son: he cuts off his daughter's head, castrates his father, castrates himself and compels his confederates to do the same.

With us it is accepted as a matter of course that every half-civilized community controls the morality of its citizens. But in Canaan in those days the cult of sensuality was regarded as the worship of the gods, men and women prostitutes ranked as 'sacred' to the followers of the religion, the rewards for their 'services' went into the temple treasuries as 'offerings for the god'.

The last thing the prophets and chroniclers did was to exaggerate. How well founded their harsh words were has only become fully understood since the great discoveries of Ras Shamra.

On the north coast of Syria exactly opposite the east tip of Cyprus lies Minet el-Beida, the 'White Haven'. The Mediterranean waves break here on dazzling snow white limestone rocks in a wonderful display of colour, changing from light green to deep violet. Inland, great banks of clouds surrounded the lonely mountain top of *Jebel Aqra*, once the holy mountain *Zaphon, abode of the divine king.*

Near the sea in 1928 a peasant who was ploughing discovered a long underground passage. Initial investigation showed that it led to a tomb. It was a sepulchral vault in the style of Mycenae.

When the discovery was announced France, which as mandatory power was in control of Syria, reacted with its customary alacrity. René Dussaud, curator of oriental antiquities in the Louvre, despatched Professor Claude F. A. Schaeffer with some other experts to the 'White Haven'. Exciting discoveries awaited them.

Three quarters of a mile (1200 metres) from Minet el-Beida rose an artificial hill. Round its base flowed a pleasant rippling brook. It had always been called by the natives Ras es Shamra, 'Head of Fennel'. Fennel was actually growing on the old heap of ruins which concealed the remains of the Phoenician royal city of Ugarit. More than 3,000 years ago it had been wiped out for good by the onslaught of the Sea Peoples.

Schaeffer had incredible luck with his excavations on the 'Head of Fennel'. For here at last the long-sought information about the religions of Canaan came to light. Between two temples, one of

many of the houses which were excavated was found a burial vault in which the inhabitants of Ugarit buried their dead. Oddly shaped clay funnels were sunk into the ground through which water, wine, oil and flesh and blood of animal sacrifices were offered to the dead.

Gruesome and ferocious are Astarte and Anath, goddesses of fertility and of war alike. The Baal-epic of Ugarit depicts the goddess Anath: *With her might she mowed down the dwellers in the cities, she struck down the people of the sea-coasts, she destroyed the men of the east. She drove the men into her temple and closed the doors so that no one could escape. She hurled chairs at the youths, tables at the warriors, footstools at the mighty men. She waded up to the knees, up to the neck in blood. Human heads lay at her feet, human hands flew over her like locusts. She tied the heads of her victims as ornaments upon her back, their hands she tied upon her belt. Her liver was swollen with laughing, her heart was full of joy, the liver of Anath was full of exultation. When she was satisfied she washed her hands in streams of human blood before turning again to other things.*

Anath is the sister and wife of Baal, the god of storm and rain. His symbol is a bull's head. Baal fertilises the cattle in the meadows with rain to make them fat. He is also concerned with their propagation. When he dies at the turn of the seasons, overpowered *like the bull under the knife of the sacrificer,* his son takes over his duties. *And the children of Israel did evil in the sight of the Lord and served Baalim* (Judges 2:11). Quite recently an

The Phoenician commercial metropolis of Ugarit (Ras Shamra) on the Syrian coast fell a victim to the 'Sea Peoples' in about 1190BC. The excavations begun in 1928 uncovered not only palace and temple areas but also extensive residential quarters (above right). The sallyport of the fortress, like the tombs underneath the houses, has a 'false' arch made of projecting courses of stones.

them dedicated to the god Baal and the other to the god Dagon, he found among the houses of rich merchants the house of the High Priest of Ugarit, who owned a handsome library, as is clear from the large number of inscribed tablets which were found there. Schaeffer's trained eye recognized at once that at some points the writers were using a hitherto unknown Phoenician alphabet. It was surprisingly quickly deciphered in 1930 by three scholars—Professor H. Bauer, of the University of Halle, Germany, and C. Virolleaud and E. Dhorme of France. The texts concerned are in a north Canaanite language, which like Aramaic and Hebrew belongs to the north west Semitic family. While the letters and contracts found in Ugarit are mostly written in the Akkadian syllabic cuneiform script, the vast majority of these tablets written in the Ugaritic alphabetic cuneiform script contain mythological and religious texts.

The myths and practices described in this unique collection of documents abounding in barbaric activities of gods and demigods, indicate the particular significance which was attached to the rites of the goddesses of fertility in Canaan.

The forms of worship which Canaan connected with fertility extended to everyday life. Under

The rich ports and trading towns of Phoenicia were places for the exchange not only of goods but also of ideas and artistic forms. The role of the cities as intermediaries between Egypt, Crete and the Aegean in the west and the Mesopotamian cultures in the east created a remarkable pluralistic culture, with much blending of religions.

The result of such international religion, in cities such as Ugarit,often proved sensuously enticing. A typical example is this ivory carving in the Louvre. The work is ascribed to a Mycenaean workshop which had established itself in Ugarit. The widespread motif of a 'mistress of the animals', later taken over by the Greek Artemis, is mixed here with the characteristics of a goddess of love and fertility.

image of one of these gods was recovered on Israeli territory at Hazor. It was found in one of the heathen shrines which according to the Bible the Israelites erected in many places for the worship of strange gods. In the centre of an area encircled with flat stones, with two altars for burnt offerings dating from the days before the monarchy, stood some weapons and a clay jar. It contained, together with other bronze votive figures, an image of a seated god—a *baal.*

Professor Schaeffer also found in Ugarit small images and amulets of Astarte. They are made of clay and gold and the goddess is naked. Snakes and pigeons, renowned in the Ancient East for their fertility, are her symbols.

The goddesses of fertility were worshipped principally on hills and knolls. There their votaries erected for them Asherim, set out 'sacred pillars', trees, under which the rites were practised, as the Bible repeatedly points out: *For they also built them high places and pillars, and Asherim on every high hill and under every green tree* (1 Kings 14:23, RV).

It is only since the results of scientific investigation into Canaanite gods and Phoenician religions have come to light that we can properly gauge the intensity of the moral struggle that the people of Israel had to face.

What temptation for a simple shepherd folk, what perilous excitement! More than once the Baal religions got a firm foothold and penetrated right into the temple of Yahweh, into the Holy of Holies.

Without its stern moral law, without its faith in one God, without the commanding figures of its

prophets, Israel would never have been able to survive this struggle with the Baals, with the religions of the fertility goddesses, with the Asherim and the high places.

That was the reason for the 'objectionable passages'. In the interests of truth the matter could not be passed over in silence.

THE END OF NINEVEH AS A WORLD POWER

Are you better than Thebes, situated on the Nile, with water around her? The river was her defence, the waters her wall. Cush and Egypt were her boundless strength; Put and Libya were among her allies. Yet she was taken captive and went into exile. Her infants were dashed to pieces at the head of every street.

NAHUM 3:8–10

In 663BC the Assyrians celebrated the greatest triumph in their whole history. King Ashurbanipal conquered,the capital of Upper Egypt, which according to Homer had 100 gates, and which until then in had been regarded as impregnable—the city of Thebes. It was an event which caused and enormous stir in the world of the ancient orient. The Assyrians plundered the metropolis, whose temples contained boundless wealth. *I conquered the whole city . . . silver, gold, precious stones, the whole contents of its palace, coloured vestments, linen, magnificent horses, slaves, both men and women, two great obelisks of shining bronze weighing 2,500 talents; I took the temple gates from their place and brought them to Assyria. Enormous spoils of priceless worth did I take with me from Thebes,* exulted Ashurbanipal.

The Assyrian war machine had devastated the far famed temple-city on the Nile. Excavations fully confirm the description of the catastrophe given by the prophet Nahum and by the victor himself. The capital of Upper Egypt never again recovered from this blow.

After this victorious expedition the world of those days lay at Assyria's feet. From the upper reaches of the Nile to the mountains of Armenia and the mouth of the Euphrates the nations were under its yoke, their peoples reduced to vassals.

But scarcely had Assyria reached the pinnacle of its might when the power of the empire began to wane. Ashurbanipal was not a conqueror or war lord of the calibre of his father Esarhaddon, to say nothing of his prodigious grandfather Sennacherib. Ashurbanipal, the *great and honourable* (Ezra

4:10), had already developed other interests.

After the long succession of bloodstained tyrants this one Assyrian did the world an inestimable service. He ordered the transcription of the masterpieces of Akkadian literature, including the Babylonian Creation story: he commissioned the production of dictionaries and grammars of the various languages which were spoken in his colossal empire. The library which he built up in Nineveh was by far the largest and most important in the Ancient East. Without this precious collection mankind would have been infinitely poorer in its knowledge of the thought and literature of the 'Fertile Crescent' from earliest times.

Nevertheless the wild streak in this last important scion of the race of Assyrian rulers was not completely tamed. As well as being a lover of art and literature he loved hunting. Ashurbanipal was a big game hunter in the proper sense of the word, and his successors in this pursuit can hardly compete with him. It was not with planes and armour-plated jeeps, not with elephant-howdahs equipped with telescopic sights which enable the fatal shot to be firmed from a safe distance where there is no threat of slashing paws or snapping teeth, that this big game hunter of the ancient world set out to attach his prey. On these wonderfully vivid larger reliefs which were found in his palaces on the Tigris he hunts in a light two-wheeled hunting car or on horseback—with bow and arrow or javelin. *30 elephants, 257 wild beasts, 370 lions,* according to the cuneiform texts, made up the splendid total of Ashurbanipal's bag.

> *Woe to the city of Blood! . . . Many casualties, piles of dead, bodies without number, people stumbling over the corpses . . . (Nahum 3:1, 3)*

So the prophet announces the end of Nineveh, the end of its world empire and centuries of bloody tyranny.

With the death of Ashurbanipal the sudden and rapid collapse began. The new great powers of Indo-Aryans and Semites gripped the gigantic structure between them like a vice, crushed it and divided the colossal spoil between them.

To the north-east the kingdom of the Medes in the mountains of Iran had come into being. Then *Cyaxares came to power,* writes Herodotus, *and united all Asia beyond the Halys under him. Then he gathered together all his peoples and marched against Nineveh to take the city.*

In the south-east of Mesopotamia a second adversary had sprung up whom the Assyrians had to take seriously. From the fringe of civilization south of the estuary of the Euphrates, where 'Ur of

The god of storm and weather, Baal, was the most important divinity in the Canaanite Pantheon. On a one-and-a-half-metre-high limestone stela from Ugarit he is depicted swinging a cudgel in his right hand and holding a thunderbolt in his left. In front of him the tiny form of the king of Ugarit appears as a petitioner. In the course of Israelite history the cult of Baal was a continual challenge to the worship of Yahweh, and despite all the polemic of the prophets it still had a considerable effect on Israel's worship.

the Chaldees' was also situated, Semitic tribes had pushed their way inland and had imported new vigour into the old kingdom of Babylon. They called themselves 'Chaldeans'. Merodach-Baladan, who a century before had made a name for himself and had plagued Assyria, was one of them.

Meantime his countrymen had succeeded in penetrating the whole country in a series of waves of invasion. In 625BC a Chaldean assumed control over South Mesopotamia. Nabopolassar became king and founder of the Neo-Babylonian Empire. The Chaldeans likewise had only one

immediate end in view, the destruction of Assyria.

At the same time as the two powers, north and south, were lying in wait to administer the death blow to Assyria, a wild horde burst out of the Caucasus into the 'Fertile Crescent,' penetrated into Media and inundated the Assyrian empire. These were the Scythians. Looting and burning, they forced their way from Mesopotamia through Palestine to the very frontiers of Egypt.

Through the maritime plain by the Mediterranean stormed this unruly mob of Scythian horse-

men. Fearful and frightening rumours heralded their approach. The prophet Zephaniah foresees with horror what will happen. *Gaza will be abandoned and Ashkelon left in ruins. At midday Ashdod will be emptied and Ekron uprooted . . . In the evening they will lie down in the houses of Ashkelon.* (Zephaniah 2:4, 7).

They headed for Egypt, Herodotus relates, *and while they were in Palestinian Syria, Psammitichus, king of Egypt, went to meet them and persuaded them with gifts and pleas to go no further. And while the*

Under a vine in the park of a palace, Ashurbanipal lies on a softly upholstered couch. With his right hand he raises a drinking-cup to his mouth, in his left he holds a flower. In front of him his consort Ashursharat sits on a precious throne. Servants bring delicacies or wave fans, and a female musician plays the harp. What a peaceful picture this would be, if not for the fact that on one tree hangs a cut-off human head. It is

the head of the king of Elam, for the Assyrian king is celebrating his victory over the Elamites in the battle of Susa. The alabaster relief in the British Museum comes from the northern palace at Nineveh.

Scythians on their way back were in the Syrian city of Ashkelon a few of them remained behind and plundered the temple of Aphrodite Urania. Those Scythians who had plundered the temple in Ashkelon together with their descendants for ever were smitten by the goddess with a gynaecological ailment.

Within ten years the Asiatic horsemen had disappeared again like an evil apparition. Archaeological traces of the Scythian incursion have of course not yet come to light; nor can the name of the city of Scythopolis be counted as proof, for it

originates from the Hellenistic period.

Then the Medes and the Neo-Babylonians bore down upon the Assyrians on two fronts. They attached from north and south at the same time. Ashur, the great city and fortress on the Tigris, was the first to fall in 614BC. *The king of Babylon and his army, which had set out to assist the Medes, did not arrive in time for the battle. The king of Babylon and Cyaxares met each other among the ruins of the city,* says a Neo-Babylonian chronicle, *and pledged themselves to friendship and a confederacy ... They*

This hexagonal clay cylinder, 37.5 centimetres tall, was discovered in Nineveh by an Englishman, Colonel Taylor, in 1830. On it is inscribed an account by the Assyrian King Sennacherib. It concerns, among other things, his attack on Jerusalem in 701BC: 'As for Hezekiah of the land of Judah, who would not bend to my yoke, I besieged and conquered forty-six of his strong walled towns . . . Himself I trapped in Jerusalem, his royal city, like a bird in a cage . . .'

took vast quantities of booty in the city and reduced it to a heap of rubble and ruins.

In 612BC the alliance of Medes and Neo-Babylonians achieved its aim. After a violent battle the city was taken: Nineveh was destroyed. *He will stretch out his hand against the north and destroy Assyria, leaving Nineveh utterly desolate and dry as the desert.* Zephaniah had prophesied this (Zephaniah 2:13) and now it had happened:—the nerve-centre of Assyrian power destroyed and reduced to ashes, the Nineveh which for centuries with its armies of conquest and occupation, with torture, terror and mass deportations had brought nothing but blood and tears to the ancient world.

The 'Fertile Crescent' breathed again. Jubilation filled its afflicted peoples—new hope began to spring up, in which Judah shared.

After the death of Ashurbanipal, when the hated Assyrian colossus as shaken by the first signs of ultimate collapse, King Josiah had without hesitation banned the practice of foreign religions in Jerusalem. (2 Kings 23) There was more to that then merely religious objections. It clearly signified the termination of the state of vassalage, of which the gods of Nineveh, imported by compulsion, were symbolic. Josiah's reforms paved the way for a renewed religious and national vitality.

Meantime something quite unexpected happened which threatened to ruin everything. . . . *Pharaoh Necho king of Egypt went up to the Euphrates River against the king of Assyria. King Josiah marched out against him in battle, but Necho faced him and killed him at Megiddo* (2 Kings 23:29). This passage from the Bible is a perfect example of how a single word can completely change the meaning of a narrative. In this case the wrong use of the little word 'against' brands Josiah as the accomplice of the hated tyrant. At some point or other in the transcription of the Hebrew the word *al* (against) has been substituted for the word *äl* (towards). In reality Pharaoh Necho went to the aid of Assyria, i.e. 'towards'. It was only through a chance discovery that the Assyriologist C.I. Gadd found out this historical slip of the pen.

The place of discovery was quite outside the normal archaeological pattern—it was a museum. In 1923 Gadd was translating a badly damaged fragment of cuneiform text in the British Museum which had been dug up in Mesopotamia many years previously.

It read as follows: *In the month of Du'uz (June–July) the king of Assyria procured a large Egyptian army and marched against Harran to conquer it . . .*

Till the month of Ulul (August–September) he fought against the city but accomplished nothing.

The *large Egyptian army* was the forces of Pharaoh Necho.

After the fall of Nineveh what remained of the Assyrian forces had retreated to Northern Mesopotamia. Their king embarked upon the forlorn hope of reconquering from there what he had lost. It was for this purpose that Pharaoh Necho had hastened to his aid. But when after two months of fighting not even the town of Harran Had been recaptured, Necho retired.

It was the appearance of Egyptian troops in Palestine that decided Josiah to prevent the Egyptians at all costs from rendering military aid to the hated Assyrians. So it came about that the little army of Judah marched against the far superior Egyptian force, with the tragic ending at Megiddo.

On the way back to Egypt Pharaoh Necho assumed the role of overlord of Syria and Palestine. He made an example of Judah, so as to leave it in no doubt whom the country now depended. Jehoahaz, Josiah's son and successor, was stripped of his royal dignities and taken as a prisoner to the Nile (2 Kings 23:31–34). In his stead Necho placed another son of Josiah upon the throne, Eliakim, whose name he changed to Jehoiakim (2 Kings 23:34).

Egyptologists have not been able so far to produce any hymns of triumph of Pharaoh Necho. Herodotus learned from Egyptian priests a century and a half later that he had presented to the temple of Apollo in Miletus *the garb in which he had accomplished these deeds* in thankoffering for the participation of Greek mercenaries in his expedition. In the land he conquered he left nothing but a stela. It bears his name in hieroglyphic script. Its fragments were left lying in Sidon.

Four years later—605BC—Necho's dream of suzerainty over 'Asia', as his predecessors had always called it, was at an end.

Even while he was collecting tribute in Palestine, decisions were being taken about his 'conquest' elsewhere. After their joint victory the Medes and the Neo-Babylonians had divided the empire of Assyria between them. The Medes annexed the north and north-east; Babylon the south and south-west. Syrian and Palestine thus fell to King Nabopolassar. But in the meantime he had grown old and was no longer fit for the fray. He therefore sent the crown prince of Chaldea, his son Nebuchadnezzar, to take possession of the new territories.

Necho made an attempt to repulse him but

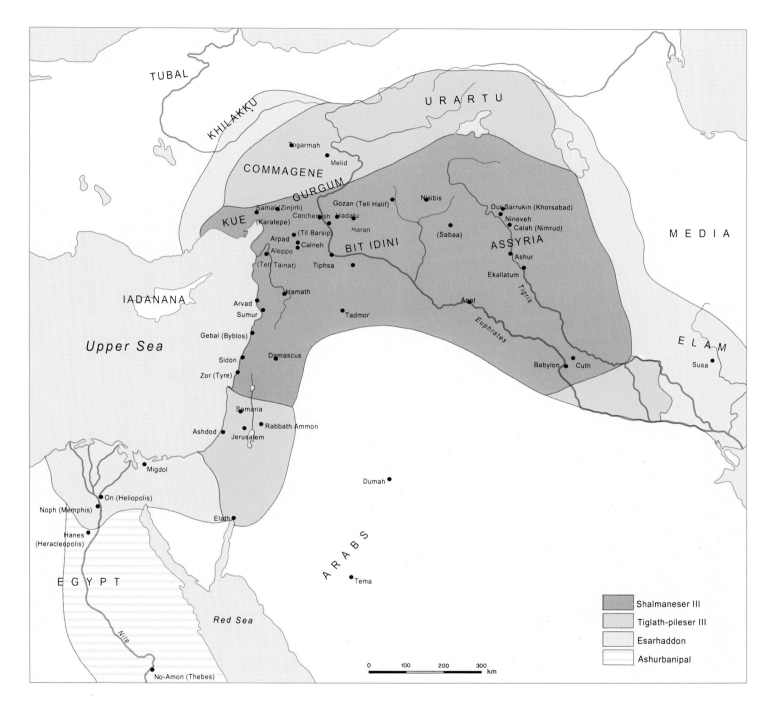

TUBAL

KHILAKKU

URARTU

COMMAGENE

Togarmah

Melid

GURGUM

KUE

Samal (Zinjirli)
(Karatepe)

Gozan (Tell Halif)

Nisibis

Dur Sarrukin (Khorsabad)

Carchemish Hadatu

Nineveh

Calah (Nimrud)

MEDIA

Arpad (Til Barsip)

Haran

(Sabaa)

Aleppo Calneh

BIT IDINI

ASSYRIA

(Tell) Tainat) Tiphsa

Ashur

IADANANA

Hamath

Ekallatum

Tigris

Arvad
Sumur

Tadmor

Arat

Euphrates

Upper Sea

Gebal (Byblos)

ELAM

Sidon

Damascus

Babylon Cuth

Susa

Zor (Tyre)

Samaria

Ashdod

Rabbath Ammon

Jerusalem

Migdol

Dumah

On (Heliopolis)

Noph (Memphis)

Elath

Hanes
(Heracleopolis)

A
R
A
B
S

EGYPT

Tema

Red Sea

Nile

	Shalmaneser III
	Tiglath-pileser III
	Esarhaddon
	Ashurbanipal

0   100   200   300
km

No-Amon (Thebes)

failed miserably. Near Carchemish, in the same region where four years previously he had endeavoured to assist the last king of Assyria, he suffered total defeat at the famous passage across the Euphrates from Mesopotamia to North Syria (Jeremiah 46:2).

Necho fled through Palestine followed by the jeers of the prophet Jeremiah: *Pharaoh king of Egypt is only a loud noise; he has missed his opportu-* *nity... Egypt will hiss like a fleeing serpent* (Jeremiah 46:17, 22).

After this shameful flight Judah saw no more of Necho. *The king of Egypt did not march out from his own country again, because the king of Babylon had taken all his territory, from the Wadi of Egypt to the Euphrates River* (2 Kings 24:7). The crown prince of Chaldea was not able to exploit his victory at Carchemish. In the course of the battle news of the

The New Assyrian Empire from the ninth to the seventh centuries BC.

263

Men, women and children of one of the towns conquered by Assyria, on the way into exile. During a rest stop the deportees are being supplied with rations by their guards. This alabaster relief, in the Museum of the Near East in Berlin, comes from Nineveh.

death of his father overtook him, and he had perforce to return to Babylon. After Nebuchadnezzar had acceded to the throne more important affairs of state kept him in his own country for the next few years. Judah was spared a fresh occupation for a time and was left to itself.

There are no contemporary records giving us the details of what happened in Judah around the turn of the sixth century. The Bible gives no clear picture of when, for example, the Chaldeans made their first appearance in the country, or of when they started to demand tribute. The Neo-Babylonian kings, unlike their predecessors the Assyrians, left no informative annals behind them. Inscriptions on buildings which have been preserved merely indicate historical events.

THE LAST DAYS OF JUDAH

During Jehoiakim's reign, Nebuchadnezzar king of Babylon invaded the land, and Jehoiakim became his vassal for three years.

2 KINGS 24:1

About the turn of the sixth century there took place the calamitous event which in a few years was to blot out Judah for ever as a nation with a place in the history of the ancient orient. Events now began to close in with frightening speed upon the tiny vassal state on the Jordan and its inhabitants, which were to result in Judah's most grievous hour of affliction. They ended with the road to exile and forcible removal to Babylon.

It began with refusal to pay tribute, and rebellion against the new feudal lord. In 598BC open revolt broke out in Judah.

At first Nebuchadnezzar did not intervene in person. Perhaps he did not think it sufficiently important: in a great empire local rebellions are no rare occurrence. He was content to leave it, to begin with to troops from Moab, Ammon and Syria, strengthened by Chaldean regular. They do not appear to have taken control of the situation however, whereupon Nebuchadnezzar himself hurried to Judah.

He was already on his way to Palestine with a considerable force when Jehoiakim unexpectedly died. It appears that so far he is the only king of Judah of whom we have a portrait. In Ramath-Rahel near Jerusalem, where a royal citadel from the time of Jehoiakim was found, a sherd with a line drawing on it was recently unearthed. This is thought to represent Jehoiakim. His son followed him upon the throne: *Jehoiachin was eighteen years old when he became king, and he reigned in Jerusalem for three months . . . At that time the officers of Nebuchadnezzar king of Babylon advanced on Jerusalem and laid siege to it, and Nebuchadnezzar himself came up to the city . . . He carried into exile all Jerusalem . . . Nebuchadnezzar took Jehoiachim captive to Babylon* (2 Kings 24:8–15).

In 597BC King Jehoiachin and his family were deported to Babylon as prisoners. But after 2,500 years who could hope to check up on the reliability of this biblical statement? Nevertheless, shortly before the beginning of the twentieth century an opportunity came the way of the archaeologists to find out something definite about the destination of the royal family of Judah.

In 1899 the German Oriental Society equipped a large expedition under the direction of Robert Koldewey, the architect, to examine the famous ruined mound of *Babil* on the Euphrates. The excavations, as it turned out, took longer than anywhere else. In eighteen years the most famous metropolis of the ancient world, the royal seat of Nebuchadnezzar, was brought to light, and at the same time, one of the Seven Wonders of the World, the 'Hanging Gardens', loudly extolled by Greek travellers of a later day, and the legendary Tower of Babel. In the palace of Nebuchadnezzar and on the Ishtar Gate, which was situated beside it, countless inscriptions were discovered.

Nevertheless the scholars were conscious of a certain disappointment. In contrast to the detailed records of Assyrian rulers, in which the names and fortunes of the kings of Israel and Judah were frequently given a historical setting, the Neo-Babylonian records hardly mentioned anything apart from the religious and architectural events of their day. They contained for example no corroboration of the fate of Judah.

Thirty years later, when the great finds at *Babil* had long since found their way into archives and museums, there emerged a number of unique documents from the immediate neighbourhood of the Ishtar Gate—in Berlin!

On Museum-Island, in the middle of the Spree in the heart of the German capital, the wonderful Ishtar Gate from Babylon had been reconstructed in the great Central Court of the Kaiser-Friedrich Museum. Menacing and sinister, the bright yellow bodies of the long row of lions stood out against the deep blue of the glazed tiles on the Processional Way of the god Marduk. As it had done by the Euphrates, so now it led astonished citizens of the twentieth century to the splendid gate dedicated to the goddess Ishtar, with its dragons and wild oxen.

While deeply impressed visitors from all over the world stood in the Central Court upstairs in front of the lofty and brilliantly coloured twin-gate, and, as Nebuchadnezzar had done long ago, turned under its arch on to the Processional Way, 300 cuneiform tablets lying in the basement rooms of the museum were waiting to be deciphered.

Koldewey's team had rescued them from the outbuildings of Nebuchadnezzar's palace near the Ishtar Gate, had numbered them and packed them in boxes. Together with masses of brightly glazed tiles, bearing reliefs of lions, dragons and wild oxen, they had made the long journey to Berlin, where, as luck would have it, the old tablets were lying in their packing-cases by the Spree, almost exactly as they had been in Babylon, only a few yards under the Ishtar Gate.

After 1933 E.F. Weidner, the Assyriologist, took in hand to look through the tablets and sherds in the basement rooms of the Kaiser-Friedrich Museum. He then translated them one by one. They contained nothing but court inventories, receipted accounts from the royal commisariat, book-entries of ancient bureaucrats, nothing but ordinary everyday matters.

Despite that, Weidner stuck it out manfully day after day in the basement under the Ishtar Gate and worked at his translations tirelessly.

Then all of a sudden his monotonous job came unexpectedly to life. Among this dull administrative rubbish Weidner suddenly found some priceless relics of red tape in the ancient world.

On four different receipts for stores issued he came upon a familiar biblical name: *Ja'-u-kinu*—Jehoiachin!

There was no possibility of his being mistaken, because Jehoiachin was given his full title: 'King of the (land of) Judah'. The Babylonian clay receipts moreover bear the date of the thirteenth year of the reign of King Nebuchadnezzar. That means 592BC, five years after the fall of Jerusalem and the deportation. In addition the Babylonian steward of the commisariat has mentioned in three cases five of the king's sons, who were in charge of a servant with the Jewish name of *Kenaiah*.

Other personnel on the ration-strength of Nebuchadnezzar's stores are noted as *eight persons from the land of Judah*, who possibly belonged to the retinue of King Jehoiachin, among them a gardener by the name of *Salam-ja-a-ma*.

Jehoiachin, the deposed king of Judah, lived with his family and his retinue in the palace of Nebuchadnezzar in Babylon. We may conclude from Weidner's discovery that the biblical account in the Second Book of Kings may be thus supplemented: *Day by day the king of Babylon gave Jehoichin a regular allowance as long as he lived, till the day of his death* (Jeremiah 52:34).

A sensational addition to the account of these events was made in 1955 through the examination of 2,500-year-old cuneiform tablets which had long lain in peaceful oblivion in the British Museum. D.J. Wiseman was engaged in deciphering these tablets when to his great surprise he came

A cuneiform tablet from Babylon gives an account of how King Jehoiachin was taken prisoner and King Zedekiah installed by Nebuchadnezzar.

Several fragments of clay tablets from Babylon record deliveries of foodstuffs to the imprisoned King Jehoiachin and his sons.

Clay 'despatch blocks' found in the rubble of the gate buildings at Lachish give us information on the dramatic last days before the conquest of the fortress by the Babylonians.

In spite of all resistance, the kingdoms of the Amorites, Edomites
and Moabites eventually came,
like their neighbours Israel and
Judah, under the domination of the
Near Eastern superpowers—the
Assyrians and then the New Babylonian Empire and the Persians.

At the foot of the citadel of
modern Amman, the biblical
Rabbat-Ammon, two statues were
discovered in 1949 which
probably portray Ammonite kings.
One (left) wears a helmet-like
head covering, which resembles
the Atef crown of the Egyptian
Osiris. On the other statue an inscription in Phoenician letters
names the subject of the portrait,
Jerach-Azar, and his grandfather
Shanib, of whom we know that he
was king of Ammon.

across the following entry in the official records of the Babylonian royal house:

> In the seventh year, in the month Chislev, the king assembled his army and advanced on Hatti-land (Syria). He encamped over against the city of the Judeans and conquered it on the second day of Adar (the sixteenth of March 597). He took the king (Jehoiachin) prisoner, and appointed in his stead a king after his own heart (Zedekiah). He exacted heavy tribute and had it brought to Babylon.

Here we have the original account in Babylonian chronicles of the first conquest of Jerusalem by Nebuchadnezzar as it has been preserved for us in the Bible in the twenty-fourth chapter of the Second Book of Kings.

Eleven years had gone by since the capture of Jehoiachin and the first deportation to Babylon. The time had now come for Judah's fate to be sealed.

> Now Zedekiah rebelled against the king of Babylon. So in the ninth year of Zedekiah's reign, on the tenth day of the tenth month, Nebuchadnezzar king of Babylon marched against Jerusalem with his whole army. He encamped outside the city and built siege works all around it. (2 Kings 24:20b–25:1)

The last scene in the tragedy of this tiny nation provides a classic example of how biblical narratives and archaeological discoveries illuminate the same event from different points of view, and how accurate are the statements of the prophet alongside the official account in the Second Book of Kings and in Chronicles. Jeremiah sketches with swift strokes of his brush scenes taken from the exciting and anxious events of the last days, which through discoveries in Palestine in our own day are confirmed as being startling in their accuracy and historically genuine.

After the first conquest in 597BC Nebuchadnezzar allowed Judah to continue its existence as a vassal state. The successor to the throne, after Jehoiachin had been led off into captivity, was his uncle Mattaniah, who was renamed Zedekiah by the Chaldean king.

The deportation of their kinsmen before their very eyes, the bitter experiences of a century and a half, the miserable fate of the northern kingdom, still only too fresh in their memories, nevertheless did not extinguish the will to resist.

Soon indeed voices were being raised, denouncing Babylon, and demanding the recovery of all that had been lost (Jeremiah 28:1–4). The prophet Jeremiah raised his voice in warning but it was the anti-Babylonian, pro-Egyptian group which was more and more heeded. They egged the people on and eventually got the upper hand of the spineless and vacillating king. Alliances were struck with the bordering vassal states. There was a meeting of 'messengers' from Edom, Moab, and Ammon as well as from the seaports of Tyre and Sidon in the presence of King Zedekiah in Jerusalem (Jeremiah 27:3).

The fact that in 588BC a new Pharaoh, Apries, ascended the throne had clearly a decisive influence on the decision to revolt (Jeremiah 44:30). The new ruler of Egypt must have given Judah assurances of armed help, for *Zedekiah rebelled against the king of Babylon* (2 Kings 24:20).

In the 'tenth month' (2 Kings 25:1) of the same year 588BC—it was 'the ninth year' of king Zedekiah—Nebuchadnezzar arrived with a strong army from Babylon. With the speed of lightning the punitive campaign against rebellious Judah was unfolded.

The Chaldean divisions of infantry, fast cavalry and charioteers smashed all resistance and conquered city after city. Except for the capital, Jerusalem, and the frontier fortresses of Lachish and Azekah in the south, the whole land was finally subdued.

Jerusalem, Lachish and Azekah were determined to fight to the end; *while the army of the king of Babylon was fighting against Jerusalem and the other cities of Judah that were still holding out—Lachish and Azekah. These were the only fortified cities left in Judah* (Jeremiah 34:7).

Impressive and enduring evidence of the last phase of this hopeless struggle lies before us. Twenty miles south-west of Jerusalem the green valley of Elah pushes its way far into the mountains of Judah. This was the scene of the duel between young David and Goliath the Philistine giant (1 Samuel 17:19ff). The little brook out of which David gathered 'five smooth stones' for his sling still runs and burbles between its oak trees.

From the river bed the hill slopes gently upwards to a height of 1,000 feet. From the top the cornfields and olive groves of the old plain of Philistia can be seen stretching away to the far horizon where they meet the silvery sparkle of the Mediterranean. On this spot Dr. Frederick J. Bliss, the British archaeologist, identified a fort with eight stout towers as ancient Azekah, one of the frontier fortresses which, as we have seen, remained unconquered. Just about 12 miles to the south the ruins of Lachish were found to contain

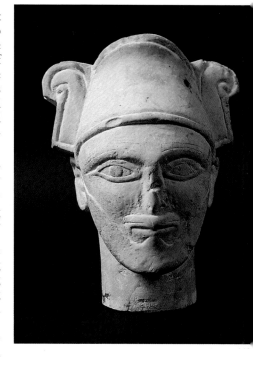

This highly stylized head from around 700BC in the Amman Museum may also represent a king of the Ammonites. The featherlike forms on either side of his helmet derive from the high conical crown of Osiris. Similar headdresses worn by high-ranking personages are recorded frequently in Syria and Phoenicia but have no implications of divinity there.

Sargon II, possibly a usurper of the Assyrian throne, whose propagandist name means 'the rightful king', publicized his successful campaigns in the form of 'letters to the god'. They are composed as speeches of thanks to the imperial god Ashur. The longest account of this type originated as a result of a war against the kingdom of Urartu and came into the possession of the Louvre Museum.

career of James Lesley Starkey, the famous excavator of Lachish. During the Palestinian troubles which had broken out he was shot by Arabs at the age of forty-three in the neighbourhood of Hebron on the road from Lachish to Jerusalem. His death was a tragic case of mistaken identity. In the course of the protracted excavations he had grown a beard and the Arabs took him for a Jew.

In 701BC the storm troops of Sennacherib, king of Assyria, had rushed the walls of Lachish with armoured siege engines fitted with battering rams. Nebuchadnezzar's special detachments adopted an entirely different technique to force the city to surrender.

Investigation of the stratum which marked the Babylonian work of destruction produced, to Starkey's astonishment, ashes. Ashes in incredible quantities. Many of the layers are several yards thick and are still—after 2,500 years—higher then the remains of the solid walls of the fortress. Nebuchadnezzar's engineers were specialists in the art of incendiarism, past masters at starting conflagrations.

Whatever wood they could lay hands on they dragged to the spot, stripped the whole area around Lachish of its forests and thickets, cleared the hills of timber for miles around, piled the firewood as high as a house outside the walls and set it alight. Countless olive-groves were hacked down for this purpose: the layer of ashes contains masses of charred olive stones.

Day and night sheets of flame leapt sky high, a ring of fire licked the walls from top to bottom. The besieging force piled on more and more wood until the white-hot stones burst and the walls caved in.

So Lachish likewise fell and only Jerusalem still offered resistance. The whole weight of the Babylonian war machine could now be directed against it. It was impossible to use the new incendiary technique in this case, for the forests around Jerusalem had, since the time of the patriarchs and of Joshua's conquest, been reduced to miserable little plantings and undergrowth (Joshua 17:15, 18). They therefore preferred to storm Jerusalem with the approved technique of battering rams and siege engines. For eighteen months Jerusalem was besieged and heroically defended: *The city was kept under siege until the eleventh year of King Zedekiah* (2 Kings 25:2).

What made the defenders hold out, despite the fact that famine had long been raging in the city and was taking a heavy toll, was a desperate hope that Egypt might come to their assistance.

It seemed that this hope was to be fulfilled, for

valuable evidence. J.L. Starkey, the archaeologist, disinterred them in the thirties when the Wellcome-Marston Expedition from the U.K. investigated the ruins of the great city gate, where the battle was fiercest. Eighteen ostraca, inscribed clay sherds, contained information about forward posts, observation posts and strong points held by Judahite troops which had not yet been overwhelmed. These despatches on clay had been sent to *Jaosh, the commandant of the fort of Lachish,* during that fateful 'tenth month' of the year 588BC. The messages, scratched out in haste, indicate with every line the frightful tension that existed just before the collapse. One of the last of these eyewitness reports reads: *May Yahweh grant that my lord should hear good tidings . . . we are watching for the signal stations of Lachish, according to the signals which my lord has given . . . we are no longer receiving signals from Azekah.* This massage told Jaosh, the commanding officer at Lachish, that Azekah had fallen. Nebuchadnezzar could now withdraw his engineers for the attack on the last fortress but one.

British archaeologists with the Wellcome-Marston expedition obtained information about the terrible end of Lachish in 1938 after six strenuous seasons of excavating.

It was the last success that was to crown the

the Babylonians suddenly withdrew. *Pharaoh's army had marched out of Egypt, and when the Babylonians who were besieging Jerusalem heard the report about them, they withdrew from Jerusalem* (Jeremiah 37:5). An army did in fact at that time come up from the Nile under Pharaoh Apries, as Herodotus also mentions. Its destination was however not Jerusalem. Apries was making an attack by land and sea against the Phoenician ports.

Fragments of Egyptian monuments testify to Pharaoh's presence in Tyre and Sidon at that time.

So it came about as Jeremiah had prophesied: *Pharaoh's army, which has marched out to support you, will go back to its own land, to Egypt* (Jeremiah 37:7). After a few days the enemy was back in front of Jerusalem, the siege continued with the utmost fury, and the end could no longer be delayed.

> *Then the city wall was broken through, and the whole army fled at night through the gate between the two walls near the king's garden.* (2 Kings 25:4)

Thanks to the result of excavations, the route taken by the defenders in their flight can now be reconstructed without difficulty.

King Hezekiah had strengthened the old fortifications of the city of David by a second wall on the south side (2 Chronicles 32:5). There is still no certainty as to the line it followed.

The moment the enemy entered the city through a breach in the walls the defenders retreated in the first instance behind the double walled southern part of the fortifications and only with the onset of darkness did they escape through an outer gate into freedom and then over the hills to Jericho. In the process King Zedekiah was captured and hauled before the great king, who was staying in his headquarters in Ribla on the Orontes. *They killed the sons of Zedekiah before his eyes. Then they put out his eyes* (2 Kings 25:7)—the harsh Babylonian martial law for traitors. This cruel punishment by blinding is frequently attested on pictorial reliefs.

Jerusalem was given over to plundering: the royal palace and the temple were set on fire, the city walls and fortifications were razed to the ground. The order to destroy was given to *Nebuzaradan commander of the imperial guard* (2 Kings 25:8), a grand vizier who appears in the Babylonian list of court officials as *Nabu-Seri-Idinnam*. Once more in 587BC part of the population was deported (2 Kings 25:11). Nebuchadnezzar deposed the royal house of David, which had reigned without interruption for 400 years.

The land of Judah became a Babylonian province. Those who were left waged a guerilla war

from their hide-outs in the mountains and claimed as their victim the Babylonian-appointed governor, a Jew named Gedaliah. The third deportation was a reprisal for this (Jeremiah 52:30). Little groups of Judahites were able to escape it by fleeing to Egypt (2 Kings 25:26; Jeremiah 43:7). If we are to believe the biblical account, the curtain of history was lowered on an empty land.

Scholars like S.A. Cook and C.C. Torrey have denied the truth of the biblical tradition of this carrying off into exile. In their view there was never a mass deportation from Judah, at the most some of the nobility were imprisoned in Babylon.

William F. Albright never tired of describing in his writings how severe was the destruction in Judah: 'Many towns were destroyed at the beginning of the sixth century and were never again resettled. Others were destroyed at that time and then partially inhabited at a later period. Others still were destroyed and only re-occupied much later. There is not a single known case of a town in Judah being continuously inhabited during the exile.'

Even though a continuing colonization can be demonstrated, as at Mizpah, for example, where the Babylonian governor resided, still the truth is established—six-and-a-half centuries after Joshua entered the Promised Land, his descendants were scattered to the four winds.

The story of the children of Israel is at an end—the story of the Jews begins.

An artist's reconstruction which attempts to reproduce the powerful impression which the city of Ashur must have made in its golden age. The peninsula-like spur of rock in the north-east of the city is surrounded by the river Tigris and an artificially created arm of the river. Behind the mighty walls of the city looms the temple of the city god Ashur (enlarged by Sargon II and Sennacherib) and to the right of this the ziggurat for the gods Enlil and Ashur. Both buildings, once rearing up so proudly, are now pitiful mounds of ruins.

From the Exile to the Maccabean Kingdom

> *Build houses and settle down; plant gardens and eat what they produce. Increase in number there; do not decrease. Also, seek the peace and prosperity of the city to which I have carried you into exile.*
>
> Jeremiah 29:5–7

EDUCATION THROUGH EXILE

It was well-considered advice that the prophet Jeremiah sent from Jerusalem to the elders, priests, prophets and to the whole nation that at Nebuchadnezzar's bidding had been carried off to Babylon. Following his counsel, they sought and found 'the peace of the city', and did not fare at all badly. The Exile in Babylon was not to be compared with the harsh existence of the children of Israel on the Nile, in Pithom and Raamses in the days of Moses. Apart from a few exceptions (Isaiah 47:6) there was no heavy forced labour. Nowhere is there any mention of their having to make bricks by the Euphrates. Yet Babylon ran what was probably the greatest brick-making industry in the world at that time. For never was there so much building going on in Mesopotamia as under Nebuchadnezzar.

Anyone who took Jeremiah's advice as his guide got on well, some indeed very well. One family which had made the grade has left to posterity its dust-covered business documents on clay. 'Murashu and Sons'—International Bank—Insurance, conveyancing, Loans—Personal and real estate—Head office: Nippur—Branches everywhere—a firm with a reputation throughout the world, the 'Lloyd's' of Mesopotamia.

The Murashus—displaced persons from Jerusalem—had done well for themselves in Nippur since 587BC. They were an old established office. Their firm still stood for something in Mesopotamia even in the Persian era. The 'books' of 'Murashu and Sons' are full of detailed information about the life of the exiles, such as their names, their occupations, their property.

Scholars from the University of Pennsylvania discovered some of the Jewish firm's deeds when they excavated its former business premises in

Like Gerasa in Jordan, many towns on either side of the river Jordan acquired a Greek flavour through colonnaded streets, temples and theatres.

In the golden age of the Hittite kingdom, tribes and clans of this people already lived in Palestine. Where local rulers with Indo-Germanic names are mentioned, as for instance in Acre, Megiddo, Sharon, Ashkelon or Gaza, we may assume they were Hittites. A series of small Hittite principalities in the border areas survived the end of the empire, and then one by one these came under Assyrian domination. The dispersed remains of this once-powerful people were gradually absorbed into the ethnic mixture of Syria and Canaan. This stone relief from Jinjirli in the Archaeological Museum of Istanbul shows a late Hittite princeling on his chariot, shooting arrows from a bow.

Nippur. They were in great clay jars, which, in accordance with security precautions in those days, had been carefully sealed with asphalt. It was not only Assyriologists who read the translations of these documents with delight.

The offices of Murashu and Sons were a hive of activity. For 150 years they enjoyed the confidence of their clients, whether it was a matter of conveyance of large estates and sections of the canals or of slaves. Anyone who could not write, when he came eventually to add his signature, put, instead of his name, the print of his finger-nail on the documents. It corresponded to putting a cross, in the presence of witnesses, as in the case of illiterates today.

One day three jewellers called on Murashu and Sons... *Elilaha-idinna and Belsunu and Hatin said to Elil-nadin-sum, son of Murashu: In the case of this emerald ring, we give a twenty-years guarantee that the stone will not fall out of the gold. If the emerald falls out of the ring before the expiry of twenty years, Elil-aha-idinna, Belsunu and Hatin undertake to pay damages to Elil-nadin-sum amounting to 10 Minas of silver.* The document is signed by seven people. Before the lawyer's name the clay bears the imprint of three finger-nails. These are

the signatures of the three jewellers who were unable to write.

An exiled Jew, Mannudannijama, came to Murashu and Sons, because he wanted to arrange a deed of conveyance with a Babylonian concerning an important herd of cattle: *13 old rams, 27 two year old rams, 152 lambing ewes, 40 year old rams, 40 year old ewe-lambs, an old he-goat, a two year old he-goat... a total of 276 white and black, large and small sheep and goats... cash on delivery... Mannudannijama to be responsible for pasture, feeding, and safe custody... Nippur, the twenty-fifth of Ulul... Signed: Fingernail of Mannudannijama.*

Securities for those imprisoned for debt were deposited with the bank. There were special departments for all eventualities of life.

The rate of interest was 20 per cent, not introduced by Murashu, let it be said. That was the normal rate in those days.

'Murashu and Sons' may serve as an example of the profession, which since the days of the Exile has been associated with the children of Israel. It became for them the profession par excellence: that of merchant and trader. In their homeland they had only been peasants, cattle breeders and tradesmen. The law of Israel had made no provi-

societies, within which they could build themselves into a community and devote themselves to their religious practices. It gave them cohesion and continuity.

The Israelites could have chosen no better training college. Babylon as an international centre of trade, industry and commerce, was the great school for the cities and capitals of the whole world, which from then on were to become the home of the homeless. The metropolis, whose ruins after 2,500 years still betray its ancient power and glory, had no equal in the ancient world.

sion for commerce: it was an alien occupation. The word *Canaanite* was for them synonymous with 'shopkeeper', 'merchant', people whom the prophets had vigorously castigated for their sins. (Hosea 12:7; Amos 8:5, 6).

The switch over to this hitherto forbidden profession was extremely clever. For it proved to be in the last resort, when added to a tenacious attachment to the laws of Yahweh, the best guarantee of the continuance of Israel as a people. As farmers and settlers scattered throughout a foreign land they would have intermarried and interbred with people of other races and in a few generations would have been absorbed and disappeared. This new profession demanded that their houses should be in more or less large

Above left **The costume and weaponry of this warrior on a relief from Jinjirli in southern Turkey are Hittite: a conical cap, an apron decorated with borders, pointed shoes, a long spear, a sword and a 'Pontic' shield. He wears his beard according to Assyrian fashion.**

Above right **This late Hittite relief, of a man throwing stones with a sling, comes from Tell Halif in northern Syria. This primitive shepherd's weapon could be thoroughly effective if aimed accurately.**

Sixty miles south of busy Baghdad the desert is churned up, scarred and furrowed. As far as the eye can see, there stretches a maze of trenches, rubble heaps, and pits which bear witness to the efforts of German archaeologists, over a period of eighteen years. As a result of this prolonged campaign Professor Robert Koldewey has been able to bring to light the fabulous Babylon of the Bible.

Seventy years after the excavations the site presented a dismal and chaotic appearance. Wind and desert sand was slowly but relentlessly covering up again the gigantic skeleton of the old metropolis. Only on one side a few block-like towers stood out with sharply defined silhouette against the sky. Their brick walls, once brightly

Etemenanki (**'foundation stone of heaven and earth'**) **was once the name of the proudest building of Babylon. The remains of the 'tower of Babel' make a mockery of this claim. At the time of the biblical account, which makes this building the incarnation of human arrogance, the staged tower was still standing; even the Persians in 479BC could not destroy its huge mass of bricks.**

Only when, in the course of centuries, thieves had carried off its cladding of fired bricks, did the core of sun-dried mud bricks begin to disintegrate. The perimeter of the building measured about ninety metres, and it is estimated that its 'peak' was of an equal height. The seventh platform bore a temple-like building, which may have served for the 'divine marriage' at the new year. The beginnings of this most famous of ziggurats go back to around 2000BC, but many restorations are recorded; the last rebuilding was the work of the New Babylonian kings Nabopolassar, Nebuchadnezzar II and Nabonidus between 624 and 539BC.

tiled, were bleak and bare. Here at the Ishtar Gate began the long Processional Way. Where it ended, a massive hump on the other side of the city proclaimed the presence of one of the greatest edifices of the ancient world, the Tower of Babel.

The pomp and glory, the power and might of the city which *sinned against the Lord* (Jeremiah 50:14) were all destroyed and disappeared.

It was never again inhabited. Could the oracle of the Prophet Isaiah have been more completely fulfilled?

> *Babylon, the jewel of kingdoms, the glory of the Babylonians' pride, will be overthrown by God like Sodom and Gomorrah. She will never be inhabited or lived in through all generations; But desert creatures will lie there, jackals will fill her houses; there the owls will dwell, Hyenas will howl in her strongholds, jackals in her luxurious palaces. (Isaiah 13:19–23)*

It is long time now since the site was un-inhabited by jackals and owls and more so by ostriches. Even the mighty Euphrates has turned its back on it and has chosen a new bed. Once upon a time the arrogant walls of the city and the lofty Tower were reflected in its waters. Now a silhouette of palm trees in the distance indicates its new course. The little Arab settlement of Babil preserves in its name the memory of the proud city: but it lies some miles north of the ruins.

The ruins preserved as their most precious treasure documents of incomparable value: it is

thanks to them that we are able today to reconstruct on accurate picture of the time of the Jewish exile which was also the period of Babylon's greatest prosperity.

Is not this the great Babylon I have built as the royal residence, by my mighty power and for the glory of my majesty? (Daniel 4:30). These words which Daniel puts into the mouth of King Nebuchadnezzar do not exaggerate. Hardly any other monarch in the past was such an assiduous builder. There is scarcely any mention of warlike activities, conquests and campaigns. In the forefront there is the constant building activity of Nebuchadnezzar. Hundreds of thousands of bricks bear his name, and the plans of many of the buildings have been preserved. Babylon in fact surpassed all the cities of the ancient orient: it was greater than Thebes, Memphis and Ur, greater even than Nineveh.

The centre of the city, which is full of three and four-storey buildings, is traversed by dead straight streets not only those that run parallel to the river but also the cross streets which lead down to the water side. So Herodotus described what he himself had seen. The town plan of Babylon is reminiscent of the blueprints for large American cities.

Coming from Palestine, even from proud Jerusalem, the exiles had only known narrow twisting streets, little better than alleys. In Babylon however they made the acquaintance of streets as broad as avenues and as straight as if they had been drawn with a ruler. Every one of them bore the name of one of the gods in the Babylonian

pantheon. There was a Marduk street and a Zababa street on the left bank of the river. In the right-hand corner of the city they crossed the streets of the moon-god Sin and of Enlil, the 'Lord of the World'. On the right bank Adad street ran from east to west, and intersected the street of the sun-god Shamash.

Babylon was not only a commercial but a religious metropolis as can be seen from an inscription: *Altogether there are in Babylon 53 temples of the chief gods, 55 chapels of Marduk, 300 chapels for the earthly deities, 600 for the heavenly deities, 180 altars for the goddess Ishtar, 180 for the gods Nergal and Adad and 12 other Altars for different gods.*

Polytheism of this kind with worship and ritual which extended to public prostitution must have given the city, in terms of the present day, the appearance of an annual fair.

But the most vicious practice of the Babylonians is the following, writes Herodotus in shocked aston-ishment (I, 199). *Every woman in the country must take her seat in the shrine of Aphrodite, and once in her life consort with a stranger . . . And only when she has been with him, and done her service to the god-dess, is she allowed to go home: and from then on no gift is great enough to tempt her. All the women who are tall and beautiful are quickly released: but the unattractive ones have to wait for a long time before they can fulfil the law: some of them have to wait three or four years.*

The abominable temptations and enticements which were part of everyday life in Babylon remained indelibly fixed in the minds of the exiled Jews. Through the centuries until the time of Christ the brilliant metropolis was for them: *Babylon the Great, the mother of prostitutes and of the abominations of the earth* (Revelation 17:5). The idea of Babylon as a cesspool of vice is rooted in the vocabulary of every modern language.

The German archaeologists had to clear away over a million cubic feet of rubble before they had exposed part of the temple of Marduk on the Euphrates, which had been rebuilt under Nebu-chadnezzar. The shrine, including its outbuild-ings, measured approximately 1,500 feet by 1,800 feet. Opposite the temple rose the Ziggurat, the staged tower of Marduk's sanctuary.

> *Come let's make bricks and bake them thoroughly. They used brick instead of stone, and tar instead of mortar. Then they said, Come, let us build our-selves a city, with a tower that reaches to the heavens, so that we may make a name for our-selves. (Genesis 11:3,4)*

The bricklaying technique described in the Bible at the building of the Tower of Babel corre-sponds with the findings of the archaeologists. As the investigations confirmed, actually only asphal-ted bricks were used in the construction, especial-ly in the foundations. That was clearly necessary for the security of the structure in accordance with building regulations. In the neighbourhood of the river the regular rise in the level of the water and

The 'Lion of Babylon' was found by Bedouins in 1776. This basalt sculpture, almost two metres high, of a lion striding away over a lying man, remained unfinished. Its con-dition suggests the half-finished state in which sculptures were customarily transported from the quarry to their destination, to be finished there. The theory that it might be a piece of booty of Hittite provenance, is probably mistaken, since at the time unfinished works of art were not seen as having any aesthetic value. It is more likely that the Persian conquest of Baby-lon interrupted the sculptor at his work.

Plan of the city of Babylon in the late Babylonian period, after E. Unger. In the course of millennia the bed of the Euphrates has risen considerably, and the water table has risen with it. This means that the Babylon of the time of Hammurabi, lying deep below the present level, can hardly be investigated. The late Babylonian town, too, has been nowhere near fully excavated. The plan of 1931 is a reconstruction based on confirmed remains, soundings and descriptions. Visitors to the excavation site cannot exactly expect to stroll around the town and get a coherent overview of it, as suggested by the plan or the models in the museum. But they still serve to aid our imagination and to help us find our way around the chaotic terrain.

The more-or-less rectangular heart of the town, about 2500 by 1500 metres in extent, was intersected by the Euphrates. The two halves of the town were linked by a bridge which was an extension of Adad Street. Outside the moat around the city walls lay suburbs. The 'summer palace' of Nebuchadnezzar II lies far outside to the north, under a heap of rubble which still bears the name of Babil. The centre with its shrines and the royal seat lay on the east bank of the Euphrates. From here alone six gates led in three directions. The palace was linked to the Ishtar Gate in the north; this was part of the town fortifications and, together with the northern fort, projected into a bend of the river. On the town side there was a moat alongside it. At the point where the processional way began is the supposed site of the famous 'Hanging Gardens' (which of course have nothing to do with Semiramis).

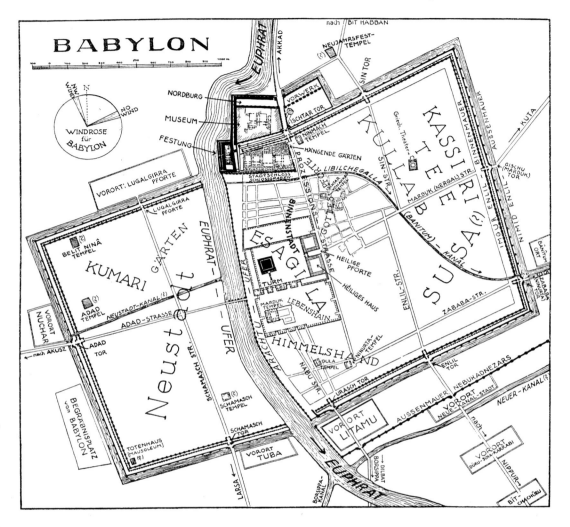

the constant dampness of the ground had to be borne in mind. Foundations and stonework were therefore made waterproof and damp-proof with 'slime', i.e. asphalt.

The biblical story of the building of the tower at the dawn of history probably originated at the time when the tower, whose top was to 'reach the heavens', was already falling into decay. It was for this reason that it could become a symbol of the vanity of human ambition. More than once it had been destroyed and rebuilt. After the death of Hammurabi the Hittites tried to raze the mighty structure to the ground. Nebuchadnezzar merely had it restored.

Seven stages rose one above the other. A little tablet belonging to an architect which was found in the temple expressly mentioned that length, breadth and height were equal and that only the terraces had different measurements. The length of the sides at the base is given as being rather

more than 290 feet. The archaeologists measured it as 295 feet. According to that the tower must have been almost 300 feet high.

The Tower of Babel was also involved in dubious religious rites. Herodotus writes: *On the topmost platform there is a spacious temple, and inside the temple stands a couch of unusual size richly adorned, with a golden table by its side. There is no statue of any kind set up in the place, nor is the chamber occupied at nights by anyone but a single native woman, who, as the Chaldeans, the priests of this god, affirm, is chosen for himself by the deity out of all the women of the land. They also declare—but I for my part do not believe it—that the god himself comes down into the temple and sleeps upon the couch. This is like the story told by the Egyptians of what takes place in Thebes, where a woman always sleeps in the temple of the Theban Zeus . . .*

On the streets and squares between the temples, the chapels and the altars, trade and com-

merce flourished. Solemn processions, heavily laden caravans, traders' barrows, priests, pilgrims, merchants surged to and fro, colourful and noisy. Religious life and business life were so closely associated in Babylon's everyday affairs that they often dovetailed into each other, as they did in the temples. What else could the priests do

with all the sacrificial animals, all the 'tithes' that were presented daily on the altars, many of them quickly perishable, apart form turning them into money as soon as possible? Just as in Ur, the temple authorities in Babylon ran their own department stores and warehouses. They also ran their own banks to invest their revenues to the best advantage.

Outside the double walls of the city, which were broad enough, Herodotus tells us, *to allow a four-horse chariot to turn on them*, lay the 'Chambers of Commerce'. It was on the river-bank that prices were fixed and exchange rates established for the commodities that arrived by boat. *Karum*, 'quay', was the name the Babylonians gave to what we now call the Exchange. As well as taking over the Quay, or Exchange, from the Babylonians the old world has also taken over its system of weights and measurements.

However much the Jews may have sought 'the peace of the city' and found it; however much they may have learned in the cities of Babylonia which would profit future generations, broaden their own outlook and raise their standard of living, all of which would benefit future generations in many ways—nevertheless their heart-yearnings for

Above **Approaching the city of Babylon from the north through the Ishtar Gate (foreground), immediately to the left on the processional way can be seen the reconstructed temple of the bird-shaped goddess Ninmah.**

Left **Only an artist's reconstruction can still allow us to imagine the main shrine of the city, the temple and the ziggurat of the god Marduk. From the new city to the west, we look across the Euphrates, with its fortified east bank, and the town's only bridge. The staged tower and the temple each lie in huge walled courts. Behind the ziggurat the Holy Gate opens onto the processional way. Behind this a huge residential quarter stretches out, so far hardly investigated.**

The Ishtar Gate was by far the most splendid gate building in Babylon; it was through this gate that the processional way led from the ziggurat to the New Year temple outside the city. Doubtless it was also meant to show off the adjoining palace. The whole gate, as well as the passage leading to it, was clad with brick reliefs decorated with coloured glazes; the originals are in the Museum of the Near East in Berlin. In Babylon a copy has been erected. The nobly pacing animals correspond to the most important deities: the lion of Ishtar, the ox of the weather god Adad, the dragon of the city god Marduk.

The hands of the cosmic clock are approaching 500BC. The ancient orient carries more than 3,000 years on its shoulders. The nations in the 'Fertile Crescent' and on the Nile have grown old, their creative impulse is exhausted, they have fulfilled their task, and the time is drawing near for them to step off the stage of history.

The sun of the ancient orient is setting and its peoples are vaguely conscious of the approaching night.

Yet there is to be a last flicker of life among these weary nations: they summon up enough strength for one last effort. From Egypt to the lands on the Euphrates and the Tigris it is as if there is to be one final attempt to rise before sinking into insignificance. Were they looking back and thinking of the leading role they had played on the world's stage? It would almost seem as if they were. Their monarchs look back to the great symbols of their glorious past. They believe that with a new display of strength they can delay the inevitable.

Pharaoh Necho and Pharaoh Apries made great efforts to reconquer Syria and Palestine. The Old Kingdom with the campaigns of Thutmosis III against Asia became the ideal of the Twenty-sixth Dynasty. Large navies were built and an attempt was made to restore the old canal between the Nile and the Red Sea.

Even if the new manifestations of strength bore no fruit, and success eluded their military exploits, nevertheless the example of the great days of the builders of the Pyramids lent vitality in other directions. Painters and sculptors copies the works of their great predecessors. Names of Pharaohs of the third millennium were engraved on new scarabs. Ancient official titles and court titles were revived, the civil service was, as it were antiquarianized.

The same thing happened on the Mediterranean coast in Phoenicia. In 814BC Carthage was founded as a North African colony of the city of Tyre. By this time the power of these Phoenician merchant sailors had reached its limit. From the Black Sea to the Straits of Gibraltar they had trading posts and bases along the Phoenician coast of the Mediterranean. A century later the Greeks had partly inherited their world trade. Sanchuniathon, the priest, wrote the history of Phoenicia. He was commissioned by a king to copy old inscriptions and texts which Philo of Byblos was to use much later as the source for his history.

With Ashurbanipal the Assyrian Empire

their distant little homeland on the Jordan left them no inward peace. They could not forget the city of David, their beloved Jerusalem. *By the rivers of Babylon we sat down and wept, when we remembered Zion* (Psalm 137). These were no empty words. For in the course of the following centuries thousands of them set out on the difficult journey home. They rebuilt their shattered city and the temple of Yahweh. Without a passionate longing for the homeland they had lost, that would never have happened.

SUNSET IN THE ANCIENT ORIENT

Look! Disaster is spreading from nation to nation; a mighty storm is rising from the ends of the earth.
JEREMIAH 25:32

reached the zenith of its power. It stretched from the Persian Gulf to Upper Egypt. The tiger of the ancient orient had eaten his fill, and the ruler of the most powerful of all conquering nations allowed himself to be painted in an arbour of grape-vines, reclining on soft cushions and being handed a goblet of wine. Collecting old books was his hobby and he had the biggest library in the ancient Orient. On his instructions the repositories of old temples were ransacked in a search for lost documents. His scribes made copies of thousands of tablets from the reign of the great Sargon I (2350BC). The hobby of his brother Shamash-Shumukin of Babylonia went even further. He had the events of his day written up in the ancient language of Sumeria.

Nebuchadnezzar too, the last great ruler on the throne of Babylon, was afflicted with this longing for old forgotten far-off things. His court chroniclers had to compose inscriptions in Old Babylonian, which nobody could either speak or read. Architecture and literature flourished once again among the Chaldeans.

Observing the sky in the interests of astrology led to undreamt of advances. They were able to predict eclipses of the sun and moon. In the Babylonian School of Astronomy about 750BC observations of heavenly bodies were recorded and continued without interruption for over 350 years, the longest series of astronomical observations ever made. The accuracy of their reckoning exceeded that of European astronomers until well into the eighteenth century.

Nabonidus, the last of the Babylonian rulers, caused ruined shrines and temples to be excavated, old inscriptions to be deciphered and translated. He restored the staged tower at Ur which had been weakened by age, as was shown by the finds at Tell at Muqayyar.

Princess Bel-Shalti-Nannar, sister of the

The bricks which make up the animal reliefs on the Ishtar Gate were factory-produced in moulds. The unglazed reliefs of the gate's foundations come from the same moulds. The brilliant enamel colours were made by mixing metal oxides, felspar and ground silica, which were applied to the already fired bricks and melted into a glaze at a high temperature. We have even inherited chemical recipes for these glazes in cuneiform texts.

In the year 540BC the Persian army of the emperor Cyrus killed the Babylonian King Nabonidus, and a year later the Persians occupied Babylon. The capital of the Babylonian empire seems to have fallen to the new rulers without a battle, indeed they were probably greeted as liberators.

A cuneiform document, the so-called Cyrus Cylinder in the British Museum, tells us about this in the Babylonian language: 'As I entered Babylon peacefully, and took up my seat of government in the royal palace amid rejoicing and exultation, Marduk, the great lord, inclined the hearts of the Babylonians towards me... The inhabitants of Babylon I freed from the yoke, which it was not seemly for them to wear...' Indeed the last Babylonian king, Nabonidus, had persistently annoyed the priests of Marduk and alienated the whole of Babylon with his wrong-headed religious policies. The innumerable foreign deportees had also become a threat. In 538BC Cyrus allowed them to return to their own countries.

Belshazzar in the Bible, had the same interests as her father Nabonidus. Woolley discovered in an annexe to the temple in Ur, where she had been priestess, a regular museum with objects which had been found in the southern states of Mesopotamia—probably the earliest museum in the world. She had actually carefully catalogued her collection piece by piece on a clay cylinder. This is, in Woolley's words, the 'oldest museum catalogue known'.

One people alone—broken up into many parts and at that time scattered far and wide throughout the 'Fertile Crescent'—did not succumb to surfeit or slackness: the children of Israel, descendants of the patriarchs, were filled with eager hope and had a definite end in view. They did not disappear: they found the strength to preserve themselves for new millennia—up to the present day.

For 1,500 years mankind's brightest light had come from the 'Fertile Crescent,' the oldest centre of civilization since the Stone Age. About 500BC darkness fell, imperceptibly but irresistibly, over the lands and peoples who had within them the seed of all that would come after them—but in other lands.

A new light was already shining from the mountains of Iran: the Persians were coming. The great Semitic states and Egypt had fulfilled their assignment in history: the most significant and decisive part of man's early existence had helped to prepare the ground for the Indo-Germanic kingdoms which gave birth to Europe.

From the extreme south-eastern tip of the continent the light travelled farther and farther west. From Greece to Rome, across the barrier of the Alps, across Western Europe and up to Scandinavia and the British Isles. Light from the East!

On its way, within a few centuries, new civili-

zations would appear, art would reach unimagined heights of beauty and harmony, the human mind in the philosophy and science of the Greeks would soar to pinnacles denied to the ancient orient.

On its way the light would also bring the varied colourful legacy of the ancient orient, from a practical system of weights and measures to astronomy. It would bring writing, the alphabet and—the Bible.

CYRUS, KING OF PERSIA

This is what the Lord says to his anointed, to Cyrus, whose right hand I take hold of to subdue nations before him and to strip kings of their armour, to open doors before him so that gates will not be shut.

ISAIAH 45:1

Seven years after Nebuchadnezzar's death, Nabonidus ascended the throne of Babylon in 555BC. He was to be the last ruler from Mesopotamia. For events in the highlands of Iran suggested that world history was quickly heading for a great revolution.

Five years after the accession of Nabonidus the new era began with the Persians' rise to power.

The Medes—who since the fall of Nineveh in 612BC had shared the stricken Assyrian empire with the Babylonians—were unexpectedly overcome by their neighbours and vassals, the Persians. Astyages, king of the Medes, was beaten by Cyrus, who according to Herodotus was his own grandson.

In the ancient world great men were wont to herald their arrival in extraordinary ways: often the remarkable circumstances of their birth took them outside the normal framework of the lives of their contemporaries. Two unusual dreams are said to have decided the destiny of Cyrus. They were gossiped around the whole of the ancient orient and in this way came to the ears of Herodotus, who recounts them:

Astyages... had a daughter who was named Mandane. He dreamt that from her such a stream of water flowed forth as not only to fill his capital but to flood the whole of Asia. This vision he laid before such of the Magi as had the gift of interpreting dreams, who expounded its meaning to him in full, whereat he was greatly terrified. On this account, when his daughter was of marriageable age, he would not give her to any

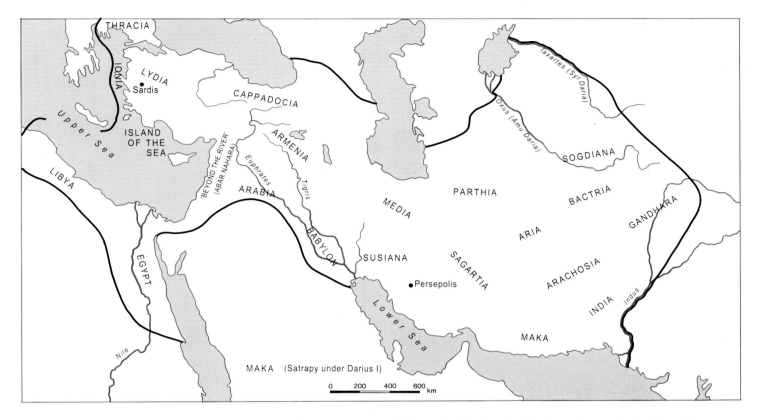

The Persian Empire with its satrapies.

of the Medes lest the dream should be accomplished, but married her to a Persian by name Cambyses...

When Mandane was living with Cambyses, Astyages in the very first year saw another vision. He fancied that a vine grew from the womb of his daughter and overshadowed the whole of Asia. After this dream, which he submitted also to be interpreted, he sent to Persia and fetched away Mandane, who was now with child, and was not far from her time. On her arrival he set a watch over her intending to destroy the child to which she should give birth: for the Magian interpreters had expounded the vision to foreshow that the offspring of his daughter would reign over Asia in his stead. To guard against this, Astyages, as soon as Cyrus was born, sent for Harpagus, a man of his own house and the most faithful of the Medes... and addressed him thus: '...Take the child born of Mandane: carry him with thee to thy home and slay him there...'

Harpagus found that he had no heart to carry out this murderous command of the child's grandfather. No more had a shepherd to whom he deputed the task. So Cyrus remained alive.

It was not only the birth and boyhood of Cyrus

that were wrapped in legend. This Persian king's son, descended from the royal race of Achaemenes, has, more than any other prince of the ancient world, caught the imagination and evoked the admiration of all nations. Xenophon, the Greek, celebrated the foundation of his empire in a complete romance, the *Cyropaedia*.

The Bible remembers him as an enlightened monarch. His unparalleled, swift and brilliant rise to power was marred by no deed of violence. His able and humane policy made him one of the most attractive figures in the ancient orient. The most repugnant feature of oriental monarchs before him, despotic cruelty, was foreign to this Persian.

The figure of Cyrus became a hard fact of history in 550BC. In that year he captured Ecbatana, capital of the kingdom of Media. His royal grandfather Astyages was banished. Cyrus amalgamated Media with the Persian kingdom. Babylonia, Lydia in Asia Minor and Sparta formed an alliance against the conqueror. Croesus king of Lydia—his name is still proverbial for great riches—attacked the Persians. Cyrus took Sardis, his capital, and defeated him.

The way to Babylonia was open and Babylon lay invitingly before him. Against the background of such a situation a strange and mysterious story got about which, since it has been recorded in the

The first Achaemenian capital city, Pasargadae ('the camp of the Persians'), was the site of King Cyrus' victory over the Median king Astyages. Cyrus had a simple tomb chamber on a terraced base erected here, as his mausoleum.

The founder of the Persian Empire was called 'the Great', and in the Bible praise is heaped on him because he arranged the return of the Israelites from their 'Babylonian exile'. A campaign against the Scythians cost him his life in 529BC. His grave was first plundered at the time of Alexander the Great; apparently the Macedonian had the culprit, Orxines, executed.

Bible, has gripped the imagination of the western world:

King Belshazzar gave a great banquet for a thousand of his nobles and drank wine with them . . . As they drank the wine they praised the gods of gold and silver, of bronze, iron, wood and stone. Suddenly the fingers of a human hand appeared and wrote on the plaster of the wall, near the lampstand in the royal palace. The king watched the hand as it wrote. His face turned pale and he was so frightened that his knees knocked together and his legs gave way. The king . . . said to (the) wise men of Babylon, 'Whoever reads this writing and tells me what it means will be clothed in purple and have a gold chain placed around his neck, and he will be made the third highest ruler in the kingdom.' (Daniel 5:1, 4–7). *Mene, Mene, Tekel, Upharsin* were the words on the wall which have become famous. They mean: *'God has numbered the days of your reign and brought it to an end.' 'You have been weighed on the scales and found wanting.' 'Your kingdom is divided and given to the Medes and Persians.'* (Daniel 5:25–28).

When Joseph in Egypt was able to interpret Pharaoh's dreams of the seven fat kine and the seven lean kine and of the ears of corn, he was made second man in the kingdom, grand vizier.

What was the meaning of the promised reward for guessing the meaning of the mysterious writing to be *the third highest ruler in the kingdom*?

This Bible passage was unintelligible and was only explained with the help of archaeology.

Who Belshazzar was has now been established by cuneiform texts from his own father. He was not, in fact, as the book of Daniel says (5:2), the son of Nebuchadnezzar, but of Nabonidus, who says in an inscription: *And put into the heart of Belshazzar, my first born son, the fruit of my loins, fear of thy sublime divinity, that he commit no sin, and that he may have fulness of life.*

Thus it is clear that Belshazzar was crown prince, therefore the second man in Babylonia. He could only therefore hold out a promise of third highest place in the kingdom.

The story of Belshazzar's Feast and the Writing on the Wall reflects through the eyes of the prophets a contemporary political situation. In 539BC Cyrus turned his attack against Nabonidus, and the Babylonian army was defeated. With that the hours of the last great Mesopotamian empire were numbered.

Go down, sit in the dust, Virgin Daughter of Babylon; sit on the ground without a throne, Daughter of the Babylonians. (Isaiah 47:1)

A year after the battle Cyrus, king of Persia, made his triumphal entry into conquered Babylon. Hittites, Kassites, Assyrians had at various times threatened the great city with the same fate. This conquest however did not not follow the normal pattern: it was without a parallel in the military practice of the ancient orient. For this time there were no columns of smoke rising from behind shattered walls, no temples or palaces razed to the ground, no house plundered, no man was butchered or impaled. The clay cylinder of Cyrus narrates in Babylonian script what took place: *As I entered Babylon in peace, and established my royal residence in the place of the princes amid jubilation and rejoicing, Marduk, the great lord, warmed the hearts of Babylonians towards me, while I for my part devoted myself daily to do him reverence. My troops wandered peacefully widespread throughout Babylon. In all Sumer and Akkad I let no man be afraid. I concerned myself with the internal affairs of Babylon and all its cities. The dwellers in*

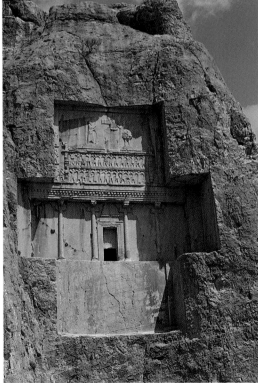

Above **At Bisotun, west of Hamadan (Ecbatana), Darius I had a victory memorial carved into a wall of rock. Here one of the battles against the rebellious Medes took place, over the magician Gautama.**

Left **The tomb of Artaxerxes I at Naqsh-I-Rustam. From Darius I on, the Achaemenian kings made themselves rock tombs with roomy chambers and an imposing facade of reliefs in the shape of a cross. The format of the facade was always the same: above the doorway with its four columns, guardsmen representing the peoples of the empire support a dais on which the king approaches the god Ahuramazda.**

The principal seat of the Persian emperors was Susa, former capital of the kingdom of Elam. Only the foundations have survived of the huge palace of Kings Darius I and Artaxerxes I. In the Assyrian and Babylonian tradition, the walls of the most important state rooms were covered with colourful brick reliefs. Striding along the wall, alongside lions, winged oxen and gryphons, we find the warriors of the 'Guard of the Immortals'. An inscription of Darius I lists the origins of the materials used, the craftsmen and artists. From this we learn that the fired bricks and glazed reliefs were made by Babylonians.

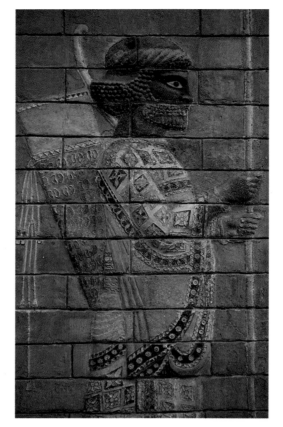

Babylon... I freed from the yoke that ill became them. I repaired their houses, I healed their afflictions ... I am Cyrus, king of all, the great king, the mighty king, king of Babylon king of Sumer and Akkad, king of the four corners of the earth...

The last sentences almost suggest that the biblical Chronicler had known the text of the clay cylinder. *This is what Cyrus king of Persia says: 'The Lord, the God of heaven, has given me all the kingdoms of the earth...'* (2 Chronicles 36:23).

That rulers should make tolerance, including religious tolerance, their motto was uncommon, and marked the Persian king out from the first.

After his entry into Babylon Cyrus at once had the images and shrines of the local gods set up again. He was concerned with *the daily worship of the chief god of the city Marduk.* In the city of Ur he did the same. On a broken cylinder which was preserved among the ruins Cyrus himself says: *Sin, the light of heaven and earth, with his favourable omens gave into my hands the four corners of the earth. I brought the gods back into their sanctuaries.*

His tolerance was also to the advantage of the Jews. After these many years of exile their dearest wish was now to find fulfilment.

RETURN TO JERUSALEM

In the first year of King Cyrus, the king issued a decree concerning the temple of God in Jerusalem: Let the temple be rebuilt as a place to present sacrifices, and let its foundations be laid. It is to be ninety feet high and ninety feet wide.

EZRA 6:3

This meant permission for them to return to Jerusalem. The text of the royal decree is in imperial Aramaic, the new official language of the Persian government. Archaeology has been able to establish the authenticity of this permit, which has been incorporated in chapter six of the Book of Ezra.

It was a matter of reparation. It is clear from the terms of the enactment that the Persians regarded themselves as successors of the Babylonians: ... *The costs are to be paid by the royal treasury. Also, the gold and silver articles of the house of God, which Nebuchadnezzar took from the temple in Jerusalem and brought to Babylon, are to be returned to their places in the temple in Jerusalem; they are to be deposited in the house of God* (Ezra 6:4–6).

The carrying out of the order was entrusted by Cyrus to Sheshbazzar, the governor (Ezra 5:14), a price of Judah, and probably a member of the house of David. It is assumed that he can be identified with Shenazzar, fourth son of King Jehoiachin (1 Chronicles 3:18).

It is understandable that fifty years after the deportation not everyone would take advantage of this permission to return to the land of their fathers. In any case it was a risky business to leave this wealthy country of Babylon where they had established themselves and where most of them had grown up and to set out on the difficult road back to the ruins of a ravaged land. Despite this, in the spring of 537BC, after long preparations a lengthy caravan set out on the trail towards the old homeland. *The whole company numbered 42,360, besides their 7,337 menservants and maidservants; and they also had 200 men and women singers. They had 736 horses, 245 mules, 435 camels and 6,720 donkeys* (Ezra 2:64–67).

Whether this list of people returning to their homeland really is that of the members of a mighty trek from the Euphrates to Judah is debatable. It is all repeated in Nehemiah almost word for word except that the number of singing men and singing women is not quite the same as there is a difference of 45. In this instance, however, the list is of a population census, a register of the Persian satrapy which Judah had become under Persian rule. However this may be and whatever the number of people who did, in fact, return to Judah after the long years in exile, we can vividly imagine their journey into the land west of the Jordan.

Almost 800 miles have to be covered between Babylon and distant Jerusalem, with the clouds of dust churned up by the caravan as a faithful companion throughout the whole journey. One day they would pass the site of old Mari. They would reach the spot where, on the opposite side of the river, the Balikh, on whose lower reaches Haran was situated, enters the Euphrates.

From then on the returning exiles were following the same track which was said to have been taken by Abraham, when he left the land of his fathers to go to Canaan, via Damascus and along the foot of Hermon to the Lake of Galilee. Then came the day when from among the brown peaks of the mountains the city of Zion, largely still lying in ruins, rose before their eyes—Jerusalem!

Soon after their arrival in Jerusalem the foundations of the new Temple were laid amid great enthusiasm. But then the work slackened off (Ezra 5:16). The great enthusiasm of the returned settlers quickly waned: life was too hard and barren in this depopulated land, where dilapidated houses provided the scantiest of shelter. Added to this was the problem of making a living, as Haggai said *each of you is busy with his own house* (Haggai 1:9). Everyone was too concerned with his own problems.

The rebuilding advanced but slowly. The first settlers were poor, and as the remains of their household belongings indicate, few in number. The objects which have been discovered clearly reflect the harshness of that first early stage.

Cyrus, the liberator, died on an expedition to the east in 530BC and was buried in the royal place of Pasargadae near Persepolis. His palace was built in the form of individual pavilions: each one lay in the centre of magnificent garden: the whole area was enclosed by a high wall.

On the southern slopes of a long range of hills there still stands among the rough grass of the highlands a small unpretentious stone building dating from the time of Cyrus. Six square blocks form the steps which lead up to a small chamber, above the entrance to which there could at one time be read the following plea: *O man, whoever you are and whenever you come, for I know that you will come—I am Cyrus, who gave the Persians their empire. Do not grudge me this patch of earth that covers my body.* Alas, the small stone chamber in which a golden sarcophagus enclosed the mortal

remains of the great Persian is now as empty as the place above the entrance which bore the inscription. Occasionally shepherds with their flocks pass unconcernedly by this forgotten spot, as they did in olden times, across the wide plateau where the lion is still lord of the chase.

Cyrus was followed by his son Cambyses II. With the conquest of Egypt Persia became under him the greatest empire that the world had ever seen: it stretched from India to the Nile.

It was not until the reign of his successor Darius I that the rebuilding of the Temple in Jerusalem was finally taken in hand. Almost twenty years had passed since the foundations had been laid. At the request of the official responsible for the administration of Judah, the Satrap of Transeuphrates, Darius I expressly confirmed the permit issued by Cyrus. The official exchange of letters with the Persian court on this matter can be found in the Book of Ezra (5:6–6:12).

Many experts, it must be said, doubt the historicity of these documents. If they are not genuine, however, they are very clever imitations both as to form and to content. The Bible here even uses the Aramaic of the empire, the commercial language of the Achaemenide Empire. However one settles this question, numerous other contemporary texts confirm the extent to which Darius fostered the indigenous cults of the peoples incorporated in his empire, not only in Palestine, but also in Asia Minor and Egypt.

For example the inscription of the Egyptian chief medical officer Usahor runs as follows: *King*

The layer of occupation from the time of Persian domination is one of the most recent in the ancient city of Susa. Deeper excavations reach right back to the beginning of the fourth millennium BC. In about 2500BC Susa became the capital of the 'Old Elamite' kingdom, which had neighbouring Mesopotamia to thank for a highly turbulent history and innumerable foreign occupations. From the thirteenth century BC, the 'New Elamite' kingdom reached out to the north-west. It was in one of the many military raids and plundering expeditions to Babylon that the Elamites brought back the famous stela containing the laws of King Hammurabi, which French archaeologists found in 1901 in Susa.

Right **Darius I and his successor Xerxes (standing behind the throne) are depicted in this relief on the pillar of a door in the palace of Persepolis. Representatives of the royal guard support the dais on which the throne stands. Above the canopy hovers the winged symbol of the imperial god Ahuramazda.**

Previous pages **Persepolis, the royal seat of the Persian emperors erected north of Shiraz by Darius I and his successors, was never the centre of the empire; the seat of government remained in Susa. The massive terraced area was surrounded by thick walls. Apart from the imposing pillared hall of Apadana and the 'hall of a hundred columns', the palace also included an extended area of storehouses, a treasure chamber, living quarters, courtyards and a library.**

Darius—may he live for ever—commanded me to go to Egypt . . . and make up once more the number of the priests of the temple and bring new life into what had fallen into decay . . .

Darius wrote to Gadata, the steward of his demesnes, in no uncertain manner. He took him sharply to task for his attitude to the priesthood of the temple of Apollo in Magnesia: *I hear that you are not carrying out my instructions properly. Admittedly you are taking trouble over my estates, in that you are transferring trees and plants from beyond the Euphrates to Asia Minor. I commend this project and the Court will show its gratitude. But in disregarding my attitude to the gods you have provoked my displeasure and unless you change your tactics you will feel its weight. For you have taken away the gardeners who are sacred to Apollo and used them for other gardening jobs of a secular character, thereby showing a lack of appreciation of the sentiments of my*

ancestors towards the god who has spoken to the Persians . . .

The efforts of the returned exiles were for many years confined exclusively to rebuilding the Temple at Jerusalem. Building operations started at the end of 520BC and by 12 March 515BC they were completed.

They had to wait for the city wall until the next century. It was not until the time of Nehemiah, who was installed as governor of Judah by King Artaxerxes I of Persia in 444BC, that they began work on the wall, which was finished in record time. *So the wall was completed . . . in fifty-two days* (Nehemiah 6:15). A new wall in fifty-two days— impossible! Nehemiah himself tells us of *the walls of Jerusalem, which had been broken down, and its gates, which had been destroyed by fire'* (Nehemiah 2:13). The walls were thus merely repaired. And that must have happened in hurry. For the neighbouring tribes, above all the Samaritans, wanted to stop the refortification of Jerusalem by every means in their power. The Jews had to be constantly on the look out: *Those who carried materials did their work with one hand and held a weapon in the other* (Nehemiah 4:17).

The speedy filling up of holes and patching up of gaps in the walls reflect the pressure of the time factor and the feverish anxiety with which the work went forward. The British archaeologist J. Garrow Duncan dug up parts of the wall on the little hill to the south-east above the Gihon spring. In his report he says: 'The stones are small, rough, irregular and unequal. Some of them are unusually small and seem to be merely chips broken off from bigger stones, just as if they were using any kind of material that came to hand. The large holes and hollow spaces are filled up with a haphazard mixture of clay plaster mixed with tiny chips of stone . . .'

During the time that Nehemiah was governor of Jerusalem, the holy fire of the altar for burnt offerings is supposed to have been rediscovered (1 Maccabees 1:19ff). According to Leviticus 6:12 it was never to be allowed to go out; it has after all fallen from heaven as a gift of Yahweh! Nehemiah *told the descendants of those priests (who hid the fire) to find the fire.* They *had found no fire but only some oily liquid.* When at Nehemiah's command they poured this liquid over *the wood and the sacrifice . . . suddenly everything on the altar burst into flames. Everyone looked on in amazement* (2 Maccabees 1:21–22). Nobody paid much attention to the observation that followed: *Nehemiah and his friends called the liquid nephthar* (2 Maccabees 1:36). Yet this passage in the Bible contains a very clear hint regarding a quite specific mineral product which must have been well known to the Israelites. It was only in the 1950s that this was recognized, when petroleum, or *naphtha*—the word is of Babylonian derivation—was found in Israel.

The rebuilding of the Temple and of the old city of David after the return from exile in Babylon make it abundantly clear that despite all messianic expectations Israel knew full well that the days of the monarchy had gone for ever and that only the inward solidarity of a religious community could guarantee the further existence of the tiny state in face of what political developments might be in store for them. With this end in view they made the holy city the centre of Jewry, both for those Jews who lived in the homeland of Judah and for those who were scattered throughout the world. The High Priest of the new Temple at Jerusalem gained a dominant position and under the Ptolemies he became the *ethnarch*, the 'ruler of the people'. The little theocracy in Palestine took no noteworthy part in the affairs of the world during the subsequent centuries. Israel turned its back on politics.

With Persian approval the Law of God became the law of Israel, indeed of Jews everywhere (Ezra 7:23–26); in other words the Jewish people was constituted as a legal community recognized by the state. What the book of Ezra says about this is borne out by another document from the same period.

In 1905 three papyrus documents were discovered on the palmcovered island of Elephantine, which lies beside the first cataract of the Nile near the Aswan dam. They are written in imperial Aramaic and date from the year 419BC. One of them is an Easter message from King Darius II of Persia containing instructions as to how the Feast of the Passover is to be celebrated. The recipients of the letter were the Jewish military colony in Elephantine. The sender signs himself Hananiah, *agent for Jewish affairs at the court of the Persian governor of Egypt*.

For two centuries the Persians were liege lords of Jerusalem. The history of Israel during this period seems to have been subjected to no violent variations. The Bible makes no mention of it, nor have the layers of rubble anything significant to tell us of this long space of time. At all events there is a complete absence of large buildings, or objects of art and craft, among the archaeological trophies recovered from the appropriate layer. Fragments of simple household utensils prove how miserably poor life in Judah must have been at that time.

Coins certainly occur in the course of the fourth century BC. They bear the proud legend *Yehud*, 'Judah'. Apparently the Persians had granted the high priest the right to mint silver coins. Following the example of the Attic drachma, they are decorated with the owl of Athens, testimony to the way in which Greek trade and influence had been able to penetrate everywhere in the Orient long before the days of Alexander the Great.

The reliefs on the stairway leading to the hall of Apadana in Persepolis show the Persian and Median warriors of the royal guard. A long procession of representatives of all the satrapies of the empire bring their tributes.

UNDER GREEK INFLUENCE

This history begins when Alexander the Great, son of Philip of Macedonia, marched from Macedonia and attacked Darius, king of Persia and Media. Alexander enlarged the Greek Empire by defeating Darius and seizing his throne. He fought many battles, captured fortified cities.

1 MACCABEES 1:1

In the fourth century BC the centre of political power gradually shifted from the 'Fertile Crescent' to the West. The prelude to this development in world history had been two famous battles in the previous century, in both of which the Greeks called a halt to any further Persian advance. At Marathon in 491BC they defeated the Persian armies of Darius I. At Salamis, off Athens, they smashed the fleet of his successor Xerxes eleven years later.

With the victory of Alexander the Great over Darius III, King of Persia, in 333BC at Issus near the northern Syrian seaport of Iskendrun, formerly Alexandretta, the Macedonians arrogated to themselves the leading role among the nations of the world.

Alexander's first target was Egypt. With a picked force of 32,000 infantry and 5,000 cavalry he marched south at the age of twentyfour, accompanied off shore by a fleet of 160 ships. Twice he was held up on the coast of Syria and Palestine.

The first occasion was at Tyre. This Phoenician city, heavily fortified and protected by stout high walls, was built on a small island which guarded the coastline. Alexander performed here a miracle of military ingenuity by building a 2,000 foot mole in the sea out to the island city. To safeguard the operations, mobile protective

When the successors of Alexander the Great divided up his empire between them, Palestine was at first allotted to the Egyptian Ptolemies. After the victory of Antiochus III (above right) over Ptolemy in the year 198BC, the Seleucids laid hold of the country and began assiduously to subject it to Greek influence. For the Jews this was a serious threat to their faith, which under Antiochus IV (above left) reached its zenith in desecration of the Temple and the forced introduction of Hellenistic religious practices.

shields, so-called 'tortoises' had to be employed. Despite this the construction of the causeway was greatly hindered by an incessant hail of missiles. Meantime his engineers were on shore building veritable monsters: *Helepoleis*. These were mobile protective towers many stories high, which held the detachments of bowmen and light artillery. A drawbridge on the front of the towers enabled a surprise attack to be made on the enemy's walls. They were the highest siege towers ever used in the history of war. Each of them had twenty stories and the topmost platform towered at a height of over 160 feet far above the highest city walls.

When after seven months' preparation these monsters, bristling with weapons, slowly and clumsily rolled towards Tyre, the fate of the maritime stronghold, which was considered to be impregnable, was sealed.

Tyre has built herself a stronghold; she has heaped

up silver like dust, and gold like the dirt of the streets. But the Lord will take away her possessions and destroy her power on the sea, and she will be consumed by fire. (Zechariah 9:3–4)

... *Gaza will writhe in agony* we read in the following verse (Zechariah 9:5) which deals with this year in Alexander's life. It was indeed the old Philistine town of Gaza which brought the Macedonian king to a halt for the second time. But this siege lasted only two months, and then the road to the Nile lay open.

The Jewish historian Flavius Josephus tells us that after the capture of the fortress of Gaza, Alexander came to Jerusalem. Received with great ceremony by the High Priest Jaddua and the people, he is said to have offered a sacrifice in the Temple and granted the people favours.

The conqueror of the world can, however, hardly have found time for a trip to Jerusalem, since he had already been held up for nine months by the resistance of Tyre and Gaza. After the fall of Gaza he hurried on by the quickest road to Egypt, leaving the conquest of the territory inland to his general Parmenio, who had no difficulty in subduing the country. Only Samaria, the seat of the governor of the province, had to be forcibly brought to heel. As a punishment it had a colony of Macedonians settled in it.

Jerusalem and the province of Judah seem to have submitted to their new masters without more ado. At all events no contemporary source has so far suggested that there was any resistance.

The visit of Alexander to Jerusalem is probably only a legend which nevertheless contains a grain of truth. It bears eloquent witness to the fact that the Greek conqueror too tolerated the way of life of the theocracy of Judah. It was left unmolested as a religious community.

This is quite in accord with what archaeology has been able to establish. There are no traces of either a Greek conquest or a Greek occupation of Judah at that time.

Only in the neighbouring city of Samaria a strong Greek fortress came into existence about 322BC. Excavations disclosed a whole series of round towers. They lean against the old casemated wall which was built in the days when Samaria was still the capital of the kingdom of Israel.

Alexander remained in Egypt, which welcomed him as a liberator, during the winter of 332-331BC. On the western tip of the Nile delta he founded the city of Alexandria, which was destined for the role of the metropolis of the new age. It quickly blossomed into the centre of a new intellectual life which attracted the best minds of the Greek and oriental world within its orbit.

At its foundation Alexander issued instructions which were to be of the highest significance in future days. He guaranteed to the Jews—descendants of the refugees in the Babylonian era—the same rights as were accorded to his own countrymen. This provision, carried on by successors of the great Macedonian, led to Alexandria becoming subsequently one of the great reservoirs of Jewish life and culture.

Cities with Jewish communities in the Seleucid and Ptolemaic empires and in Greece.

During excavations in front of the Herodian south wall of the Temple Mount, the foundations of a stairway were found leading to the gate above 'Robinson's Arch'.

The name of the city founded by Alexander does not appear in the Bible earlier than the Book of Acts: *a Jew named Apollos, a native of Alexandria, came to Ephesus. He was a learned man, with a thorough knowledge of the Scriptures* (Acts 18:24).

On the way to one of the greatest and most successful military expeditions known to history, Alexander marched once more through Palestine. Every country in the Ancient East fell before him. He pressed on to the Indus, almost to the foot of the Himalayas. On the way back he was attacked by a fever. Alexander died in Babylon at the age of 33 on the thirteenth of June 323BC.

In view of the fact that, long before Alexander, the Greeks had been stretching out their feelers in a thousand ways in the direction of Mesopotamia and Egypt, we can only shake our heads in amazement at the ignorance of the ways of the world which this question reflects. Time seems to have been standing still in the little theocracy and the life of its tiny religious community appears to have been influenced only by the Torah, the Law of God.

A long way back there had been Greek mercenaries in the armies of Pharaoh Psamtik II and Nebuchadnezzar, king of the Chaldeans. It was also a long time since the first Greek forts and trading stations had started to spread along the coast of Syria and Palestine. In the fifth century BC there were already highly educated Greeks traveling and studying in all countries of the ancient orient: Herodotus and Xenophon, Hecataeus and Ctesias.

Were these men in their theocratic community no longer able to recognize or understand the signs of the times? Or did they intentionally shut their eyes and hope to keep the future at bay?

If so they must have had all the ruder awakening when they came face to face with Greece, but a few steps from the sanctuary of the Temple and could disguise from themselves no longer that Jewish youth had fallen completely for the sport of throwing the discus, which had been imported from Greece. Athletic contests on the Greet pattern quickly found an enthusiastic response among the young people.

Greece was not a danger to the Jews by reason of its growing ascendancy, or militarism, or seductive temptations. The danger lay far more in the freer atmosphere of a fabulous modern world. Hellas, with its Pericles, Aeschylus, Sophocles, Euripides, with its Phidias and Polygnotus, its Plato and its Aristotle, had climbed up to a new stage in human development.

Undisturbed by the new era of mankind the tiny theocracy went on obstinately in its own way, held tenaciously and inflexibly to its traditions and to the past. Despite all this it was forced to join issue with the new ideas.

> When Alexander . . . was about to die he called together his generals . . . and divided his empire, giving a part to each of them. After his death, the generals took control, and each had himself crowned king of his own territory. The descendants of these kings ruled for many generations and brought a great deal of misery on the world. (1 Maccabees 1:7–9)

The idea behind the struggle for power of Alexander's captains—the Diadochi—is not unknown even in twentieth century politics. In its original form it was no more of an advertisement for the profession of army commanders. Alexander's generals had no scruples about getting rid of his whole family by murdering them: Philip Arrhidaeus his half brother, his mother Olympia, his widow Roxana and his posthumous son. The conflict came to a head in the division of the empire into three kingdoms. The kingdom of Macedonia in Northern Greece was ruled by the dynasty founded by Antigonos. The Kingdom of the Seleucids extended from Thrace through Asia Minor and Syria to the borders of India. Antioch, on the lower reaches of the Orontes in the north of Syria, and Seleucia, on the Tigris, were founded as capitals of this second and by far the largest of the successor states.

The third was the Ptolemaic kingdom on the Nile with Alexandria as its capital. It was ruled by a dynasty whose last representative, Cleopatra, has ever since enjoyed a certain amount of fame for having so successfully turned the heads of her distinguished contemporaries Julius Caesar and Mark Antony.

Two unusually far-sighted rulers, Ptolemy I and his son Ptolemy II Philadelphus, developed their capital city of Alexandria into a nursery of Hellenistic culture and learning whose fame extended far beyond the borders of their own kingdom. It drew emigrants from Judah, among others, into its charmed circle; and in this crucible they steeped themselves in the beauty of the Greek language. It was this language alone that allowed them to enjoy the prodigious advances of the human mind and the human spirit. The international language of learning and of commerce became the language of tens of thousands of Israelites who knew no other home.

The rising generation no longer knew Hebrew as their mother tongue. They could no longer follow the sacred text in the services of the synagogue. Thus it came about that the Jews in Egypt decided to translate the Hebrew scriptures. About 250BC the Torah was translated into Greek, a fact of immeasurable import for Western civilization.

The translation of the Bible into the Greek tongue was for the Jews in Egypt such an incredible step forward that legend took hold of it. The story is told in an apocryphal letter of Aristeas of Alexandria.

Philadelphus, the second of the Ptolemaic dynasty, took great pride in the fact that he possessed a collection of the finest books in the world. One day the librarian, the legend tells us, said to the monarch that he had brought together in his 995 books the best literature of all nations. But, he added, the greatest books of all, the five books of Moses, were not included among them. Therefore Ptolemy II Philadelphus sent envoys to the High Priest to ask for a copy of these books. At the same time he asked for men to be sent who could translate them into Greek. The High Priest granted his request and sent together with the copy of the Torah 72 learned and wise scribes. Great celebrations were organized in honour of the visitors from Jerusalem, at whose wisdom and knowledge the king and his courtiers were greatly astonished. After the festivities they betook themselves to the extremely difficult task which had been assigned to them, and for which there was neither prototype nor dictionary. They set to work out at sea, on the island of Pharos off Alexandria, at

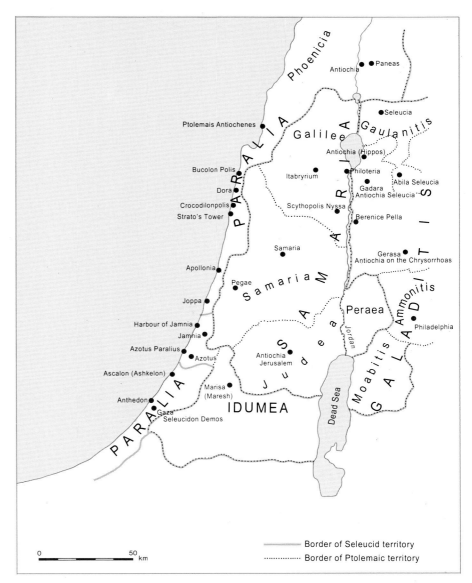

the foot of one of the seven wonders of the world—the 300 feet high lighthouse which Ptolemy II had erected as a warning for shipping far and near. Each of them worked in a cell by himself. When the scholars had completed their work and the translations were compared with one another all seventy-two are said to have corresponded exactly, word for word. Accordingly the Greek translation of the Bible was called the *Septuagint*, meaning 'the Seventy'.

What had previously been made known only in the sanctuary, only in the old tongue, and only to the one nation was now all at once available and intelligible for people of other tongues and other races. The hitherto carefully guarded door into the 'tents of Shem' was thrown wide open, and

Greek towns in Palestine in the third and second centuries BC.

293

Right 'The treasure house of Pharaoh' is the name the Arabs give to one of the rock tombs with Hellenistic pillared facades at Petra.

Previous pages **Petra, which lies south-east of the Dead Sea protected by huge rock masses, was an important junction and trading centre on the route of the caravan traffic and incense trade from southern Arabia to Syria. Here lived the kings of the kingdom of Nabatea, which was established during the decline of the Seleucid kingdom.**

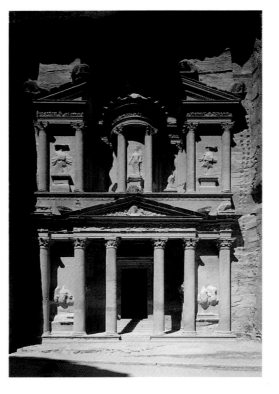

Judaism, which had admitted proselytes since the Persian period, could now gain new adherents in the Hellenistic/Roman world.

Judah's attachment to the kingdom of the Ptolemies lasted for more than 100 years. Then the Seleucids of Antioch forced their way southwards, an expansion for which they had long been striving. After a victorious battle against Ptolemy V at the sources of the Jordan, Antiochus III, called the Great, took over Palestine in 195BC, and Judah thereby once more came under a new sovereignty.

Gradually the foreign seed began to sprout even in the theocracy. The manifold and enduring influence of the Greek attitude of mind, which had been infiltrating since Alexander's victorious campaigns, became more and more apparent.

When *Antiochus Epiphanes . . . became king of Syria in the year 137* (1 Maccabees 1:10) and *Jason . . . became High Priest by corrupt means . . . he made the people of Jerusalem change to the Greek way of life . . . he built a stadium near the Temple hill and led our finest young men to adopt the Greek custom of participating in athletic events . . . the craze for the Greek way of life and for foreign customs reached such a point that even the priests lost all interest in their sacred duties. They lost interest in the Temple services and neglected the sacrifices. Just as*

soon as the signal was given, they would rush off to take part in the games that were forbidden by our Law (2 Maccabees 4:7–14).

This place of exercise—Luther even translated it as a 'gaming-house'—was nothing more or less than a stadium. Why then so much excitement over a sports ground? Gymnastics in Jerusalem—discus throwers and sprinters in the holy city—it sounds perhaps unusually progressive, but why should Yahweh be displeased at it, how could a High Priest be denounced as ungodly on that account?

Between the method of playing games today and playing games in those days there is a slight but very essential difference. It has nothing to do with the exercises themselves, which have remained practically the same for over 2,000 years. The difference lies in dress. True to the Olympic pattern, games were played completely naked. The body could only be 'covered' with a thin coat of oil!

Nakedness itself must have been regarded by all orthodox believers in Judah as a challenge. They firmly believed in the corruption of human nature from youth onwards and in the sinfulness of the body. It is impossible that athletics in full view of the Temple, only a few steps from the Holy of holies, should not have been regarded as an outrageous insult or that it should not have given rise to vigorous opposition. According to contemporary sources the High Priest, Jason, had located the stadium in the heart of Jerusalem, in the valley which bordered the Temple hill.

But that was not the end of the scandal. It was not long before Jewish athletes were guilty of a serious crime against the Law, they *had an operation performed to hide their circumcision* (1 Maccabees 1:15). The Greek conception of beauty and the circumcision of Jewish athletes displayed in full view of the public eye were two irreconcilable things. Jewish teams—not in Jerusalem among their own people naturally—met with scorn and ridicule, and even aversion, as soon as they appeared in contests away from home. The Bible speaks of *the athletic games that were held every five years in the city of Tyre* (2 Maccabees 4:18), although this does not refer to a Jewish team but to a ceremonial delegation whose duty was confined to the presentation of gifts.

Many of them must have suffered so much from the disgust which they encountered that they sought a remedy and through a surgical operation restored the natural state.

Nakedness had come for a second time to be Judah's great temptation. Nakedness had been the outstanding characteristic of the fertility

goddesses of Canaan, nakedness was now paraded by the athletes in the sports grounds which had sprung up all over the country. In those days a much deeper significance was attached to athletics than to sport in the modern sense. They were religious exercises, dedicated to the foreign Greek gods Zeus and Apollo. The reaction of orthodox Judaism to this revival of a real threat to their religion could only be uncompromising. Their new overlords, the Seleucids, gave them all too soon every reason to be so.

THE BATTLE FOR RELIGIOUS LIBERTY

With his filthy and unholy hands, Antiochus swept away the sacred utensils and the gifts which other kings had given to increase the glory and honour of the Temple.

2 MACCABEES 5:16

King Antiochus IV, called Epiphanes, plundered and desecrated the Temple in Jerusalem in 168BC. Plundering temples was his speciality, so his contemporaries tell us. Polybius, the Greek historian, observed in his forty-volume *History of the World* that Antiochus IV had *despoiled most sanctuaries*.

However, the treasures of the Temple were not enough for the Seleucid king. He sent in addition his chief tax collector Apollonius with an armed force to Jerusalem. This man, *plundered the city, set it on fire and tore down its buildings and walls. He and his army took the women and children as prisoners and seized the cattle* (1 Maccabees 1:29–32;

Above **The architectural style of the synagogues which were erected in the centuries immediately before and after the birth of Christ, with their Hellenistic collonades, show the far-reaching Greek influence on the culture of Palestine.**

Left **Corinthian capital with Jewish religious symbols, from the synagogue in Capernaum.**

2 Maccabees 5:24ff).

Throughout the chances and changes of its past history Israel had been spared none of the horror and ignominy which could befall a nation. But never before, neither under the Assyrians nor under the Babylonians, had it received such a blow as the edict issued by Antiochus Epiphanes by which he hoped to crush and destroy the faith of Israel.

The king also sent messengers with a decree to Jerusalem and all the towns of Judaea, ordering the people to follow customs that were foreign to the country. (1 Maccabees 1:44)

The worship of Olympian Zeus was set up in the Temple of Yahweh. For taking part in any Jewish religious ceremonies, the traditional sacrifices, the sabbath or circumcision, the penalty was death. The holy scriptures were destroyed. This was the first thoroughgoing religious persecution in history.

But Israel gave the world an example of how a nation that refuses to be untrue to itself can and must react to a violation of its conscience of this kind.

There were of course even in those days weak characters who chose the way of least resistance. Nevertheless many *preferred to die rather than break the holy covenant* (1 Maccabees 1:63). But it was the resolute and fervent faith of an old man which first kindled the torch of revolt in the land.

Modin was the name of a small village, 20 miles from Jerusalem on the western fringe of the highlands of Judah. Today it is the market town of el-Medieh. Here lived the priest Mattathias with his five sons. When Antiochus' officers came to Modin to force the inhabitants to 'abandon (God's) Law', to offer sacrifices and to burn incense, Mattathias steadfastly refused to obey the

Above left **One of the carvings from the synagogue at Capernaum shows a little 'temple' on wheels, perhaps the Ark of the Covenant or a mobile Torah shrine.**

Above right **The Maccabean kingdom at the time of Alexander Jannaeus (103–76BC).**

order, and when he saw one of his countrymen offering a sacrifice he *became angry enough to do what had to be done. Shaking with rage, he ran forward and killed the man right there on the altar. He also killed the royal official who was forcing the people to sacrifice, and then he tore down the altar* (1 Maccabees 2:1–25). This act was the signal for open resistance, for a life and death struggle for religious freedom—the 'Wars of the Maccabees'.

Mattathias and his sons escaped. In their secret haunts in the mountains and in caves they gathered round them a band of those who shared their beliefs and with their assistance waged bitter guerilla warfare against the occupying power. After the death of the old priest his son Judas,

whose surname Maccabaeus means 'the Hammer', became the leader.

It was in the highlands of Judah that the rebels achieved their first successes. Their achievements were indeed remarkable. This small untrained and badly equipped band mastered the well drilled and numerically superior occupation troops. Beth-Horon, Emmaus and Beth-Zur were captured. The Seleucids had to retreat until reinforcements arrived from Antioch. Judas Maccabaeus liberated Jerusalem in 164BC and restored the old order in the Temple. The altar was rebuilt and sacrifices to Yahweh were offered as in former times (1 Maccabees 4:36ff).

In the course of military expeditions which took him more and more across the frontiers of the province of Judah, Judas Maccabaeus entered Galilee and Transjordan and wherever there were Israelites who remained true to the old faith. On the way to Idumaea, the old town of Hebron in southern Judah was besieged and destroyed. This continuing good fortune of Judas Maccabaeus in battle compelled King Antiochus V Euaptor, son of Epiphanes, to intervene with a large armed force.

In the decisive battle, which took place a few miles south-west of Bethlehem near Beth-Zachariah, the Seleucids employed elephants, flanked by detachments of cavalry. The Maccabees were unable to cope with this colossal superiority and were defeated. Dissension amongst themselves, however, drove the victors to make peace with surprisingly favourable terms for the vanquished. The decrees of Antiochus IV Epiphanes of 167BC were rescinded, liberty of worship was guaranteed and the religious community at Jerusalem was once more recognized (1 Maccabees 6:30ff, 58ff). The aims of the Jewish rebellion had been achieved.

Not content with that, the Maccabees wanted political independence as well as freedom of religion. The successors of Judas Maccabaeus, his brothers Jonathan and Simon, began the struggle anew. It ended in 142BC under Simon, with Syria granting them also political freedom (1 Maccabees 15:1ff).

A fortress which was in the midst of the struggle and changed hands several times was Beth-Zur. The results of excavation

The mosaic floor of a synagogue in Beth-Shan shows the Torah shrine flanked by seven-branched candelabra, shofar horns and sacrificial shovels (Israel Museum, Jerusalem).

Right **Phoenician graves in Amrit from the first century BC.**

Opposite **View of the Mount of Olives and the valley of Kidron with the 'Tomb of Absalom' (left) and the 'tomb of Zechariah' (right). These Hellenistic pillared mausolea were carved out of the living rock around the time of Christ.**

correspond to the historical circumstances described in the first book of the Maccabees.

'Khirbet et-Tubeka' is the modern name of this once hotly contested spot. It controls the old road from Jerusalem to Hebron on the frontier between Judah and Idumaea which lies to the south of it. In 1931 the American archaeologists W. F. Albright and O. P. Sellers found here a large collection of coins. One hundred and twenty-six out of a total of over 300 were stamped with the names of Antiochus Epiphanes and Antiochus Eupator.

The hill still bears the foundations of a powerful fortress in which three stages of construction can be clearly distinguished. Only fragments remain of the lowest and oldest. They date from Persian times. The next stage above it is of oriental character.

This is the work of Judas Maccabaeus dating from the first period of his successful revolt. *Judas placed a detachment of soldiers there (Jerusalem) to guard the Temple. He also fortified the town of Bethqur, so that the people of Israel would have a fortress facing Idumea* (1 Maccabees 4:61). After the Battle of the Elephants near Beth-Zachariah, Antiochus V Eupator occupied this border fortress: *The king occupied Bethqur and stationed a body of troops there to guard it* (1 Maccabees 6:50).

The troops of the Seleucids likewise have left unmistakable traces of their stay. As the archaeologists were able to establish, these consisted of relics of their catering arrangements, which were found among the ruins of the walls erected by Judas Maccabaeus. Part of the rations of these soldiers was wine of excellent quality from the hills of Greece. From the handles of the jars, which lay about among the mass of broken earthenware, Albright and Sellers were even able to tell where the wine came from. A wine merchant in Rhodes must have been the army's principal supplier.

That was in 162BC. A year later the Seleucids fortified Beth-Zur anew. A new citadel, with characteristic Hellenistic masonry, arose upon the ruined Maccabean walls. Their general Bacchides *built fortifications with high walls and barred gates for a number of towns in Judaea ... He also strengthened the fortifications of the towns of Bethqur and Gezer and of the fort in Jerusalem. He placed army units in them and stored up supplies there* (1 Maccabees 9:50–52).

The biblical record ends with the murder of Simon, brother of Judas Maccabaeus. The spiritual and political leadership of Judas was transferred, with the office of High Priest, to Simon's son John. He was called John Hyrcanus. *John, the High Priest, and the Jewish people* and *John the High Priest, Head of the Jewish people* are the inscriptions on coins which he had minted and which have since been found.

We are indebted to Flavius Josephus' careful account of the history of the period for accurate information about this Maccabean and his successors.

By dint of incessant and purposeful fighting the frontiers of Judah were extended farther and farther. Under Alexander Jannaeus they enlarged their territories until they almost covered the area previously occupied by the kingdoms of Israel and Judah.

As time went on the Seleucids became less and less serious adversaries. They lacked the strength to cope with the Maccabeans when Rome—now, having overthrown Hannibal of Carthage, undisputed mistress of the Western Mediterranean—had expanded its sovereignty beyond Greece into Asia Minor.

Pompey, the Roman general, marched through the kingdom of the Seleucids into Palestine. After a three months' siege Roman legions entered Jerusalem in 63BC. Judah became a Roman province.

With this event the political independence of Israel came to an abrupt end.

Gazeteer of Bible Places

Alexandria, on the western shores of the Nile delta, was a cosmopolitan city from the date of its foundation by Alexander the Great in the year 332BC. As a worldwide centre of trade, where both goods and ideas were exchanged, the magnificent royal seat of the Ptolemaic rulers drew an international clientele who were strongly influenced by Hellenistic intellectual life and shied away from any narrow nationalism. This 'modern' freedom of thought was not without its effect on the large and highly active Jewish community in Alexandria: it was here that the Old Testament was first translated into Greek and that many daring modifications of traditional teaching were developed. Jewish erudition, the lure of philosophical and sophistical speculation, and the extraordinarily complex ancient Egyptian lore of the gods, joined forces in Alexandria; their mingling issued in the subleties of early Christian theology, whose diverging tendencies were to give rise to so many church councils later on.

Wars, uprisings and conquests, as well as the rising level of the Nile, have left few visible remains of the city which was once of world importance.

Amarna, in Middle Egypt, was, under the name of Akhetaton, the royal seat of King Akhnaten (1364–47BC). Apart from the foundations of the temple, palaces and dwelling houses, the rock tombs of highly placed officials can still be seen on the edge of the mountains. The wealth of archaeological finds there went to Cairo and Berlin. The numerous small tablets covered in cuneiform writing, from the archives of the foreign office, are particularly informative. They are mostly letters from Near Eastern princes, who complain in lively language of the chaotic conditions in the area which was increasingly dominated by the Hittite empire, and of the laissez-faire foreign policy of Akhnaten. Whether these letters were ever answered, we do not know; the financial or military help requested of Egypt was certainly never given.

Amman, the capital of the Hashemite Kingdom of Jordan, is on the site of the ancient Rabbah, capital of the Ammonites, whose history began in about 2000BC. The oldest level of settlement is the citadel, below which the 'water city' spread out. Although the Ammonite language was related to Hebrew, their relations with the Israelites always remained tense and often hostile. While Joshua failed to conquer Rabbah at the time of the entry of the Israelites into the land, he did defeat and kill King Og of Bashan, reputed to be a giant, whose 'ironstone' sarcophagus in Rabbah was a cause of amazement. King David finally captured the city, and it seems to have paid tribute to the kings of Judah for a time. The discovery of richly furnished graves has led to the conclusion that Amman enjoyed a particular time of prosperity under the Assyrian occupation; however the Babylonian campaigns apparently resulted in the town being largely deserted. The Egyptian king Ptolemy Philadelphus re-founded it in the third century BC under the name of Philadelphia. The development of the town as a Hellenistic metropolis, begun by him, was continued after its conquest by Antiochus III (218BC) and under Roman rule. Most of the visible ruins of the town date from this period: for example the theatre, the Odeon and the Nymphaeum, as well as the remains of a shrine of Baal-Ammon on the citadel, and parts of the fortifications.

Antioch, on the Orontes, (now Antakya, southern Turkey) was founded in 300BC by Seleucus I Nicator, and quickly developed into one of the most flourishing cities of the Diadochi, the successors of Alexander the Great. Jews, who were actively encouraged to settle there by the Seleucids, played a significant part in this economic boom. The clearest impression of the city's prosperity in the Hellenistic/Roman period is given by the finds exhibited in its museum, particularly the exquisite mosaics.

Despite the dominance of a famous, and orgiastically celebrated, cult of Apollo and Daphne, one of the largest Christian congregations flowered in Antioch.

Ashur was the first capital of the Assyrian kingdom. The city, whose history reaches back to the beginnings of the third millennium BC, lay on a peninsular promontory on the west bank of the river Tigris, commanding both the Tigris and a man-made arm of the river. Under the rule of Sumer, Babylon and Mitanni, Ashur was wealthy on account of its trade, but without historical significance. It probably acquired its first walls around 2300BC, and a renewal of the fortifications can be dated to the time of the Babylonian king Hammurabi about 1700BC. In the course of succeeding centuries, Ashur extended its trade links and its sphere of influence, but it became a dominant power only under Shalmaneser I (about 1273–1244BC), who conquered Urartu, and his son Tukulti-Ninurta (about 1243–1207BC), who succeeded in storming Babylon. During his reign the capital was rebuilt with great magnificence, a moat was dug in front of the walls and a ziggurat with a temple was dedicated to the national god and god of war, Ashur. Internal political disputes delayed the further rise of the kingdom for almost a century, until Tiglath-pileser I (about 1112–1074BC) renewed its splendour. It was only in the ninth to the eighth centuries BC that Assyria became the terror of the whole Near East, as its campaigns of plunder and conquest overran, with unprecedented ferocity, all the regions to its west and advanced through Palestine and as far as Upper Egypt. Ashur did lose its status as the main royal seat in the ninth century BC, but it became instead a sacred temple city. Thirty-four temples are listed in an account which has been described as an 'address book of the gods'. The German excavations of 1903–14 confirmed a great deal of the information given in this account.

After the fall of the Assyrian empire, Ashur disappeared from history. Under the Parthians the town again enjoyed a modest prosperity, but then suffered heavily under the conquests of Trajan (AD116) and Septimius Severus (AD198); after its destruction by the Sassanid king Shahpur I (AD257) it was finally deserted.

The most impressive building in the ruins of Ashur is the ziggurat, which was originally dedicated to the god Enlil, but re-assigned in the 13th century BC to the god Ashur, whose equally ancient temple was not far away from it. West of this the remains of the temple of Anu-Adad have been found, which had two adjoining staged towers. Between these buildings lie the ruins of the old royal palace of the second millennium, in whose foundations various kings were buried from the 11th century BC on. The new palace in the western part of the city was probably built in or after the 13th century BC, and a third palace, that of Sennacherib, lay on the bank of the Tigris, but has largely fallen into the river. Another significant shrine was the temple of Ishtar; the goddess however had several places of worship in Ashur.

Avaris was, according to Egyptian sources of the 17th and 16th centuries BC, the royal seat of the Asiatic 'Hyksos', who gave the land of the Nile its troubled 'Second Intermediate Period' and for a century ruled the whole of Lower Egypt. According to these accounts Avaris lay in the eastern Nile delta. It was thought for a long time that it could be identified with Tanis. More recently Tell ed-Daba (near Kantir) has been regarded as the ancient Hyksos city; at any rate, the ruins of a substantial fortress can be attributed without doubt to this period.

Babylon, the biblical Babel, lies about 50 miles south of Baghdad on the river Euphrates. Its name is translated as 'Gate of the Gods'. The city may have been founded as early as the Sumerian period, but remained insignificant until the era of the Amurru Dynasty (from about 1830BC), whose most famous king, Hammurabi, developed Babylon into a splendid royal seat and made it the capital of all 'Sumer and Akkad'. Despite the fall of the kingdom as a political power in the time of the Kassites and Assyrians, and its repeated destruction, the city remained a significant religious and cultural centre. In 612BC, under Nabopolassar, Babylon became the capital of the Neo-Babylonian Empire, to whose most famous ruler, Nebuchadnezzar (605–562BC), it owed its second golden age. Under his successor Belshazzar the kingdom passed to the Persians; Cyrus captured Babylon in 539BC. In an uprising against Xerxes the city was laid waste. Alexander the Great's plan to rebuild it and make it a major city of his Greek/Oriental empire was frustrated by his early

death in Babylon. The city decayed into a barren ruin, and brick thieves carried a large proportion of it away. Nevertheless Babylon was never forgotten; travellers of the late ancient world and the Middle Ages give accounts of it. In 1850 research into it began, and in 1899 German excavations were started, which were taken over by Iraq in 1960.

Since the Old Babylonian layers of occupation now lie almost entirely below the water table, the visible remains belong to the Neo-Babylonian period. The greatest disappointment for the visitor is the famous 'Tower of Babel', whose vestigial remains lie in the water, surrounded by croaking frogs. On the basis of measurements given on a cuneiform clay tablet, we know that the seven-staged ziggurat was once nearly three hundred feet high. Apart from a few temples to the gods and the ruins of the city palace of Nebuchadnezzar II, excavations have also brought to light the city's double encircling walls. These were interrupted by nine towers built for military use, named after the most important gods. The most magnificent design was lavished on the Ishtar Gate and the Processional Way, over three hundred yards long with their glazed brick reliefs of the sacred animals: the bull of Hadad, the dragon of Marduk and the lion of Ishtar.

Byblos, a Phoenician seaport now in Lebanon, is 25 miles north of Beirut. The Semitic name Gebal (a hill) describes its position above the coast. The town's most important means of subsistence was, from earliest times, overseas trade with the Aegean region and above all with Egypt, whose main purchase from Byblos was cedar wood. The importance of this importation of wood from Lebanon is frequently documented in Egyptian sources, particularly at times of political instability, when the loyalty of the Phoenician local rulers waned and trade stagnated. Building and handicrafts were also flourishing branches of industry in Byblos, and it was from there that Solomon engaged specialists for the building of the Temple. The excavations, begun in 1919, brought to light a thick city wall, the temple of the city goddess Balaat Gebal with many votive offerings to her, and the richly furnished royal tombs. Luxury articles found there are mostly of Egyptian provenance.

The greatest cultural and historical achievement of the city was the development of a purely alphabetic script, which soon overtook the complicated methods of writing devised by the other great civilizations. Adapted by the Greeks, it became a forerunner of our own alphabet. The Greek word *biblion*, 'a book', which became the name of the Holy Scriptures, preserves the name of Byblos to this day.

Damascus, capital of Syria, lies in a fruitful river oasis between Mount Hermon and the Syrian desert, on an important caravan route. The city is mentioned frequently in the Amarna letters. From the end of the 11th century BC it was the capital of the kingdom of the Arameans and belonged briefly to King David's empire. However by the time of Solomon, Damascus had slipped out of Israel's grasp again, and from then on it was an uncomfortable neighbour on Israel's northern border. Conquered by Tiglath-pileser in 732BC, Damascus became the capital of an Assyrian province. Foreign rule by the Persians, Seleucids, Nabateans and Romans meant that the city had no continuing political status or power, but did allow it economic progress and a high standard of living. At this time a large Jewish community lived in this city, before whose gates Paul was converted. As a result of multiple rebuildings in the last two millennia, ancient Damascus is almost impossible to investigate archaeologically; what is left of it can be seen in the museum.

Ebla (Tell Mardikh), forty-five miles south of Aleppo, was a flourishing city-state from about 3000–1400BC. This trading centre was ruled by kings in whose palace the Italian archaeologists in 1975 found the state archive with more than 18,000 cuneiform tablets dating from 2400 to 2250BC. Some of the texts are written in an as yet incompletely researched 'palaeo-Canaanite' language; the readable Sumerian records give accounts of trade in timber, grain, textiles and copper with Palestine. At the same time Canaanite towns such as Megiddo, Lachish, Gaza, Hazor and Urusalima (Jerusalem) are named. At the moment there is fierce dispute over early Semitic personal names such as Abrama, Ismael, Ishrael or the royal name Ebrum, which

Israeli historians would like to be able to identify with Eber, an ancestor of Abraham; for it is to Eber, or Heber, that the Hebrews trace their name.

Ecbatana is the Greek name of the Median capital Hangmatana (now Hamadan in Iran), which the Persian and Parthian kings later used as their summer residence on account of its position at a height of 5800 feet. Almost nothing remains of the city which Herodotus praises effusively, with its 'seven circles of walls', although thorough investigations have not yet been made. According to tradition Esther, the wife of Xerxes (485–465BC) founded a Jewish colony here. The population of Hamadan to this day venerate a 'grave of Esther' and of her uncle Mordechai. According to another version of the story, the Jewish colony only goes back to the Jewish wife of Jezdegerd I (AD399–421).

Elephantine, the capital of the first Upper Egyptian province, lay on an island in the Nile at the outlet of the first cataract at Aswan. In the most recent excavations the original shrine of the goddess of the cataract, Satet, has been found, which goes back to at least 3000BC. Together with her consort Chnum and the Nubian goddess of fertility, Anuket, Satet forms one of the customary triads of gods. On this spot, which the Egyptians thought to be at least one of the sources of the Nile, it fell to the gods to perform the important duty of ensuring the annual flooding of the Nile, which was vital to life.

While the political power of the provincial princes was broken after the end of the Middle Kingdom, Elephantine retained great significance as the departure point for expeditions into Nubia, as a loading station for pink granite, and as a place of worship of Chnum. During the Persian Empire a Jewish garrison was stationed at Elephantine and had a temple of Yahweh there. Papyri from this period give important information on Jewish religious practice in the Aramaic language and script. Under the rule of Darius the priests of Chnum destroyed the temple of Yahweh, because they saw the slaughter of the Passover lamb as a sacrilegious insult to their god, who was worshipped in the form of a ram. However the

garrison shrine was rebuilt on the order of the emperor.

En Gedi lies west of the Dead Sea, 35 miles south of Jericho. So far five layers of occupation have been excavated, which go no further back than the time of King Josiah, the seventh century BC. The modest tell allowed no space for a larger town. Finds of pottery allow us to conclude that the inhabitants were involved in perfume manufacture; the area was known for its fragrant herbs.

During the Babylonian invasion the town was destroyed in 580BC and it was abandoned for a time. More recent layers of occupation date from the Persian, Herodian, Roman and Byzantine periods.

Fayum (ancient Egyptian Merwer, Greek Moeris), the great oasis south-west of Cairo, is a depression which lies about 140 feet below sea level. The oasis draws its water from the so-called 'River of Joseph' (Bahr Yusuf) which is often falsely described as 'Joseph's Canal'. It branches off from the Nile in the heights of Dairut, flows roughly parallel to the Nile for about 180 miles and finally falls into the depression, which has no outlet. Fayum was thus originally a great lake; its name derives from the Old Egyptian word *pajom*, sea. To cultivate the water-filled and marshy lands of Fayum, it was thus necessary to regulate the River of Joseph. This was undertaken by the kings of the Twelfth Dynasty. Amenemhet III (1844–1797BC) in particular availed himself of the oasis; he had his pyramid built on its shores, at Hawara, and was revered as a god in Fayum. By building further sluices, Ptolemy II (282–246BC) and his consort Arsinoe, were able substantially to extend the fertile land around Fayum. Of the former lake-filled landscape, Birket Karun (Lake Karun) remains to this day on the northern edge of the oasis.

Gezer was one of the oldest and most important cities of Canaan. The tell lies 19 miles north-east of Jaffa; it was identified as early as 1873 and has been investigated by various archaeologists since then. According to the latest findings made by William Dewer (Hebrew Union College, Jerusalem, 1965–73), Gezer was settled from the third millennium BC at the latest. In the 16th

century BC a religious 'high place' with monolithic stelae was erected. The city is mentioned in the lists of the conquests of Thutmosis III (about 1468BC) as well as in the Amarna letters and on the 'Israel stela' of Merenptah. In the 12th century BC it appears to have become Philistine (under Egyptian domination). Joshua at any rate did not conquer Gezer, and neither, probably, did David, for apparently the town only came into Solomon's possession as the gift of a princess of the Twenty-first Dynasty of the Pharaohs. During Solomon's time Gezer acquired a thick casemate wall; particularly impressive even today is an enormous gatehouse with three chambers on each side. Whether the 215 foot long tunnel to the watering-place is Solomonic or was only installed under Ahab, is still a matter of debate. Gezer was conquered not only by Pharaoh Sheshonk but also by Tiglath-pileser III; nevertheless it was always re-settled. It is only since the Hellenistic period that the town has gradually disappeared from history.

Haran was once a wealthy trading town on the road from Nineveh to Aleppo. The site, now in Turkish territory, lies 20 miles south of Edessa (Urfa) on the Balich, a tributary of the Euphrates. The excavations undertaken in the 1950s established the existence of a settlement dating from about 2000BC, thus confirming the information in a text from Mari which mentions a temple of the moon god Sin at Haran at about the same time. This shrine, which was restored under Shalmaneser III, Ashurbanipal and Nabonidus of Babylon, probably lies under the walls of the medieval Fatimite and Crusader fortress. It is in Haran that Abraham and his father Terah are first supposed to have settled on leaving Ur. From here Abraham is said to have set out for Canaan, and here Jacob too is supposed to have lived with Leah and Rachel, the daughters of Laban. The ancient ruins around the little village of Haran, with its 'termite hill houses', mostly originate from the Roman period, when the place then named Carrhae played a significant role in the conflicts with Parthians and Armenians. The emperor Caracalla was murdered here in AD216 The town walls with their seven gates, whose erection goes back to King Adad Nirari I of Assyria (about 1300BC), are still recognizable.

Hattusa was the capital of the Hittite empire. Its ruins lie near the Turkish village of Boghaskoi about 95 miles east of Ankara. The town was heavily fortified, particularly to the north, where the only entrance was situated. On the other sides of the inhabited area the slopes of the 3900-feet-high mountain ridge fall steeply away. The excavations carried out by the German Oriental Society in 1906–07, 1911–12 and 1931–39, and taken up again in 1952, established five layers of occupation. The earliest settlers in the middle of the third millennium BC were described as 'proto-Hattian'; their area of origin and ethnic group is unknown. About 2000BC the town was conquered by the Hittites, and it was probably raised to the status of capital city of the 'Old Kingdom' in the 17th century BC. In the 'New Kingdom' which established itself about 1450BC through a change of dynasty, it enjoyed its golden age. At least five main temples and the great royal palace were built. From here the Hittites subdued large areas of the ancient Orient. The suffering of the Mitanni and the local rulers of Phoenicia and Canaan under the Hittites are vividly brought before us in the Amarna letters. After the laissez-faire Egyptian foreign policy towards the end of the Eighteenth Dynasty, King Sethos I and his son Rameses II tried to re-assert their political interests. After the indecisive battle of Kadesh on the river Orontes in 1285BC, the threat of a migration of peoples from the north did force the Hittite king Chattusili to make a peace treaty with Egypt, the text of which was made public in identical words in Hattusa and Karnak. The new friendship was sealed with the marriage of Rameses II to a Hittite princess. However towards 1200BC the Hittite empire succumbed to the onslaught of the 'Sea Peoples'. During the era of the Phrygians and Persians the capital, Hattusa, maintained no more than a twilight existence, and was finally abandoned.

Among the most impressive remains of Hattusa are the city walls and the walls of the royal palace, the temple ruins and parts of the residential quarter. Not far from the city lies the rock shrine of Yazilikaya, in which the chief Hittite god, the storm god Teshub, was worshipped together with his extensive family and thus almost the whole of the Hittite Pantheon. The mobile finds from these excavations are exhibited in the Museum of Ankara. Of particular importance is the state archive from the royal palace; we owe its historical usefulness to the deciphering achievements of the Czech linguist B. Hrozny (1915).

Hazor lies 14 miles north of Tiberias on a once-important road connecting Egypt to Mesopotamia, the Via Maris. Egyptian and Syrian sources mention the city as early as the 19th–18th centuries BC, and the oldest of the nine strata of occupation which have been investigated also go back to this time. The most impressive relics of this Canaanite city are the powerful earth walls which protect the tell. After its destruction by Joshua in the 13th century BC, the lower town was abandoned, while the upper town was rebuilt several times and considerably developed under Solomon and Ahab. The splendid citadel gate from the 10th–9th centuries BC, with its 'proto-Aeolian' curled capitals, can today be seen in the Israel Museum in Jerusalem, but there are also impressive remains left on the site, such as a great triple-naved hall from the time of Ahab and the four-roomed houses (the 'House of Yahel', the 'House of the Machbiram Family') from the era of Jeroboam II. In 763BC Hazor was afflicted by an earthquake, whose effects can still be clearly seen on the excavation site in the form of crooked walls. The layer of ash marking the destruction by the Assyrian king Tiglath-pileser III in the year 732BC is almost three feet thick. Later rebuildings continue to the Hellenistic period, but are without great significance.

The greatest discovery in Hazor was made by the archaeologist Yigael Yadin in 1968: the town's water supply installation, provided by King Ahab. A shaft with steps, leading to a tunnel through the rock, goes down 130 feet under the tell. The tunnel is so wide that it is even possible that donkeys could have been used to transport the water.

Heliopolis ('City of the Sun') is the Greek name for the time-honoured shrine of sun worship, Inunu (the biblical On) on the southern tip of the Nile delta. Its major importance reaches back at least to the Third Dynasty (about 2700BC). It is true that its priests did not command as much power and influence later as they had in the Old Kingdom, but nevertheless it still enjoyed the greatest prestige. So it is a mark of the status to which the biblical Joseph rose, that he became the son-in-law of a high priest of Heliopolis. Only modest remains can still be seen, in the village of Matariya north-east of Cairo, of the former splendour of the shrine. Apart from a fragment of an obelisk of King Teti (Sixth Dynasty), a great obelisk of Sesostris I (Twelfth Dynasty) indicates the site where the sun god Ra once held sway.

Jericho is thought to be the oldest city in Palestine; the fruitful oasis in the Jordan valley has been inhabited since at least the early Stone Age. What remains of this early culture is exhibited in the Rockefeller Museum in Jerusalem. As early as 7000BC the settlers joined in a communal life bearing the marks of a city, and fortified their settlement. The oldest architectural evidence found at the excavation site known as Tell es-Sultan is a massive stone tower, which still stands to a height of about thirty feet. Only a little younger is the six-foot-thick city wall, which even then enclosed an area of at least 97,500 square feet. A fortress of the Bronze Age is likely to belong to the third millennium BC. The first excavators (Sellin and Watzinger, 1907–09) established six levels of occupation; in 1930–36 Garstang found the necropolis and further walls— however all the investigators searched in vain for the walls of Jericho which are supposed to have collapsed under the onslaught of the Israelites' trumpet blasts. Even the painstaking excavations of Kathleen Kenyon (1952–58), to which we owe the early dating of the oldest fortifications, could not find any evidence of destruction from the time of Joshua. Jericho seems already to have sunk into insignificance at that time and never flourished again after the Israelite entry into the land. It could be that the 'walls of Joshua' were built of dried bricks, and that their ruins have been carried off by rain and wind.

Also under the name of Jericho, an Israeli excavation is under way at the mouth of the Wadi el-Qelt in the Jordan valley. Under the winter palace of King Herod, who died there in 4BC, Ehud Netzer found in 1980 a Hasmonean palace, a double structure which may have belonged to the warring brothers Aristobolus II and Hyrcanus II.

305

Jerusalem is, from the end of the third millennium BC, frequently mentioned in Syrian and Egyptian sources as Urusalim. This Jebusite city was small but strategically placed, lying in an unusually favourable position on a ridge between the Kidron valley and the Tyropoeon valley (Greek for 'valley of the cheesemakers'). Moreover, the Jebusite Acropolis on Mount Ophel commanded a spring which supplied water all year round, the spring of Gihon.

In the 15th century BC the city was conquered by Thutmosis III and probably stayed dependent on Egypt for a long period. In the conflict with Joshua, King Adoni-sedek was defeated and killed, but his city successfully defended itself against capture and was only conquered by King David in about 1000BC. According to the biblical account David's commander-in-chief Joab stormed the city through the tunnel which the Jebusites had bored in the rock to give access to the spring. Though it was now, as the *City of David*, the religious and political centre of the kingdom, Jerusalem at first stayed within the borders of the strengthened Jebusite encircling wall. It was King Solomon who first extended the city to the north, from 975BC on, erecting his palace more or less where today's Al-Aqsa Mosque stands, and immediately to its north the Temple, whose foundation stone is traditionally identified with the great block of stone under the Dome of the Rock. To keep up with the growth of the city's area and population, the fortifications too had to be considerably extended; the course of the walls at this time is however still a long way from being confirmed at all points.

Because of the many layers of re-building on top of the ancient Jerusalem, and the Muslim religious authorities' prohibition against excavations on the Temple Mount, the archaeologists are severely hampered in their work. Nevertheless through French/English and Israeli excavations since the 1960s we have gained many new understandings and refuted some formerly revered theories. Above all, on the steep slopes of the Kidron Valley, substantial parts of the ancient walls have been exposed, among them the ominous stone pyramids which served as a surrounding wall below the palace of Solomon. Here too the greatly damaged so-called 'royal graves' have been

unearthed, as well as innumerable Israelite private houses, which stand on Jebusite foundations.

The division of Solomon's kingdom and military attacks such as the plundering expedition of Pharaoh Sheshonk I hindered the development of Jerusalem. There is still debate about whether the extension of the city to the slopes of the valley of Hinnom happened in the 10th century BC or only in the time of Hezekiah (725–697BC). At any rate, under Hezekiah and his successor Manasseh (697–642BC) the fortifications of Jerusalem were greatly strengthened, and Hezekiah had a long tunnel bored through the rock as a conduit from the Gihon Spring to the Pool of Siloam. These measures protected Jerusalem from the Assyrian conquests led by Sennacherib (701BC) but not from the catastrophe of 587BC, when Nebuchadnezzar destroyed the city and the Temple and deported the top strata of society into the 'Babylonian exile'. Only when the Persian Empire under Cyrus had taken over the empire of the Babylonians, was the restoration of the Temple begun by the decree of the emperor in 520BC; and in the middle of the 5th century BC the restoration of the city walls (though within a smaller compass) was also begun. Apart from a section of wall above Solomon's staged stone pyramids, hardly anything can now be seen from the time of the Second Temple.

After the conquests of Alexander the Great, Jerusalem first became Ptolemaic, then Seleucid. In 169BC the city was conquered and plundered by the Seleucid ruler Antiochus IV, who erected an altar to Zeus in the Temple. This desecration was removed by the uprising under Judas Maccabeus in 164BC, but Jerusalem only began to flourish again under the rule of Herod the Great, who was put in charge of his kingdom by the Roman Senate in 37BC.

The king lavished vast expenditure on refurbishing his capital—naturally in the Hellenistic/Roman style. The palace, the forum, the theatre, the amphitheatre, and the hall of pillars were rebuilt, and from AD20 the Temple too; this however was still unfinished in AD64. The enormous extension of the Temple platform alone was a huge undertaking; gigantic blocks of stone were used for the supporting walls. The famous 'Wailing Wall' belongs to this period of building.

While research has until recently concentrated exclusively on the Temple Mount, latterly some dwelling houses of the Herodian period have been unearthed as well, and in part made accessible. The 'Burnt House', the 'Palatial Mansion' and the 'Herodian House' are examples of this period, which came to a sudden end with the destruction of Jerusalem by Titus in the year AD70.

Kantir is a village in the eastern Nile delta, near which German and Austrian excavators have found the so far scanty, but highly interesting remains of the royal seat of Rameses II. Moulds for shields, 'blast furnaces', parts of chariots, horses' bridles, and inscribed wall tiles, all leave us in no further doubt that the city of Rameses, Pi-Raamses, lay near Kantir. It had formerly been believed that Tanis could be identified as the royal seat of the great Pharaoh. There were indeed building blocks and obelisks with his name lying there, but they had in fact been carried off by the rulers of the Twenty-first and Twenty-second Dynasties to their new capital, from Pi-Raamses, which lay only twelve miles south. Since Rameses II is identified with the 'Pharaoh of the captivity', Kantir would thus be the town in whose construction Israel had to undergo forced labour, and it would have been from here that the Exodus, the departure of the Israelites from Egypt, took place.

Lachish (Tell ed-Duweir) lies on the edge of the Judean mountains, 20 miles east of Ashkelon. The tell can only be approached from the south-west, as on all other sides it is surrounded by deeply carved valleys. Its strategic position on two trunk roads made Lachish an important town, though never a metropolis. In 701BC it was besieged by the Assyrian king Sennacherib. The conquest by the Babylonian king Nebuchadnezzar II in 586BC must have wrought even greater devastation. It is in the layer of ashes resulting from this catastrophe that the Lachish letters, pottery fragments with notes written by the despairing defenders of the city, were found.

The excavations of 1932–38 (J L Starkey) and from 1966 on (Archaeological Institute, Tel Aviv) unearthed numerous strata of occupation, of which the oldest go back to the third millennium BC. On top of a monumental Canaanite building, the Israelite fortified palace was built, beginning in the 10th century BC; of this only the foundations remain. A well, 140 feet deep, supplied the town with water even in wartime; it lay within the impressive fortifications. The gates, stormed by the troops of both Sennacherib and Nebuchadnezzar, are also still clearly visible. After the Babylonian exile Lachish was re-settled in the Persian period, from about 520BC; however it remained a very modest city, which was gradually deserted after the second century BC.

Mari, the Syrian town which fell as early as the second millennium BC, experienced its greatest prosperity between 2000 and 1700BC. At that time the kingdom of the Amorites controlled from Mari the connections between Mesopotamia and the Mediterranean. The chance find of an inscribed statue in 1933 directed the notice of French archaeologist André Parrot to the large Tell Hariri near the river Euphrates. In 1933–39 and 1951–64 he excavated the remains of this once powerful city.

The layers of occupation of Mari go right back to the fourth millennium BC. Despite being under the rule of various powers (Akkad, Ur, the Amorites) the city always maintained an important status, which came to an abrupt end only when it was destroyed by Hammurabi of Babylon in 1695BC. Later there were small settlements of Assyrians, Seleucids and Parthians on the ruins, but these had no significant role.

Among Parrot's sensational finds are the remains of a twice-restored staged tower, whose oldest parts date from the beginning of the third milennium BC; various temple buildings, including two temples of Ishtar; and the extensive palace of King Zimri-Lim. In this many-roomed building Parrot found wall-paintings depicting religious scenes, statues and a comprehensive archive containing over 20,000 clay tablets which give important information on the trade and traffic of the time of the patriarchs.

Marib was for many centuries the capital of the southern Arabian Sabaeans, who probably migrated to the area in the 13th century BC. East of Sana'a, modern capital of Yemen, situated at a height of 3700 feet, Marib controlled several 'incense roads' as well as the important Wadi Dana. Earlier than the mentions of Marib in Assyrian sources, the biblical story tells us of the Queen of Sheba, or Saba, and her visit to King Solomon. An Ethiopian legend says that after her stay in Jerusalem the Queen bore a son called Menilek who later became king of Ethiopia, and who, when he visited his father Solomon in Jerusalem, stole the tablets with the Ten Commandments from the Ark of the Covenant. Until recently the Ethiopian royal house traced its origins back to Solomon. Up to the fifth century BC the kingdom of Saba was a theocracy under the leadership of priest-rulers with the title Mukarrib. Only in 420BC did Karib il Watar II take the title of 'king', Malik. In his time Saba began to engage in an imperialism which led to the colonization of Ethiopia.

Of the temple of the moon god Ilmuqah there still remains in Marib an imposing row of closely placed monoliths. But the most amazing building is the great coffer dam with its ingenious system of sluices, which twice a year collected the water from the brief monsoon in the Wadi Dana and directed it to the higher-lying fields of the oasis. The dam at Marib was built in the 6th century BC, but was based on considerably earlier irrigation traditions. The dam was in service for over a thousand years; damage and repairs are frequently mentioned. In AD575 however the walls collapsed. The flood disaster is mentioned in the Qu'ran. The once fertile area became barren, and Marib was abandoned.

Megiddo was one of the strategic points on the Via Maris, and was accordingly often conquered. The archaeologists (Gottlieb Schumacher 1903–05, Chicago Oriental Institute 1925–39, from 1960 on the Hebrew University, Jerusalem) unearthed no fewer than twenty layers of occupation, which allowed them to trace Megiddo's varied history back to the fourth millennium BC.

Three shrines, city gates and the remains of palaces have been found from the time of the Canaanite kings. In 1479BC Megiddo was conquered by Thutmosis III, and remained strongly under Egyptian influence until nearly 1150BC (Strata VIII–VI). Apart from the base of a stela of Rameses VI, this period yielded above all a wealth of ivory carvings, which were taken to the Rockefeller Museum in Jerusalem. Megiddo resisted conquest by Joshua. Stratum V is clearly Philistine. King David was the first to capture the city for the Israelites, and Solomon built it up into the capital of the fifth province of his empire. It was to this stratum (IVa) that the Israeli archaeologists naturally devoted the most attention: the casemate wall, the northern city gate, the north and south palaces as well as the private houses are the most impressive remains of this period. The famous 'Solomon's Stables' probably only date from the time of King Ahab, who had to restore Megiddo after plundering by Pharaoh Sheshonk. He also took action to ensure the city's water supply, digging a 120-foot-deep shaft leading to a 215-foot-long tunnel to the underground spring. From 733BC Megiddo was Assyrian and served as the provincial capital. In 609BC King Josiah of Judah was defeated here by Pharaoh Necho II and lost his life. After that the tell remained uninhabited.

Nimrud is mentioned in the Old Testament under the name Calah and is counted there among the cities founded by the legendary Nimrod. The layers of occupation of the city do indeed go back at least to the third millennium BC. However Nimrud only acquired any significance as one of the great royal seats of the Assyrian kings.

The gigantic excavation area lies 25 miles south of Nineveh and was investigated by British archaeologists in 1845–48 and 1949–63; since 1970 a joint Polish/Iraqi team has been working on it. Interest of course centres on the golden age of Nimrud, which lasted from the 13th century BC to its fall in the Babylonian conquest of 612BC.

Until recently the excavations were devoted mainly to the upper town with its temples and palaces. It was surrounded by an exceptionally strong wall, which in places remains standing to a height of nearly forty feet. To the north-west the ziggurat and the temples of Ninurta and Ishtar reared up. The north-western palace has been identified as the royal residence of Ashurnasirpal II.

In the 'central palace' of Shalmaneser III accounts of the attacks on Israel and Judah have been found. Many of the sculptures, ivory carvings and metal vessels which were displayed here were booty from Palestine. On the 'Black Obelisk', a basalt stela with reliefs and inscriptions which was found in 1846 and came into the possession of the British Museum, King Jehu of Israel is shown kneeling before Shalmaneser. Next to the 'burnt-down palace', probably from the 13th century BC, stood the temple of the god of scribes, Nabu. Here the treaties giving vassal status to conquered peoples were kept.

Nineveh lies on the east bank of the river Tigris, opposite modern Mosul (Iraq). Although the city is mentioned in writing only after 2200BC, the Bible counts Nineveh among the prehistoric foundations of the mythical Nimrod. Excavations have confirmed a first settlement dating from about 4500BC, above which later strata of the city tower to a height of almost 80 feet.

The striking mound of rubble attracted the notice of scientific travellers as early as the 17th century, but the first investigations in 1820 and 1842–43 yielded little. It was only with the excavations carried out by Layard and Rassam in 1845–54 that the archaeologists stumbled on the palaces of Sennacherib and Ashurbanipal and confirmed the identification of the tell with Nineveh by the inscriptions they found. Since then numerous excavations have been undertaken under the supervision of the British Museum; since the 1960s Iraq itself has continued the work, and its end is still not in sight.

Among the oldest buildings in Nineveh is the temple of Ishtar, which was founded at the latest by Sargon's son Manishtusa (about 2300BC), and was later restored several times. With the blossoming of the Assyrian empire under Shalmaneser I Nineveh became the royal seat in about 1260BC and rose to become a city of world importance. Almost every significant king built a palace here. In its most flourishing period, under Sennacherib (705–681BC) Nineveh needed a city wall over seven miles long with fifteen monumental gates. The inscriptions on its buildings mention the conquest of Lachish as well as the (unsuccessful) assault on Jerusalem. The last great palace was built by Ashurbanipal; he also established the clay tablet archive with 25,000 cuneiform texts.

The fall of Nineveh, predicted by the prophets Nahum and Zephaniah, took place in 612BC. The united forces of Medes and Babylonians destroyed the city so thoroughly that from that point on it remained a deserted heap of debris. At the time of the Romans the Syrian Lucian could no longer even identify the geographical position of this city which had once been so famous.

Nuzi, today Yorghan Tepe in Iraq, was already a flourishing commercial town in the third millennium BC, under the Sumerian name of Gasur. The town had its golden age under the rule of the Hurrite Mitanni in the 15th and 14th centuries BC. By now called Nuzi, it is said to have sheltered seven temples within its walls. Remains of frescoes from a palace have even been found. More than this, the American excavators (1925–31) found over 4,000 inscribed clay tablets from the 15th century BC with contracts and business records, which give detailed information about trade and legal customs of this time. Of particular interest are the private legal documents dealing with inheritance and wills, marriages and dowries, adoption, transfer of land or employees and other matters; many parallels can be found in them to the legal practices portrayed in the biblical accounts of the time of the patriarchs.

Persepolis was probably the most magnificent royal seat of the Persian Achaemenian kings; at any rate, even today its imposing remains still offer the visitor a striking sight. Darius I gave up the old palace in Pasargadae and began the new building in 520BC; his son Xerxes continued and completed the splendid work. Although Persepolis, well off the beaten track, never attained the political or economic significance of Susa, it seems to have been the favourite residence of its founders and their successors. When Alexander the Great conquered Persepolis in 330BC, the palace burned down; the cause seems to have been arson. An attempt was made to justify the barbaric act as retribution for the destruction of Athens by the Persians in the year 480BC. Later the lower city was re-settled, but the ruins of the palace were gradually sanded over.

The excavations, beginning in 1931 under the direction of E. Herzfeld, laid bare an extensive area of pillared halls, courtyards and magnificent gates. Alongside Oriental styles, Egyptian and Ionic/Greek influences were clearly visible. The reliefs on the northern staircase of the Apadana, with the 'Guard of the Immortals', and on the eastern staircase, with bringers of tribute from all the satrapies of the empire, are particularly well preserved.

Samaria in central Palestine is one of the few cities which the Israelites themselves founded. The commanding height, almost 425 feet high, amazingly remained uninhabited until the time of Omri, apart from a modest early Bronze Age village. Omri and his son Ahab walled the town, built a citadel, a palace (ivory finds from this are in the Rockefeller Museum in Jerusalem), and a temple of Baal. In the ninth century BC the strongly-built fortress withstood an attack by the Arameans from Damascus, but in 722/21BC, after a three-year siege, it was taken by the Assyrians and became the administrative centre of the province which was now called Samaria. The visible remains of the first golden age of Samaria are meagre; the destruction by John Hyrcanus in 107BC was all too thorough. The impressive ruins to be seen in Samaria today overwhelmingly originate from the time of Herod and that of Septimius Severus. Caesar Augustus gave the town to Herod in 25BC, and in gratitude for this Herod from then on called it Sebaste (the Greek Sebastos corresponds to the Latin Augustus) and erected a shrine to Augustus over the old temple of Baal. A wall at the foot of the hill now enclosed a large urban area, which was extremely splendidly furnished with pillared streets, forum, basilica, theatre and stadium. It was in Samaria that Herod married his favourite wife Mariamne, and here too that he had her assassinated. According to a legend of the fourth century AD, John the Baptist was buried in Samaria, and because of this a cult of the saint continued into the Middle Ages in the decaying town.

Shikmona was the only Israelite port on the northern Mediterranean coast. The excavations, begun in 1963 under the direction of Yosef Elgavish, near the Oceanographic Institute of Haifa, are still far from complete.

The city was probably founded by Egypt

in the 14th century BC, in order to control the coastal road along this narrow corridor between Carmel and the sea. In about 1000BC this key post became Israelite; the casemate wall, 16 feet thick, of which a whole section has been unearthed, fits the general profile of Solomonic fortification architecture. Two large buildings could be interpreted as a governor's palace and an inn, and streets and private houses have also been discovered. Shikmona came to an end with the Assyrian period in the 8th century BC, but was re-settled after the Persian Empire took over and was only finally destroyed and abandoned after the Arab conquest in AD638.

Sidon was a Phoenician port 28 miles south of Beirut. The idyllic little town of Saida hardly gives a hint of its great past. Its older buildings date from the Crusades or from the Muslim period. The excavation sites are scattered, some of them far outside the town. Even so the areas of settlement go back to the early Stone Age and in Genesis Sidon is called, not without reason, the 'firstborn of Canaan'. At the peak of trade with Egypt, Sidon seems to have been the leading Phoenician town, even if its fleet had to deal with Cretan competition from the 17th century BC on. After its conquest by Tiglath-pileser I in 1100BC, Sidon lost its pre-eminent position to Tyre, and fell under the rule of various foreign powers: the Assyrians, the Babylonians, the Persians, the Greeks and the Romans. In an unsuccessful uprising against Artaxerxes III in about 350BC, the town was destroyed and 40,000 inhabitants are reported to have died in the resulting fire. Although the profitable overseas trade was long gone, Sidon repeatedly recovered through its glass industry and above all through the production of purple dye, with which it supplied Israel among others. A memorable witness to this is the murex heap south of the citadel, made up of the piled-up shells of the murex, or purple snail, rising to a height of nearly 150 feet.

Susa, now Shush, in the south-western Iranian province of Chusistan, was once the capital of the kingdom of Elam. About 645BC it was destroyed by Ashurbanipal, but then flourished again magnificently as the royal seat of the Persian Achaemenians.

Darius I built himself a winter palace here in the mild lowlands. In a trilingual account (Neo-Babylonian, Neo-Elamite, Old Persian) the recruiting of labour from the various peoples of the Persian Empire for the building of the palace is recorded. After being conquered by Alexander the Great, Susa continued to enjoy considerable status under the Seleucids, Parthians and Sassanids, but it gradually lost its political and economic significance. Today Shush is more of a provincial town.

Archaeological research begun in 1884 has revealed a city covering about 440 acres, but it has been estimated that the total area of settlement was at least five times as big. The deepest strata of ancient Susa go back to the beginning of the fourth millennium BC. In 1901 the famous stela containing the laws of Hammurabi of Babylon, which had been carried off to Susa by the Elamites, was found. The city probably reached its greatest size under the Persians. The individual quarters—the Acropolis, the palace area, the craft workshops and the commercial town—were strictly separated from each other. In this the findings of the excavations to a large degree confirmed the account in the Book of Esther, from the time of Xerxes. According to this the Jewish community in Susa, as in Ecbatana, enjoyed considerable respect and great influence. It is from Susa that the introduction of the feast of Purim probably originates, celebrated in March in imitation of the Persian new year festival.

It is 'in the citadel of Susa in the province of Elam' that the prophet Daniel experiences one of his visions, and according to Shi'ite tradition he is also buried here. His mausoleum in Shush is to this day an important place of pilgrimage for Iranian Muslims, and at times it resembles a caravanserai.

Tell Arad lies six miles west of the modern Israeli town of Arad. The Canaanite city of the third and second millennia BC lay on a double hill and consisted of ample stone houses arranged in regular rows. Arad probably flourished mainly from its ceramics industry. The city centre indicates that there was a large reservoir.

After its conquest by Joshua, Arad was fortified under Solomon with a casemate wall typical of its time. The temple which has been identified on the citadel could be a little

older. A large altar of uncut stones, channels for draining away sacrificial blood in the courtyard, a hall with storage facilities, a shrine, altars for burnt offerings and a pillared portico, confirm beyond doubt the venerable status of the town. The Israeli excavators, beginning in 1962, have partly restored their finds and thus made them easily understood by lay people. In 587/586BC the city and the temple were destroyed by Nebuchadnezzar. It was not until the Hellenistic period that a new fortress was erected, and it soon fell into disrepair again.

Tell Beersheba ('The Well of the Seven'), according to tradition, goes back to the time of the patriarchs. Excavations are still in train in a well shaft outside the city wall, and up to now, at a depth of 130 feet, its bottom has not yet been found. Whether this is the well where Abraham swore an oath has yet to be confirmed.

The earliest layer of occupation of the town, which has been under investigation since 1969 by Aharoni, goes back at the most to the time of the Judges; the fortifications with casemate walls originate only from the 10th century BC. Despite destruction by Pharaoh Sheshonk and Sennacherib, the layout of the city can be quite fully reconstructed. A 'ring road' runs parallel to the city wall; along it lie the foundations of typical Israelite four-roomed houses. Near the massive city gate, capacious storehouses for wine, oil and grain have been found. A network of canals fed the great cistern below the gatehouse. Figurative religious objects of an Egyptian style indicate an older place of worship which has not yet been unearthed.

After the destruction by Sennacherib during the Assyrian invasion a new, unfortified settlement was built at the foot of the hill; this however remained insignificant, little more than a village.

Tell Dan lies near one of the sources of the Jordan in the north of Israel; at the time of the Israelite entry into the land it was the northernmost settlement within the Aramean border area. Here Israelites of the tribe of Dan took over a much older city which appears in Egyptian texts as early as the 19th century BC under the name of Lais. A well-preserved gate from this time made of clay bricks can still be seen. In the strata of the Canaanite city, as well as those of the Israelite one, many cast bronze cooking-pots were found. Metalworking must have been a substantial branch of industry in Dan.

The first Israelite layer of occupation at Tell Dan reveals a modest, probably semi-nomadic existence. Even so the inhabitants reinforced the earth walls of their houses with layers of pebbles, from which silos were also built. It was only in the next phase of settlement that firm foundations were built for houses, mostly on slabs of basalt. After a fire disaster towards the end of the 12th century BC, the city was walled during the 11th and 10th centuries BC. A marked shrinkage in the ground plan of houses suggests that space was limited due to population growth. Under King Ahab in the 9th century stronger fortifications were built, probably against the threat from the Arameans, including an impressive gate and bastions. In the 8th century BC Dan was conquered by the Assyrians and from this time it sank into political insignificance. However the town continued as a centre of worship until the Roman period.

The Israeli excavators under the direction of Avraham Biran, who began their work in 1966, devoted particular attention to the 'high place' (*bama*). It was found in the northern part of the tell and its core probably goes back to King Jeroboam I, founder of the kingdom of Israel. As a religious counterweight to Jerusalem, according to the Bible's account, he set up golden idols in the form of bulls ('golden calves') in Bethel and Dan respectively. The great platform was extended twice (under Ahab in the 9th and under Jeroboam II in the 8th centuries), measures over 60 feet square and is surrounded by a wall built of carefully arranged courses of stones. Pitchers and sacrificial vessels leave no doubt as to the religious function of the construction. In the Hellenistic period the city god Dan seems to have been worshipped here. The Romans probably erected a 'Nymphaeum' on the high place.

Tell Qasile is today the heart of the Ha'aretz Museum in Tel Aviv. The excavations began in 1948 and unearthed streets, houses, a public building and smelting ovens of the 10th to 8th centuries BC. It was from the port of Tell Qasile, the excavators believe, that Solomon once had the cedar wood collected for the building of the Jerusalem Temple and delivered in carts. Meanwhile the strata of the Philistine town which preceded the Israelite one have also been excavated. They go back to the 12th century BC; their most striking relics are the remains of a temple, the bases of whose pillars are still easily recognizable.

Thebes (Thebai) is the Greek name for the imperial capital of Upper Egypt, which from the Middle Kingdom served at times as a royal seat, but principally as the main shrine of the imperial god Amun. The Egyptians called it Weset or simply Nut (city); in the Bible it is called No, while in the Roman period it bore the title Diospolis Magna, the Great City of Zeus. The city stretched out on both sides of the Nile and embraced the royal palace, residential quarter and temple districts in the area today covered by Luxor, as well as the extensive cemeteries on the west bank, the Temple of the Dead and the palace of Amenophis III. At the time of the Ramessid Dynasty the two halves of the city were administratively separate, and today only the west side, Western Thebes, is referred to as Thebes. The temple area of Karnak, north of Luxor, embraces the massive shrine of Amun as well as individual temples to the divine consort Mut, the child god Chons and the god of war, Month. Since the shrines were built, extended, altered or restored from the Eleventh Dynasty right up to the time of the Ptolemies, the history of their construction and appearance is extraordinarily complex and confusing.

According to ancient Egyptian theology, wars and campaigns of conquest were basically undertaken on the orders and to the honour of Amun, who also demanded the booty and a record of events. So the expeditions of the Egyptian kings to Palestine and the Near East, too, are recorded for us on the temple walls at Karnak. Thutmosis III alone (1490–1436BC) undertook no fewer than 17 campaigns into the Near East and in the process conquered Megiddo. His successes are preserved (in a fragmentary form) in the so called 'annals' and lists of foreign peoples. Moreover, in a building dedicated to the purpose, the 'Botanical Garden', foreign animals and plant varieties are depicted, which had been discovered in the Near East and to some extent imported to enrich the Egyptian landscape.

After the era of Akhnaten, Sethos I (1303–1290BC) also had occasion to force the rebellious city-states of the Near East back into subjection. On the outer northeast corner of the great pillared hall, the capitulation of the fortress of Canaan and the felling of the cedars which were so important to Egypt are depicted. On the northern outer wall the events of the war and above all the victory are recorded: endless rows of prisoners and precious pieces of booty appear. A graphic picture of the renewed border defences between Egypt and Palestine concludes the record.

The customary formula of Egyptian depictions of victory, with the slaying of enemies, cities personified as prisoners, and the dedication to Amun, is also adhered to by the monumental record of Sheshonk I (946–924BC), the biblical Shishak, on the southern outer wall of the hall of pillars. His looting expedition to Palestine, his victory over Rehoboam of Judah and the theft of the Temple treasures, remained isolated episodes and did not lead to a lasting sovereignty over the land.

The temple of Luxor served mainly for the fest of Opet, the annual celebration of the sacred marriage between Amun and Mut. On the gateway, Rameses II recorded his campaign against the Hittites and the battle of Kadesh.

While the graves of rulers in the 'Valley of the Kings' are exclusively devoted to the afterlife of the kings, and depict the underworld in detail, in the so-called Temples of the Dead on the edge of the gigantic necropolis, history too is included. Thus in the temple of Merenptah (1224–1204BC), the son of Rameses II, archaeologists found the famous 'Israel stela', the only Egyptian document on which the name of Israel appears. The north wall of the Temple of the Dead of Rameses III in Medinet Habu portrays in particular detail the rout of the 'Sea Peoples', among whom were the Philistines.

Most informative, too, are the depictions of the work of high-ranking officials. So for instance Rechmire, vizier under Thutmosis III and Amenophis II, has in his grave at Shech Abd el-Kurna pictures of long rows of foreign emissaries with their tribute—even if in reality they are quite ordinary trading partners or contractors bringing deliveries. Among them people from the Syria/Palestine area can also be found. The fact that in the time of the kings Amenophis III and Amenophis IV/Akhnaten, foreigners too could rise to the highest honours at the Egyptian court, is illustrated by some highly expressive heads of Semite courtiers, who appear in the grave of the vizier Ramose, taking part in a distribution of 'gold of honour'.

Tyre on the coast of Lebanon was one of the most important ports and commercial cities of the Phoenicians. Tradition dates the foundation of the city to prehistoric times, but so far archaeology has been unable to confirm this, since large areas are very difficult to investigate as a result of flooding, sanding over and rebuilding. Its island location made Tyre almost impossible to capture. Its centuries-long loyalty to Egypt must have been dictated by commercial interests and can hardly be interpreted, as it is in Egyptian sources, as political dependency. After the fall from power of Sidon in the 11th century BC, Tyre grew into the leading power of Phoenicia. The city maintained friendly relations with Kings David and Solomon and supported the construction of the Temple in Jerusalem with deliveries of materials and specialist workers. The High Priest of Astarte and King, Ittobaal I, gave Ahab of Israel his daughter Jezebel as a wife; she introduced the cult of Baal into Israel. At this time Tyre also established itself as a colonial power on the Mediterranean. The crown of this expansion was the foundation of Kart Hadasht (Carthage) by Dido-Elisa. As the colonies gradually claimed their independence, Tyre was lastingly weakened. So the city fell briefly to the Assyrians in 700BC; nevertheless it stood out against a thirteen-year siege by Nebuchadnezzar of Babylon. At that time the mainland city was finally abandoned, the embankment connecting it to the island was broken off and New Tyre was magnificently extended and strongly walled by King Ittobaal III.

Alexander the Great's seven-month siege in 332BC could only be brought to a successful conclusion by the building of a new connecting embankment. Under the rule of the Seleucids and the Romans Tyre remained wealthy, but never recovered its old importance. In the Crusader period the city again became important for its strategic position; nevertheless in 1291 it was given up and since then it has been used as a quarry.

Ugarit was known as an important Phoenician royal city as early as 1887 from the Amarna letters. A chance find made by a peasant while ploughing near Ras Shamra on the Syrian coast of the Mediterranean drew French archaeologists to the 65-foot-high tell, and by 1933 Claude Shaeffer was able to identify it as ancient Ugarit. The archaeologists have identified five clear layers of occupation, each subdivided several times.

The fortifications and palace walls visible today mainly originate from the city's last period of prosperity in the 14th–13th centuries BC. The two lowest strata show heavy dependence on Mesopotamia, but after a layer of fire damage about 2300BC, Phoenician settlement is evident. Like the other coastal towns of Canaan, Ugarit lived to a large extent by trade with Egypt, Crete and the Aegean; however it also depended on a highly developed bronze industry.

About 1365BC earthquakes and fire destroyed the town (according to a letter from Tyre to Amenophis IV) and a little later Ugarit had to ally itself with the Hittites, and even join the battle of Kadesh against Rameses II in 1286/85. Around 1200BC the city fell to the migrating hordes of the 'Sea Peoples'. Only from the 6th to the 4th centuries BC was it lastingly re-settled by the Greeks.

The rich archives of Ugarit, with a large number of mythological texts, are of particular importance.

Ur was in the third millennium BC one of the richest and most powerful cities of Mesopotamia and for a time ruled the whole of Babylon. The oldest traces of settlement go right back to about 5000BC. A decisive factor in the importance of the city was its position on the river Euphrates, which was navigable for seagoing ships up to that point, so that the foundation of the city's prosperity was foreign trade, which reached its zenith between 3000 and 1600BC. About 1,000 years later the Euphrates changed its course, and with the loss of its port Ur lost its means of subsistence and was gradually abandoned. The excavation site today lies about seven miles from the river.

The main attractions of the site in southern Iraq are the imposing remains of a ziggurat and temple buildings to the moon god Nannar, as well as the famous royal graves, whose extremely lavish furnishings have been transferred to the museum in Baghdad. The very first excavator, J. E. Taylor, was already convinced that here he had found the biblical Ur of the Chaldeans, the home of Haran and birthplace of Abram, who left Ur for Canaan.

Uruk is first mentioned in the Bible under the name Erech and is there assigned to the area ruled by Nimrod, the first tyrant on the earth. In Uruk the legendary hero Gilgamesh, whose deeds are sung in the earliest known great epic, also ruled.

The German excavations in the extensive area of ruins at Warka (near the river Euphrates, south-east of Babylon) have substantially confirmed the ancient traditions: the area was settled from the end of the fourth millennium BC, its first significant period of prosperity began about 3000BC, and there are shrines to the high god Anu including a ziggurat, and to the highly-venerated goddess of love, battle and the constellations, Eanna (Ishtar), as well as palace buildings and city walls. As late as the Greek period Uruk (Orchoe) was regarded as a centre of astronomy, and it is possible that it was here that astronomers first developed a method of calculating the courses of the planets.

ISRAEL'S SPRINGTIME, THE UNITED KINGDOM

Israel

About 1230 the Israelite tribes under Joshua invade and settle Canaan

Around 1200–1012 time of the judges up to Samuel; wars with the Philistines

1012–1004 Saul

1004–998 David king in Hebron

997–965 David king in Jerusalem

965–926 Solomon

962–955 Building of the Temple

926 The kingdom divides

Surrounding nations

1290–1224 Rameses II

1224–1214 Pharaoh Merenptah; end of the Hittite Empire

1193–1162 Rameses III; victory over the 'Sea Peoples'

About 1116 Tiglath-pileser I establishes Assyria's ascendancy

About 950 Hiram I of Tyre

THE DIVIDED KINGDOM

Judah	Israel	Surrounding nations
926–910 Rehoboam	926–907 Jeroboam I	922 Palestinian campaign of Pharaoh Sheshonk (Shishak)
910–908 Abijah	907–906 Nadab	King Mesha of Moab
908–868 Asa	906–883 Baasha	
	883–882 Elah	
	882–878 war between Zimri and Omri	
	882–871 Omri	
	876 Samaria established	
868–847 Jehoshaphat	871–852 Ahab	873–842 Ittobaal (Ethbaal) of Tyre
	Prophet Elijah	858–824 Shalmaneser III of Ashur
	Ahab killed at Carchemish in alliance with Damascus against Shalmaneser III	
852 Jehoram's regency	852–851 Ahaziah	
847–845 Jehoram	851–845 Jehoram	
845 Ahijah	845 Jehu's revolt	
845–840 Athaliah	845–818 Jehu	845–801 Hazael of Damascus
840–801 Joash	841 Jehu pays tribute to Shalmaneser III	
801–787 (773) Amaziah	818–802 Jehoahaz	
About 788 war between Amaziah and Joash	802–787 Joash	After 801 Ben-Hadad of Damascus
787–736 Azariah (Uzziah)	787–747 Jeroboam II	
756–741 Jotham regent and king	Prophet Amos	
	Prophet Hosea	
	747 Shallum	
	747–738 Menahem	745–727 Tiglath-pileser III (Pul) of Ashur

Judah	Israel	Surrounding nations
741–725 Ahaz regent and king	738 Tribute to Tiglath-pileser III	
736 Death of Uzziah, Isaiah's call	737–736 Pekahiah	
	735–732 Pekah	734 Campaign against the Philistines
733 war with Syria and Israel	732–723 Hoshea	733–732 Campaigns against Damascus and Israel
725–697 Hezekiah	722 Fall of Samaria End of the Kingdom of Israel	726–722 Shalmaneser V of Ashur

JUDAH UP TO THE DESTRUCTION OF JERUSALEM

Judah

725–697 Hezekiah

701 Jerusalem besieged by Sennacherib, the prophet Micah
696–642 Manasseh

641–640 Amon
639–609 Josiah, the prophet Zephaniah
628 Beginning of Josiah's reform
627 Jeremiah's call to be a prophet
622 Finding of Book of the Law; sacrificial cult centralized in Jerusalem
609 Josiah falls in battle against Necho at Megiddo, Jehoahaz king
608–598 Jehoiakim
605 The words of the prophet Jeremiah are written down

604 Jehoiakim revolts against Nebuchadnezzar
601 Fall of Jehoiakim
About 6.12.598 to 16.3.597 Jehoiachin
16.3.597 Jerusalem taken, Jehoichin made prisoner
First exile
597–587 Zedekiah
594 Coalition against Babylon
593 Ezekiel's call to be prophet
589 Babylon attacks again
January 588 Beginning of Nebuchadnezzar's siege of Jerusalem
588 The Egyptians under Hophra driven back by Babylon
About August 587 Jerusalem conquered
Second exile
March 560 Jehoiachin released

Surrounding nations

721–705 Sargon of Ashur
711 The Tartan's mission against the Philistines
704–681 Sennacherib of Ashur
690–669 Tirhakah of Egypt
680–669 Esarhaddon of Ashur conquers Egypt in 671 (Memphis)
655 Elam under Assyrian control

612 Nineveh conquered by Babylon and Media
609–594 Pharaoh Necho of Egypt

605 Victory of crown prince Nebuchadnezzar over the Egyptians at Carchemish
604–562 Nebuchadnezzar of Babylon
604 Campaign against Syria; Ashkelon taken
601 Indecisive battle between Nebuchadnezzar and Egypt

597 Nebuchadnezzar's campaign against Jerusalem

594–588 Psamtik II of Egypt

588–569 Hophra of Egypt
561–560 Amel-Marduk (Evil-Merodach)

JUDAH IN THE PERSIAN PERIOD

Judah

Prophet Isaiah of Babylon (Isaiah 40–55)

538 Edict of Cyrus
First return of the exiles to Jerusalem
Beginning of the Second Temple
520 Zerubbabel's governorship
Joshua is high priest
Prophets Haggai and Zechariah
1.4.515 The prophet Haggai consecrates the Temple

458 Ezra (398?)
445–433 Nehemiah; the walls rebuilt

Persia

558 Cyrus king of Persia, from 553 king of Media
29.10.539 Enters Babel
24.3.538–August 530 king in Babel
12.4.529–522 Cambyses, 525 conquers Egypt

521–486 Darius I

485–465 Xerxes (Ahasuerus)
464–424 Artaxerxes

BETWEEN THE TESTAMENTS

Palestine

332 Alexander in Jerusalem
332–323 Palestine under Macedonian control
323–312 Palestine under the control of different successors of Alexander

The Empire of Alexander

336 Alexander the Great becomes king of Macedonia
332 Alexander conquers Tyre and occupies Syria and Egypt
331 Founding of Alexandria; Babylon taken by Alexander
323–301 Alexander's empire divided between his successors, the Diadochi.

Palestine

312–198 Palestine under Egyptian control

218–217 Palestine under Syrian control

217 Ptolemy IV defeats Antiochus III and forces him to cede Palestine

198 Battle at Paneas. Palestine finally under Syrian control

175 Jason installed as high priest

Egypt

323–283 Ptolemy I Lagus,
Ptolemaic dynasty established (to 30BC)
285–246 Ptolemy II Philadelphus
274–271 First Syrian war over occupation of Palestine
260–253 Second Syrian war
246–221 Ptolemy III Euergetes
246–241 Third Syrian war
221–205 Ptolemy IV Philopater
205–181 Ptolemy V Epiphanes

181–145 Ptolemy VI Philometor

Syria and Mesopotamia

312–280 Seleucus I Nicator,
Seleucid dynasty established (to 64BC)
280–261 Antiochus I Soter

261–246 Antiochus II Theos
246–226 Seleucus II

226–223 Seleucus III
223–187 Antiochus III the Great

190 Antiochus III succumbs to the Romans in battle of Magnesia
187–175 Seleucus IV Philopater
175–164 Antiochus IV Epiphanes

Palestine

171 Menelaus becomes high priest

169 Antiochus robs the Jerusalem Temple

168 Apollonias plunders and destroys Jerusalem. Building of the Akra fortress in Jerusalem. Jewish worship forbidden and heathen sacrifices introduced into the Temple.

166–161 Judas Maccabeus leader of the Jewish struggle against the Syrians

166/5 Antiochus IV charges the imperial regent Lysias with the conduct of the battle against the Jews

165 Lysias concludes a peace with Judas. Jerusalem, except the Akra, ceded to the Jews. Purification and reconstruction of the Temple

163/2 Judas and his brother fight Syrian troops in various regions of the country

Antiochus V and Lysias draw up forces against Jerusalem. Alcimus becomes high priest

161 Judas defeats Nicanor, but falls soon after to Baccides. Jonathan, brother of Judas, takes up the conduct of the battle

153 Jonathan takes on the office of high priest

151/50 Jonathan recognized as dependent regional governor

148/45–139 Demetrius, son of Demetrius I, moves against Alexander

146–140 Battle for power between Demetrius and Tryphon, guardian of Antiochus VI

143 Jonathan murdered by Tryphon

142/3 Simon, brother of Jonathan and Judas, high priest and prince of the Jews. Acknowledged as independent by Demetrius II

141 Simon declared hereditary high priest by decision of the people, also commander of army, and prince. Maccabean dynasty called Hasmoneans.

135 Murder of Simon

135–104 John I Hyrcanus, son of Simon, overthrows Idumeans and Samaritans

104–103 Aristobulus I takes title of king

103–76 Alexander Janneus, brother of Aristobulus, fights against Nabateans and Pharisees

76–67 Salome Alexandra, widow of Aristobulus and Janneus, made queen. Her son Hyrcanus II becomes high priest. The Pharisees become dominant party

67–63 Aristobulus II, high priest and king

63 Hyrcanus and Antipater make alliance with Nabateans. Pompey takes Aristobulus prisoner and storms the Temple. Hyrcanus II reinstated as high priest and Roman superintendent. End of Maccabean kingdom. Palestine under Roman control.

Syria and Mesopotamia

169 First campaign against Egypt

168 Second campaign against Egypt

164–162 Antiochus V Eupator

162–161/50 Demetrius I

153 Alexander Balas rises against Demetrius

151/40 Alexander II Balas

139–128 Antiochus VII Sidetes

133 Pergamum falls to Rome

129 The Parthians occupy Babylon

64 Pompey makes remnant of Syria a Roman province

319